I

you can

*

BATT
10/16
NOR

-8 J

Plea

SHIPS OF THE
WHITE STAR LINE

RICHARD DE KERBRECH

Ian Allan
PUBLISHING

First published 2009

ISBN 978 0 7110 3366 5

Published by Ian Allan Publishing

an imprint of Ian Allan Publishing Ltd, Hersham, Surrey, KT12 4RG

Printed in England by Ian Allan Printing Ltd, Hersham, Surrey, KT12 4RG

Code: 0904/C

Visit the Ian Allan Publishing website at www.ianallanpublishing.com

Contents

Preface   4

Acknowledgements   5

Explanatory Notes   6

Abbreviations   7

Origins: a new steamship company and early iron-hulled ships   8

New companies, new routes and new partners   34

Golden Jubilee, birthday and donations   41

Ownership, coal, stokers and wireless   67

Men of Vision and the advent of the 'Olympic' class   135

Titanic, war years and aftermath   181

Class of travel, takeover, money matters and Depression   209

Merger, absorption, loss of identity and demise   236

Epilogue   238

Bibliography   239

Appendix 1   240

Preface

The White Star Line passed from existence in 1934, but due largely to the on-going interest in the *Titanic* disaster of 1912, its name is perpetuated. The Company started as a sailing ship concern, trading to Australia, but its name and goodwill was bought by Thomas Henry Ismay who started to operate a purely steamship company across the Atlantic as the Oceanic Steam Navigation Company (OSNCo), but trading under the banner of the White Star Line.

Although a comparative latecomer on the North Atlantic in 1871, it soon established a reputation for comfort, luxury, speed and reliability. At the end of the 19th century, White Star was one of the premier shipping companies in existence. Not only this but their status was enhanced because many of the Company's Masters and officers held commissions in the Royal Naval Reserve (RNR) that entitled their vessels to sail under the Blue Ensign (from 1866 the requirement was the Master plus a minimum of 10 of the complement, after 1914 it was the Master and a minimum of 6). It was rumoured that the only time White Star vessels wore the Red Ensign (the 'Red Duster') was when they underwent trials or during the delivery voyage! Indeed, up until World War 1, White Star's navigating officers wore rank insignia similar to that of the Royal Navy with the 'executive curl' (engineers, pursers and surgeons did not).

By 1902, the Company had been taken over by John Pierpont Morgan's large American shipping combine, the International Mercantile Marine Company (IMMCo). From here through the Edwardian era, it went from strength to strength until it reached its zenith with the introduction of the *Olympic* and *Titanic*. The loss of the *Titanic* in 1912 damaged the Company's reputation almost beyond repair, and was followed by World War 1 in which they incurred the loss of the *Olympic's* other sister, the *Britannic*. Following the war's end, the company bounced back with the confiscated German liners *Majestic, Homeric* and the *Arabic*. It managed to survive the era under the Royal Mail group of companies up until the Depression only to be absorbed by its largest rival, Cunard, in 1934.

This publication is at best a tribute to the White Star Line rather than a definitive company history; that will be left to those who are more competent, expert and qualified to write the 'full' story. It primarily concerns the steamships and later motorships operated by White Star, and also touches on events political and non-political, national and international, that affected the fortunes of the Company. It does not seek to deal with the complicated and labyrinthine business side in any depth but rather to give a chronological potted career and brief history of each vessel that was owned or acquired by White Star. For some of these vessels information is scant which is reflected in the text. Other ships like the *Olympic*, which became White Star's standard bearer well into the 1930s, are covered in greater detail. It is intended that the story will give a bigger picture of the White Star Line.

Also featuring are some of the main characters who influenced the fate of the Company and are given due mention such as Thomas Henry Ismay, Joseph Bruce Ismay, John Pierpont Morgan, Harold Sanderson and Lord

Below: **The *Titanic*, White Star's legacy for posterity.**
Richard de Kerbrech Collection.

Acknowledgements

Kylsant. Also intertwined with White Star were Harland & Wolff of Belfast, the builders of almost every White Star vessel. They too prospered from White Star's reputation in a close partnership that lasted 62 years. Their leading lights were Gustav Schwabe, Lord Pirrie and Thomas Andrews. Cuthbert Coulson Pounder, a former Chief Technical Director of Harland & Wolff, many years later said of the builders: 'If the time ever comes for a balanced story of contemporary British marine engineering achievement to be told, the part played by the workers in the design and drawing offices of Queen's Island, Belfast – whom it has been my destiny for so many years to lead – will be one of which neither the marine engineering community nor the nation need be ashamed.' He was right; a tribute to White Star also reflected in the skill and quality in the innovative ships of their preferred builders.

The combination of financial irregularities within the Royal Mail group, the Depression and pressure to merge with its rival Cunard had unwittingly conspired to cause White Star's downfall and its premature demise from the North Atlantic. When White Star was absorbed by the Cunard merger of 1934, some of its liners were hastily dispatched to the breakers with the exception of three that remained up until World War 2. The Company's livery and nomenclature passed to Shaw Savill & Albion which for 51 years had maintained a joint service on the New Zealand route.

They're all gone now – those ships in their distinctive White Star livery so well known in Liverpool, Southampton, New York, Australia and New Zealand, but their names were perpetuated by Shaw Savill up until the late 1970s. Cunard became Cunard White Star Line but later reverted to its former title, and up until the late 1960s, their liners flew the White Star burgee below that of their Cunard houseflag. Perhaps the only vestigial remnant of White Star is the tender *Nomadic* which was returned to Belfast in 2006.

Hopefully this story will make a suitable epitaph to a Company that has now passed into history.

Richard de Kerbrech

Gurnard, Isle of Wight

February 2009

I should like to extend my gratitude and acknowledgement to the following persons, firms and institutions for their kindness in contributing information and illustrations or in providing other help and without whose assistance this book would certainly not have been written.

Of necessity, a project of this nature draws heavily on a vast wealth of well-known published sources. Chief among these being the White Star Line history on the Red-duster website and the late Extra Master Mariner, John H. Isherwood's *Steamers of the Past* that appeared in the magazine *Sea Breezes* over a number of years; also Eaton & Haas's *Falling Star* and many others. One of the lesser-known little 'gems' that manifested itself during research was a privately published book called *The Man who Sank the Titanic?* by Gary Cooper. Apart from the *Titanic*, topics such as the class of people who travelled on the North Atlantic, officers in the Royal Naval Reserve and ice flow patterns, amongst other fascinating facets, were covered in this thoroughly well researched publication.

My thanks also go to the late David K. Brown RCNC, the retired Deputy Chief Naval Architect of the Ministry of Defence at Bath for allowing me to use his technical paper, *The Titanic and Lusitania: A Final Forensic Analysis*. For photographs I have mainly used those from my own collection. Included among these are photos taken by B & A Feilden of Stockport, the Nautical Photo Agency (NPA), Real Photographs and those from the collections of the late Tom Rayner and Alex Duncan. My appreciation to Mike Foreman and his support for this project and his offer of photographs from his White Star history on his Shawsavillships website. Also to Mr R. A. Smith of the World Ship Photo Library. To Peter Roberts of Brighton for his published recollections on a cruise he made on the *Adriatic* in 1934. The late Laurence Dunn had kindly granted me permission to use his profile drawing of the *Olympic*.

And finally a little help from my friends, all members of the World Ship Society, namely Bert Moody, David Williams, David Hutchings and Tony Westmore.

Explanatory Notes

For clarification, the Oceanic Steam Navigation Company mentioned in the text was established for the sole purpose of operating and owning steamships. It was the official title and holding company of the White Star Line. Initially, with the prevalence of sailing ships, the OSNCo was part of White Star but was referred to by and traded under the more well known title. By the end of the 19th century, as sail gave way to steam, the Company no longer operated commercial sailing ships. The firm of Ismay, Imrie & Co., was set up initially as shipbrokers and were also managing agents for the White Star Line.

One of the anomalies of White Star was that, as progressive and innovative as it was, it still used antiquated sailing ship orders for steering up until World War 1 and highlighted following the *Titanic* disaster. As the vast majority of their navigating officers were apprenticed in sail, in the early days custom and practice was probably expected. In these orders, the steering was done by the tiller (the horizontal beam at the top of the rudder post). For example, if the ship's heading was desired to be full over to port, the order was given 'Hard to starboard'. In this the ship's wheel (helm) was spun to port, the tiller moved to starboard, and the rudder and ship's heading was to port also.

These commands were further perpetuated by White Star buying a sail training ship, the *Mersey*, which they operated between 1908 and 1914. In this 1,824 gross ton, steel-hulled, three-masted sailing ship, 60 deck cadets destined to serve on steamships were versed in the handling and navigation of a sailing vessel. As a form of future investment in the Company's navigating personnel this can be understood, but to have acquired a sailing ship with its old ways and practices must surely remain a mystery of corporate decision making.

It was not until 1 January 1931 that most nations began to adopt the practice of relating helm orders to the rudder and no longer to the tiller so that an order of say 'starboard 20' meant turning the wheel, the rudder and ship's head to starboard. Masters of White Star vessels were given the courtesy title Captain and most held commissions as Commander and Lieutenant Commander in the RNR, indeed Captain E. J. Smith held the former. That said the Masters were often referred to in White Star literature as Commander, a title that Thomas Ismay himself used.

The British Board of Trade (BoT) was the Government department chiefly concerned with safety at sea, the survey of ships in its hands and the examination of Merchant Navy officers for their Certificates of Competency ('tickets'). Up until the time of the *Titanic* disaster under the Merchant Shipping Act of 1894, BoT rules stated that any vessel over 10,000 tons should be fitted with a minimum of 16 lifeboats. Both the *Olympic* and *Titanic* each carried 20. At the subsequent enquiry into the disaster, Harold Sanderson, a White Star director, stated: 'In fact, the *Titanic* carried more than necessary under Board of Trade requirements...'

Below: **The 3-masted barque *Mersey* had originally been built for J. Nourse in 1894. She was manned by cadets, including some from HMS *Conway* and made six initial voyages to Australia for White Star.** *Nautical Photo Agency.*

Throughout the text ships have been referred to by the female gender.

Each vessel has been prefixed by the following particulars where known. All dimensions and quantities are in imperial units.

Ship's Name (Period with White Star) Gross Registered Tonnage; Length Between Perpendiculars (Length Overall) x Beam
Type of machinery, Number of Screws, Horsepower, Speed in knots (given by whole number and decimal)

Passengers:
Builders   Builder's Yard No.

Abbreviations

AMC	Armed Merchant Cruiser
bhp	brake horsepower
BoT	Board of Trade
BP	length between perpendiculars
ft	feet
grt	gross registered tonnage
HAPAG	Hamburg America Line
HP	High pressure
ihp	indicated horsepower
IMMCo	International Mercantile Marine Company
in	inches
IP	Intermediate pressure
LP	Low pressure
MoWT	Ministry of War Transport
nhp	nominal horsepower
OA	length overall
OSNCo	Oceanic Steam Navigation Company
psi	pounds per square inch (lb/in²)
PSNC	Pacific Steam Navigation Company
rev/min	Revolutions per minute (rpm)
RMSP	Royal Mail Steam Packet Co. Ltd
RNR	Royal Naval Reserve
shp	shaft horsepower
SR	Steam Reciprocating

'A collision at sea can ruin your entire day.'
Thucydides

1869-1881

Origins: a new steamship company and early iron-hulled ships

The origins of the White Star Line can be traced back to a sailing ship company engaged in the Australian trade since 1845, which later expanded with the Australian gold rush of 1851. The Liverpool shipowners and brokers, John Pilkington and Henry Threlfall Wilson, who had set up their offices at 61 Waterloo Road, Liverpool, used the business name White Star Line and the red swallowtail houseflag with a five-pointed, white star upon it. These symbols first manifested themselves on a sailing poster of the clipper ship *Red Jacket*, chartered by Pilkington and Wilson in 1853. The poster displayed a Red Indian Chief with the emblem of a white star tattooed on his chest. Held in his left hand was a spear from which flew a red pennant bearing a similar star. Pilkington & Wilson had adopted the name White Star for their line and extended the association in 1854 by having a wooden clipper built in Canada, which they named *White Star*.

By 1857, John Pilkington retired from the White Star Line and was replaced as a partner by James Chambers, from Ullcoates in Cumberland, and further innovation led to them acquiring their first steamship in 1863, the 2,033 ton *Royal Standard*. Ironically, the following year on 4 April, whilst returning from her maiden voyage to Melbourne and steaming via Cape Horn, she struck an iceberg in the Southern Ocean but survived the collision. Expansion and innovation had meant severe financial and commercial risks. In 1867, the Company owed the Royal Bank of Liverpool £527,000 and was subsequently forced into liquidation and ripe for takeover. The Company's remaining assets, name, houseflag and business goodwill were up for grabs.

The company's White Knight, if one can use that term, came in the form of Thomas Henry Ismay who was born in Maryport on 7 January 1837. Maryport in Cumberland was, in those days, a thriving seaport with a substantial trade to the Baltic. It was also a fishing port and a busy shipbuilding town. By the time he was 16, Thomas Ismay had grown up in a town surrounded by shipping commerce and trade, for his father had been a Foreman Shipwright in a local shipyard close to the River Ellen. At Whitehaven, Thomas and John Brocklebank had established a thriving trade to North America with the company founded by their father. So little wonder that in 1853 he left Maryport for Liverpool where he served his apprenticeship alongside shipowners William Imrie with Messrs Imrie & Tomlinson. With the completion of his indentures, he sought to widen his experience by sailing aboard a Maryport company vessel, the *Chas. Jackson*, which departed on a 10-month voyage around Cape Horn to Chile and Peru and other ports on the west coast of South America.

Upon his return to Liverpool he set up in business as a shipbroker on his own account and soon became friendly

with another Maryport 'exile' in the trade, Phillip Nelson. Nelson was a shipowner and a useful member of the Liverpool Dock Board who was held in high esteem by the leading lights in Liverpool shipping circles. Ismay joined Nelson in the business which became Nelson, Ismay & Company. He was soon to observe that in spite of the already numerous steamship lines engaged on the Atlantic trade, like Cunard and Collins, that here was a service that promised an increasing development which would keep pace with the nation's industrial progress. He foresaw opportunities and initiatives there for the taking.

In order to add to his shipping experience, especially of the trade he planned to enter into, in 1864 he joined the board of the National Steam Navigation Company. This had been formed in 1863 to cater principally for the immigration and cargo traffic to North America. By 1867, Ismay saw an opportunity to acquire the floundering White Star Line and bought the business for £1,000 from its receivers as a going concern. Thus on 18 January 1868, ownership of the White Star Line passed to him. He immediately made his influence felt by introducing iron ships instead of the wooden vessels formerly employed on their Australian service.

During 1869, Ismay formed a partnership with two other shipowners, Mr William Imrie, late of the firm of Imrie, Tomlinson & Co. and a fellow apprentice of Ismay's, and Mr George Hamilton Fletcher. Together they formed Ismay, Imrie & Co, managers of White Star. In this capacity Ismay devoted himself to the development of the steamship department, while Imrie concentrated on the sailing ship part of the business. Another prominent Liverpool merchant and financier, Gustav Schwabe, who moved in the same circles as Ismay, entered the fray. Schwabe owned considerable stock in the Bibby Line which operated to the Mediterranean and was also the uncle of Gustav Wolff, the junior partner of the Harland & Wolff shipbuilders in Belfast. It was Schwabe who had put up much of the capital to finance the shipyard as a viable concern. It is said that whilst playing a game of billiards at Gustav Schwabe's house, he and Ismay sowed the seeds of one of the major steamship companies on the North Atlantic, the White Star Line.

Schwabe wanted a larger stakeholding in the expanding shipping business and he had plenty of money. His business proposition was simple, and with Ismay's knowledge of shipping and ownership of White Star, the proposition was put. With the nucleus of the White Star Line a new Atlantic company would be set up. Ismay would have all his ships built by Harland & Wolff in Belfast and Schwabe would guarantee the finance. The agreement with the yard was that ships were to be built of the best materials, no fixed price being quoted.

White Star would pay the cost, plus an agreed margin for profit, provided that Harland & Wolff did not build ships for potential competitors on the same route. This proposal fitted in with Ismay's vision and an agreement was struck.

To this end on 6 September 1869, the Oceanic Steam Navigation Company (OSNCo), as the White Star Line was to be officially known, was registered with a capital of £400,000 in £1,000 shares. The first £156,000 of issue was taken up by Ismay and his friends with Ismay having £50,000 worth. The offices of OSNCo were at 10 Water Street, Liverpool, and from its formation the sailing vessels of the fleet were not included in its organisation but flew the same houseflag under the ownership of T. H. Ismay & Company. (The new holding company always being referred to as the White Star Line and very rarely by its official registered name.) Ismay, Imrie & Co. solemnly contracted to give each adult a separate berth, to allow 10 ft³ of luggage space free and to do the cooking and provide all the food, the meals being breakfast at eight o'clock, dinner at one, supper at six, and, if required, oatmeal gruel at eight in the evening. Furthermore, they stipulated: 'all passengers are liable to be rejected who, upon examination, are found to be lunatic, idiot, dumb, blind, maimed, infirm or above the age of 60 years, or any woman without a husband with a child or children…' For this well ventilated and relatively spacious luxury, the cost was around six guineas (£6-30p), and children travelled half-price.

Around 1835 the marine steam reciprocating engine had become a prime mover but was still in its infancy, and it was not for another fifty years that the steam engine could said to be dominant. Experience gained had demonstrated the impracticality of being able to build a wooden ship of 300 ft long, especially if it were steam propelled. The same experience had shown that a wooden vessel propelled by paddles might operate satisfactorily, but when the power was applied by a screw propeller to the extreme end of the ship, it was difficult to combine sufficient fine lines with the necessary rigidity to resist continuous 'working' and vibration. Rigidity was of major importance in merchant ships that were usually run at full speed or as near as could be.

For high powers therefore, either the screw propeller had to be abandoned or iron replace wood for the hull. The so-called 'composite' system was then introduced, whereby the ship's frames were made from wrought iron and the planking wood. (The Royal Navy's HMS *Gannet* of 1878 and its class of sloops were of this type of construction.) This system of construction soon gave way to the all-iron ship, with a saving of about one-third of the hull weight. Although primarily introduced for screw propelled steamers, the all-iron construction proved equally beneficial to sailing ships. A generation later, steel began to replace iron, thereby reducing hull weights by a further fifteen per cent. Ironically, Gustav Schwabe encouraged Ismay to purchase and share joint ownership of an iron sailing barque from a bankrupt customer of Harland & Wolff, for Ismay, Imrie & Co. It had been built in 1868, 165 ft length of keel and fore-rake; 27 ft 8 in beam; 18 ft 4 in depth, top of ceiling to top of beams, 603 gross tons and 580 net tons. This was probably the first vessel acquired by the new owners of the White Star Line and was named *Broughton*.

In November 1869, the Anglo-French Suez Canal was opened, thereby considerably shortening the long voyage to India, the Orient, Australasia and beyond. The globe was rapidly shrinking and the influence of international events, wherever they occurred, had its ultimate effect throughout the world on trade and on the minds of travellers, who were made aware of events almost as soon as they happened by the introduction of the submarine cable. Radical departures in naval architecture and marine engineering had been achieved 10 years earlier when Isambard Kingdom Brunel's *Great Eastern* was completed in 1859 – a veritable giant iron steamship in its day with a tonnage of 18,900, an overall length of 692 ft and a beam of 82 ft 8 in. She was propelled through the water by a combination of sails, paddle wheels and a single screw propeller. The *Great Eastern* was a ship way ahead of its time whereby the builders had taken advantage of the technology and material resources available to them during her construction. By 1869, however, the single cylinder expansion steam engine, having gained acceptance, had given way to the wider use of steam propulsion, especially the compound engine powering an iron hull with a screw propeller.

Harland & Wolff had developed their expertise on a plethora of different types of machinery; for example, original vertical engines were engines with the cylinders at the bottom and the crankshaft above them. Gradually the steam hammer design prevailed; it was an inverted vertical engine, i.e. the crankshaft was underneath the cylinders. The builders also had a wealth of experience in hull design as well. In wooden hulls the ratio of length to beam was about 7:1, sometimes less, this breadth being necessary for providing the required restoring action to counteract the overturning moment of the wind against the sails. The *Broughton*'s ratio was 6:1. Many of the earlier Harland & Wolff steamships were made with a ratio of 10:1, and on occasion 11:1, thus increasing the relative payload. This new practice in length/beam ratio soon became general for their large steamships.

Meanwhile, back in Liverpool, Ismay and his partners were negotiating for the building of their first Atlantic steamer with Harland & Wolff, an association between the White Star Line and the Belfast shipbuilders which lasted for some 62 years. Such was the trust between the two firms that no written contract was drawn up. Once the price and delivery were agreed it was formalised by a handshake and this became the established custom and practice for many years to come. Ismay had met Gustav Wolff in Liverpool when he became acquainted with his ideas and those of his partner, Edward Harland, which were radical and departed from certain accepted features of traditional ship design. Quite apart from the agreement struck with Schwabe, it appears that Harland & Wolff convinced Ismay of the soundness of their ideas and proposals, for it led Ismay to place an order for four iron-hulled passenger ships for the North Atlantic operating out of Liverpool.

When the first of his intended six-liner fleet, the *Oceanic*, appeared on the Mersey in February 1871, she attracted a great deal of comment and criticism, favourable and otherwise aimed at her unusual features, both from those in

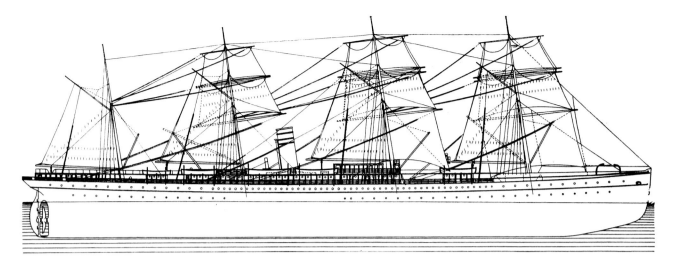

Liverpool shipping circles and assembled spectators on the waterfront. She was an imposing vessel with her four raked masts and single buff funnel with a black top band. (Buff may be defined as a colour between that of yellow and orange, although in the *White Star Line Official Guide of 1877* it identifies their funnel marks as ' Cream, with black top'. The *Oceanic* began the White Star system of nomenclature by introducing the suffix 'ic' for their ships. When Digby Murray was appointed Master of the *Oceanic* he was served with the following memorandum:

To Captain Digby Murray:

Dear Sir, when placing the steamer Oceanic under your charge, we endeavoured to impress on you verbally, and in the most forcible manner we were capable of, the paramount and vital importance above all other things of caution in the navigation of your vessel, and we now confirm this in writing, begging you to remember the safety of your passengers and crew weigh with us above and before all other considerations. The most rigid discipline on the part of your officers, should be observed, whom you will exhort to avoid at all times convivial intercourse with passengers, or with each other, and only such an amount of communication with the former as is demanded by a necessary and businesslike courtesy. We must also remind you that it is essential to successful navigation that the crew be kept under judicious control.

Ismay, Imrie & Co, 1871

With due ceremony the future schedule for the service was advertised thus:

'The new first-class, full-powered screw steamships *Oceanic, Baltic, Atlantic, Pacific, Arctic* and *Adriatic*. Sailing on Thursdays from Liverpool, and calling at Queenstown on Fridays to embark passengers. Will sail as under for New York, via Queenstown. *Oceanic*, 4,500 tons, 3,000 horsepower, Captain Digby Murray, to sail tomorrow, Thursday 2nd March 1871. These steamships have been designed to afford the very best accommodation to all classes of passengers, and are expected to accomplish quick and regular passages between this country and America. The staterooms, with saloons and smoking rooms, are placed amidships, and cabin passengers are thus removed from the noise and motion experienced in the after part of the vessel. Passengers are booked to all parts of the States, Canada, and Newfoundland, Nova Scotia, India, etc., at moderate through rates. A surgeon and stewardess carried on each ship…'

For the new concern the Third class or 'steerage' passengers generally formed the bulk of those crossing the Atlantic. Theirs were the cheapest berths on the ship, but it was these passengers that earned White Star its bread and butter as most steerage travellers would probably not cross the Atlantic again, for most were emigrants. In fact, in 1879 some 118,000 steerage passengers left Liverpool for the United States with various companies. However, the First class and Second class passengers formed a regular core of income. The cabin fare in the *Oceanic* and *Britannic* was only eighteen guineas (£18-90p). Their ranks were being made up not only of nobility, but also such people as salesmen, writers, journalists, lecturers, theatrical actors and politicians whose business demanded a great deal of travel. So the more comfortable a shipping company could make its journeys, the more they were likely to think well of the line and use it again. By 1895, steerage class was being relentlessly marketed to 'Americans of small means', who were beginning to spend their vacations abroad.

During 1872, OSNCo's share capital increased twice, a further issue of 100 and later another 250, making a total share capital of 750 shares of £1,000 per share. It may be of interest to note that Thomas Ismay was always proud of his roots. Whenever young men from Maryport intended on a seafaring life left home for Liverpool, they were pretty certain that a visit to the White Star Line offices would guarantee them employment when they stated they were natives of Maryport. One of Ismay's boyhood friends was John Cockton, a son of the local chemist. The friendship continued for many years and when John inherited his father's business, all White Star's medical supplies were purchased from him. A brass plaque was placed on Cockton's wall which proclaimed: 'Agents for Ismay, Imrie & Co'. Early on in the Company's existence, Ismay was so concerned about safety at sea, potential collisions and designated sea lanes across the Atlantic that on 1 January 1876 he wrote a letter to Mr Gray Hill of the North Atlantic Steam Traffic Conference stating his concern:

LANE ROUTES

Dear Sir,

Referring to the failure to agree upon an International Rule obliging all steamers passing between Europe and North America to follow fixed Lane routes (which, personally, I much regretted at the time), and having since given a good deal of consideration to the matter during four Transatlantic passages, made within the past eighteen months, I have determined, as far as practicable, with this Company's steamers, to follow Maury's Steam Lanes, [*routes recommended by Lieutenant Maury USN*] and would suggest that a conference be called, to consist of a nautical and a lay representative from such of the European lines as may respond to an invitation to be issued by the North Atlantic Steam Traffic Conference, and that a Committee thereof make a joint report, to be unanimously adopted, the responsibility of non-agreement to rest with those who do not accept the Committee's recommendation.

These Lanes, if generally adopted, would, I think, materially lessen the risks of collision and of ice.

Pending the discussion of this subject on the part of the Conference, the commanders of the White Star steamers are instructed to follow the routes named.

I am, dear Sir

Yours faithfully
THOMAS H. ISMAY

Indeed in one of the regulations issued to White Star Masters in the Company's *Official Guide of 1877*, they were: '...enjoined to remember that whilst they are expected to use every diligence to secure a speedy voyage, they must run no risk which might by any possibility result in accident to their ships. It is to be hoped that they will ever bear in mind that the safety of lives and property entrusted to their care is the ruling principle that should govern them in the navigation of their ships, and no supposed gain in expedition, or saving of time on the voyage is to be purchased at the risk of accident'.

And so it was that Ismay's OSNCo under the banner of the White Star name became one of the most famous and exalted shipping companies to enter the North Atlantic service.

OCEANIC (I)

(1871-1896)
3,707 grt; 420 ft 4 in BP (432 ft OA) x 40 ft 10 in
Compound expansion SR engine, Single screw,
 1,990 ihp, 14 knots.
Passengers: 166 First class, 1000 Third class
Harland & Wolff, Belfast Yard No. 73

The *Oceanic* was an historic milestone in maritime history as she was the first steamship to be built for the White Star Line and the lead ship of a class of four, appropriately named to inaugurate the Oceanic Steam Navigation Company (OSNCo), as the White Star was officially registered. Built at Harland & Wolff's Belfast shipyard, she was constructed of wrought iron frames and beams and the hull of riveted wrought iron plates. The *Oceanic* was launched on 27 August 1870 and six months later was delivered to White Star on 24 February 1871. The *Oceanic* began not only the White Star nomenclature by introducing the suffix 'ic' to its vessels but an association between the Company and Harland & Wolff that was to last for 62 years.

The *Oceanic's* innovations were an outstanding contribution to the eventual development of the modern passenger liner. She was officially designated as a 'Four-masted iron barque (single screw)' with the following technical particulars. As Harland & Wolff had not yet developed their engine expertise, the *Oceanic's* single, 4-cylinder, compound steam reciprocating engine was supplied by Maudslay, Sons & Field of Lambeth. This was shipped to Belfast in pieces and installed onboard by Maudslay's own engineers. The respective compound cylinder bores were two high pressure cylinders of 41 in placed directly above two low pressure cylinders of 78 in with a stroke of 5 ft which developed 1,990 ihp. The pistons for the upper and lower cylinders were on a common piston rod so that there were only two cranks. A single valve rod and link motion worked the main slide valves for each pair of cylinders. The *Oceanic* had a depth of hold of 31 ft 6 in and a loaded displacement of 7,940 tons.

One of the salient features was that her length/breadth ratio was more than 10:1 and she carried more cargo than her contemporaries of the same tonnage. Furthermore, the passenger accommodation was moved amidships for the first time in a steamship. Hitherto it had been built up and under the poop, a legacy from the days of sail, but Ismay and his associates were quickly convinced of the advantage of having the accommodation sited amidships. In this position passengers would be away from the vibration of the propeller and the extreme motion experienced far aft with the ship pitching, yawing or pooping in rough weather. Gone too were the heavy old bulwarks stretching around the edge of a single flush deck, rather like a wall around a flat space. This feature had been replaced by a row of neat stanchions supporting guardrails, much like ships of the present. The early isolated wooden deckhouses had grown together to form a single structure which itself supported a deck extending to the ship's sides. Below decks, the *Oceanic's* designer had gone further still to make her a distinctive ship by installing electric bells, and in the dining saloon individual chairs had replaced the older bench style seating and was constructed with larger than normal sized portholes to give more light. In addition to this, there were bathtubs provided with running water for the passengers. Whilst in general the First or Saloon class passengers travelled in great luxury, the 1000 or so in Third or Steerage class accommodation which, although lacking the additional comforts provided for First class, was a great improvement

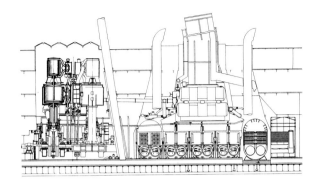

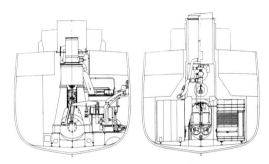

Above: **Side elevation of the *Oceanic's* innovative engines.** *Richard de Kerbrech.*

than that which had been previously been afforded this class of passenger previously. The Thomas Maudslay tandem compound engine that was a bought-in item was supplied by 12 double-ended oval boilers, operating at 65 psi and consumed around 70 tons of anthracite coal a day. (More technically rated as a coal consumption of 3 lb/ ihp hr.) An independent centrifugal pump circulated the condenser.

In those days coal was a plentiful commodity in the UK, but a sufficient supply had to be carried in the ship's bunkers to complete the voyage as well as to act as reserve in case of slippage due to wind, current, tide, drift and chart errors. Once in its port of destination the ship's bunkers could be replenished by 'coaling the ship' when all available manpower 'turned to' until the task was completed. An onerous task – as well as a potential health hazard in its day – in which coal dust settled in places it shouldn't have. Although the *Oceanic's* service speed was rated at 13.5 knots, on a good day she could 'crack on' at 14.5 knots.

On 26 February 1871, the *Oceanic* arrived at Liverpool arousing great interest. To onlookers her stem was straight and raked slightly aft instead of being dead vertical. The counter stern had a good overhang and gave her a clean run aft. She had a pleasing sheer and sat rather low in the water with every suggestion about her of slimness and speed. She appeared to the press 'more like an Imperial yacht' than a passenger vessel. In the *Liverpool Daily Post* of 1 March 1871, the following advert appeared:

> Tomorrow, 2nd March there will sail for New York
> The new First class, full powered steamship
> *Oceanic* of the White Star Line under the
> Management of Ismay, Imrie & Company.

A single fare was advertised as 18 guineas (£18-90p) and return being 25 guineas (£26-25p) and Third class 6 guineas (£6-30p). However, only 64 passengers opted to sail with the new company on the Atlantic, whereas 300 passengers embarked on the longer established Cunard ship *Calabria* that sailed for New York on the same day. On 2 March 1871, under the command of Captain Digby Murray, the *Oceanic* departed Liverpool on her maiden voyage. However, after entering the Irish Sea off Holyhead, her bearings overheated so she put into Holyhead before returning to Liverpool. Here the offending components were 'bedded in' and adjusted and the *Oceanic* resumed her maiden voyage to New York via Queenstown (later Cobh). She arrived in New York after a favourable but slow passage on 28 March and the interest aroused by her entry into service was even greater; apparently over 50,000 people visited the new steamship whilst there.

After making a few voyages, the *Oceanic* returned to Belfast in January 1872 for her first annual overhaul and to incorporate various modifications based on the operational experience gained thus far. These included the shortening of her masts to reduce rolling as well as an additional two boilers to generate more steam and increasing her coal bunker capacity accordingly. In heavy sea states water was slow at clearing her forecastle. In order to alleviate this problem a 72ft turtleback breakwater was built on her forecastle. This feature became the standard for all White Star's liners until the *Teutonic* of 1889. These modifications greatly improved her seakeeping qualities in a heavy seaway.

In all, the *Oceanic* completed some 33 round voyages on the Atlantic, making her last voyage on this route on 11 March 1875. During this time she had gained a high reputation for safety, reliability and comfort. White Star's first passenger liner helped to establish the Oceanic Steam Navigation Co. (OSNCo) on the North Atlantic. However, in 1875, the newer *Britannic* entered service with the growing fleet and the *Oceanic* was released from her Atlantic service and transferred to the longer trans-Pacific run. She was chartered to the Occidental & Oriental Steamship Co.,

Left: **Sometimes referred to as the 'Mother of Modern liners', the *Oceanic* was the first ship to have protected decks and bathtubs with running water for passengers.** *Nautical Photo Agency.*

a subsidiary of White Star, for service between San Francisco, Yokohama and Hong Kong. She augmented two other ships, the *Belgic* and the *Gaelic* already operating on this route. On 17 April 1875, she departed Liverpool for San Francisco via the new Suez Canal, Hong Kong and Yokohama. For this service she carried an all Chinese crew overseen by White Star officers. Upon her arrival in San Francisco on 29 June, she had made a record passage from Yokohama of 16 days, 10 hours. The following year during December 1876, the *Oceanic* made another record passage between Yokohama and San Francisco of 14 days 15 hours at an average speed of 13 knots. This meant that with a crossing of the United States by the Union Pacific Railroad in 7 days and an Atlantic crossing time of 9 days, it was possible to travel from Yokohama to London in 32 days compared with 90 days via Singapore and Suez. By so doing, the *Oceanic* gained a further reputation for comfort and speed. On the downside, during the following year on 25 July, the *Oceanic* lost her single screw whilst on passage between Yokohama and Hong Kong. She had to complete the voyage under sail. Two months later on 19 September 1877, whilst about to sail from San Francisco loaded with mail for Japan and China, she experienced problems with her engines and was delayed for sailing for ten days while the problem was rectified.

In late 1879, she returned to Liverpool for a major refit which included reboilering and resumed her Pacific service on 16 March 1880 when she sailed out to Hong Kong via Suez and arrived at San Francisco after 75 days on passage. On 22 August 1888 while inbound to San Francisco and in the foggy mid-channel of the Golden Gate, the *Oceanic* collided with and sank the Pacific Coast SS Co 1,106 ton steamer, the *City of Chester*, with a loss of 16 lives – 50 were resuced by the *Oceanic* and more were saved by other vessels. Once again, she arrived at San Francisco on 11 November 1889 after she made another record Pacific crossing from Yokohama to San Francisco of 13 days, 14 hours and 6 minutes, and maintained the service for another six years. It was proposed that the *Oceanic* return to her builders for re-engining to enhance her performance built upon her reputation and bring her up to date with newer vessels operating on the route. Upon her arrival at Belfast on 17 May 1895 and subsequent hull and engine survey, it was decided against major re-engining. She was instead marked for disposal and sold for scrap for £8,000. She departed Belfast on 10 February 1896 under the tow of L. Smit & Co's tug *Ocean II* for the River Thames where she was broken up.

The *Oceanic* proved a success both in operational performance on long haul voyages and as a passenger ship; her sister, the *Atlantic*, did not prove so fortunate. The *Oceanic*'s first Master, Captain Digby Murray, rose to become Commodore of the White Star Line and was later selected by the Board of Trade (BoT) as the marine adviser of the department, the highest nautical office in the Civil Service of the Crown.

OCEANIC: *Named after the Oceanic Steam Navigation Co. Of or pertaining to the ocean.*

ATLANTIC

(1871-1873)
3,707 grt; 420 ft 4 in BP (432 ft OA) x 40 ft 10 in
Compound Expansion SR engine, Single screw,
1,990 ihp, 14 knots
Passengers: 166 First class, 1000 Third class.
Harland & Wolff, Belfast Yard No. 74

The *Atlantic* was built by Harland & Wolff as a sister ship to the *Oceanic* and launched on 26 November 1870. However, unlike the *Oceanic*, the *Atlantic* was supplied by engines manufactured by G. Forrester & Co. of Liverpool and completed on 3 June 1871 at a cost of £120,000. She sailed on her maiden voyage from Liverpool to New York via Queenstown on 8 June 1871. After eleven voyages the *Atlantic* entered drydock at Liverpool to have her three-bladed propeller replaced by a four-bladed one in an attempt to reduce vibration and blade fatigue fractures that had plagued her and her sister ships. As White Star's second ship on the North Atlantic passenger service, like her sister, she proved a safe and comfortable ship on that route. As such, she completed eighteen crossings without incident and there was no reason to suppose that the next would be any different when she arrived in Liverpool on 13 March 1873. One of the first of White Star Line's officials to come aboard was the Company's Superintendent Engineer, Stewart Gordon Horsburgh. He was tasked with checking the *Atlantic*'s fuel consumption, estimating how much coal remained in the bunkers and ensuring adequate supplies for the next voyage, her nineteenth. The Chief Engineer, John Foxley, had entered in his engine room log that 132 tons remained. This was at variance with the 160 that Horsburgh had estimated, but he accepted the Chief's figure and ordered fresh bunkers based on this. 860 tons of coal was ordered by White Star for the *Atlantic* and 863 tons was actually delivered. However, 16 tons were diverted for use on White Star's Mersey tender, the *Traffic*, leaving 847 tons to be loaded in the *Atlantic*. The total amount carried including the estimated amount from the previous voyage was around 979 tons. On 20 March 1873, the *Atlantic* departed Liverpool under the command of Captain James Agnew Williams. On board were 636 passengers made up of 31 First (Saloon) class and 605 Third (Steerage) class including 78 children. A further 175 largely Steerage joined at Queenstown. These together with 141 members of the crew meant that there were 952 persons officially aboard although figures do vary and no account is taken of the unknown number of stowaways, thought to be around 14 but who were not accurately counted.

From the start of the voyage when the *Atlantic* left the Irish port the weather was foul. Gale-force winds and rough seas pounded the ship and one of her wheelhouse windows was smashed by the impact of a wave. Also, two lifeboats were seriously damaged and at one critical stage the *Atlantic*'s steering gear was disabled. Captain Williams was not unduly worried by his ship's seaworthiness as she had previously crossed the Atlantic in bad weather and heavy seaways and would do so again, provided she had enough coal for the

boilers. However on 31 March, after 11 days from Queenstown and driven through heavy seas at a reduced speed of 5 knots, there was cause for concern. Not only had passengers been uncomfortable and seasick, seasoned sailors became a little disorientated by the extreme motion of the ship. In position latitude 41°39′ N; longitude 63°54′ W, Captain Williams requested that Chief Engineer Foxley together with three senior watchkeeping engineers were to individually estimate the amount of coal left in the bunkers. One engineer calculated there was between 150 and 160 tons remaining while one reported 160 tons in supply whereas another quoted 150 tons. Mr Foxley concurred with their estimates; he had made 16 voyages on the *Atlantic* and based on his experience he believed that the remaining coal could raise steam for two days with some left over. This meant that with a coal consumption of 70 tons per day, 140 tons would be used. The chief's engine log showed a lower figure as can be seen from the following extract:

Start of Voyage No. 19	979 tons
Seven days in Liverpool @ 6 tons per day	42 tons
To enter Mersey from dock and stem tide	38 tons
Nine days steaming @ 70 tons per day	630 tons
Four days use of donkey boiler @ 5 tons per day	20 tons
Two days @ reduced consumption, say 60 tons per day	120 tons
Total consumed to date	850 tons

COAL REMAINING   **129 tons**

Each day in accordance with White Star standing orders, Mr Foxley had reported to Captain Williams a report of how much coal remained based on these figures. Now he was faced with the indisputable evidence of his fellow engineers that there was at least 150 tons of coal remaining that would have been enough to get the *Atlantic* to her destination of New York, some 460 miles away. However, the chief's log showed the somewhat lower amount of 129 tons, which if

it were correct would mean that the ship would either be towed ignominiously into New York or, worse still, left powerless and drifting on the Nantucket shoals.

Notwithstanding the fact that all senior engineers had agreed that there was enough coal for two day's steaming, and contrary to Captain Williams' request that the coal report was to be based on their personal estimation, the chief wrote out a chit saying there were 129 tons remaining in the bunkers. Working to this figure, Captain Williams made the decision to alter course for Halifax, Nova Scotia. The Canadian port was much nearer than New York being some 170 miles distant, was well stocked with coal supplies as a bunkering station and it was much used by transatlantic liners dangerously low on coal reserves. To put into Halifax for coal was not uncommon, although the *Atlantic* was the first White Star liner to attempt to do so. Unbeknown to them and as a result of the lack of sun sights due to bad weather, the ship was miles off course. At 1am on 1 April, they were searching for the Sambro Light that should have been visible from 20 miles; it was clear but cloudy weather with high seas running.

At that time none of the *Atlantic*'s mates had any intimate knowledge of the approaches to the port with the exception of the ship's quartermaster, Robert Thomas, and he was deeply concerned at the speed with which the *Atlantic* was approaching an unfamiliar landfall. Risking reprimand, he advised the Second Mate, Henry Ismay Metcalfe, that the ship had run far enough and that they ought to heave to. The Second Mate replied, 'I am not the Captain and you are not the Mate.' The quartermaster then appealed to the Fourth Mate John Brown who shared the watch with Metcalfe and suggested to him that he should climb to the main yard and look for land.

Brown told Thomas, 'You won't see any. We haven't run our distance yet.'

Thomas replied, 'You won't feel the land until you strike it.' But Brown forbade him to go aloft and check.

Captain Williams had left orders that he was to be called at 3am when it was, in fact, his intention to heave to until daylight. Fifteen fateful minutes later, Metcalfe entered the chartroom where the Master lay asleep on the settee, but hardly had he entered when the lookout on the forward deckhouse saw a streak of white showing through the dark night.

'Breakers ahead! Breakers ahead!' he yelled.

Thomas spun the wheel to starboard, which would bring the ship's head around to port. Simultaneously, Metcalfe rung the telegraph so hard to 'Full Astern' that it repeated off the order indicated in the engine room. However, although the engineer on watch responded instantly to the order, it was too late. Ploughing on through the waves with her engines on Full Ahead, the *Atlantic* rode up on the rocks, pounded on them four or five times, shattered her iron plates and came to a grinding halt. She had gone aground on Marr's Rock, Meagher's Island, near Halifax, a low-lying reef near the fishing village of Lower Prospect some 20 miles off the *Atlantic*'s course to Halifax. In the pandemonium and confusion that ensued as crewmembers attempted to clear the lifeboats, she slipped off the rocks and heeled to starboard minutes later. With the fore part and most of the rigging out of the water, many were swamped by the cold water which surged through the gashes in her iron hull and lifeboats were torn away by the heavy seas.

The situation was becoming the survival of the fittest and it was every man for himself. At great risk and in a selfless act of bravery, the Third Mate, Brady, and quartermasters Speakman and Owen swam to the shore with a rope – by dawn, five lines had been rigged via the rock to the shore. One passenger saw a sea of heads in the seas which he mistook for floating cargo as they were huddled together. As each wave burst over the mass there were many who lost their grip and were carried out to sea and lost from view. Gradually the passengers were dragged by hauling lines to the shore, but many of the cold and exhausted were swept away. As the situation further deteriorated, the Master, Captain Williams, told the passengers to climb into the rigging until they could be pulled ashore. However, in the biting wind many more fell into the sea and were lost whilst others died where they hung. As dawn broke many of the islanders rallied to help with the rescue. The loss of life was staggering; out of 952 people on board, 585 had died through drowning or exposure. Although 370 men were saved, only one of 90 children survived and every woman was lost. Survivors were taken to Halifax in the steamship *Lady Head*. At the time the *Atlantic* was the worst shipping disaster in history and was to remain so until the loss of the *Titanic* in 1912.

At the subsequent enquiry in Halifax, Captain Williams was severely censured for negligent navigation, mainly on the grounds that he had failed to take frequent soundings – only his efforts to save lives during the disaster prevented his Master's certificate from being withdrawn and he was suspended for two years. The Second Mate Metcalfe lost his life and the other officer of the watch, Fourth Mate Brown, survived but his Second Mate's certificate was suspended for three months. The White Star Line also came in for criticism as the Canadian court of enquiry stated 'The inference seems inevitable that she had not sufficient coals on board when sailing for a ship of her class.'

These findings caused uproar and indignation back in the *Atlantic*'s homeport of Liverpool. However, worse was to follow when a relative of one of the victims wrote: 'Such culpable dereliction of duty approximates more to murder than to manslaughter. I hope, therefore, to hear that a judicial inquiry of the most searching character has been, or

immediately will be, ordered to be held in England.' White Star, who denied emphatically that the *Atlantic* was short of coal, welcomed the prospect of an inquiry, but were told that the inquiry had already been held in Halifax and there were no grounds for reopening it. In the face mounting criticism, the Board of Trade realised that it was their surveyors who had signed the *Atlantic*'s clearance certificate stating that she was 'strong, seaworthy and fit in all respects for her intended service, namely the carriage of passengers to New York.'

Thomas Gray, Head of the Marine Department of the Board of Trade, ordered the British inquiry to be made – not into shipwreck disaster however, but into 'whether the provisions of the Merchant Shipping Acts and of Passenger Acts have been complied with in the case of the survey and inspection of the steamship *Atlantic* and of her rigging and equipments, and of her stores, fuel and provisions put on board of her.' Clearly, if the *Atlantic* had been short of coal, then she had not been 'fit in all respects' and the Board of Trade needed to clear its yardarm.

On 10 May 1873, the British inquiry was convened at the Liverpool's Sailor's Home chaired by Rear Admiral Charles Schomberg, the Queen's Harbour Master of Holyhead, assisted by Mr William Waldron Ravenhill QC, Recorder of Andover. Schomberg had never served on a merchant ship and only briefly in a coal-burning warship. Ravenhill was not familiar with naval architecture, marine engineering or ship construction. At the end of four days, during which White Star produced evidence to show the amount of coal on board the *Atlantic* and gave details of her consumption in all weathers, the court issued its findings with the comment:

'It would have been more judicious to have had a larger amount, say, at least 100 tons, more fully on board her.'

White Star protested that the findings were totally at variance with the evidence and demanded that the inquiry be reopened so that they might produce more proof of their innocence. The Board of Trade agreed and on 28 May 1873 and over the following nine days Schomberg and Ravenhill chaired a re-run of the proceedings in the boardroom of the Sailor's Home while expert witnesses were paraded before them. White Star had summoned before them noted shipowners like Alfred Holt of the Blue Funnel Line, Bryce Allan of the Allan Line, Edward J Harland, senior partner of Harland & Wolff together with the Superintendent engineers of famous transatlantic shipping companies, and consulting engineers in private practice. All the surviving engineers of the *Atlantic* gave evidence including the Chief, Foxley, and the engine room firemen. Even the captains of the coal barges that supplied the coal to the *Atlantic* were called to swear an oath that they hadn't stolen any. At the summing up, Schomberg apologised for differing with 'several gentlemen of well known position and experience' but, he said, 'no passenger ship of her class should be short of coals on the 11th day of her voyage to New York, as the *Atlantic*, in our opinion undoubtedly was.'

Throughout the proceedings, Thomas Ismay had a shorthand writer take a verbatim note of everything which was said. Following the court's adverse findings, the reporter transcribed his notes and White Star's engineers made an analysis of the salient points contained therein. The transcript, which contained 12,353 questions and answers, together with the analysis, were forwarded to the Board of Trade with the pointed request that they be submitted to a judge who knew something about coal-fired steamships.

Thomas Gray, himself far from satisfied with the way the inquiry had gone, passed the papers to J MacFarland Gray, the Board of Trade's Chief Examiner of Engineers, and Thomas W Traill, their Chief Engineer Surveyor. These two experts made a deeply reasoned appraisal of the evidence presented and their conclusions were cold, logical, mathematical, precise and objective. But with their scientific approach to the evidence they also brought to bear their vast experience as sea-going engineers on the behaviour of ships in bad weather, in addition, their knowledge of the custom and practice of firemen and stokers and the heating qualities of various types of coal. They were fully aware of the log-keeping habits of Chief Engineers, having come up through that route themselves. By this knowledge they exposed Mr Foxley's obstinacy.

At the end of their report they concluded: 'We are satisfied that the steamship *Atlantic* on her last voyage was supplied with sufficient coal for a voyage to New York at that season of the year. And, that at the time the vessel's course was altered for Halifax, there still remained sufficient coal to have taken her to New York and to leave 70 tons in the bunkers, even if the weather did not improve.' From their calculations, in fact, they arrived at much the same figure as Foxley and the other engineers had done. Foxley had erred towards the cautious in wanting to 'keep his powder dry' and his professional pride let him submit the lower figure to the Master. This set into action a chain of events based again on caution, error of judgement and the wrong deduced reckoning of the ship's position. The *Atlantic* was self insured and the Company's smaller liners, the *Asiatic* and *Tropic*, also built in 1871, had to be sold to recover the lost capital in addition to the lost trade through loss of confidence by Atlantic travellers.

The manner of the loss of the *Atlantic* raised a great outcry in Britain against iron steamships, but not by any means for the first time; there had been other disasters but not of the magnitude of the *Atlantic*.

ATLANTIC: *Named after the Atlantic Ocean. Of or pertaining to the lost continent of Atlantis.*

BALTIC (I)

(1872-1888)
3,707 grt; 420 ft 4 in BP (432 ft OA) x 40 ft 10 in
Compound Expansion SR engine, Single screw
1,990 ihp 14 knots
Passengers: 166 First class, 1000 Third class
Harland & Wolff, Belfast Yard No. 75

White Star's third iron-hulled passenger ship was built at Harland & Wolff and launched as the *Pacific* on 8 March 1871. Like her sister the *Oceanic*, she was engined with compound steam reciprocating engines built by Maudslay, Sons & Field of London. There was an appreciable improvement in these compound engines which worked at a pressure of 70 psi and were much more economical. In addition she had greater boiler power, larger bunkers and better passenger accommodation than the *Oceanic*. As the press of the day followed the progress of the ship they also made reference to the Collins wooden paddle steamer *Pacific* that had sunk in the Atlantic in 1856. In light of this, White Star thought it prudent to change the name to *Baltic* in order to allay the travelling public's superstitions, prior to her completion on 2 September 1871. It was as the *Baltic* that she sailed on her maiden voyage from Liverpool to New York via Queenstown on 14 September 1871.

After nearly a month in service, the *Baltic* suffered her first scrape when completing only her second voyage to New York on 7 October 1871. She collided at the Harbour's approaches with the French brig *Confiance* which was anchored off Sandy Hook. The brig's foremast was broken and a lifeboat smashed. The French brig started to take in water and had to be towed to the Atlantic Dock for repairs.

During January 1873, the *Baltic* made a record crossing from New York to Queenstown of 7 days 20 hours 9 minutes at an average speed of 15.09 knots. In so doing she became a Blue Riband holder for the fastest crossing of the Atlantic and beat the previous Eastbound record held by Inman Line's *City of Brussels*. The following year, the *Celtic*'s passengers were transferred to the *Baltic* and they left Queenstown bound for New York on 23 January 1874. The *Celtic* had shed its propeller blades after striking some floating wreckage thus delaying her voyage. Later that year while lying alongside at Granton, New York on 23 November 1874, an upset paraffin lamp led to a fire aboard the *Baltic*. The blaze was not threatening and extinguished without serious damage.

Nearly a year later on 18 November 1875 whist returning to Liverpool, she encountered the foundering sailing vessel *Oriental* in the mid-Atlantic and picked up her stranded crew of the Master and fifteen men. Another minor collision occurred in Liverpool, when on 3 February 1876, the *Baltic* ran into the steamer *Prince Llewelyn* from Buenos Aires while berthing at the Princes Dock. The *Prince Llewelyn* had her jib boom wrenched off whilst the *Baltic* remained unscathed. Again the *Baltic* was visited by misfortune when, whilst departing for New York on 17 August 1880, she was in collision in the River Mersey with the steamer *Longford* inbound from Dublin. The *Longford* was towed ashore and took on water and the *Baltic*, which had been badly damaged in the collision, had to put back into dock for repairs which required much of her cargo to be discharged. A month later on 20 September 1880, the *Baltic* was delayed four hours by fog off Sandy Hook. When the fog cleared, as she was steaming to her pier in New York, she ran into a schooner, the *Sarah Burns* and punched a hole in its side. Again, two years later on 17 November 1882, whilst under the command of Captain Parsell, the *Baltic* was sailing to her New York berth off West 10th Street, when she collided with the *Peter Reuter*, a barge under tow carrying iron. As the *Baltic* manoeuvred astern the barge heeled over jettisoning her crew of four into the Hudson. One man was severely injured and taken to hospital.

During 1883, White Star's rivals on the Atlantic, the Inman Line, returned their new passenger ship the *City of Rome* to its builders as she was not up to her design speed and because of her reduced cargo capacity for her draught, during her inaugural voyages. The *Baltic* was chartered by them, initially for two round voyages, starting on 3 April 1883. Again, two years later, when the Inman Line had to sell their *City of Paris* in order to stave off financial collapse, they chartered the *Baltic* on 10 March 1885 for a further fourteen round voyages. Whilst on her second voyage for Inman they went into voluntary liquidation, but the liquidators continued to extend the charter for a further ten voyages and she commenced on her last charter passage for them between Liverpool and New York on 29 March 1887. The *Baltic* once again resumed her service for White Star on the Atlantic but it was short lived for she made her last crossing for them on 5 May 1888. This was not without incident, for on the 7 May she had to return to Queenstown when her low pressure cylinder shuttle valve spindle broke. The repairs took ten hours before she resumed the crossing, and after the return voyage she was laid up at Birkenhead pending disposal.

She was sold to the Holland America Line for £32,500 in October 1888 who renamed her the *Veendam*. As such, she sailed on her first voyage for Holland America on 3 November 1888, from Rotterdam to New York via Cherbourg. During 1890, she was re-engined by Dutch shipbuilders to triple expansion reciprocating machinery which increased her gross tonnage to 4,036. She further established a good name and reputation for Holland America over the next seven years but on 6 February 1898, while on a westbound crossing, she struck a submerged derelict in position 49º 19′ N, 19º 47′ W. The *Veendam* foundered the following day without loss of life.

BALTIC: *Named after the Baltic Sea.*

REPUBLIC (I)

(1872-1889)
3,707 grt; 420 ft 4 in BP (432 ft OA) x 40 ft 10 in
Compound Expansion SR Engine, Single screw,
1,990 ihp, 14 Knots
Passengers: 166 First class, 1,000 Third class
Harland & Wolff, Belfast Yard No. 76

The *Republic* completed the Oceanic Steam Navigation Co's initial group of four ships and as she was launched on 4 July 1871 she was named partly as a goodwill gesture on the United States' Independence Day.

As with her sister, the *Atlantic*, she was engined by compound steam engines supplied by G. Forrester & Co, Liverpool and completed on 21 January 1872. She sailed on her maiden voyage from Liverpool to New York via Queenstown on 1 February 1872. During the crossing the *Republic* encountered extremely rough weather and high seas, so much so that a lot of superficial damage was caused. Large volumes of seawater were swept into the ventilator cowls and the engine room skylights were smashed by a wave, causing some boilers to be extinguished. During the gale force conditions a lifeboat broke loose and crushed the Second Mate, James Agnew Williams, breaking his left leg and fracturing ribs. As a result of his injuries sustained and the damage incurred, White Star changed its policy regarding the stowage of lifeboats. It had been observed that during such extremely rough weather, lifeboats that had been securely lashed down were smashed to pieces whereas those lifeboats that were lightly tethered and free to move about suffered less storm damage.

Below: **Lying at anchor in the River Mersey is the *Baltic*. She was originally launched as the *Pacific* but as a Collins Line vessel of that name had previously sunk in the Atlantic, was later renamed *Baltic*.** *Nautical Photo Agency*

Later that year, White Star decided to inaugurate a service to Chile and Peru in South America with their new *Republic*, and muscle in on the Pacific Steam Navigation Co's monopoly on this route. Having caught wind of White Star's intentions, the Pacific Steam Navigation Co. scheduled their brand new steamship the *Tacora* to embark on her maiden voyage a day before White Star's service started. Sadly, the *Tacora*, which left Liverpool on the 4 October 1872, was wrecked near Montevideo on 28 October.

With some of the cargo space turned over to carry extra coal bunkers for the long journey, the *Republic* departed Liverpool on the new service on 5 October to South America calling at Bordeaux and Vigo en route and after the Atlantic crossing called at Rio de Janeiro, Montevideo and via the Magellan Straits to Valparaiso. Any re-bunkering would have to be done at coaling stations on the way, like Port Stanley in the Falkland Islands. She then continued north up the Chilean and Peruvian coast. Two smaller cargo ships, the *Tropic* and *Asiatic*, were also employed on the route and the *Atlantic* was scheduled to sail to South America in January 1873. This sailing was cancelled and other schedules were repeatedly postponed and it became apparent that this route was not a viable proposition.

When the larger liners *Britannic* and *Germanic* entered service in 1875, the *Republic* became the Company's reserve ship. The *Republic*'s career in reserve proved very busy and she was not idle for long. On 17 February 1879, whilst at anchor in the River Mersey, the schooner *Ocean Queen* ran into her. The subsequent damage to the schooner meant it had to be towed clear and beached near Newferry. Towards the end of that year on 22 December 1879, the *Republic* ran into five days of strong gales and heavy seas as she steamed westward from Queenstown. A very high wave struck her port quarter and stove in her funnel and smashed a lifeboat to matchwood, at the same time damaging the deck. By

improvising and using oars as splints and sheets of canvas as bandages, the ship's engineers managed to re-rig the funnel as a temporary measure; later, when the seas subsided, using thin iron sheet to replace combustible materials used.

On 10 December 1880, the *Republic* hove to with a machinery breakdown in latitude 41º 86′ N, longitude 63º 40′ W (ironically near the same position that the *Atlantic* took stock of her coal, prior to her fateful alteration off course). Whilst repairs were being carried out, the Master hailed a passing German steamship, the *Mosel*, with the request that the *Mosel* tow them to New York. On learning that the German ship had insufficient coal to do so the *Republic*'s Master rescinded his request. After on board repairs the *Republic* reached New York on 14 December. Just three months later the much active *Republic* was inbound in the Mersey on 20 February 1882, when she was in collision with an anchored American vessel, the *Palestine*, which had its bowsprit broken. The *Republic* suffered a damaged lifeboat.

In 1885, she was chartered to the Inman Line for three months for two round voyages between Liverpool and New York in place of the *Baltic* which had been on charter to them. Whilst on this charter and leaving New York on 20 September 1885, she was in a violent collision with Cunard's outward bound *Aurania*. The Cunarder's bow smashed into the side of the *Republic*'s nose which caused her to heel over to port until her lowest row of portholes were at the water's edge before returning to even keel. A wedge-shaped hole 4 ft wide at the gunwales tapering down to 1 ft at the waterline rent the *Republic*'s bow, causing her voyage to be cancelled while she was drydocked at New York. The *Aurania*, which

Below: **A rather rare photograph of the *Republic* thought to be alongside at Liverpool in a lightly loaded condition. Her name was inspired by the United States as she was launched on 4 July 1871.** *Tom Rayner Collection.*

had swung around, received a heavy blow to its stern and was left with a V-shaped buckle in her port quarter but continued on her voyage. The cause was orders given by both vessels' pilots in not anticipating the other ship's movements and course during manoeuvring in port.

Two years later in the early morning of 10 December 1887 when entering New York harbour after her westbound crossing, the *Republic* ran into the Italian barque *Rosa Madre*. The barque, carrying a cargo of liquorice root, was lying anchored in the harbour's quarantine when she was struck on her starboard quarter by the incoming liner. All equipment on the barque's deck was broken by the impact, the wreckage in turn jamming the steering gear and putting it out of action. The *Republic* lowered a lifeboat but it was not required, as the *Rosa Madre*'s hull was not damaged in the collision.

During an overhaul in 1888, Second class accommodation was introduced at the expense of a quantity of Third class berths. Notwithstanding this improvement her days as a White Star liner were numbered and she made her last sailing for them on 16 January 1889 under the command of Captain Edward J. Smith. When off the Sandy Hook and about to enter New York on 27 January, the *Republic* ran aground. After five hours of trying she was eventually refloated and made all speed into New York to make up for her delay to disembark her passengers. Later that day whilst berthed at her White Star pier, one of the fire tubes (flue pipes) to a lower forward boiler fractured. The mixture of smoke and steam shot into the engine room, which was busy with firemen and stokers at the time. Three men were killed instantly and seven others injured by burns and scalding. Ambulances were called for and the injured were able to walk to them from the ship. In the meantime the fire was brought under control, the boiler drawn down and damped and the steam pressure vented off from the boilers before the dead were able to be removed and an investigation carried out. An inspection was made of the damage done to the ship and it was found to be minimal. The inspectors predicted that it could be fully repaired in several hours and the ship made ready for sea.

Following the *Republic*'s return crossing to Liverpool she was laid up at Birkenhead pending disposal. In June 1889, she was sold to the Holland America Line for £35,000 and renamed *Maasdam*. Prior to entering her new service, she remained in Liverpool where she was re-engined by G. Forrester & Co. with new triple expansion steam reciprocating machinery. In addition her accommodation was refurbished for 150 First, 60 Second and 800 Third class passengers. The *Maasdam* sailed on her first voyage with Holland America on 15 March 1890 from Rotterdam to New York. She seems to have had a fairly successful career with the Dutch company maintaining a regular schedule for it wasn't until twelve years later on 6 March 1902 that her itinerary was extended to include Boulogne on the Westbound crossing. However, later that year the *Maasdam* was sold to La Veloce Navigazione Italiana of Genoa and renamed *Vittoria*. Once again in 1902 she was renamed *Citta di Napoli* by the same company for use on the Genoa–Naples–Palermo–Gibraltar–New York service carrying Italian and Sicilian emigrants; with an accommodation for 1,424 in Third class only. She undertook thirty round voyages in this capacity between 30 September 1902 and 27 April 1907. Following the earthquake at Messina in Sicily on 28 December 1908, the La Veloce company placed the *Citta di Napoli* along with its other ships, the *Nord America* and the *Savoia* at the disposal of the Italian Government for use as an accommodation ship to house the survivors and homeless from the disaster. She was returned to her owners in 1909 and sold the following year, and upon her arrival in Genoa was broken up during 1910. A Harland & Wolff-built ship for White Star had served three owners for nigh on 38 years!

REPUBLIC: *Named to honour the USA. A democracy that is no longer a Monarchy.*

Below: **The Republic anchored in the River Mersey ready to sail with what appears to be a barge or tender alongside her.** *Nautical Photo Agency.*

TROPIC (I)

(1872-1873)
2,093 grt; 326 ft 5 in BP (350 ft OA) x 35 ft 2 in
Compound Expansion SR Engine, Single screw,
1,500 ihp 12 knots
Passengers: 10
Thos. Royden & Sons, Liverpool Yard No. 137

Although not originally ordered by White Star, the *Tropic*, along with her sister, the *Asiatic* was bought on the stocks whilst under construction at the Liverpool shipyard of Thomas Royden & Sons (the shipbuilders were also shipowners) and launched on 14 October 1871, essentially purchased to tap shipping markets other than the North Atlantic. The new Suez Canal had been opened in 1871 across Egypt, linking the Mediterranean Sea with the Red Sea and short cutting the route to India. It was on this trade, hitherto dominated by the P & O SNCo, that the *Tropic* first entered service in 1872, sailing from Liverpool to Calcutta via Suez, in competition with Thomas Royden's Indra Line. This route was abandoned and later she was transferred to the South American service and made her first voyage from Liverpool to Valparaiso on 5 November 1872. As this route also proved financially unviable, given the complicated logistics of bunkering for the cargo returns, it was also dropped. The *Tropic* made her last voyage to Valparaiso from Liverpool on 4 June 1873 after which she was sold to J. Serra y Font of Bilbao and renamed *Federico*.

She was again sold in 1886 to Cia. de Nav. La Flecha of Bilbao who retained her name. After a further eight years service with them she was sold for scrap and broken up at Lytham St. Annes in Lancashire during October 1894.

TROPIC: *After the tropics Capricorn and Cancer.*

ASIATIC

(1872-1873)
2,122 grt; 326 ft 5 in BP (350 ft OA) x 35 ft 2 in
Compound Expansion SR Engine, Single screw
1,500 ihp 12 knots
Passengers: 10
Thos. Royden & Sons, Liverpool Yard No. 136

Like her sister the *Tropic*, the *Asiatic* was purchased whilst under construction by White Star while building by Thos. Royden & Sons of Liverpool. She was launched on 1 December 1870 and bought in 1871 while being fitted out. In March 1872, she entered the unsuccessful Liverpool to Calcutta trade via the Suez Canal. On 25 February 1873, the *Asiatic* made her first voyage from Liverpool to Valparaiso but it too proved unprofitable. It was during the *Asiatic's* crossing that the *Atlantic* was wrecked on the Canadian coast and upon her return to Liverpool she was sold to the African Steamship Company of London and renamed *Ambriz*. She was the largest ship owned by the African SS Co. at the time and she sailed on her first voyage for them from Liverpool to West

Africa on 12 September 1873. After ten years in the trade, the Africa SS Co. had become Elder Dempster and the *Ambriz* was refitted during December 1883 at Belfast. She was re-boilered, the engines overhauled and converted to carry an extra 200 tons of cargo and in 1884 was employed on the Liverpool to New Orleans cotton run. She was sold in 1895 to Cie Francaise Charbonnage et de la Batelage a Madagascar of Majunga. In this capacity she served as a mobile coal depot ship that steamed to Europe, mainly Cardiff, when coal stocks needed replenishing. During February 1903, she was wrecked near Majunga on the Madagascar coast.

ASIATIC: *Of or pertaining to Asia.*

ADRIATIC (I)

(1872-1898)
3,888 grt; 437 ft 6 in BP (452 ft 4 in 0A) x 40 ft 10 in
Compound Expansion SR Engine, Single screw,
3,500 ihp, 14 knots
Passengers: 166 First class, 1,000 Third class
Harland & Wolff, Belfast Yard No. 77

The first sister of a pair of larger ships built for White Star, the *Adriatic* was launched on 17 October 1871. Her engines, like previous ships, were supplied by Maudslay, Sons & Field of London. During construction, there was an innovative departure from the usual on board lighting of candles and paraffin lamps which in service were dim, dirty and unsafe. She was installed with gas lamps of open flame type and the gas was generated on board in a special retort in which oil was heated by coal fire; all supplied by Aveling, Porter & Co. of Lincoln. As such she was the first Atlantic liner to be lit by gas and the on board unit could generate sufficient gas for 300 lamps. Sadly, the concept proved unsuccessful when the *Adriatic* was in service, owing to the number of pipe leaks and fractures that the system developed caused by vibration as the ship moved in a heavy seaway.

The *Adriatic* was completed on 31 March 1872 and sailed on her maiden voyage on 11 April 1872 from Liverpool to Queenstown and New York. A month later during May she took the Atlantic westbound crossing between Queenstown and Sandy Hook with a record passage of 7 days, 23 hours and 17 minutes at an average speed of 14.53 knots. She took the record from Cunard's *Scotia* which had held it since 1863. During a particularly stormy westbound passage in December 1872, the *Adriatic* under the command of Captain Hamilton Perry was late arriving at New York when she shed two of the four removable blades from her single screw. This propeller, with its bolt on blades, with a diameter of 22 ft 6 in, was one of the largest fitted to any merchant ship of the day. Despite being partially disabled by the blade loss, the *Adriatic* managed to attend a sailing vessel, the *Allan*, which was foundering due to punishment by heavy seas, and rescue 20 seamen. Eventually the *Adriatic* arrived off Sandy Hook on 22 December after a 15-day voyage and landed her 47 First and 141 Third class passengers safely.

Nearly two years later on 24 October 1874, the *Adriatic* was leaving New York at the same time as Cunard's *Parthia*. She was approaching Sandy Hook and was passing the *Parthia* on her port side at a cable's length with both ships steering a parallel course. When the *Adriatic* was almost half her length past the *Parthia*, the Cunard vessel appeared to be turning to starboard towards the *Adriatic* and on an imminent collision course. Captain Perry, the Master of the *Adriatic*, took evasive action by also turning to starboard. The *Parthia's* starboard bow struck the *Adriatic's* port quarter, forward of the jigger rigging, causing considerable damage. If the *Adriatic's* lifeboats had been slung out, as was the normal procedure, the damage could have been far worse. The *Adriatic* then turned immediately to port to prevent her propeller from striking the *Parthia's* bows. The *Adriatic* hove to and decided to anchor and put back to port to carry out repairs. A party of engineers worked around the clock to effect repairs and the *Adriatic* departed New York four days later on 28 October. Although both the ships' Masters shared the blame for the collision, they had each obeyed the rules of the road and each taken the appropriate evasive action to avoid collision. What was not known at the time (and which will be dwelt upon more in the career of the *Olympic*), was that a hydrodynamic phenomenon known as 'canal' or 'shallow water effect' had drawn the hulls of the two ships together while they were underway in the same direction and only a cable (600 ft) apart.

A string of unfortunate incidents marred the *Adriatic's* career. With Captain Perry still in command, on 8 March 1875, while inbound to Liverpool and having picked the Mersey pilot up and having just passed the Crosby light vessel, she ran into the small American schooner *Columbus* and sank it. Although the night was clear and the *Adriatic*

Above: **The *Adriatic* at rest in the River Mersey preparing to sail for New York. Note the steaming pennant flying from her after mast, originally to alert passing sailing ships that she is a steamship.** *Nautical Photo Agency.*

was steaming at dead slow ahead, with the schooner looming up ahead the *Adriatic* swung hard aport but struck the schooner on its starboard quarter. Another steamer, the *Enterprise*, rescued the schooner's Captain and crew. All but the Captain's child were saved.

Later that year Captain Jennings relieved Captain Perry as Master of the *Adriatic* and departing Liverpool on 30 December 1875 for New York she was involved in another collision this time in the St. George's Channel off Minehead, County Waterford. At 2.30am on 31 December, the *Adriatic's* lookout spotted a green light off her starboard bow which then changed to red then green (presumably a ship tacking under sail) while closing in on the *Adriatic*. The light then changed to red again as the sailing vessel attempted to cross the liner's bows. The Master at the bridge put the *Adriatic's* engine full astern but her port anchor stock hooked the sailing ship's port jib guy ripping it away. Blocks, tackle and sail sheets fell on to the *Adriatic's* foredeck as the darkened sailing ship passed into the night. The *Adriatic's* Master ordered lifeboats to be lowered but after 45 minutes searching the area there was no trace of the unidentified vessel or of any wreckage. The mysterious vessel was later thought to be C. H. Marshall & Co's *Harvest Queen* which was later reported overdue at Liverpool and never seen again. She was on passage from San Francisco to Liverpool and had called at Queenstown and left the Irish port on the evening of 30 December and would have brought her into the vicinity of the *Adriatic's* route. In addition to this a former

Mate from the *Harvest Queen* identified the rigging debris on the *Adriatic*'s deck as that of the sailing ship. To this end the owners of the *Harvest Queen* sued White Star Line for £35,000, the writ being served when the *Adriatic* arrived at New York on 13 February 1876. A bond for twice this amount had to be lodged with the plaintiff by White Star before the ship was allowed to sail.

Once again misfortune struck, for having left Liverpool late on 18 July 1878 and whilst in thick fog at 4.30am the following morning, she collided with the *Hengist* under tow off Holyhead, Anglesey. The *Hengist*'s starboard quarter was damaged and her main brace torn away but she continued on tow to Liverpool. Undamaged the *Adriatic* proceeded to St. George's Channel where she anchored and waited for the fog to lift. Later that day on 19 July while contemplating getting underway, a brigantine, the *G. A. Pike* owned by W. Glenn of Ardrossan, and bound for Dublin came under full sail out of the fog and struck the *Adriatic* when both were off the Tuskar Rock. The brigantine sunk with the loss of five of her six man crew. The *G. A. Pike*'s owners blamed the *Adriatic* for the collision for travelling at excessive speed!

During 1884, Second class was added. A very special dinner was held on board the *Adriatic* whilst she was anchored in the Mersey on 16 September 1885 given in honour of Messrs Ismay and Imrie by an appreciative group of White Star shareholders. At this Thomas Ismay was presented with a silver gilt dinner service, commissioned at a cost of £4,000, and a portrait of himself painted by Sir J. E. Millais whilst Imrie was presented with two oil paintings that he had chosen. Following a spate of trouble free crossings, it was not until 4 October 1889 when the *Adriatic* was involved in another incident, this time she ran into her pier at New York whilst docking. The flood tide caused her stern to swing around so that her bow hit the pier with great force. In this impact her starboard anchor snagged with a new dock house built on the pier, wrenching it away for nearly 50 feet before the anchor stock broke and sent the anchor through the roof of the pier making visitors on the pier below scatter and run for cover.

Five and a half years later whilst under the command of Captain E. R. McKinstry she ran into a severe storm whilst in mid-Atlantic. The storm delayed her crossing time to ten days and the heavy seas stove in three lifeboats and tore No 11 from its davits. She eventually arrived in New York on 1 April 1895 with no serious injuries among her 834 passengers. The *Adriatic* made her last voyage from Liverpool to New York on 17 November 1897 and upon her return was laid up in reserve at Birkenhead. She was sold for scrap during 1898 and on 12 February 1899 arrived at the Preston yard of Thos. W. Ward where she was broken up.

ADRIATIC: *After the Adriatic Sea between Italy and the former Yugoslavian states.*

CELTIC (I)

(1872-1893)
3,867 grt; 437 ft 6 in BP (452 ft 4 in OA) x 40 ft 10 in
Compound Expansion SR Engine, Single screw
3,500 ihp 14 knots
Passengers: 166 First class, 1,000 Third class
Harland & Wolff, Belfast Yard No. 79

Originally ordered and laid down at Harland & Wolff's yard as the *Arctic* a sister to the *Adriatic*. Although similar her engines were supplied by G. Forrester & Co. of Liverpool. Because of press exposure at the time about the former Collins liner *Arctic* which had sunk in 1854 with the loss of 322 lives, it was decided to rename the vessel *Celtic* while still on the stocks. This decision coincided with the renaming of the *Pacific* to the *Baltic* for the same reason. And so the *Celtic* was launched on 8 June 1872 with her new name and completed on 17 October 1872. Ironically, the following day after being handed over to White Star, she grounded on the mud of the Belfast Lough after leaving Harland & Wolff's yard. She moved off on the following tide. Six days later on 24 October, she sailed from Liverpool on her maiden voyage to New York via Queenstown and settled into her regular service.

On 15 January 1874 after leaving Liverpool, the *Celtic* fouled some floating wreckage in the Irish Sea and lost all of her propeller blades that were sheared off in the encounter. A smaller White Star liner, the *Gaelic*, towed her to Queenstown where her passengers were disembarked and had to wait to board the *Baltic* which left there for New York on 23 January. In the meantime the *Celtic* was towed to Birkenhead's Alfred Dock for repairs. Harland & Wolff and White Star had settled on prefabricated propellers whereby iron blades were originally bolted onto the cast iron propeller boss rather than the more popular fully cast iron (or later bronze) screw. In this manner it was cheaper in material and labour costs for repairs to lose an occasional blade and have a new one bolted on rather than wreck a complete cast propeller. Also, with vessels of the Company having the same size propellers, the bolt on blades could be interchangeable and spares readily made and stored in Liverpool and Belfast to be used on different ships. The use of closely related metals like cast iron, wrought iron and later steel were compatible but later with the introduction of steel blades bolted onto bronze bosses another factor crept in. Although steel and bronze were stronger metals their close contact in the presence of seawater introduced the onset of electrolytic or galvanic corrosion. Over a period of time the nuts and bolts corroded and a blade would shed. Regular drydocking and maintenance during refit ensured the propeller condition was checked and changed if necessary. This would be later overcome by using bronze bosses together with detachable bronze blades.

On 9 June 1874 while anchored in thick fog off New York's quarantine, a coastal steamer, the *Matteawan*, ran into the *Celtic* stoving the former's bow in, and wrenching off railings and its decking and showering her passengers with wood splinters. There were no injuries but damage to the *Matteawan* was put at £400 or so and that to the *Celtic* as £100. Again, on 31 January 1879, whilst eastbound at 48° N latitude, 34° W longitude, the *Celtic* reported a loose propeller. Five days later and at 51°N latitude, 19° W longitude, she reported that the blades of her propeller were broken. Hailing her plight to passing vessels, news was

passed on to her port of landfall and on 7 February, several tugs from Queenstown sailed out to tow her into port. On 6 December 1881, the *Celtic* arrived at New York with 302 passengers aboard having endured being battered by hurricane force winds for six days. The winds had continually swept along her decks and smashed her lifeboats. After a seeming nine years trouble free service, during January 1883, when only 24 hours out of New York, the *Celtic's* propeller shaft sheared. The four masts were rigged for sail and she continued the voyage under canvas. She completed the passage by being towed into Liverpool by the larger 5,004 grt *Britannic*.

The following year both vessels were together again but this time in a collision. On 19 May 1887, the *Celtic*, with 104 First and 765 Third class passengers on board, was under the command of Captain Peter J. Irvine and inbound for New York. Meanwhile the *Britannic*, with Captain Hamilton Perry as its Master, had departed New York the previous night with 176 First and 300 Third class passengers aboard. Later around 5.30pm that day, both vessels entered thick fog 350 miles east of Sandy Hook. At the time neither ship had slackened speed. Both ships sounded their whistles at one-minute intervals and the *Celtic's* speed was reduced to dead slow ahead. Each ship could hear the other's whistle but watchkeepers could only guess at the direction from which it was coming; small course alterations to starboard were made by both ships. The *Celtic* came looming out of the fog towards the *Britannic* and collided with her beam on abaft the mizzenmast. The *Britannic*, holed with a four foot wide vertical gash which extended to four feet below the waterline just missing her engine room compartment and her No 4 hold, carrying grain, soon flooded. In addition three lifeboats were stove in. The *Britannic's* passengers were transferred to the less damaged *Celtic* whose bow had been

Below: **Seen here letting off steam whilst in the River Mersey, the *Celtic* had originally been laid down as the *Arctic*. She was the last of the initial batch of six liners built for White Star.** *Nautical Photo Agency.*

broken off and plates stove in. In the impact of the collision four of the *Britannic*'s Third class passengers were killed and nine severely injured. Carpenters aboard the *Britannic* had shored up the hole with temporary repairs which staunched the flooding. Both liners returned to New York slowly under their own steam and were later towed, the *Celtic* to her New York pier and the *Britannic* to a drydock at Brooklyn for repairs. At the subsequent Court of Enquiry held in New York on 9 June 1887 both Masters were reprimanded for: 'not observing regulations for preventing collisions at sea'. The *Celtic*'s Captain Irvine was censured for failing to reduce speed while steaming through fog and Captain Perry was censured for failure to sound his whistle before the collision. Another more far reaching recommendation was that Mariners separate 'in and out' passage lane be extended right across the Atlantic.

Second class was added during repairs to the *Celtic*, and along with the *Adriatic*, they could offer a return fare of £13 which was inclusive of bedding and mess utensils and where: 'the dining apartment is very similar to the old type of saloon'. Children under 12 travelled at half-fare and infants under 12 months were carried for £1 each way. On 4 February 1891, she made her last voyage from Liverpool to New York calling at Queenstown and upon her return was laid up at Birkenhead pending disposal. Two years later on 6 April 1893 she was sold to Danish shipping company, Thingvalla Line and renamed the *Amerika* under the Danish flag.

She made her first voyage as the *Amerika* on 27 May 1893 from Copenhagen to New York via Christiania and Cristiansand but the service was not a success as was considered too big for that route. Consequently she only made eight voyages during the peak summer seasons. She commenced on her last round voyage from Copenhagen on 7 September 1897 and was sold and scrapped in 1898 at Brest. She was the last vessel acquired by Thingvalla Line, for following her disposal they were taken over by Det Forende D/S, the forerunner of DFDS. One of the *Celtic*'s former Masters, Captain W. W. Kiddle, later received the appointment of Chief Surveyor for the Board of Trade (BoT) under the provisions of the Merchant Shipping Act in Ireland.

CELTIC: *Of or pertaining to the Celts.*
N. B. Originally pronounced with a soft 'c' as 'Seltic', as in the Glasgow football club. In more recent years it has become fashionable to pronounce it with the hard 'c' as 'Keltic'.

GAELIC (I)

(1873-1883)
2,658 grt; 370 ft BP x 36 ft 4 in
Compound Expansion SR Engine, Single screw
1,800 ihp 12 knots
Passengers: 40 First class
Harland & Wolff, Belfast Yard No. 80

The *Gaelic* was originally one of a pair of ships built for the Liverpool based shipping company J. J. Bibby. She was bought on the stocks by White Star for employment on their South American route and her engines were supplied by J. Jack, Rollo & Co. of Liverpool. The *Gaelic* was launched on 21 September 1872 and completed on 7 January 1873. Her length/breadth ratio of 10:1 made her narrow and sleek for seakeeping and was consistent with White Star's and Harland & Wolff's design ideas of the day. Although primarily built as a cargo ship she had accommodation for 40 First or 'saloon' class passengers. The *Gaelic* sailed on her maiden voyage from Liverpool to Valparaiso on 29 January 1873, calling at intermediate ports and coaling stations en route. However, on White Star's decision to abandon this route, she was transferred to the Atlantic run and made her first voyage on this route from Liverpool to New York on 10 July 1873. She made eight round voyages on this route and during an eastbound trip on 15 January 1874 she went to the assistance of the larger company liner the *Celtic* which had shed her propeller blades after striking wreckage in the Irish Sea. The *Gaelic* towed the *Celtic* into Queenstown. From 3 June 1874, the *Gaelic* operated on the London to New York run where she made four round voyages over the summer season, departing London on the last of these on 2 November that year. She then returned to Liverpool and resumed service on that run from 24 December 1874 for two round trips, departing on the latter on 11 February 1875.

When White Star's newer ships came into service, and with six ships maintaining the weekly service to New York, the *Gaelic*, along with her sister the *Belgic*, were redundant along with the pioneering *Oceanic*. From 29 May 1875, the *Gaelic* was chartered along with the other two ships to the Occidental & Oriental Steamship Co. initially for a five-year term. She entered the trans-Pacific route between San Francisco, Japan (Yokohama) and Hong Kong. Later that year on 20 November, while returning to San Francisco from Hong Kong, the *Gaelic* was caught by a fierce gale, which blew away her trysail and smashed in the after part of her wheelhouse.

Some eight years later, on 11 May 1883, while still on the Pacific run, the *Gaelic* had to put into Hankow in mainland China after her propeller shaft had sheared. She was steaming from San Francisco to Hong Kong at the time and it may well be that she had to complete the remainder of her journey under sail after the event. Later that same year, the *Gaelic* was sold for £30,000 along with the *Belgic*, to the Cia. de Nav. la Flecha of Bilbao and renamed *Hugo*. Some thirteen years later on 24 September 1896, the *Hugo* stranded on Terschelling Island in the Netherlands where she became a constructive total loss. She was later refloated and auctioned for scrap on 9 December 1896 after which she was towed to Amsterdam and broken up.

GAELIC: *Of or pertaining to the Gaels i.e. the Scottish or Irish Celts. The language of the Celtic inhabitants of the Scottish Highlands and Islands.*

BELGIC (I)

(1873-1883) 2,652 grt; 370 ft BP x 36 ft 4 in
Compound Expansion SR Engine, Single screw
1,800 ihp 12 knots
Passengers: 40 First class
Harland & Wolff, Belfast Yard No. 81

The *Belgic*, like her sister the *Gaelic*, was originally a cargo ship laid down for Liverpool shipowner J. J. Bibby, but acquired by White Star whilst under construction. Her engines were also supplied by J. Jack, Rollo & Co. of Liverpool and she was launched on 17 January 1873 for White Star's incursions into the South American route. The *Belgic* was completed on 29 March and sailed on her maiden voyage on 16 April 1873 from Liverpool to Valparaiso with calls at intermediate South American ports. However, her career on this route was short-lived, and following White Star's decision to quit the service, she was transferred to the North Atlantic run after making her last voyage to that continent on 17 December 1873. The *Belgic* made only one round trip from Liverpool to New York on 30 May 1874 before being switched, along with the *Gaelic*, to the London to New York run on 10 July for four round voyages over the summer season. Whilst returning from the first run and having left New York, she encountered the disabled Spanish steamer *Tornas* on 20 July and towed her back into New York. Later whilst departing London on the last of the summer service on 24 November 1874, the *Belgic* was leaving the Victoria Dock when she collided with and sank two barges, one empty and the other loaded with the rudder of an ironclad warship. The *Belgic* was undamaged and proceeded on her intended departure, albeit a little late.

She transferred back to the Liverpool to New York for a single round trip starting on 25 January 1875. After the entry into service of newer ships and with White Star having six ships to maintain the regular North Atlantic service, the *Belgic*, along with the *Gaelic* and the *Oceanic*, became surplus to requirements. The *Belgic*, together with the other two, was chartered on 29 May 1875 to the Occidental & Oriental Steamship Co., initially for a five year term and entered service on their San Francisco – Japan (Yokohama) – Hong Kong service. The *Belgic*'s charter was extended and it appears that she had a longer more regular career on the Pacific run. The *Belgic* was sold for £30,000, along with the *Gaelic*, to the Cia. de Nav. la Flecha of Bilbao during 1883 and renamed *Goefredo*.

Her career under the Spanish flag was short-lived, for on 27 February 1884, she went aground at Santiago de Cuba. Three days later the *Goefredo* was refloated and she sailed to Liverpool for repairs. Only a month later, she sailed out of Liverpool on 26 February 1884 bound for Havana, Cuba, and whilst in thick fog in the River Mersey she became stranded on the Burbo Bank at the mouth of the river. The grounding caused the *Goefredo* to break her back and she became a total loss.

BELGIC: *Of or pertaining to the Belgae, the tribe of people once occupying what is now Belgium and the Netherlands.*

TRAFFIC (I)

(1873–1896)
155 grt; 101 ft 10 in BP x 23 ft 7 in
Compound Expansion SR Engine, Single screw 8 knots
Speakman & Co., Runcorn.

The *Traffic* was built of all-wood construction for White Star as a baggage and stores tender and launched on 22 September 1872. She was used to tender White Star's Liverpool service liners to speed up loading and discharge of passengers' luggage. She performed these tasks for many years until replaced on these duties by the newer *Pontic* of 1894. She was sold to the Liverpool Lighterage Co. during 1896 for further port duties which continued for another 20 years. In 1919, her engines and enclosed area were removed when she was converted to a sullage barge. Later during World War 2 in the Blitz of 5 May 1941, she was sunk in Liverpool Docks by German aircraft. She was later raised and returned to service until 1955 when she was broken up at Tranmere Beach near Birkenhead.

TRAFFIC : *To trade, carry on commerce or barter.*

BRITANNIC (I)

(1874–1903)
5,004 grt; 455 ft BP (468 OA) x 45 ft 2 in
Compound Expansion SR Engine, Single screw
4,970 ihp 15 knots
Passengers: 220 First class 1,500 Third class
Harland & Wolff, Belfast Yard No. 83

A radical improvement on the previous liners ordered by White Star and the largest ship owned by them to date, she was laid down as the *Hellenic*. The *Hellenic* along with her sister the *Germanic* (1875), were largely designed by Sir Edward J. Harland and were the last iron-built ships for White Star. She was later renamed *Britannic* while still under construction and launched on 3 February 1874 under her changed name.

The *Britannic* was rigged as a four-masted barque and was the first of the Company's vessels to sport two funnels. She was propelled by inverted two-stage (compound) expansion, direct acting engines supplied by Messrs Maudslay, Sons & Field of Lambeth. The two high pressure (HP) cylinders of 48 in diameter, and the two low pressure (LP) cylinders of 83 in diameter, were arranged in tandem pairs with the former on the top. They each had a common stroke of 60 in.

The main slide valves of each set were moved by a single valve rod worked by the usual link motion, but on the back of each high pressure slide valve was an expansion valve worked by a separate eccentric, and provided with an arrangement by which the cut-off of each could be simultaneously adjusted. The link motion was fitted with a screw reversing gear assisted by a steam cylinder. Both engines exhausted their steam into a single surface condenser, which was cylindrical in form and was arranged behind them. Steam at 70 psi was supplied by eight double-ended oval fire tube type boilers with a total heating surface of 19,500 sq ft, developing some 4,970 ihp. The boilers were installed in two separate watertight compartments. The various steam inlet and exhaust pipes were provided with a form of bellows expansion joint to allow some flexibility under the stresses due to uneven temperatures. Coal consumption was 96 tons per day at full speed which worked out to 1.8 lb/ihp/hour. The ship was constructed with eight watertight bulkheads dividing her into nine watertight compartments.

The propeller, which rotated at 52 rev/min, had a diameter of 23 ft 6 in and a pitch increasing from 28 ft to 31 ft 6in. The *Britannic* was originally fitted with a universal type mechanism (probably similar to an Oldham coupling that connects and drives shafts whose centrelines are parallel) so that it could be raised for shallow water to its high point and lowered when clear of land. This was an attempt to avoid the propeller 'racing' when it lifted out of the water in a heavy sea, which in the past had added to the passengers' discomforts. The mechanism for lifting the propeller in its integral bracket was constructed at the after end of the shaft tunnel and arranged such that the portion carrying the screw could be raised and lowered as required along a 'dovetail' slideway cut in the stern. By this mechanism the propeller blades were below the level of the keel when the shaft was in its lowest and normal position, taking full advantage of what there was in the way of propeller thrust. It also meant that the engines had to be tilted in order that the whole shaft should form a single straight line in this position. In addition to this, little advantage was gained during pitching in a very heavy sea state, as the result of the screw lifting out of the water was the same. After nine voyages the *Britannic*'s innovative propeller was removed at Belfast and the screw reinstalled on the conventional direct drive method. The machinery output gave the *Britannic* a maximum speed of 16 knots, which was capable of cutting White Star's normal North Atlantic crossing time by almost a day.

She had a net tonnage of 3,152 and a loaded displacement tonnage of 9,100. Her load draught was 24 ft 6 in and her depth of hold was 33 ft 8½ in. The *Britannic* was completed on 6 June 1874 at a cost of £200,000 and she

Below: **The *Britannic* as she originally appeared with yards on her foremast. She is photographed in the River Mersey ready to sail for New York**. *Nautical Photo Agency.*

had a crew of 130. She sailed on her maiden voyage from Liverpool to New York on 25 June 1874 and on the leg from Queenstown to Sandy Hook she took 7 days 20 hours at an average speed of 15 knots. Together with her sister, the *Germanic*, they would prove worthy rivals to the Inman Line's *City of Berlin* and quickly established a reputation on the North Atlantic for comfort, speed and reliability.

Following modifications to her propeller shaft, she returned to her regular service on 9 June 1876 and her speed and reliability ran like clockwork for the next decade. In November 1876, the *Britannic* made a record westbound crossing from Queenstown to New York with a time of 7 days 13 hours 11 minutes at an average speed of 15.44 knots, knocking some 5 hours off the *City of Berlin*'s previous crossing time. On her return crossing in December that year from New York to Queenstown, she made an eastbound record crossing of 7 days 12 hours 41 minutes at an average speed of 15.94 knots, a creditable turn of speed given the normal weather conditions on the North Atlantic for that time of year. By the following year she further reduced her westbound crossing time to 7 days 10 hours 53 minutes at an average speed of 15.25 knots. On a good day's run the *Britannic* could steam 468 miles over a 24-hour period.

The *Britannic* had good fortune for she ran without incident for almost seven years but on 31 March 1881 this changed. After leaving Liverpool on an evening departure, she collided off Belfast with the schooner *Julia*, belonging to W. Hinde of Dublin. The schooner sank but its crew was saved and the undamaged *Britannic* resumed her voyage. Later that year another incident almost caused her loss when so near to home. The *Britannic*, under Captain Hamilton Perry had left New York on 25 June 1881 and had called at Queenstown on 3 July. The next morning whist in heavy fog off Kilmore, near Wexford, Ireland, Captain Perry set his course North Easterly for Holyhead around 7.30am after hearing the fog signals of a gun fired at 5 minute intervals which he thought was coming from the Tuskar Rock Lighthouse in the St. George's Channel. The gun was actually that of Hook Point lighthouse being fired at 10 minute intervals! Five minutes later lead soundings indicated that the water was getting shallower and the engines put to full astern; but it was too late and the *Britannic*'s momentum due to her speed caused her to ground. No injuries resulted and at first it was felt that there was no damage to the ship. Later on that day passengers and mail were put ashore by the ship's lifeboats and taken to Wexford and then on to Dublin to sail for Liverpool. In an attempt to further lighten the ship to help float her off on the tide, the Master ordered some of the cargo to be jettisoned into the sea. However, later on in the

afternoon, while still in shallow water, the *Britannic* sprang a serious leak in her No2 hold and soon took on a 12° list to port. A team from the hastily dispatched Liverpool Salvage Association set to work with divers and pumps to save the ship from sinking. Over the next two days a further 1,500 tons of cargo was unloaded into lighters and barges and shipped to Waterford, further lightening the ship. By 6 July, the *Britannic* was back on even keel and on 8 July she was refloated at 12.30 pm.

The following day the *Britannic* was taken in tow by four tugs to Liverpool, when at 8.30am while off the Barrels Rock, she sprang another leak in her engine room which flooded within the hour. Her tow was immediately diverted to South Bay where she was beached on a smooth sandy bottom; here she settled the water gradually flooding up to her Saloon deck. Some more pumps arrived from Liverpool and with further pumping and shoring up of leaks she was again refloated by 12 July and on the afternoon of that day proceeded to Liverpool under tow for drydocking and repairs. Upon her arrival in Liverpool on 14 July, she was inspected and her damage assessed as being superficial with no serious damage to the keel and bottom plates. After patching up and drying out she departed for New York on schedule on 18 July 1881.

In January 1883, the *Celtic*, when only 24 hours out of New York, suffered a sheared propeller shaft. Her four masts were rigged for sail and she completed the remainder of the

Below: **A full broadside view of the *Britannic* anchored in the River Mersey with a tender alongside. In this later photograph she has had her funnels heightened**. *Tom Rayner Collection.*

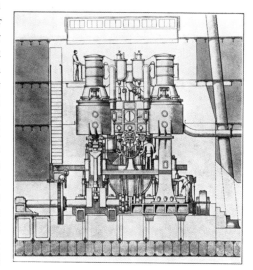
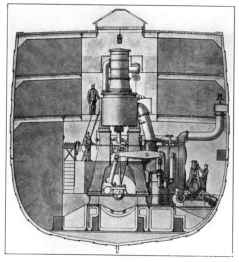

Above: **Arrangement of the propelling machinery of the *Britannic* of 1874. The engines were designed and built by the firm of Maudslay, Sons and Field.**
Richard de Kerbrech Collection.

voyage under sail. The *Britannic*, inbound from New York caught up with the *Celtic* and took her in tow, thereby assisting her safe return to Liverpool for repairs. The *Britannic* herself also fell victim to this phenomena of fatigue. On 27 May 1883, she had just set out on her scheduled voyage from Liverpool when a 'squeaking' noise was heard from her propeller shaft prior to a crack being discovered. The voyage on which she just embarked was cancelled. The same occurrence happened on the 1 April 1886 which caused the westbound trip to be cancelled for repairs.

During 1883 it is believed that Bram Stoker, the Irishman and author, later famous for his book *Dracula*, crossed the Atlantic as manager of the Lyceum Theatre Company at the start of an annual season on tour of the New York stages. The *Britannic* was to encounter further incidents, for on 14 January 1887, having just left Liverpool and steaming down the Mersey, she was involved in a scrape with the British steamer *St Fillans*, inward bound from Baltimore. The *St Fillans* sustained major damage to several of her plates that

required her to be drydocked for repairs. By contrast, the *Britannic*'s davits and a small boat were damaged but she proceeded on her journey.

On 19 May 1887, the *Celtic*, with 104 First and 765 Third class passengers on board, was under the command of Captain Peter J. Irvine and inbound for New York. Meanwhile, the *Britannic*, with Captain Hamilton Perry as its Master, had departed New York the previous night with 176 First and 300 Third class passengers aboard. Later, around 5.30pm that day, both vessels entered thick fog 350 miles east of Sandy Hook. At the time neither ship had slackened speed. Both ships sounded their whistles at one minute intervals and the *Celtic*'s speed was reduced to dead slow ahead. Each ship could hear the other's whistle but watchkeepers could only guess at the direction from which it was coming, small course alterations to starboard were made by both ships. The *Celtic* came looming out of the fog towards the *Britannic* and collided with her beam on abaft the mizzenmast. The *Britannic*, holed with a four foot wide vertical gash which extended to four feet below the waterline just missing her engine room compartment and her No 4 hold carrying grain, soon flooded. In addition three lifeboats were stove in. The *Britannic*'s passengers were transferred to the less damaged *Celtic* whose bow had been broken off and the plates stove in. In the impact of the collision four of the *Britannic*'s Third class passengers were killed and nine severely injured. Carpenters aboard the *Britannic* had shored up the hole with temporary repairs which staunched the flooding. Both liners returned to New York slowly under their own steam and were later towed, the *Celtic* to her New York pier and the *Britannic* to a drydock at Brooklyn for repairs.

At the subsequent Court of Enquiry held in New York on 9 June 1887 both Masters were reprimanded for: 'not observing regulations for preventing collisions at sea'. The *Celtic*'s Captain Irvine was censured for failing to reduce speed while steaming through fog and Captain Perry was censured for failure to sound his whistle before the collision. Another more far reaching recommendation was that Mariners separate 'in and out' passage lane be extended right across the Atlantic. On 5 September 1889, the *Britannic* was at Queenstown having made the homeward voyage, when a small fire in her cargo of cotton was discovered. Several bales were dumped over the side and the fire suppressed only to break out the following day. This smouldered until she reached Liverpool where her cargo was unloaded and the fire fully extinguished. While inbound for Liverpool on 2 January 1890, the *Britannic* collided in Liverpool Bay with J. Marshall's brigantine *Czarawitz*. The sailing vessel, on passage from Fowey to Runcorn, was cut in two and she quickly sank; whereas the *Britannic* slipped into port undamaged. Much later in 1890 whilst on her 318th passage across the Atlantic, the *Britannic* made her fastest ever Atlantic crossing from New York to Queenstown in 7 days 6 hours 50 minutes, at a mean speed of 16.08 knots. The speed of both the *Britannic* and her sister *Germanic* seemingly increased with age.

She made her last voyage for White Star on their Atlantic service, departing Liverpool on 16 August 1899, from then on she was surplus to White Star's requirements. However during October 1899 the first Boer War in South Africa had begun and during that month she was chartered to the British Government as a troopship, designated HM Troopship *No. 62*. As such she was painted in white hull. She departed on her first voyage from Queenstown on 26 October 1899 with nearly 1,000 troops, horses, munitions and supplies for Cape Town. Following this she made ten round voyages from Southampton, including two to Australia, despite her relatively small bunker capacity for the Atlantic! On 12 November 1900, still sporting her white hull, the *Britannic* departed Liverpool for Australia with a Guard of Honour to represent Great Britain at the inauguration of the Australian Commonwealth. She was to take part in a fleet review in Sydney Harbour to mark the occasion, and among the passengers on board was the honour guard. Whilst transiting the Suez Canal en route she

Below: **An interesting photograph of the *Britannic* during her requisition for Boer War service as HM Troopship *No 62*.** *Real Photographs Co Ltd.*

grounded, thereby delaying the southbound convoy in the Canal, prior to being refloated and resuming the transit.

By 28 October 1902, the *Britannic* arrived back in Southampton on the completion of her trooping duties and was released from government service. White Star then sent the *Britannic* to her builders in Belfast for a survey with the intention that she might be modified for further service. It was proposed that she might be re-boilered and re-engined with new triple expansion engines and her passenger accommodation refurbished. The builder's report revealed that the expenditure to bring such an old vessel up to standard would not be cost effective. Brand new ships like the Company's second *Celtic* and the *Cedric* were being fitted out for service and in July 1903 the *Britannic* was sold to German shipbreakers for £11,500. On 11 August 1903, she left Belfast under tow for Hamburg to be scrapped. Perhaps it is fair to say that the *Britannic* was a successful and innovative ship, the sort which won White Star its clientele.

BRITANNIC: *Of or pertaining to Britannia, the Latin name for Britain.*

GERMANIC

(1875-1904)
5,008 grt; 455 ft BP (468 ft OA) x 45 ft 2 in
Compound Expansion SR Engine, Single screw
4,970 ihp 15 knots
Passengers: 220 First class 1,500 Third class
Harland & Wolff, Belfast Yard No. 85

The *Germanic* was built as a sister to the *Britannic* and launched on 15 July 1874 and like the earlier ship, her engines were supplied by Maudslay, Sons & Field of London. However as the *Britannic* had entered service and made a few voyages it was decided to remove the *Germanic's* adjustable propeller during construction based on her sister's operational experience with this innovation. As White Star did not require her until the following summer season, she spent an extra three months at Belfast being finished off and painted, before final completion on 24 April 1875 and her builders' trials two days later. One of her pioneering features was an early type of air-conditioning in the primitive form of forced ventilation, which was intended to alleviate the discomfort of the passengers when confined below decks in rough weather. She would be the last iron-hulled ship built for White Star and upon her completion the Company would not order a purpose-built ship for the North Atlantic service for another thirteen years. The *Germanic* sailed on her maiden voyage from Liverpool to New York via Queenstown, on 20 May 1875. Upon her entry into service on the North Atlantic; she replaced the four-year-old *Oceanic* which had been placed on charter.

In February 1876, the *Germanic* made a record eastbound crossing from New York to Queenstown in 7 days 15 hours 17 minutes at an average speed of 15.81 knots, just minutes short of that previously held by Inman Line's *City of Berlin*. This record became to be known as the Blue Riband. On 29 August 1876, whilst leaving Liverpool for New York

and still underway in the Mersey, the *Germanic* fouled the British steamship the *Circassian* which was due to dock in Liverpool after arriving from Quebec. In the encounter the *Germanic's* rigging was slightly damaged.

The following year during April 1877, the *Germanic* again made a record, this time westbound from Queenstown to New York in 7 days 11 hours 37 minutes at an average speed of 15.76 knots. Both *Germanic* and *Britannic* were recognised as among the best liners on the North Atlantic service and although both vessels enjoyed a friendly rivalry; over the years their speed and reliability improved with age. On Friday 18 October 1878, the following advertisement appeared in the Maryport Advertiser and Weekly News. (Maryport being Thomas Ismay's hometown):

WHITE STAR LINE
ROYAL & UNITED STATES MAIL SERVICE
NOTICE

The steamers of this Line take the Lane Routes recommended by Lieutenant Maury both on the Outward and Homeward passage.

LIVERPOOL to NEW YORK
Forwarding Passengers to all parts of the United States and Canada.

These well known magnificent steamers are appointed to sail weekly as under, carrying Her Majesty's and the United States Mails.

BALTIC	October 22nd
ADRIATIC	October 29th
BRITANNIC	November 7th
CELTIC	November 12th
GERMANIC	November 21st

From Queenstown the following day.
From New York.

ADRIATIC	October 12th
BRITANNIC	October 19th

These splendid vessels reduce the passage to the shortest possible time and afford the highest degree of comfort hitherto attainable at sea.

Average passage 8½ days in summer and 9½ days in winter. Each vessel is constructed in seven water-tight compartments.

The Saloon, Ladies' Boudoir, State Rooms and Smoking Rooms, are amidships, and are luxuriously furnished and finished with all modern conveniences, pianos, libraries, electric bells, bathrooms, barber's shop etc.

Saloon Passage 15 guineas, 18 guineas, and 21 guineas. Return tickets at reduced rates.

The Steerage accommodation is of the very highest character, the rooms are unusually spacious, well lighted, ventilated, and warmed, and the passengers of this class will find their provisioning unsurpassed.

Stewardess in Steerage to attend the women and children.

Drafts issued on New York free of charge.

For freight or passage apply to: - John Cockton, Chemist, Agent for Maryport
Ismay, Imrie & Co.,
10, Water Street, Liverpool and
34, Leadenhall Street, London E. C.

Perhaps in this advert a hint of the future policy of White Star with the emphasis on safety and comfort rather than speed; 'shortest possible time…' being mentioned rather than record time. On 7 November 1880, the *Germanic* departed New York a day later than scheduled due to persistent fog in the port. Whilst underway she collided with the Dutch cargo ship *Samarang*, a fully rigged sailing ship of 1,076 tons. The *Samarang* was holed in its port side amidships and rapidly sank down to her main deck and spars; the *Germanic* picked up the crew.

In January 1883, whilst on a scheduled eastbound passage from New York, her propeller shaft sheared and she resorted to completing the voyage under sail. She was overhauled by Donald Currie's vessel *Westmoreland* whose offer of a salvage tow was refused. In the days before the introduction of wireless the *Westmoreland* would report the *Germanic*'s plight when the former made landfall; in this way relatives and authorities could be forewarned as to the ship's delay. The *Germanic* completed her voyage at Waterford. Two years later on 5 April 1885, the *Germanic* had left Queenstown after embarking some 850 passengers for New York when she encountered mountainous seas on entering the Atlantic, some 500 miles west of Fastnet. In these her lifeboats were torn away and the engine room skylights smashed in together with the pilot house being stove in by the force of the waves. Further waves pounded the *Germanic* and water cascaded through her reading room breaching the adjoining bulkhead to the saloon and staterooms. The Master thought it prudent in the interests of safety for his ship and all aboard to put back to Liverpool to avoid further punishment and effect repairs. It is believed that this was the first time that one of White Star's ships had to return to port because of the weather.

On 20 November 1886 while unloading cargo at Liverpool, a fire broke out in the cargo hold. In this and the attempt to extinguish it, 53 bales of cotton and numerous boxes of cheese were destroyed. After 15 years in service the *Germanic* had gained a reputation among the regular White Star clientele but her crossing schedules were not without incident. Whilst on an eastbound crossing, on 19 July 1890, the forward spindle on her engine fractured and she had to heave to in mid-Atlantic in order for her engineers to carry out repairs. These took several hours before she got underway, eventually arriving at Queenstown on 24 July.

The following year brought further dramas. Again whilst eastbound, the *Germanic* ran into a storm on 1 November 1891, when en route to Queenstown; in this one of her lifeboats was smashed in and washed overboard although no one was hurt. Outward bound to New York on 24

December 1891, the *Germanic* was about to anchor at Queenstown when her crankshaft sheared. She had to be towed back to Liverpool where her Saloon passengers along with 900 sacks of mail were transferred to Cunard's *Bothnia* and the Steerage passengers and the cargo were transferred to the *Adriatic*. After twenty years in service, the *Germanic* was returned to Harland & Wolff's yard during 1895, to have her operational life extended with a complete overhaul and refit. New higher pressure boilers were installed along with new triple expansion steam reciprocating engines built by Harland & Wolff. The funnels were increased in height and an extra deck added by building up the superstructure. The refit and modification increased the *Germanic*'s gross tonnage to 5,066.

Returning to service on 15 May that year she became the first ship to embark passengers at Liverpool's new floating Princess Landing Stage at the Pierhead. Later that year on 11 December 1895, the *Germanic* left Liverpool for New York in dense fog and standard precautionary procedure was taken of doubling the lookouts. However on leaving the River Mersey, the *Germanic* ran into the Glasgow-registered steamer *Cumbrae*, penetrating her between the forehatch and forecastle by some 14 feet. The *Germanic*'s Master kept his ship underway at Dead Slow Ahead so that both ships remained locked together and in order that the *Cumbrae*'s 28 passengers and crew could scramble aboard to safety. Upon separation the *Cumbrae* rapidly heeled over and sank. The collision resulted in the *Germanic*'s bow being badly twisted, and she was withdrawn from service pending repairs, thus cancelling the scheduled round trip. She returned to routine service during January 1896.

Three years later in early February 1899, whilst on passage to New York with Captain Edward R. McKinstry as Master, she ran into a blizzard eventually arriving in port with her upperworks and rigging laden with ice and snow. This gave her a starboard list of around 4º and because of ice in the Hudson she made her way to her berth instead of going to Quarantine. Immediately ice was chipped away from ropes and gangways by frozen crewmembers in order to allow passengers to land and to try to alleviate the list which was away from New York's Pier 45. The *Germanic* was then warped some 25 feet or so off from the pier to allow access to the coaling barges to come alongside and commence bunkering. On 11 and 12 February high winds and snow blizzards swept New York which caused temporary suspension to the bunkering. On 13 February, the bunkering continued with some 362 tons of coal being loaded and all cargo landed. However the preceding day's snow had accumulated more ice to the *Germanic*'s topsides, deckhouses and masts and rigging, in fact and added topweight of around 1,800 tons! With the ship practically in ballast and the added mass of the ice this made the *Germanic* extremely 'tender' in stability; in fact under these conditions she would have had a negative metacentric height and been unstable. Any slight minor load would literally 'tip the balance'. The crew turned to in order to chip away the ice but conditions were bitter. Due to movement of personnel and their weight distribution the ship heeled from an 8º list to port then over 8º to starboard. Coaling ports on both

sides were open, and coal was being evenly distributed; cargo of frozen bacon was loaded in an attempt to trim the ship and improve her stability.

By evening, the weather had again deteriorated to high winds and heavy snowfall which caused her to heel another 2° to starboard. Then on the flood tide and with the wind blowing she returned momentarily to upright before suddenly heeling over to 8° to port. The action caught all aboard off guard and water poured in through the port side coaling ports flooding her and filling the holds. Efforts to put counterbalancing ingots, due to be loaded, onto the *Germanic*'s starboard side proved fruitless as did trying to secure the coal ports. So the *Germanic* continued to sink alongside her pier until she came to rest almost upright and leaning against the dock wall. The following day on

Below: **A photograph taken later in her career shows the *Germanic* alongside Liverpool's Prince's Landing Stage, sporting her longer funnels.** *Real Photographs Co Ltd.*

Above: **The *Germanic* in her original configuration with yards on fore and mainmasts and short funnels. She is seen here anchored in the River Mersey in readiness to sail to New York.** *Tom Rayner Collection.*

14 February, salvage efforts were under way as the temperature had risen to enable work to be started. Ice was removed from her hull and deck by stevedores prior to a salvage vessel arriving with pumps to start pumping water only from her flooded compartments. Five days later this was completed and her hull made sound and secured for watertightness; the water had not reached or damaged the Saloon passenger accommodation. After a further two days she was towed to Brooklyn's Erie Basin where she was drydocked until 26 February. The water was drained and the hull's structural integrity inspected and approved. Following this a cargo of grain was loaded aboard the *Germanic* and she sailed for Belfast. Upon arrival on 17 March 1899 (St Patrick's Day), her crew were paid off

Above: **On 11 February 1899, the *Germanic* sunk at her New York pier and rested on the harbour bottom. This photo shows her with salvage vessels alongside helping to raise her, a task that took just over a week.** *ILN.*

and she shifted to Harland & Wolff's Queens Island yard for repairs, drying out and repainting.

The salvage and repairs to the *Germanic* cost White Star some £40,000, a huge sum for the day that ate into the Company's profits but no blame was apportioned to Captain McKinstry or his officers for her near loss. After three months refurbishment the *Germanic* returned to the Liverpool–Queenstown–New York run on 7 June 1899. After a record time in service of 28 years, the *Germanic* made her last voyage for White Star on their North Atlantic service on 23 September 1903 prior to being laid up for winter. During 1904 she was transferred to the International Mercantile Marine Company (IMMCo), the new holding group that had bought White Star in 1902. Under this she was switched to the American Line and hence to their Southampton terminal from where she sailed on her first voyage for them on 23 April 1904, to New York via Cherbourg. In this service she completed six round voyages the last being from Southampton on 2 October that year. Following this she was sold to the Dominion Line (another company within the IMMCo Group), and converted to carry 250 Second class and 1,500 Third class passengers only. On 5 January 1905 she was renamed *Ottawa* and placed on Dominion's Canadian service making her first voyage for them from Liverpool to Halifax service and deployed on this route for the winter months. From 27 April 1905, her itinerary changed to Montreal and Quebec during the summer months when the St Lawrence was ice free.

At the end of the 1909 summer season, the *Ottawa* made her last crossing from Liverpool on 2 September before being laid up during October. In 1910, the *Ottawa* was sold to the Turkish Government for £20,000 for use as a troop transport. On 15 March 1911 she sailed from Liverpool to Constantinople as the renamed *Gul Djemal*, operated by the Administration de Nav. a Vapeur Ottomane of Istanbul. Under the Turkish flag she immediately commenced carrying troops to quell the uprising in the Yemen, the

south-eastern extremity of the Ottoman Empire. Later in 1912 she was transferred to the Black Sea and whilst at the time considered to be too big to operate in that area, her presence gave prestige to the Turkish Navy. After the start of World War 1 in which Great Britain and Turkey were enemies, the *Gul Djemal* was used to transport troops and during April 1915 she was used to carry them to the Gallipoli peninsula following Anglo-French landings there.

At 2030 hrs on 10 May, whilst in the Sea of Marmara along with another transport, the *Patmos*, with a full complement of 1,600 troops, she was torpedoed by the British submarine *E-14* which struck her bow, the damage however was not serious but she was down slightly by the head. The *Gul Djemal* was assisted back to the safety of Istanbul by Bosporus ferries *No 26* and *No 46* where her bow was found to be broken completely through. But even after 40 years this was by no means the end of the former *Germanic*, for she was repaired with German assistance, refitted and re-entered service. When salvaged the crew of the submarine shared a bounty of £31,000 based on £5 per Turk soldier plus the vessel's assessed value. At first she was used as a naval auxiliary in the Black Sea, then in November 1918 to repatriate 1,500 German troops from Turkey after the Armistice. Upon her unannounced arrival at the Allied Control point off Dover, she caused much concern and confusion to the authorities there! She was, however, disarmed and allowed to proceed on passage to Germany. During 1920 the *Gul Djemal* transferred to the Ottoman–America Line for further use as an emigrant ship on the Istanbul (formerly Constantinople) to New York service. She commenced her first voyage in this service on 6 October 1920 for four round trips; the service was terminated on 21 October 1921 when she sailed on the last of these trips. She later operated regularly along Turkey's Black Sea coast to Trabzon. Later during 1928 and whilst still government owned, she was operated by Turkiye Seyrisefain Idaresi and her name spelling amended to *Gulcemal*.

Once again, during 1931, she ran aground in the Sea of Marmara. This might well have been the end of a new ship, but the 57-year-old vessel was refloated to sail again. Later, in 1939, she was still in service although apparently her voyages were few and far between. During 1949 the *Gulcemal* was being used as a store ship at Istanbul with her engines intact. The following year, 1950, she was being used as a floating hotel for a short time. Following this she left Istanbul on 29 October under tow for Messina for breaking up, where she arrived on 16 November. White Star's last iron-built steamship had lasted some 75 years, 40 of which had been in the service of the Turkish Government; a remarkable record and tribute to her Belfast builders.

GERMANIC: *Of or pertaining to, the Germans. Of or pertaining to the Teutons or their language.*

Above: **The *Arabic* was sold in 1890 to Holland America Line to become the *Spaarndam*. Although in Holland America livery, her profile betrays her White Star origins.** *ScanpixTR.*

ARABIC (I)

(1881–1890)
4,368 grt; 427 ft 10 in BP (430 ft 2 in OA) x 42 ft 2 in
Compound Expansion SR Engine, Single screw,
2,000 ihp, 13 knots
Passengers: Cargo only
Harland & Wolff, Belfast Yard No. 141

On 30 April 1881, Harland & Wolff launched White Star's first steel-hulled vessel, the *Asiatic*, which was completed as the *Arabic* on 12 August that year. Iron when alloyed with a very minute percentage of carbon produced steel. Steel is stronger, tougher and more ductile than iron. Consequently it meant a further reduction in the ship's scantlings or dimensions of the various plates and frames in hull construction, and a reduction in the cost of building, with a relative increase in carrying capacity.

The *Arabic* along with her sister, the *Coptic*, was originally designed as a cargo ship and with a return to the four masts and one funnel profile was an improved version of the earlier *Oceanic* class of 1871. Whilst able to accommodate the normal mixture of steerage and more affluent passengers they were also designed primarily for the carriage of cargo and live cattle. This was a lucrative source of income for the shipping lines, as cattle did not require the usual trappings of comfort and ablutions as the passengers. Following the trend, the *Arabic* was of the 10:1 length/beam ratio, but J. Jack & Co. of Liverpool engined her. Although designed with a service speed of 14 knots, she often averaged 13 knots.

White Star had originally intended the *Arabic* to be chartered to the Occidental & Oriental Steamship Co. for

operation on their trans-Pacific route, but before sailing for San Francisco, she was pressed to make three end-of-season round voyages from Liverpool to New York, making her maiden voyage on 10 September 1881. Whilst departing the Mersey on the last of these crossings, she was in collision with the steamer *Plove*. The following year on 4 February 1882, the *Arabic* departed Liverpool and sailed east to Hong Kong via the Suez Canal then onwards to San Francisco to take up station on the trans-Pacific service.

No sooner had the *Arabic* settled into her new itinerary than two years later, on 2 June 1884, she arrived at Hong Kong via Yokohama with a damaged propeller. This required drydocking prior to her making the return journey to San Francisco. During 1886, she returned to the UK and on 26 October she sailed from London to Melbourne and Sydney via Cape Town, making the one round voyage to Australia for Occidental & Oriental. Upon her return early in 1887, the charter was completed and she returned to Belfast to have 50 new Second class berths installed, which were advertised as Intermediate class. She was placed in White Star's service from London to Queenstown and New York and commenced on this on 30 March 1887 but later on 12 May she resumed the Liverpool–New York run.

A year later she made her last voyage departing Liverpool to New York on 19 April 1888. The following month she reinstated her Occidental & Oriental charter until February 1890 when the *Arabic* was sold to the Holland America Line for £65,000 and renamed *Spaarndam*. As such, she sailed on her first voyage in her new Holland America colours on 29 March 1890 from Rotterdam to New York. She remained under the Dutch flag for 11 years, making her last voyage for them on 7 February 1901. Later that year during August she was sold for demolition and broken up at Thos. W. Ward's yard at Preston.

ARABIC: *Of or pertaining to the Arabs, i.e. Arabian.*

A Ship: '…designed by geniuses to be run by idiots.'
Herman Wouk, *The Caine Mutiny.*

1881-1886

New companies, new routes and new partners

By 1882, two new shipping companies were formed, the Atlantic Transport Line and Shaw Savill & Albion. Both were to have significant trading links with the White Star Line. Robert Ewart Shaw and Walter Savill were shipping clerks, who in 1858 formed a partnership and started chartering vessels to New Zealand. The two partners did what many other entrepreneurs of their ilk were doing at the time; they chartered previously owned ships and managed them to run a regular shipping service. Many of the early migrants to New Zealand sailed in Shaw Savill ships, and for the homeward run the accommodation was taken out, and such cargo as was available was carried back to the United Kingdom. Over the period of some years the practice of shipowners changed, and Shaw Savill began to purchase shares (64ths) and later ships outright.

Around the same time, Patrick Henderson's Albion Line of Glasgow, which had been trading as early as 1855, was in strong competition with Shaw Savill & Co. This kept high the standard of efficiency and comfort of passengers and the prices competitive. The two companies between them enjoyed almost a monopoly of the New Zealand trade. This was disliked by a number of colonial merchants and in 1873 they formed the New Zealand Shipping Company (NZSCo). This new competition, rendered more intense by local patriotism, was met by Shaw Savill and Paddy Henderson by chartering, buying and building ships. In 1881, the Government of New Zealand offered a subsidy of £20,000 a year for the establishment of a service of refrigerated 50-day boats and for direct steam communication between the UK and New Zealand. The inducement was too slight to attract shipowners, nevertheless the growing competition of the New Zealand Shipping Company brought about the amalgamation of the two rival British Lines and in November 1882 the Shaw Savill & Albion Company Ltd. was formed. The honour of opening New Zealand's frozen meat trade fell to them, pioneered by the newly merged Company's sailing vessel *Dunedin.*

During the formation of Shaw Savill & Albion, White Star had some surplus tonnage and was looking for the challenge of seeking out new markets and trade routes to take on. It was therefore suggested and agreed between Walter Savill and Thomas Ismay, that with White Star Line's experience of operating steamships and that of Shaw Savill on the New Zealand trade there might be some common risk. This seemingly ideal combination would save both parties from committing many mistakes and it was arranged such that the two firms could run an amicable partnership by operating a combined service. Apparently White Star had

no financial stake in Shaw Savill and White Star vessels so employed were identified by their wearing both house flags on the main and mizzenmasts. All the White Star ships were crewed by their men but the ships managed and marketed by Shaw Savill. For the service White Star initially provided three vessels, the *Ionic, Doric* and *Coptic* and Shaw Savill the *Arawa* and *Tainui,* all fitted with refrigerating plant. These vessels, with a tonnage of between 4,000 and 5,000 tons, were capable of speeds up to 14 knots. They made the outward voyage by way of Cape Town and Hobart to New Zealand, and homeward via Cape Horn and Rio de Janeiro, along the 'Clipper Way'.

The time on passage from New Zealand was reduced from 90 to 100 days to around 40 by the steamships, enabling them to 'catch the market' in the UK. On the long haul route followed by the steamers, they frequently encountered heavy seas and it was not uncommon for them to suffer the occasional broken propeller shaft and its inevitable delays. This route was maintained by the combined service up until the opening of the Panama Canal. In 1918, when commercial service was resumed after World War 1, the direct shorter route through the Panama Canal was used in both directions.

Across the Atlantic in the United States, and partly as a form of protectionism against the rise of British and European steamship companies operating across the Atlantic, the Jones Act came into force in 1886. Also known as the Passenger Services Act, it related to cabotage in which it stated that: 'No foreign vessels shall transport passengers between ports and places in the United States, either directly or by way of a foreign port, under penalty of $300 for each passenger so transported and landed'.

COPTIC

(1881–1906)
4,448 grt; 427 ft 10 in BP (430 ft 2 in OA) x 42 ft 2 in
Compound Expansion SR Engine, Single Screw,
2,000 ihp 13 knots
Passengers: Cargo only (as built)
Harland & Wolff, Belfast Yard No. 142

The *Coptic* was launched by Harland & Wolff on 10 August 1881 and delivered three months later on 9 November. She was built with a steel hull and machinery to the same dimensions and service speed as the *Arabic,* and like her sister was destined for the trans-Pacific service with the

Occidental & Oriental Steamship Co. However, instead of sailing for San Francisco, she made her maiden voyage from Liverpool to New York on 16 November 1881 under the command of Captain Edward J. Smith. Whilst on the return leg, on 23 November, she ran into a hurricane that lasted 12 hours. During this encounter several of the lifeboats and her after turtleback were stove in and two seamen were swept overboard and drowned. She remained on the transatlantic for two round voyages only and later on 11 March 1882 she sailed from Liverpool to Hong Kong via Suez on charter for the Pacific service.

By 1883, there was a surfeit of vessels operating with Occidental & Oriental and as a result the *Coptic* became surplus to requirements on that route and she was chartered by the New Zealand Shipping Co. while that company's ships were still under construction. Prior to the *Coptic* entering the joint White Star-Shaw Savill service, a 750 ton capacity insulation space and refrigerating machinery were installed forward of the engine room for the carriage of frozen meat. It was reckoned that five steamships would be required to maintain the regular service, with White Star providing the *Coptic* along with the *Ionic* and *Doric*, and Shaw Savill the *Arawa* and *Tainui*.

Because Shaw Savill had definitely decided to enter steam navigation, it had a claim on the UK-New Zealand mail contract, and in spite of the fact that it had been arranged to grant this to the New Zealand Shipping Co, Shaw Savill came into it. Shaw Savill's directors were cautious to avoid any cut-throat competition from their rivals on this route at all costs and therefore approached them for an amicable agreement. The New Zealand Shipping Co's directors were willing and it was not difficult to fix and draw up detailed arrangements.

So the Shaw Savill and White Star joint steam service got under way, which was not so much a combined service in the normal sense as White Star provided their ships and crews for Shaw Savill to manage and advertise. It had been planned that the route should start from the Royal Albert Dock, instead of the East India Dock from where the sailing ships and most of the chartered steamers normally sailed, as it had excellent loading and discharge facilities.

Above: **The long haul demands on single screw ships were considerable and they coped. Here the *Coptic* is at anchor in the River Thames with a tug alongside making ready to sail for New Zealand. She is flying the Shaw Savill houseflag from her mainmast and White Star's from her mizzen.** *Nautical Photo Agency.*

The scheduled outward voyage was from London via Plymouth, by way of Tenerife, Cape Town (where bunkers would be taken) then via Hobart, Tasmania to the New Zealand coast, for Port Chalmers, Lyttelton, Wellington and/or Auckland and occasionally Napier. The homeward journey would return by way of Cape Horn, Montevideo, Rio de Janeiro and Tenerife with a call at Plymouth to land passengers. This itinerary not only afforded a balanced service which would take the best advantage of the physical properties of the sea along the 'Clipper Way', but it also offered further opportunities of profit en route to South Africa outward, and from South America homeward.

So the four-masted, barque-rigged *Coptic* was the first White Star ship to enter the New Zealand service. She loaded in the South West India Dock as the berth in the Royal Albert Dock was not ready in time. She sailed from London on 26 May 1884 under the command of Captain Kidley, calling at Plymouth on the 28th, arriving at Tenerife for bunkers on 2 June. From here the *Coptic* steamed via Cape Town and arrived at Hobart on 9 July and Otago on the 13th, then sailing on to Wellington, Napier and Auckland. However, it was not until the *Coptic*'s second sailing from London, on 8 October 1884, that the joint Company's regular, four-weekly service between London and New Zealand was truly established. Fares for the service ranged from 70 guineas (£73.50p) in First class to 16 guineas (£16.80p) for Steerage, with a First class 'Round the World' ticket costing £105; a veritable fortune back in 1884! For this, passengers could travel outward to New Zealand by the White Star-Shaw Savill joint service steamships, with an option to travel homeward via the Pacific Mail to San Francisco. Thence overland to New York and ultimately across the Atlantic by White Star steamship to Liverpool.

During 1887 the Master at the time, Captain R. E. Bence, died on board. Between 1889 and 1894, Captain Edward J. Smith was Master of the *Coptic* and in December 1890 on a return trip, she was departing Rio de Janeiro for Plymouth, when she ran aground. She had stranded on Main Island and flooded her forward compartments and was later repaired by local shoreside engineers. By 1894, she finished on the joint service to New Zealand and during the same year her original compound engines were replaced by triple expansion machinery along with the installation of new boilers. At the same time her funnel was heightened and her accommodation was modernised.

However, during the mid-1890s, there was a downward movement in trade on the route and instead of returning to the New Zealand service, when work was completed in 1895 she relieved the *Oceanic*, which was due for re-engining, on the Occidental & Oriental service between San Francisco and Hong Kong once more. Whilst on this run, during September 1897, the *Coptic* collided in Kobe harbour with a Japanese steamship, the *Minatogawa Maru*. Several of the *Coptic's* plates were buckled and her stem twisted in the encounter. Three years later, on 12 September 1900, whilst on a return journey from Hong Kong to San Francisco, the *Coptic* ran aground at Shimonoseki, Japan and was refloated undamaged.

Moving on to 3 January 1903, the *Coptic* was berthed in San Francisco when a water tank adjacent to No 3 starboard hold ruptured and damaged some of the cargo therein. This did not prevent her from sailing without repairs. On 30 October 1906, the *Coptic* made her final sailing from San Francisco for Occidental & Oriental and terminated her charter upon her arrival in Hong Kong. In the following December she was sold to the American-owned Pacific Mail Steamship Co. and renamed *Persia*. She was re-registered at London and was employed on the same trans-Pacific service and as such she still sailed under the red ensign, as she had not been built in the United States.

As the *Persia*, she was again refitted in 1911 and four years later she was sold to Toyo Kisen Kabusiki Kaisha of Tokyo for their trans-Pacific service and renamed *Persia Maru*. Following World War 1, by 1922, she operated on the Japan to the Dutch East Indies service but was later laid up at Yokohama in December 1924. Her furnishings and fittings were sold off for auction and she was broken up at Osaka during 1926. The career of the *Coptic/Persia/Persia Maru* had spanned some 44 years; some of her earlier Masters during her time as the *Coptic* were H. S. Lindsay (1894-1896), J. H. Rinder (1899-1904), F. H. Armstrong (1904-1905) and W. Finch (1905-1906).

COPTIC: *Of or pertaining to the Copt Christians of Ethiopia. Following the Joint New Zealand service with Shaw Savill the Coptic's name became a Shaw Savill & Albion nomenclature and was not used again by White Star.*

IONIC (I)

(1883–1900)
4,753 grt; 428 ft BP (439 ft 11 in OA) x 44 ft 2 in
Compound Expansion SR Engine, Single Screw,
3,280 ihp 13 Knots
Passengers: 70 First class
Harland & Wolff, Belfast Yard No. 152

On 11 January 1883, Harland & Wolff launched the *Ionic*, the first of a pair of cargo-passenger ships for the joint White Star-Shaw Savill service to New Zealand. By this time marine engines had progressed to the multi-expansion, inverted vertical, double-acting engine; together with a definite design of boiler; the Scotch (fire-tube) boiler. A major step was that Harland & Wolff were now building their own engines, and so it was that their single, 2-cylinder, compound steam engine, which could develop 3,280 ihp and give an average speed of 13 knots, was built into the *Ionic*.

Below: **The *Ionic* is seen here photographed very early in her career, after entering service on charter to the New Zealand Shipping Co. She is anchored in the River Thames making ready to sail for New Zealand.** *Nautical photo Agency.*

With a gross tonnage of 4,753, an overall length of nearly 440 ft and a beam of 44ft 2 in, she was a larger version of the two previous built steel ships of the 'Arabic' type. The *Ionic* was handed over on 28 March 1883 and sailed from Belfast, arriving at London on 1 April. Three weeks later on 23 April, while alongside and loading general cargo for the outward voyage, she was officially visited by the Prince of Wales (later to become King Edward VII). The *Ionic* and her sister the *Doric* were essentially 'fast' cargo ships with a limited passenger accommodation for 70 First class passengers. Like the earlier *Coptic*, the *Ionic* was chartered by the New Zealand Shipping Co. who were awaiting delivery of their new ships. On 26 April 1883, the *Ionic* sailed on her maiden voyage under charter to NZSCo from London to Wellington, via the Cape of Good Hope. Her sustained speed of 14 knots on passage enabled her to complete the journey in a record time of 43 days, 22 hours and 5 minutes, eventually arriving in Wellington on 11 June.

The *Ionic* entered her intended White Star-Shaw Savill joint service on her first voyage departing London on 4 December 1884 and settled into the five-ship regular service. On 13 May 1889, having departed Lyttelton and steaming North along the New Zealand coast for Wellington, the *Ionic's* crankshaft sheared. She had to put back into Lyttelton for repairs and her return voyage was cancelled. The spectre of a breakdown at sea occurred again on 8 February 1893 when her propeller shaft sheared two days out from Cape Town. Being square-rigged on three of her four masts, she started to sail back to Cape Town, but wind and current were against her and after three days of battling these she was taken in tow by Donald Currie's *Hawarden Castle*. Both vessels arrived back into Cape Town on 15 February and £7,000 salvage was awarded to the crew of the *Hawarden Castle*. Following repairs the *Ionic* resumed her voyage in April.

In 1894, the *Ionic* returned to Harland & Wolff's for extensive alteration and refurbishment in which the opportunity was taken to re-arrange her passenger accommodation entirely, on the lines of the new larger *Gothic* that had entered service that year. She was also installed with newer refrigerating machinery capable of dealing with very much larger quantities of meat and dairy produce. Her old compound engines were replaced by 4-cylinder quadruple expansion engines. These, combined with new boilers, gave her a steady sea speed of 14 knots with much greater economy. She was, in fact, capable of 15 knots, but the Directors of both Companies finally decided that 14 knots was the economical maximum to New Zealand and that it would be far better to save on coal. The *Ionic's* yards were removed from the main and mizzenmasts and her funnel heightened. All this capital investment and she only continued in the New Zealand joint service for a further five years; making her last voyage from London to New Zealand in December 1899. She loaded troops, cavalry horses and stores for Cape Town where they were to be deployed for action in the Boer War.

Following this, the *Ionic* did not remain idle for long, for in April 1900 she was chartered by the Spanish Government to repatriate troops and officials back from Manila, following the Spanish-American War of 1898, whereby the Philippines gained their independence from Spain. That same year she was sold to the Aberdeen Line for £47,500 and renamed *Sophocles*. As such she replaced the *Thermopylae* (the sister to the *Cutty Sark*), which had been lost in September 1899, and sailed on her first voyage for them on 23 October 1900. As the *Sophocles*, she made her last voyage for the Aberdeen Line on 21 August 1906. She was sold for scrap and broken up during April 1908 by Thos. W. Ward's Morecambe yard in Lancashire. Some of the *Ionic's* Masters included Captain W. H. Kidley (1887-1894) and Captain C. H. Kempson (1894-1900).

IONIC: *Of or pertaining to Ionia, an ancient district in Asia colonised by the Greeks.*

Below: **The *Ionic*, thought to be photographed anchored in the River Thames with her heightened funnel. She is making ready to sail. Out of view and moored alongside her starboard side is a two-funnelled tug or tender flying the Shaw Savill houseflag from its mast.** *Tom Rayner Collection.*

DORIC (I)

(1883-1906)
4,744 grt; 428 ft BP (440 ft 11 in OA) x 44 ft 2 in
Compound Expansion SR Engine, Single Screw,
3,280 ihp, 13 Knots.
Passengers: 70 First Class
Harland & Wolff, Belfast Yard No. 153

The *Doric*, sister to the *Ionic*, was launched by Harland & Wolff on 10 March 1883, and was also destined for the New Zealand trade, to complete the trio of White Star's commitment to the joint service with Shaw Savill. Her size and dimensions were almost the same as the *Ionic's* and she was capable of a maximum service speed of 14 knots. Following trials, she entered service on 4 July 1883, and whilst on the positioning trip between Belfast and London she called in at Holyhead to pick up Thomas Ismay and a party of dignitaries who travelled on to London. The junket must have been somewhat of an austere affair for a cargo-passenger ship, but Ismay was a shrewd businessman and was proud to show his ships off, no matter what their function. It was also a good opportunity to advertise the Company and secure future trade!

Like the *Coptic* and *Ionic* before her, the *Doric* embarked on her maiden voyage on 26 July 1883 from London to Wellington via Cape Town, under charter to the New Zealand Shipping Co. A month later, on 27 August, a baby was born on board and baptised (presumably in the ship's bell), William Doric Jenkin. The *Doric* completed a further year on charter then entered the White Star-Shaw Savill joint service, departing London to New Zealand on 6 January 1885 on her first voyage for them. In 1891, she carried Mr Rudyard Kipling from Cape Town to New Zealand as one of her passengers, and it is generally believed that the *Doric's* Chief Engineer, Mr

Above: **The third of the joint service trio, the *Doric* is photographed anchored in the River Thames whilst on charter to the New Zealand Shipping Co. between 1883 and 1884.** *Nautical Photo Agency.*

Robert Reid was the prototype of McAndrew in 'MacAndrew's Hymn' (also spelt M'Andrew), composed in 1893.

*Lord, Thou hast made this world below the shadow of a
    dream.
An', taught by time, I tak' it so –exceptin' always steam.
From coupler-flange to spindle-guide I see Thy Hand,
O God–
Predestination in the stride o' yon connectin'-rod.
John Calvin might ha' forged the same
–enormous, certain, slow–
Ay, wrought it in the furnace-flame- my 'Institutio.'
I cannot get my sleep to-night; old bones are hard to please;
I'll stand the middle watch up here- alone wi' God an' these
My engines, after ninety days o' race an' rack an' strain
Through all the seas of Thy world, slam-bangin'
    home again.*

In May 1895, she was returned to her builders Harland & Wolff and, like the *Coptic* had been earlier, re-engined with new triple expansion machinery. This together with modifications to her accommodation increased her gross tonnage to 4,784 and improved her service speed to 14 knots! However during the mid-1890s there was a downward movement in trade on the route and following the refit, in 1896 she was transferred, along with the *Coptic*, to the Occidental & Oriental Steamship Co. and placed on their San Francisco-Yokohama-Hong Kong service.

On 24 February 1902, whilst on passage from San Francisco to Japan she encountered 'fearful storms' in

Above: **A rather rare photograph of the** *Belgic* **anchored in the River Mersey prior to sailing. She spent some 13 years on charter to the Occidental & Oriental Steamship Co.** *Nautical Photo Agency.*

mid-Pacific and was a day late in arriving in Honolulu. The *Doric* maintained the Pacific run for 10 years, making her last voyage under charter from San Francisco on 4 August 1906, before being sold, along with the *Coptic*, to the Pacific Mail Steamship Co. and renamed *Asia*. Following a short refit, the *Asia* made her inaugural sailing for Pacific Mail on 11 June 1907. Four years later, on 23 April 1911, whilst en route from Hong Kong to San Francisco and steaming through fog, she was wrecked on Finger Rock, Taichow Island (200 nautical miles south of Shanghai in an approximate position 28º 30′N, 121º 50′E in the East China Sea). There was no loss of life and the survivors were taken on to Shanghai by China Navigation's *Shaoshing*, whilst the wreck of the *Asia* was looted and set on fire by local fishermen.

And so White Star's *Coptic*, *Doric* and *Ionic* set a partnership into motion which would last for some 50 years. They were later augmented by the *Gothic* on the service, but by so doing White Star had diversified its shipping activities in the Southern Hemisphere. Among the *Doric's* early Masters were Captain Jennings (1884-1894), Captain C. H. Kempson (1894), and Captain W. Sowden (1894-1895).

DORIC: *Of or pertaining to Doris, a small mountain state in Greece.*

BELGIC (II)

(1885-1899)
4,212 grt; 420 ft 4 in BP x 45 ft 5in
Compound Expansion SR Engine, Single Screw,
2,800 ihp, 13 knots
Passengers: Cargo only.
Harland & Wolff, Belfast. Yard No. 171

The shipbuilding liaison between White Star and Harland & Wolff flourished and in 1885 a further pair of sisters were launched, the *Belgic* and the *Gaelic*. The *Belgic* was launched on 3 January 1885, and was very similar in size as the *Ionic* trio but intended to carry cargo only. Although designed for a service speed of 14 knots, she could average 12.5. The *Belgic* was delivered to her owners on 7 July 1885 and chartered to Occidental & Oriental Steamship Co's Pacific service, and would later be joined by the *Gaelic* when she was ready. Just prior to taking up her position in the Pacific, she made her maiden voyage from Liverpool to New York. Following this she sailed on her first crossing on 28 November 1885 from San Francisco to Hong Kong via Yokohama.

Later on 28 January 1886, while on the return trip between Hong Kong and Yokohama, one of her piston rods broke, and repairs whilst at Yokohama delayed her schedule by eight days before the *Belgic* resumed her crossing. On 17 February 1893, when the *Belgic* arrived in San Francisco after her eastbound crossing from Japan, several cases of smallpox were reported among the crew, she had to remain in quarantine until fumigated and allowed to dock. The following year, on 26 May 1894, while loading tea from barges in Amoy Harbour, the *Belgic* was accidentally rammed by Blue Funnel's steamship *Ulysses*. Neither ship was damaged but a barge loaded with tea that was

Above: **The second** *Gaelic,* **of 1885, was very similar in profile and size to the** *Coptic, Ionic* **and** *Doric.* **She was destined to spend 20 years on the Pacific on charter to Occidental and Oriental.** *World Ship Photo Library.*

sandwiched between them sank. Again, a year later on 9 September 1895, while bound for Yokohama from San Francisco, the *Belgic* went aground at King's Point in Sateyama Bay, Japan. After a month grounded she was refloated and entered drydock in Yokohama for repairs to her bottom.

The *Belgic* made her last trans-Pacific run in 1898 and returned to the United Kingdom; in the following year she was sold to the Atlantic Transport Line and renamed *Mohawk.* She undertook her first voyage for her new owners on 7 September 1899 from London to New York and no sooner was she in the swing of things when she was requisitioned as a transport ship for the Boer War in South Africa the following December. In 1902, following the war, she was released from Government service but her owners decided against having her refitted and she was sold for breaking up at Garston by Liverpool in 1903.

GAELIC (II)

(1885-1905)
4,205 grt; 420 ft 4 in BP x 42 ft 5 in
Compound Expansion SR Engine, Single Screw,
2,800 ihp, 13 knots
Passengers: Cargo only
Harland & Wolff, Belfast. Yard No. 172

The *Gaelic* was launched as a sister to the *Belgic,* on 28 February 1885 and as such her career paralleled that of her sister. She was built as a cargo ship only and intended to operate under charter to the Occidental & Oriental Steamship Co, but following her delivery on 7 July 1885, she made her maiden voyage from London to New York on 18 July. She made her first voyage for Occidental & Oriental on 10 November that year sailing from San Francisco to Yokohama and Hong Kong in consort with the *Belgic.*

On 15 August 1896, the *Gaelic* went aground on a mudbank at Shimonoseki, Japan. Springing some plates, her forward hold flooded up to 12 ft with water. She was refloated and drydocked at Nagasaki on 28 August where repairs were carried out. The passage of the first 102 Korean immigrants to the US began when the *Gaelic* sailed from Nagasaki, Japan, on 29 December 1902 and arrived at Honolulu on 13 January 1903. During May 1904, Occidental & Oriental gave six months notice that they were terminating the charter contract. The *Gaelic* departed San Francisco on 13 December 1904 on her final trans-Pacific crossing then returned to Belfast for overhaul and refurbishment during the first quarter of 1905.

Following this refit, in March she was sold to the Pacific Steam Navigation Co. of Liverpool and renamed *Callao.* As such she entered Pacific Steam's South American West coast service from Liverpool, Valparaiso via Cape Horn and Callao route as a stopgap until their new vessel, the *Quillota,* entered service. Upon the *Callao's* withdrawal she was broken up at Briton Ferry in September 1907.

'The designer sees little of the ship he designs after a few hours' trial trip, generally
under the most favourable circumstances…'
Thomas Walton-*Know your Own Ship*. In other words the Naval Architect does not have to
live or work on the ships he designs!

1886-1889

Golden Jubilee, birthday and donations

With White Star firmly established on the North Atlantic and the New Zealand route in conjunction with Shaw Savill, and also on the Pacific with the Occidental and Oriental Steamship Co, it had an extensive service across the globe. By 1896 White Star's shareholding in Shaw Savill was just £1,000. The year 1887 marked Queen Victoria's Golden Jubilee, and in January that year Thomas Ismay celebrated his 50th birthday. He marked both by donating £20,000 to found the Liverpool Seamen's Pension Fund for aged and infirm and destitute sailors trading into and out of Liverpool. (By the time of Ismay's death in 1899 this sum had grown to £40,000 and had already provided pensions of £20 a year each to over 100 old seamen). This donation was supplemented by a gift of £10,000 from Mrs. T. H. Ismay to establish the 'Margaret Ismay' Widows' Fund, which provided grants of £10 per annum to widows of pensioners; also the Andrew Gibson Memorial Home with accommodation for 44 widows of seamen. For its time an extremely generous donation on behalf of the Ismays!

In commemoration of this Fund Thomas Ismay was presented with an illuminated address by the Mercantile Marine Service Association (MMSA), and also commissioned a portrait for his rooms. Over the years that White Star had been building up its international trade routes, companies like Cunard had been making inroads into the North Atlantic route and attracting the cream of passenger traffic with liners like the *Umbria* and *Etruria*, entering service in 1884. These two were the last iron-hulled, single screw ships to be built. But White Star kept a keen eye on their operational performance with the intention of matching them.

As early as 1880, Sir Edward Harland had proposed plans for what were later to be the *Teutonic* and *Majestic* of 1889. Thomas Ismay was too shrewd to force the pace and was content to keep reasonably abreast of their rivals rather than build expensive ships unnecessarily. The Russian War scare of 1885 gave him his opportunity. The impending threat resulted in a number of liners being taken up by the Admiralty and fitted up as auxiliary cruisers, at tremendous cost and expense only to prove quite unsuitable for their intended task!

Seizing upon this opportunity, the White Star Line put forward a proposal for a reserve of auxiliary cruisers, pointing out that they had the plans ready for a ship faster than any of those the Admiralty had previously requisitioned, and very much more manoeuvrable because she would be built with twin screws. The Admiralty was suitably impressed by the proposal such that in 1887 they had completed negotiations with the Cunard Line that all future express liners would be ready for conversion to auxiliary cruisers for which the Admirality would pay an annual subsidy or retainer, one stipulation being that any vessel taken up for such duties should be designed with a capability of maintaining 18 knots for 16 days steaming duration. A tall order for any single screw vessel!

For this strategic role the White Star designated the *Britannic*, setting her value at £130,000; the *Germanic*, £130,000; the *Adriatic*, £100,000; and the *Celtic*, £100,000. William James Pirrie had risen up through Harland & Wolff from 'gentleman' apprentice to Chief Draughtsman to become a partner in the firm. It was he who was also a strong advocate of twin screws, the adoption of which was followed in the large vessels built at the shipyard. Concurrent with this was an improved arrangement of the after part of the hull in which the bossing formed part of the outside of the hull and protected the main shafts. These were carried inside right to the outer bearing, thus avoiding the need for external 'A' brackets. Later he became a keen advocate of the diesel oil engine as a form of marine propulsion.

CUFIC (I)

(1888-1896; 1898-1901)
4,639 grt; 430 ft BP (430 ft 8 in OA) x 45 ft 2 in
Triple Expansion SR Engine, Single Screw,
3,050 ihp, 13 knots
Passengers: None, Livestock only.
Harland & Wolff, Belfast. Yard No. 210

In an attempt to capitalise on the lucrative cattle trade from the United States, the *Cufic* was launched on 10 October 1888 as a livestock carrier and was installed with Harland & Wolff's Triple expansion steam reciprocating machinery, White Star's first vessel fitted with this type of propulsion that would make most efficient use of steam as it expanded through the cylinders. The high pressure cylinder bore was 27 in, the intermediate pressure bore was 44½ in and the low pressure bore 72 in with a stroke of 60 in. The working pressure was 180 psi. Economy both in men and fuel was the main objective of her design and in this Harland & Wolff had succeeded. These engines could give a service speed of 13 knots and indeed on her first voyage she demonstrated that she could maintain this speed in all weathers with what was then considered extraordinary economy.

The *Cufic* and her sister ship *Runic* were the last two White Star ships to be built with a single screw and were of the three-island type, with separate raised poop, bridge deck

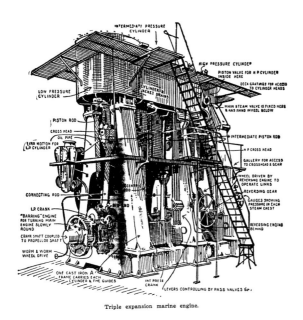

Triple expansion marine engine.

Above: **Illustration of a triple expansion steam reciprocating engine, a later version of that installed in the *Cufic*.**

and forecastle, with the hull divided by seven bulkheads. The *Cufic* was delivered on 1 December 1888 and on 8 December made her maiden voyage from Liverpool. She had loaded general cargo for New York and carried 1,000 head of cattle on the return crossing. In order to cater for this volume of cattle the *Cufic* was fitted out with special stabling facilities for livestock. In fact she was the most up-to-date cargo carrier on the North Atlantic with a cargo capacity for 6,000 tons. Even though the *Cufic* was essentially a cargo ship, she could offer comfortable accommodation for a limited number of passengers.

Past experience of livestock carriers had revealed overcrowding, poor ventilation and insufficient feed and water during carriage, and indifferent if not cruel handling during loading, unloading and during rough weather. Many steers perished on passage and many were made lame by rough and cruel herding. White Star's mission was to improve shipboard facilities and try to alleviate some of the hitherto inhumane practices. The cargo was money, the higher the percentage of cattle arriving safely at market the higher the profit margin.

So it was for the years to come that the *Cufic* would be engaged in this growing trade for the next 10 years as a successful carrier. However, on 17 January 1895, Captain Edward J. Smith reported the loss of 75 head of cattle as the *Cufic* arrived in Liverpool from New York. In July 1896, she was chartered by the Compania Trasatlantica Espanola of Cadiz for use as a horse remount carrier between Spain and Cuba during the Cuban revolution just prior to the Spanish-American War. She was renamed *Nuestra Senora de Guadalupe* and was on charter to the Spanish company for two years. On completion of the charter in 1898 she reverted to her original name *Cufic*, returning to her North Atlantic livestock duties.

On 16 December 1900, the *Cufic* shed her propeller in the Atlantic at position 51°34′ N, 21° 24′ W whilst steaming in heavy weather and high seas. Fortunately Bristol City Line's *Kansas City* spotted the stricken vessel but for three days was unable to get a line aboard the *Cufic* because of the heavy weather. When they did, the two hawsers

Below: **The *Cufic* of 1888. This view shows her under tow in the River Mersey ready to depart for the United States.** *Richard de Kerbrech Collection.*

parted. In the second attempt, the *Cufic's* Chief Officer, Mr Crosby, jumped overboard with a line but was drowned. A while later with the *Cufic* under tow the two ships were joined by the steamer *Throstlegarth* which also aided the rescue and escorted the *Cufic* into Queenstown and then on to Liverpool for repairs. For this the *Kansas City* received a £6,800 salvage reward. Her return career with White Star was short-lived as in 1901 she was sold to the Mississippi & Dominion Line Steamship Co. for their Liverpool to the United States and Canada run in the winter months and Liverpool to New Orleans run during the summer season, for the carriage of cotton. She was renamed *Manxman*.

When the Dominion Line demerged from the original New Orleans company to be absorbed into J. Pierpont Morgan's International Mercantile Marine Company (IMMCo) in February 1902, the move did not affect the *Manxman's* service. She was again sold in 1915 to Elder Dempster for their Liverpool-West Africa route until October that year when a Canadian company, R. Lawrence Smith of Montreal bought her for Canadian Government service without a name change. They sought to capitalise on her cargo-carrying capability until required for Government service. During the latter part of World War 1 in April 1917, the British Shipping Controller commandeered her under the Liner Requisition Scheme. In this capacity she transported wheat and horses from the United States and Canada, carried coal for the Royal Navy, and made one voyage to South Africa to load maize. In February 1919, she was released from Government service and was sold to the Universal Transport Company of New York which later became the United States & Canadian Transport & Trading Co. of Toronto.

On 17 December 1919, whilst carrying a cargo of wheat on a voyage from Portland, Maine to Gibraltar, she started listing in heavy seas and was taking in water when she was encountered by the tanker *British Isles*. The tanker attempted to take the *Manxman* in tow, but did not succeed in getting a line across. Early the next morning of the 18th while standing by the tanker lost sight of her for a few minutes during a heavy snow squall. After it passed there was only wreckage to be seen, with the crew of a lifeboat doing their best to pick other crew members out of the water. Eventually the Second Officer and 15 men were rescued by the *British Isles*. The *Manxman* had sunk in heavy seas with a loss of over 40 hands. It is believed that the *Cufic* laid the foundations of White Star's policy of moderate speed and extreme comfort.

CUFIC: (or KUFIC). *Of or pertaining to Cufa, an ancient city near Babylon and seat of Mohammedan learning before the building of Baghdad. Of, in an early, angular, form of Arabic script, found in early copies of the Koran, and much used as decoration.*

Below: **An unusual photograph of the *Runic* as the *Tampican*, in which role she spent seven years.** *Scanpix TR.*

RUNIC (I)

(1889-1895)
4,833 grt; 430 ft BP (430 ft 8 in OA) x 45 ft 2 in
Triple Expansion SR Engine, Single Screw,
3,050 ihp, 13 knots
Passengers: Livestock only.
Harland & Wolff, Belfast. Yard No. 211

The *Runic* was also built by Harland & Wolff as a livestock carrier and launched on 1 January 1889. As the *Cufic's* sister ship she had the same dimensions, and was fitted with the same Harland & Wolff triple expansion engines and capable of sustaining a similar speed. Following her completion on 16 February 1889, she entered the Liverpool to New York service on her maiden voyage on 21 February in the cattle trade, but only a year later on 18 April 1890, she had to put back to Holyhead when her engine developed a fault. Repairs were swift and she sailed for New York the following day.

A month later on 28 May the *Runic* was at Liverpool loading general cargo for New York. She had just loaded a cargo of 2,000 bags of sulphur, bales of jute, and a consignment of caustic soda in drums, when a fire broke out. The hold had to be flooded to bring the fire under control and put it out. Again, a minor fire broke out aboard her while she was at her berth in Liverpool, on 27 March 1892, but it was quickly extinguished. Moving on to 17 August 1895, whist the *Runic* was manoeuvring in the Mersey prior to her departure for New York, she ran into the Liverpool Landing Stage but sustained only slight damage. During the following month of September 1895, she was sold to the West India & Pacific Steamship Co. of Liverpool and renamed *Tampican*, for their West of India and Central American trade.

Just over four years later, on 31 December 1899, the *Tampican* was transferred to Frederick Leyland & Co, along with other vessels in the Company and she ran on their Liverpool-New York service without a name change. H. E. Moss & Co. of Liverpool purchased her during March 1912 with the intention of using her for their non-tanker fleet under the ownership of the Sefton Steamship Co. However she was sold by Moss only days later, on 13 March, to the Norwegian whaling concern, the South Pacific Whaling Co. of Christiania (later Oslo). She then became the *Imo* and as such was converted for the carriage of whale oil during the Antarctic whaling season. (For some reason a small number of White Star's vessels gained a secondary career in the whaling industry. No doubt their proven sea-keeping qualities and reliability may have contributed in some small way to their selection).

Five years later the *Imo* was to be involved in one of the world's biggest explosions and the largest experienced by North America in a pre-nuclear age, and what came to be known as the Great Disaster of 1917! During World War 1, Halifax harbour was open to neutral ships as well as Allied ones. At the time the *Imo* was on the way to New York to load relief supplies for Belgium. As a non-belligerent, neutral vessel she had 'Belgian Relief' painted on her sides to emphasis her neutrality to any lurking U-boats. She was delayed on her sailing schedule having had to wait for coal, and being in ballast she may have been steaming at a slightly faster speed than was normal when she left the Bedford Basin.

French Line's *Mont Blanc*, under the command of Captain Le Medec was inbound from New York where she had loaded a consignment of explosives. These included 2,300 tons of picric acid, 200 tons of TNT, 10 tons of gun cotton and a large number of drums of Benzol stowed on her decks. The *Mont Blanc* was on her way to the Bedford Basin but arrived too late to be let through the anti-submarine net and had to wait until the next day to enter the harbour. At 08.45am on the morning of 6 December 1917, the *Imo* weighed anchor and headed for the open sea, just as the *Mont Blanc* entered harbour and they collided in a bottleneck known as the 'narrows'. In the impact some of the Benzol drums burst open, spilling their contents onto the deck, and then some caught fire. Because of the imminent danger from fire and the volatile cargo, the Captain ordered his crew to Abandon Ship. By then the *Mont Blanc* was on fire and drifted towards Halifax where she came to rest against Pier 6.

At 09.05am the *Mont Blanc* blew up; the ship itself disintegrated. The force of the blast flattened the immediate area for 2 square kilometres, and devastated an area of 325 acres and most of the windows in Halifax were shattered. The explosion, which was felt some 260 miles away, obliterated the suburb of Richmond where 3,000 buildings were destroyed; some 1,600 were killed, 2,000 people were missing, presumed dead and 8,000 were injured. Just across the harbour in the village of Dartmouth thousands of buildings were also damaged by the blast. The overall damage was estimated at around Canadian $30million. Although the *Mont Blanc* had been blown to smithereens, the *Imo*, which had drifted clear, was struck by a combination of the blast and the ensuing pressure wave and swamped. This impact caused her to lose all but one of her lifeboats, and her tall funnel.

The *Imo*, however, survived, running aground on the shore at Dartmouth and heeled over to starboard. She was sent for repairs and rebuilding during 1918. By 1920 she was again sold to other Norwegian owners in the whaling trade, and renamed *Guvernoren*. She sailed from Sandefjord on what was to be her last voyage to the Antarctic on 26 October 1921. Five weeks later, on 30 November, while steaming in fog, she ran aground on rocks 20 miles from Port Stanley in the Falkland Islands and became a total loss. The ex-*Runic* was not the only former White Star vessel to find further trading as a whale oil ship/factory ship.

RUNIC: *Of, in, marked with, runes; (of poetry etc.) such as might be written in runes, especially ancient Scandinavian or Icelandic.*

TEUTONIC

(1889-1921),
9,984 grt; 565 ft 10 in BP (582 ft OA) x 57 ft 10 in
Triple Expansion SR Engines, Twin Screw,
17,000 ihp, 19 knots
Passengers: 300 First class, 190 Second class, 1,000 Third class
Harland & Wolff, Belfast. Yard No. 208

By 1887, Queen Victoria's Golden Jubilee year, White Star's main New York service was in urgent need of replacement tonnage as the pioneering *Oceanic* and *Britannic* class had come of age. They had been eclipsed by larger competition from rival companies such as Cunard's *Etruria* and *Umbria*, and Inman Line's *City of New York* and *City of Paris*. The *Teutonic* had been designed by the Rt Hon Alexander Montgomery Carlisle, Harland & Wolff's Chief designer and of its design the Admiralty stated 'it was the finest ever put forward'. They oversaw the building under the Auxiliary Armed Cruiser Agreement.

The construction of the *Teutonic* began at Harland & Wolff's yard with the laying of the keel during March 1887. Thomas Ismay had negotiated with the Admiralty for financial assistance from the British Government. Thus, while being overseen by the Admiralty while she was under construction, the Company took the opportunity to incorporate certain innovations and luxuries into her construction, and also into her sister, the *Majestic*. The *Teutonic* was launched on 19 January 1889 and, as with all White Star liners at that time, without ceremony, but was their first vessel to be built with twin screws.

Because of the *Teutonic*'s relatively narrow beam being a little under 58 ft the two 19 ft 6 in diameter propellers of 29 ft 6 in pitch, overlapped each other by 5 ft 6 in, the starboard propeller shaft was extended 6 ft further aft than the port one. It was considered that the propulsive efficiency would

be increased by this arrangement as it permitted the fitting of these maximum sized propellers without their 'discs' protruding beyond the beam of the ship. A considerable amount of trial and error had been undertaken in finding the right type of outward turning screw, and both engines had always to be run at different speeds on account of the higher 'slip' of the starboard propeller, (at full speed the revs varied between 79 and 82 rev/min). Each propeller was of manganese bronze and there were no external 'A' brackets in which the shaft was supported. Instead, the hull was bossed out to take the tail end shaft bearings, and the shaft tunnels were long rectangular chambers with ammonia refrigerating machinery between the shafts and the centreline bulkhead dividing them.

The *Teutonic*'s triple expansion engines, which were built by Harland & Wolff, had a high pressure (HP) cylinder bore of 43 in, an intermediate pressure (IP) bore of 68 in and a low pressure (LP) bore of 110 in. The engine stroke was 5 ft. The cylinders were not steam jacketed. The engines' crankshafts each weighed 41 tons and the after thrust blocks against which they acted each had 11 collars. They were supplied by steam at 180 psi from 12 double-ended and four single-ended boilers which were aided by huge steam-driven forced draught fans manufactured by Howden. The use of these forced draught fans enabled the coal to be burned more efficiently and it was claimed that they reduced the coal consumption of the *Teutonic*, normally 320 tons a day, by 10 tons! To convert the steam back to water, there were two condensers 20 ft long and 7 ft in diameter, built of brass

Below: **An early photograph of the *Teutonic* taken circa 1890 whilst at anchor in the River Mersey. She appears to be in pristine condition with a twin-funnelled paddle tug alongside her starboard bow. All masts are rigged with yardarms and she is flying what appears to be a 'steamer pennant' from her after yardarm.** *Pamlin Prints.*

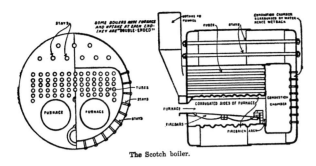

Above and below:. **Sketch of a single-ended and double-ended Scotch boiler.**

with 20 miles of ⅞ in Admiralty brass tubing in their nests. The seawater circulating pumps had a capacity of around 4,000 tons/hour. Her engines developed a total of 17,000 ihp which gave her a trial speed of 20 knots. As a result of the *Teutonic* being fitted with twin screws it meant that there was no longer any need to carry sail as an auxiliary form of power. Although she was completed with three masts without square rig and yards, the masts carried three gaffs.

The Auxiliary Cruiser requirement resulted in the engine and boiler rooms being compartmented as in warship fashion and to this end; she was built with a longitudinal watertight bulkhead which ran fore and aft throughout the length of the machinery space in the engine and boiler rooms. This centreline bulkhead rose to above the waterline and was level with the cylinder heads. It had a platform along its top from which the engineers could look down into either engine room. In addition to this there was complicated redundancy and duplication of steam, pumping and piping systems, in case of being laid open to the sea. This was incorporated and added to her cost. Under the Armed Merchant Cruiser (AMC) Agreement terms, White Star would receive a subsidy of 15 shillings (75p) per gross ton per annum from Her Majesty's Government, i.e. this worked out to £7,488 per annum for each of the *Teutonic* and her sister the *Majestic*.

When the *Teutonic* was nearing completion, it was decided that she should be present at the 1889 Naval Review at Spithead to mark Queen Victoria's Golden Jubilee. Following her delivery from the builders on 25 July 1889, she sailed for Liverpool under the command of Captain Henry Parsell and whilst at anchor she was converted to an AMC in the fast time of two days. It was intended that she be armed with twelve 5 in guns, one of the earliest breech-loaders in the British armed services and it was planned that in the mounting of these that six would be fitted on either side of the Promenade deck. However, at Spithead she only mounted four of these, one on each corner of the deck. The Naval Stores were unable to come up with the balance of the armament allocated to her. Later 4.7 in guns were substituted for the cumbersome 5 inchers.

On 1 August with Thomas Ismay and a party of guests aboard, the *Teutonic* sailed from Liverpool for The Solent where she later arrived and anchored at Spithead in a line of merchant ships. Later on 4 August, the Prince of Wales (later Edward VII) and Kaiser Wilhelm II, the German Emperor who was also attending Royal Cowes Week, boarded the *Teutonic* for a detailed inspection. The Kaiser himself had already considered the possibility that Germany should include a number of liners sufficiently fast to act as cruisers in time of war. Although one can only speculate that he warmed to and felt at home with the liner's name, the Kaiser was sufficiently impressed that in his speech he said that he had not the least doubt that she would prove a very useful cruiser; a self-fulfilling prophecy that was to be to his disadvantage in 1914. The inspection took up most of the Kaiser's time but one salient point he did take issue with was the steering of the ship. He realised that helm orders were given against the ship's head, that is to say the order to port the helm put the ship's head to starboard, a vestigial remnant from White Star's sailing ship steering. The Kaiser remarked that he would not have anything so illogical in his own Merchant service; starting the helm order controversy which lingered on up until the *Titanic* disaster. Notwithstanding this, he is rumoured to have said: 'We must have one of these!'

Most commentators of the day approved of the concept of the Armed Merchant Cruiser (AMC), for at that time the Royal Navy boasted a strength of 31 cruisers, with a nominal speed of 18 knots and over. But in reality, the great majority of these were under construction and some of those that were in service could not be relied upon achieving their predicted service speeds! The *Teutonic*'s participation at the Naval Review prevented her carrying out her speed trials. The actual Review itself was postponed until the following Monday because of bad weather. (*Typical Cowes Week weather, according to local 'caulkheads*). However, the *Teutonic* had to leave on the Sunday to return to Liverpool to be disarmed ready to enter her scheduled service, and so she was not present for the actual Naval Review line up.

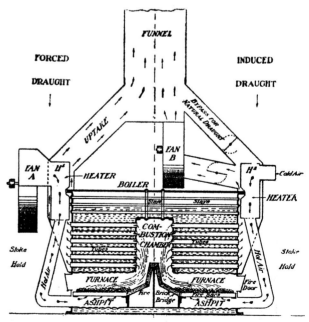

The double-ended Scotch boiler.

Accommodation was provided for 300 First class passengers, 175 Second and over 850 in Third or Steerage as it was more popularly known. That for the First class was situated amidships as the funnels were widely spaced so that the dining saloon, which could seat all 300 at one sitting, could be positioned where the ship's motion was not so extreme. Another innovative facility was that because of the 'ingenious arrangements of the First class accommodation', a passenger could 'procure the privilege of having a room to himself'. In addition, 400 tons of fine cargo could be carried.

Other technical aspects of the *Teutonic* were that she was fitted with steam-driven steering gear and steam reciprocating prime movers for the electrical generating plant to supply the lighting system. The draught arrangement for the boilers also played an important part. The traditional high funnels which enabled boilers to draw a natural draught were replaced with slightly shorter funnels because the forced draught was supplied to the boilers by fourteen large steam-driven double fans similar to those used in the ventilation system but capable of supplying 16,000 ft³ of air per minute. The air was drawn into these from the engine and boiler rooms and in this way natural air circulation was effected in these spaces from ventilators in the upper deck. The forced draught blowers were installed to feed the Scotch boilers via air heaters. It was claimed by Howden, the manufacturer, that this method reduced the coal consumption of the *Teutonic* and the *Majestic* by 10 tons per day under their predicted consumption had they used natural draught! In North Atlantic liners of the day which could carry well over 1,400 passengers and crew, ventilation between decks was an essential requirement. The opening of ports could prove dangerous to the ship in rough seas. Even with all the ports open, not all public rooms could be adequately ventilated, not even with 'air scoops' fitted. In order to meet the need, the *Teutonic* (and also her sister the *Majestic*) were fitted with similar fans used in the boiler forced draught system, 14 steam-driven, forced draught double fans but of lower capacities.

Above: **Another view of the *Teutonic* at anchor in the River Mersey with two of her lifeboats in the water. The arrow-like features just aft of the base of her mainmast are 'wind sails' used for the ventilating the hold.** *Nautical Photo Agency.*

Because of the higher speed, the *Teutonic* was fitted with refrigerating machinery as well as provision rooms. She had two meat holds of 40,000 ft³ total capacity situated aft between the main and mizzenmasts. Each hold had its own Linde refrigeration plant employing ammonia as the primary refrigerant; circulating air was blown over cold coils through which the compressed and cooled ammonia expanded. The installation also allowed for the cooling of the provision rooms via the forward air circulating system. This installation proved to be very successful and profitable on the *Teutonic* and her sister ship that during 1892, White Star removed the older *Britannic* and *Germanic* from service to have them fitted with refrigerated spaces. In order to simplify the installation into the existing holds, an indirect carbon dioxide refrigeration system was chosen. In this method, the gas was used to cool brine, which was circulated through pipes laid in the hold. Carbon dioxide was chosen in preference to ammonia as the latter caused corrosion of the copper pipes through which the brine passed.

The main differences in hull form between the White Star duo and the rival Inman Liners *City of New York* and *City of Paris* were that the length/beam ratio of the former was 9.7:1, a long fine form sporting a straight stem, whereas the Inman sisters were broader and with a curved hull and with clipper bow, giving a length/beam ratio of 8.3:1. As regards the engine power in the White star pair, the proportion of ihp to gross tonnage was 1.7 compared with the Inman ships 1.8. In the matter of speed, there was very little to choose between the White Star sisters or indeed any of the four. On the balance, the *City of Paris* was the speediest of the lot, while the *Teutonic* was faster than the *Majestic*.

The *Teutonic* eventually departed on her maiden voyage from Liverpool on 7 August 1889. On this she made a fast

Above: **The *Teutonic* in Southampton's No 6 (Trafalgar) drydock. This photo clearly shows her port propeller is forward of the starboard one.** *Pamlin Prints.*

passage to New York of 6 days 17 hours and 25 minutes, at an average speed of 17.59 knots, in spite of encountering fog and heavy seas. The *Teutonic's* entry marked a return of new liners to the Atlantic after an absence of 13 years, and quickly recaptured some of White Star's lost trade, the earlier pioneering liner the *Baltic* was made redundant by her entry into service. Later in 1889, new propellers of a smaller diameter were fitted and brought improved performance. On 31 January 1890, while berthed at Liverpool, a fire broke out in some mattresses stored between decks; the flames were brought under control with some minor damage.

Whilst on an eastbound crossing, on 14 February 1891, the *Teutonic* encountered gale force winds and high seas for 48 hours. She had broken out her foresail to make headway against the buffeting seas but it was torn to shreds. Water crashed through the companionways and poured into passengers' staterooms causing panic and discomfort. Having weathered this, upon her arrival at Liverpool she encountered thick fog and had to anchor outside the Mersey Bar for some 30 hours. Gradually the vying for the Blue Riband became more widely known not only in shipping circles and among passengers but also to the wider public. This in turn encouraged keen rivalry between Inman's *City of New York* and the *Teutonic* which caught the public's attention and it was to last as long as either of the two ships were both in the front line. The *Teutonic's* best record effort was in August 1891 when she crossed between Queenstown and New York in 5 days 16 hours and 31 minutes, making the 2,778 nautical mile crossing at an average speed of 20.35 knots; a record she held for the following 12 months.

The following month, the *Teutonic* under Captain P. J. Irving, set off on her thirteenth crossing from Liverpool while the *City of New York* was commencing on her seventeenth. The *Teutonic* left Queenstown at 2.58pm and the *City of New York* at 2.45pm on 4 September. They both arrived at New York on 10 September after a time on passage of 5 days 20 hours and 54 minutes and 5 days, 20 hours and 5 minutes respectively. The average speed was 19.5 knots, the distance steamed by the *Teutonic* being 2,774 nautical miles and 2,779 by the *City of New York*. The best day's run for the *Teutonic* was 509 miles. The homeward run was equally as exhilarating. The two ships left New York on 17 September within 25 minutes of each other and both arrived at Queenstown on 23 September. On that occasion the *Teutonic* steamed 2,794 miles in 6 days and 19 minutes, and the *City of New York* steamed 2,773 miles in 6 days and 31 minutes. Perhaps one can wonder what all the fuss was about back in those times, but bearing in mind that both ships were 'cracking on' at full speed in the busy North Atlantic seaway, without the use of radar or the Global Positioning System (GPS) aids. Small wonder that the public was wildly excited over these contests and took more interest in Atlantic travel and the liners than it had ever done before.

The *Teutonic* was the last liner in the Company to hold this record, for from this time on White Star placed their emphasis on comfort, reliability and safety. The case for the Auxiliary Cruiser role had vindicated Thomas Ismay's predictions, however, after 40 years in the shipping and allied businesses, in December 1891, he retired from the firm of Ismay, Imrie & Co. of which he had been a founder but continued to control the destinies of the White Star Line as its Chairman. In 1896, the tonnage of the various Atlantic companies had improved so much since the Admiralty's original Auxiliary Cruiser Agreement of 10 years before, that the rubric was reviewed and updated. Hence Cunard's newer *Campania* and *Lucania* were paid an annual subsidy of £7,500 each whilst White Star's *Teutonic* and *Majestic* were given a different rating, the former being priced at £7,285 and the latter at £7,396. At the same time the old 5 in muzzle-loading guns, then obsolete for their original purpose, were replaced by 4.7 in breechloaders backed up by a number of 0.45 in Nordenfeldt machine guns, which were then considered quite sufficient to stop a torpedo boat.

Only the crack liners were actually subsidised, but in order to secure the agreement Cunard and White Star promised to hold other ships at the disposal of the Government without extra payment, as a matter of goodwill. In the case of Cunard it covered their liners *Etruria*, *Umbria* and *Aurania*; and for White Star, the *Britannic*, *Germanic* and *Adriatic*. It is not widely known but during this period the potential value of auxiliary cruisers was increasing rapidly owing to the increased efficiency of the Royal Naval Reserve, which was beginning to be treated as a serious force by the regular naval officer class.

On 26 March 1892, whilst berthed at Liverpool, the *Teutonic* was struck by the steamship *Indiana* which buckled three of the *Teutonic*'s plates; the *Indiana* continued on to ram a collier whilst under the same manoeuvre. Moving on to 26 June 1897, the *Teutonic* took part in Queen Victoria's Diamond Jubilee Fleet Review at Spithead. To mark the 60th year of Queen Victoria's reign, an album for private circulation only was printed of guests invited aboard the *Teutonic*. Guests of Thomas Ismay included many from Cumberland which also included his family and his son Joseph Bruce Ismay, as well as Mr and Mrs. H. Senhouse of Maryport, the Earl and Countess Lonsdale, cadets from the training ship HMS *Conway* and 100 boys from the training ship *Indefatigable*. On the cover was a picture of the vessel with the caption: 'HIM The Emperor of Germany and HRH The Prince of Wales inspecting the *Teutonic* at Spithead on August 4th 1889'. For this Review she was again armed as an AMC with her eight 4.7 in guns mounted at White Star's expense as the Admiralty was unwilling to foot the bill. Also in attendance was the Company's tender *Magnetic*.

During the Review Sir Charles Parsons demonstrated his experimental yacht *Turbinia* through the lines of warships assembled for the Review. With his little vessel powered by three shafts each carrying three screws, he piloted the *Turbinia* through the lines of ships at 32 knots, thereby capturing the Admiralty's attention. The *Turbinia* later moored alongside the *Teutonic* and Thomas Ismay and his son Bruce were given a trial run at '40 miles per hour'. Although the *Turbinia*'s pioneering propulsion was later adopted by the Royal Navy, Allan Line and Cunard, it was not readily taken up as a main form of power plant by White Star until 1926 other than as an exhaust turbine after steam had been expanded in reciprocating engines. Later that year, on 17 August 1897, whilst manoeuvring astern from her

New York dock, the *Teutonic* ran into and sank an ice barge which was being towed by the tug *Peter Nevins*. The following year, on 21 September 1898, she was again in collision at New York, this time with the US Transport *Berlin* which was outward bound with stores and provisions for the United States' forces at Ponce in Puerto Rico. The *Teutonic*'s bows caught the *Berlin*, which later resumed her voyage with minimal damage to the *Teutonic*.

In 1900 with the disturbances in the Transvaal and the onset of the Boer War, the *Teutonic*, which had been earmarked for government service because of its Naval subsidy was taken up for service as a troopship. She was one of four mail ships totalling 33,280 gross tons supplied by White Star. As such the *Teutonic* was commended for the speed at which she carried some battalions of troops to South Africa at a time when they were greatly needed.

On 11 June 1900, whilst under the command of Captain E. R. McKinstry, the *Teutonic*'s starboard engine suffered a breakdown. On board at the time as a passenger was shipowner J. Pierpont Morgan who would later merge White Star with his International Mercantile Marine combine (IMMCo). He was travelling with his daughter at the time and they both helped to placate concerned passengers. The *Teutonic* proceeded at half speed over the following 24 hours whilst repairs were effected. Early in the following year on 24 February 1901, whilst steaming westbound, the *Teutonic* ploughed into a large tidal wave which appeared seemingly from nowhere but likely as not may have been generated by an earthquake. In this impact the two lookouts in the crow's nest were thrown to the deck and the officers' quarters were flooded. A deckhouse was flooded and railings and ladders twisted by the sheer volume of the water. Fortunately, this incident happened at night, had it been during the daytime there is the likelihood that many passengers on deck may have been lost overboard. Nineteen months later on 25 September 1902 she was at Liverpool and collided with the Dublin mail ferry *Mayo* which was damaged in the impact. Again on 13 December 1903 the *Teutonic* was in the Atlantic steaming in heavy westerly gales and driving snow when just before dinner time lightning struck her mainmast. The trunk of the mast was damaged and wreckage fell through a skylight above the dining saloon, shocking the assembled passengers. On 28 July 1905, whilst alongside at New York, a fire broke out in the electrical switch gear room, thought to be caused during fumigation at the time. It took over two hours to extinguish but fortunately no lives were lost.

Concerning the rival company, the American Line, they had been one of the first companies to realise the paramount importance of the French trade, and the possibility of working it economically with the United Kingdom run. After a good deal of discussion with the United States Post Office, permission was obtained for the Eastbound mail steamships to land their mail at Plymouth, where the Great Western Railway was sufficiently keen on the business to run a train service to London. The ships then continued to sail to Cherbourg for the convenience of their Continental passengers before they went on to Southampton, which remained the terminal port. This was a very important change and, when official permission had been obtained to drop the Plymouth call a little later, it became the regular run for their main Atlantic service. The White Star Line took a leaf from the American Line's book and followed their example. It moved its operational express passenger service to Southampton from Liverpool in the summer of 1907. In this manner the move satisfied the growing demand for direct connection between the United States and English Channel ports.

Along with the *Teutonic*, White Star sent three of their largest liners to Southampton, the *Majestic* (1890), *Oceanic* (1899) and the *Adriatic* (1907). By this move White Star also maintained their Wednesday mail service. The *Teutonic* made her first voyage from Southampton to New York via Cherbourg on 12 June that year. In 1911, the Company, under the policy of internal transfers within the International Mercantile Marine Company (IMMCo), decided to place her on the Dominion Line's (later known as the White Star-Dominion service) Canadian service, terminating at Montreal in the summer season and Portland, Maine during the winter. To facilitate the new itinerary she underwent an extensive refit at Belfast during which much of her upper and promenade decks were plated in to give better protection for the colder weather that might be expected on that route. In addition her passenger accommodation was re-graded to carry 550 Second class and 1,000 Third class passengers, the First class being discontinued. She reverted to Liverpool as her UK terminus and commenced on the Montreal service on 6 May 1911. During one of her winter passages from Liverpool to Halifax and Portland, Maine she ran into heavy weather. In this a broken ventilator allowed water to flood a hold thereby damaging some of her cargo.

Following the outbreak of World War 1 on 4 August 1914, the *Teutonic* was taken up for service and requisitioned

as an Armed Merchant Cruiser (AMC) on 20 September in the 21-ship 10th Cruiser Squadron under the command of Captain G. C. Ross. She was pressed into service to replace the *Aquitania*, which had been damaged following a collision with Frederick Leyland's *Canadian*. In her warship role she took up her station with the Cruiser Force 'B' on the Northern Patrol which operated in the Faeroes to the ice belt and in the Denmark Strait between Iceland and Scotland. Later during the War, on 16 August 1915, she was bought outright from White Star by the Admiralty and equipped with large 6 in guns. However by December 1916 she was placed in reserve for 10 months. She was reactivated again in October 1917 and recommissioned to join the 10th Cruiser Squadron as a White Sea convoy escort.

In 1918, following the Armistice, the *Teutonic* was taken over by the Shipping Controller, under White Star management, and used for trooping duties between the UK and Alexandria in Egypt, with a capacity for 1,500 troops. She was offered for sale in the spring of 1920 but soon afterwards the sale was withdrawn to carry out further transport duties into the early part of 1921. She was later laid up in Cowes Roads off the Isle of Wight for several months in 1921, before being sold to Dutch shipbreakers in July that year. Two months later in September she was again resold to German shipbreakers for scrapping in Emden during that year. Notwithstanding her war service with the Admiralty and the Shipping Controller, the *Teutonic* was one of the longest serving ships to be owned by White Star.

TEUTONIC: *Of or pertaining to the Teutons; of the Germanic group of Indo-European languages.*

Below: **A later view of the *Teutonic* anchored in the River Mersey, minus her yard arms and with enclosed promenade decks.** *B&A Feilden.*

MAJESTIC (I)

(1890-1914)
9,965 grt; 565 ft 10 in BP (582 ft OA) x 57 ft 10 in
Triple Expansion SR Engines, Twin Screw,
17,000 ihp, 19 knots
Passengers: 300 First class, 190 Second class,
1,000 Third class
Harland & Wolff, Belfast. Yard No. 209

Above: **An early photograph of the *Majestic* at anchor in the River Mersey with what appears to be a paddle tug or tender alongside her starboard well deck and a sailing barge moored forward of the bridge. She is in her original configuration with yard arms rigged on all masts with the after one flying a "steaming pennant". Her paintwork appears in pristine condition with the sun reflecting on it.**
Richard de Kerbrech Collection.

The *Teutonic*'s sister was ordered in March 1887, launched on 29 June 1889 and delivered to White Star on 22 March 1890. Like the *Teutonic*, the *Majestic* was designed with the capability of being converted to an Armed Merchant Cruiser (AMC) in time of war. Unlike the *Teutonic*, she was not constructed with the longitudinal bulkhead for watertight integrity and compartmentalisation. Operational experience in the earlier vessel had led to very high temperatures in the boiler rooms with a degree of discomfort for the firemen and engineers in that space, so the innovation was dropped. She was fitted with two main condensers 20 ft long and 7 ft in diameter built of brass with ⅞in brass tubes. The total length of condenser tubing used was rumoured to be around 20 miles! The circulating pumps had a flow capacity of around 4,000 tons of seawater per hour. She also sported the fore, main and mizzenmasts without the crosstrees for auxiliary sail and it is believed that for the first time in an Atlantic liner no yards were fitted or sails carried. Her steam steering was duplicated, with port and starboard engines. The hull was stiffened and reinforced for eight gun positions.

Her net tonnage was originally 4,340 and displacement 16,740 tons. Although built expressly for passengers and mails, 4,000 tons of cargo could be carried and this could be handled through five hatchways: three forward and two aft. The *Majestic* was exceptionally strong in its construction of Siemens-Martin steel with the plate butts triple and quadruple riveted – in some places quintuple. There were three overall decks with an orlop deck forward and 10 main

bulkheads including the bunker bulkheads. Her saloon was 60 ft long and 57 ft across, with a dome that extended up into the library above. Three long tables fore and aft down the centre and numerous shorter tables were arranged athwartships along the sides. There were a number of single berth staterooms with many rooms having double bedsteads. All the public rooms were a veritable exhibition of diverse art tastes in mouldings, carving, statuary, fine woods, gilt, crystal, rich hangings, tapestry, wrought iron work, paintings and coloured glass. There were 'bas-relief' figures of tritons and nymphs gambolling, around the library on the promenade deck. The smoking room was panelled in mahogany, the 'walls in embossed leather, richly gilt'. The barber's shop had 'electric motors to drive revolving hair brushes'. First class staterooms had coloured glass screens over the ports. The Second class abaft the mainmast had their own open promenade deck, while the Third class, fore and aft on the lower decks, were for that time, well catered for and had baths, a smoking room, some family rooms, mechanical ventilation, and also 'an elaborate system of lavatories planned with a view to the utmost delicacy'. All these works of art, painstaking labour and décor were the work of individual skilled craftsmen and the cost must have been astronomical.

The *Majestic* sailed on her maiden voyage on 2 April 1890 from Liverpool to New York via Queenstown and by doing so replaced the earlier *Republic* of 1872 on the route. At once upon her entry into service she vied for a fast

Above: **A full broadside view of the *Majestic* taken c1890 whilst anchored in the River Mersey. Moored alongside her port side are what may be two water/coaling vessels (one might well be the *Pontic*), and further aft a paddle tug/tender by the well deck.** *Pamlin Prints.*

crossing and upon her return voyage from New York, made a record eastbound passage of 6 days 8 hours 58 minutes at a speed of 18.31 knots. However, the following year in July 1891, she broke the westbound record between Sandy Hook and Queenstown with a time on passage of 5 days 18 hours 8minutes at an average speed of 20.1 knots. This was to be her only record. On 26 February 1893, the *Majestic's* starboard engine broke down and she was forced to steam on for several hours on at reduced speed on her port engine only; the design of liners with twin screws came into its own on occasions like this.

The *Majestic* settled along with other units of White Star in maintaining the North Atlantic ferry service. An incident of excitement in the career of the *Majestic* occurred during 1894, when she raced her rival, the *City of Paris* from New York to the English Channel. Upon their reaching the western approaches to the Channel the honours were even, with no outright victor. She was requisitioned as a troop transport vessel during the Boer War which had broken out, and on 13 December 1899 she departed Liverpool for Cape Town. This was followed by a second voyage which set out from Southampton for the cape on 12 February 1900. For the two round trooping voyages, the *Majestic* and the Company received a warm commendation from the authorities for the speed with which she dispatched some much-needed battalions of troops on time!

She returned to commercial service but this was not without incident. Whilst westbound, on 7 April 1901, a big end connecting-rod bolt fractured on her starboard engine. This forced the *Majestic* to continue on at reduced speed on

her port engine only, whilst repairs were carried out. This breakdown caused her to be over a day late on her scheduled arrival at New York. Four months later on 7 August, whilst under the command of Captain Edward J. Smith, and just before reaching her New York destination fire broke out aboard. Around 5am in the morning, it occurred in one of the ship's linen closets, and was thought to have been caused by faulty electrical wiring which ran through the closet. A hole had to be cut in the decking and water poured in to extinguish it. However it smouldered on for a few more hours before eventually reigniting (presumably the same 'electrical fault' still persisted). This time steam hoses dowsed the fire.

In 1902, she returned to Harland & Wolff for a major refit, in which new boilers were fitted and her funnels raised by 10 ft. At the same time the large house at the foot of the foremast was extended out to the ship's sides and forward to join up with the forecastle, giving a forecastle 150 ft long. This created an awkward knuckle in it where the turtleback merged into the side plating. A light deck was added over the second class promenade. In addition, the main and mizzenmasts were removed and the mainmast restepped on the fore end of the second class desk; upon completion in 1903 her gross tonnage had increased to 10,147. Whilst alongside at Liverpool on 28 May 1905, she was damaged by a fire in her bunkers, which proved not to be too serious. By contrast, some six weeks after this, on 6 July 1905, four Engineers were scalded in a steam explosion in *Majestic's* engine room.

Along with the *Teutonic, Oceanic* and *Adriatic* (1907), the *Majestic's* terminal port was transferred to Southampton in 1907 and as such she made her first voyage from Southampton to New York on 26 June that year. Seven months later on 31 January 1908 whilst in port at Southampton, she suffered a fire on board which gutted her Smoking Room and several cabins before it were extinguished, thus throwing out her schedule. Despite her major refit of 1902-1903 she was placed in reserve in November 1911 and laid up in Bidston Dock at Birkenhead. The decision to retain a reserve ship came into its own some six months later when she was reactivated in May 1912, following the *Titanic* disaster the previous month, and maintained the service. Perhaps an older, more established ship was what the travelling public needed to boost their confidence in White Star, after the *Titanic*'s loss! On 17 October 1913, the *Majestic* rescued the crew of the French schooner *Garonne*.

The *Majestic*'s last sailing from Southampton to New York was on 14 January 1914 following two years unexpected service. Upon leaving Cherbourg later that day, one of the tenders bumped into her wrenching away one of her coal ports. After repairs were effected she departed for New York. Upon her arrival at New York, six days later, one of her propellers struck and sank an attending tug, the *John Nichols*. Somewhat ironically, she was sold to Thos. W. Ward for £25,000 on 5 May 1914 and broken up at Morecambe. In hindsight, the decision to scrap her just three months before the outbreak of World War 1 seems a bit premature, but by August, demolition was well advanced.

It is rather strange that, with the advent of World War 1 just three months away, that she was not taken up for duties as an AMC like the *Teutonic*, or as a troopship. Even more ironical is that she was not used in her intended auxiliary role for which the Admiralty had continually subsidised White Star throughout the liner's 24-year career! Perhaps then, as now, the shipbreaker's scrap value offer was too good to refuse.

MAJESTIC: *Having majesty or great dignity.*

Below: **A photo of the *Majestic* in later years, seen outward bound for the United States. Her after mast has been removed and her mainmast re-sited aft and she has taller funnels.** *FGO Stuart.*

NOMADIC (I)

(1891-1903)
5,749 grt; 460 ft 10 in BP x 49 ft 1 in
Triple Expansion SR Engines, Twin Screw,
3,500 ihp, 13 knots
Passengers: None. Livestock carrier.
Harland & Wolff, Belfast. Yard No. 236

Following on from the success of the earlier single screw, livestock carriers *Cufic* and *Runic*, White Star further developed the purpose-built vessels and what emerged was the *Nomadic* and her sister the *Tauric*. The pioneering pair were of the three-island type, with raised poop, bridge deck and forecastle. Later ships starting with the *Nomadic*, were all twin screw and differed in having the weather deck topped by a bridge deck, usually plated in and with more superstructure above.

The *Nomadic* was launched on 11 February 1891 and delivered two months later on 14 April. She sailed on her maiden voyage from Liverpool to New York on 24 April 1891. After settling into her intended service, three months later on 10 July, she collided with the pier head at Liverpool and damaged her stem. A year later on 13 October 1892, the *Nomadic* was on the return voyage to Liverpool when one of her engines broke down, but she continued on to her destination at reduced speed. Misfortune again struck, when the *Nomadic* arrived at Liverpool on 12 June 1897 from New York, and collided with the cargo ship *Barnesmore* which was departing for Montreal. The *Nomadic*'s stem, no stranger to damage, was twisted but did not delay her next departure. The *Barnesmore* had to put back to Liverpool to make good repairs to a damaged port bow.

The *Nomadic* was the first White Star vessel to be requisitioned as a troopship for the Boer War during October 1899 and as such she was designated HMT *No. 34*. Although what the soldiers thought of being transported in a livestock carrier, one can only guess. During her three round voyages she made to South Africa, she also transported hundreds of horses commandeered from London horse-bus operators for use serving the artillery and pulling the supplies wagons. After White Star was taken over by the International Mercantile Marine organisation (IMMCo), the *Nomadic* was transferred to the Dominion Line under the holding group's Steamship Amalgamation Plan during 1903. On 14 March that year, whilst berthed at Portland, Maine, a fire broke out on the ship's upper cattle deck and the forward part of No 5 hold. Although the damage was minor, 73 bales of scorched and water-damaged wool were thrown overboard. Fortunately there were no livestock loaded at the time.

Above: **In October 1899, the livestock carrier *Nomadic* was the first White Star ship to be requisitioned as a Boer War troopship and horse transport. This photograph shows her as HMT *No 34*. Note the large cowl type ventilators on the fore and well deck to aerate the livestock holds and take away the smell of methane from the animals' dung.** *Nautical Photo Agency.*

In 1904, the *Nomadic* was renamed the *Cornishman* and operated on the United States and Canadian routes for many years. By 1921, the *Cornishman* was internally transferred to Frederick Leyland & Co., still on the same route. After a career of nearly 35 years she became surplus to requirements and on 12 May 1926 she arrived at Hayle in Cornwall and sold for scrap for £10,500. She was subsequently broken up at Lelant in the Duchy.

NOMADIC: *Of or pertaining to a nomad or wanderer.*

TAURIC

(1891-1903)
5,728 grt; 460 ft 10 in BP x 49 ft 1 in
Triple Expansion SR Engines, Twin Screw,
3,500 ihp, 13 knots
Passengers: None. Livestock carrier.
Harland & Wolff, Belfast. Yard No. 237

Built by Harland & Wolff as a livestock carrier, the *Tauric* was launched on 12 March 1891 and delivered two months later on 16 May. Like her sister the *Nomadic*, the *Tauric* was an improvement on the earlier cattle ships, the *Cufic* and the *Runic*. Besides being almost 1,000 grt larger the *Tauric* was some 30 ft longer and with just a small increase in draught from 30 ft to 30 ft 11 in.

She sailed on her maiden voyage from Liverpool to New York on 22 May 1891. That year was fairly fraught for the *Tauric*, for barely six months after her entry into service, on 14 November, whilst inbound to New York, she ran aground in the Romer Shoals, two and a half miles east of Sandy Hook. In order to shift her from being stranded more than 800 head of cattle on board had to be transferred to a cattle boat, the *General McCullum*. At the same time a large quantity of cargo was offloaded onto a lighter by the *Tauric*'s derricks. Once the ship had been sufficiently lightened, after 25 hours and with the assistance of five tugs, the *Tauric* was eventually dragged off. Just two weeks after this, on 28 November, she collided with the steamship *Baltimore* in the Mersey. In this the *Baltimore*'s bows were damaged but the *Tauric* survived with negligible damage.

A year later on 27 November 1892, she again collided in the Mersey, this time with the Allan liner *Buenos Ayrean*. On this occasion the *Tauric*'s bow was stove in, while the Allan liner's stem was twisted in the encounter. Another unfortunate incident occurred on 30 January 1895 when a faulty electrical wire sparked, causing a fire in the *Tauric*'s No 4 hold, whilst she was alongside at Liverpool. The fire was brought under control by means of a hole cut through the deck above and the fire blasted by steam hose. In the attempt to extinguish the fire, the ship's electrician was suffocated by the smoke; in addition to this, the hold's cargo was badly damaged. The following month on 10 February whilst en route to New York, the *Tauric* went to the rescue of a sinking ship, the *Rialto*, and rescued the 14 people aboard. For this act the Life Saving Benevolent Association of New York (Incorporated 29 March 1849) had a special medal struck by Samuel Hammond & Co. which they presented to the *Tauric*'s Master. On its reverse was engraved: 'Presented to William Jones of steamship TAURIC in recognition of his courage and humanity in manning with other seamen the boat which rescued 14 persons from the foundering ship RIALTO in mid-Atlantic Ocean, February 10th 1895.'

Above: **The improved cattle carrier** *Tauric* **departs Liverpool for the United States.** *World Ship Photo Library.*

After a particularly rough eastbound crossing on 6 February 1899, the *TAURIC* arrived back in Liverpool from New York with her deck damaged and a large part of her deck cargo lost overboard by heavy seas. As with her sister the *Nomadic*, under the International Mercantile Marine organisation (IMMCo) Steamship Amalgamation Plan of 1903, the *Tauric* was transferred to the Dominion Line. She made her first voyage for this company on 12 March 1903 from Liverpool to Portland, Maine. Later in 1904, she was renamed the *Welshman*. For some 16 years the *Welshman* successfully traded in her role until 1921 when she was transferred to Frederick Leyland & Co. in which she spent a further eight years in service. In 1929, she was sold for scrap and broken up at Bo'ness on the Firth of Forth in December that year.

TAURIC: *Of or pertaining to Tauris, the name sometimes given for the Crimea in ancient times. Perhaps in view of the TAURIC's role, it might well be pertaining to Taurus i.e. bovine or bulls.*

MAGNETIC

(1891-1932)
619 grt; 170 ft 6 in BP x 32 ft 11 in
Triple Expansion SR Engines, Twin Screw,
1,200 ihp 13.5 knots
Passenger Tender
Harland & Wolff, Belfast. Yard No. 269

The *Magnetic* was built primarily for use as a passenger tender at Liverpool to serve the Company's passenger ships. But equally she could double up when equipped to do so as White Star's tug and as a water carrier. She was launched at Belfast on 28 March 1891 and delivered on 6 June that year.

On 26 June 1897, she was the tender to the *Teutonic* at the Spithead Review to celebrate Queen Victoria's Diamond Jubilee.

She was also used as tender and tug for other companies' ships and occasional coastal and cruises on the Mersey extended her itinerary. On 25 November 1907, while White Star's cargo vessel *Armenian* was docking at Liverpool having arrived from New York, she was being towed by the *Magnetic* when the tow rope parted. The momentum of the *Armenian* under way carried her against the wall of Sandon Dock's half tide entrance. In the ensuing collision, several plates on her port quarter and starboard side amidships were dented and it was necessary for her to be berthed in the Canada Dock for survey. The *Magnetic* was the first White Star ship to be converted to oil burning in the early 1920s. However on 3 October 1925 she caught fire and had to be beached at Tranmere where she was subsequently repaired.

In December 1932, she was sold to the Alexander Towing Company of Liverpool and renamed *Ryde*. She was refitted for similar duties and it was originally intended for her to be

Below: **White Star's first purpose-built passenger tender, the** *Magnetic,* **was in the Company's service for 41 years.** *B&A Feilden.*

placed in service at Southampton but this plan was cancelled and she was retained at Liverpool. For her new owners, she was painted with a white hull. When the No 2 Stanlow Oil Dock was opened on the Manchester Ship Canal in 1932, the *Ryde* carried the dignitaries and guests but two years later in 1934 she was transferred to Llandudno in North Wales where she continued as an excursion and coastal cruise steamer. By the following year she was sold after 44 years service and on 20 August 1935 she left the Mersey for Port Glasgow to be broken up.

MAGNETIC: *Of or pertaining to or acting as a magnet. Very attractive. Perhaps the company saw it as the larger ships of their fleet with the little tug/tender alongside giving the illusion of being magnetic or drawn towards each other.*

NARONIC

(1892-1893)
6,594 grt; 470 ft BP x 53 ft
Triple Expansion SR Engines, Twin Screw,
3,700 ihp, 13 Knots.
Passengers: 12. Livestock Carrier
Harland & Wolff, Belfast. Yard No. 251

The *Naronic* was launched from Harland & Wolff's yard on 26 May 1892 and delivered on 11 July. Upon her entry into service she was the largest cargo steamship afloat. The *Naronic* was constructed of steel with three decks, nine bulkheads and 16 water ballast tanks capable of holding 1,193 tons. The *Marine Engineering* journal of the day described her as: '…The spacious accommodation provided for 1,050 cattle, which she will be able to carry on her upper and main decks, will comprise every improvement that the most careful consideration and experience can suggest. The stalls, fresh water supply, and ventilation will be unsurpassed…'

She was a slightly larger improvement of the *Nomadic* pair and although built as a livestock carrier, she was fitted out with extra accommodation for 15 passengers to meet increased demand on the non-New York routes although in effect she was certified to carry 12. She carried a crew of 60. With an increased gross tonnage over the *Nomadic* and *Tauric* she was completed at a cost of £121,685 a rather expensive cargo ship for the day. The practice of carrying both passengers and cattle was never very popular among travellers for obvious reasons, quite apart from the smell! Notwithstanding this the Company had to capitalise on its opportunities wherever it could and the *Naronic* sailed on her maiden voyage from Liverpool to New York on 15 July 1892.

Later that year on 27 November the *Naronic* arrived back in Liverpool having lost 34 head of cattle on the voyage. The following year, during February, the North Atlantic experienced a spate of violent gales bordering on the hurricane, making the crossing not only uncomfortable but also perilous for those ships plying this route. And so it was

when the *Naronic* departed on her 13th voyage from Liverpool's Alexandra Dock on 11 February 1893, under the command of Captain William Roberts. On board were 74 persons, including 14 returning cattlemen. In addition she had been loaded with 1,017 tons of Welsh coal and 3,572 tons of general cargo which included some volatile chemicals; potassium chloride, sodium sulphide and carboys of acid. Apart from a consignment of bundles of iron, two horses were loaded in the pens. An additional 200 tons of coal was stowed on deck as the *Naronic*'s bunkers were full and to compensate for this topweight No 7 port ballast tank was filled with 140 tons of water to provide stability.

After dropping the Mersey pilot at Point Lynas near Holyhead she rang Full Away and steamed out into the Irish Sea. She was due to arrive in New York 11 days later but was never seen again! It was not uncommon for steamers to be overdue in port after encountering heavy seas, or even notwithstanding mechanical breakdown to the engines or, as we have already seen, the loss of a propeller. In so busy a seaway as the North Atlantic, a stricken vessel could be encountered by a passing ship, and could either be taken in tow if possible or the stricken vessel's plight reported at her port of destination. But by the end of February no word had been received as to the *Naronic*'s fate.

The ship's loss had prompted those with a sick sense of humour to play a hoax such as planting a message in a bottle. Two such were found. On 3 March one was found at Bay Ridge an inlet to New York Harbour, it read: 'March 1 1893. The *Naronic* is sinking with all hands. We are praying to God to have mercy on us. L. Winsel.' Another bottle was found on the beach at Ocean View on the Virginia coast, with the message: 'February 19 1893. The ship is sinking fast. It is such a storm that we can never live in the small boats. One boat with its human cargo has already sunk. We have been struck by an iceberg in the blinding snow. The ship has floated for two hours. It is now 3.20 in the morning and the deck is level with the sea. Will the finder of this message please forward it to the White Star agent at New York. Mr Maitland Kearsey.' It was purported to have been written by one of the cattlemen, John Osborn. Both the letters were thought to be false as neither of the above authors was among those listed as being aboard. Quite apart from this it is ironic that both bottles were found on the United States coast so near to the *Naronic*'s destination, and appeared to use the American system of dating with the month before the day. As if anybody on a fast sinking vessel in a storm would have time to write such a lucid message then conveniently find a bottle to put it in!

It was not until 19 March when Sivewright, Bacon's steamship, the *Coventry*, arrived at Bremerhaven from Newport News, Virginia, that her Master, Captain Wilson, reported that on 4 March his ship had passed one of the *Naronic*'s lifeboats floating upturned in position 44°02′ N, 47°37′W at 02. 00am. Twelve hours later, the *Coventry* passed another, half-submerged in position 44º 34′ N, 46º 24′ W, some 500 miles east of Halifax, Nova Scotia and roughly on the 'great circle' route. Although both lifeboats were reported as being far apart, the last sighted one was trailing a sea anchor, which might well have reduced its rate of drift. Ironically, neither boat was hoisted aboard. The latter reported had the name on its bows: '*Naronic, Liverpool.*' The ship's intended route was well south of the recognised iceberg zone.

It is speculation on the part of the author, but if the *Naronic* had been struggling in mountainous seas, it is possible that the coal may have shifted giving her an angle of loll. If she were then subjected to further punishment from beam on waves, these could combine to cause an already listing ship to capsize without time for the lifeboats to be unshipped. All in all a recipe for disaster no matter how good or experienced the crew. A theory was put forward that that some of the volatile chemicals had broken loose and formed an explosive cocktail combined with hydrogen which could be generated from spilt acid containers and bundles of iron cargo and seeping seawater into the hull. It is felt that any combustion that may have occurred from these may well have possessed fast flame propagation rather than an explosive pressure wave with the capability of blowing apart the hull.

At a subsequent Court of Enquiry, the subject of the *Naronic's* stability was called into question. To clarify this, heeling trials on her sister ship of similar dimensions, the *Bovic*, were carried out. The outcome from these proved the *Naronic* to be in a stable condition both laden and unladen. The Court cast doubt on the validity of the messages in the bottles as it was thought that the ship's position was well south of the Newfoundland iceberg field and it was believed that there was probably no ice within 100 miles of her scheduled route. The harsh reality of the *Naronic's* loss was that all 60 British and 14 Americans aboard had perished. The ship, valued at £121,685, was not insured whereas the cargo was insured for £61,855.

Below: **The *Bovic* of 1892 was one of the last livestock carriers built for White Star. This photograph shows her rather utility design.** *Tom Rayner Collection*

BOVIC
(1892-1922)
6,583 grt; 470 ft BP x 53 ft
Triple Expansion SR Engines, Twin Screw,
3,700 ihp, 13 knots
Passengers: 12. Livestock Carrier
Harland & Wolff, Belfast. Yard No. 252

Thirty-three days after the *Naronic* was launched, her sister ship, the *Bovic* was launched from an adjacent slipway on 28 June 1892. She was delivered on 22 August and departed on her maiden voyage on 26 August 1892 from Liverpool to New York, under the command of Captain Thompson, the *Naronic's* former Master. Following the loss of the *Naronic* in February 1893, heeling trials were carried out on the *Bovic* to establish if the ship when laden might be in an unstable condition, she was not though. Correlating this data with an identical ship inferred that the *Naronic* could not have been. Indeed the *Bovic's* Captain Thompson said that when he was Master of the *Naronic* for her first three voyages, that during rough weather the *Naronic* was not tender (*a small metacentric height which helped restore a rolling ship to the upright quite slowly*), and did not require further stiffening to her construction.

On 27 November 1893, whilst discharging cargo at Liverpool, it was found that several bales of hay had been soaked with cattle urine and seawater and had to be condemned. The following year, on 6 April 1894, whilst outward bound from Liverpool, the *Bovic* was in collision with the Norwegian barque *Duen* in Carnarvon Bay but sustained very little damage. Some four years later on 28 February 1898, after having landed her cargo at Liverpool, the *Bovic* struck the dock entrance and damaged her bows. On 4 August 1900, the *Bovic* was berthed at New York's Pier 49. Adjacent to her at the next Pier was the Company's flagship the *Oceanic*, which had entered service 11 months previously. In *Bovic's* No 3 hold was a cargo of cotton.

A small fire broke out in the adjacent hold. The *Bovic's* Master, Captain Thomas Jones then mustered the ship's fire party and sent for the New York Fire Department in case the fire got out of control and spread to the nearby *Oceanic*. In the event the fire was brought under control and No 3 hold's cotton was thrown overboard onto the quay and street below. The damage to the *Bovic* was around £200.

After a relatively incident-free seven years, on 12 October 1907 she was again in collision, this time with the schooner *Excelsior* off the Tuskar Light, in the St. George's Channel off Southern Ireland. The schooner ran into the *Bovic's* port side but there was no damage to either vessel. On 14 February 1914, the *Bovic* was seconded to the new White Star-Leyland-Lamport & Holt joint service to operate from Manchester to New York. She was White Star's contribution to this service and her masts were subsequently shortened so that she could pass under the bridges of the Manchester Ship Canal. In connection with this, she operated in consort with Leyland's *Memphian* and Lamport & Holt's *Canning*.

It was well into World War 1 when the British Shipping Controller under the Liner Requisition Scheme commandeered the *Bovic* during April 1917. As such she was employed on war service until 1919 when she was returned to White Star. From 1921 the *Bovic* resumed the Manchester to New York service until 16 January 1922 when she was transferred to Frederick Leyland & Co. and renamed *Colonian*. As the *Colonian* she remained in service with Leyland's until she was eventually broken up in Rotterdam during 1928.

BOVIC: *Of or pertaining to cattle. (Not a surprising choice of name considering the Bovic's role).*

GOTHIC

(1893-1926)
7,755; 490 ft 8 in BP x 53 ft 2 in
Triple Expansion SR Engines, Twin Screw,
4,400 ihp , 14 knots
Passengers: 104 First class; 114 Third class
Harland & Wolff, Belfast. Yard No. 267

The *Gothic* was launched on 28 June 1893 and although intended primarily with the North Atlantic service in mind, the decision was made for her to augment the joint White Star-Shaw Savill service to New Zealand via Cape Town, along with the earlier *Coptic*, *Doric* and *Ionic*. Because of her larger size to her predecessors, every effort was made in her design to incorporate the latest luxurious appointments in her public rooms, to carry 104 First class and 114 Steerage on the 7½-week voyage. In order that she could carry frozen produce back from New Zealand, she was fitted with the latest refrigerating plant whereby the secondary refrigerant was circulated brine to its primary refrigerant, carbon anhydride. One of the considerations in the frozen meat trade was its ability to carry the maximum number of carcasses

possible. From 1885 to 1888 a 4,000 ton deadweight steamer was considered a big vessel. Ships were then constructed to carry the maximum quantity of deadweight on the minimum net register. Consequently they had the minimum amount of cabin capacity within their dimensions.

When frozen meat became a factor in the steam carrying trade, it was found that, as it required 160 ft³, including refrigerating apparatus and insulation, to carry 20 cwt. of meat, it was advisable to increase the number of decks within the dimensions of the vessel. This was effected by the construction of a shelter deck, which filled the space between the forecastle and the short bridge deck thereby making it a continuous deck. In this way another deck was created which increased the ship's cubic capacity by twenty-five per cent to thirty-three per cent from the earlier ships. On top of the shelter deck a forecastle and bridge with accommodation for the officers was built. Increasing the beam to counteract the extra height gained by the shelter deck provided for the question of stability. In addition she had a 33 ft 6 in depth of hold.

The *Gothic* was the first twin screw ship to enter the New Zealand service. At that time, broken propeller shafts or shedding a propeller completely were the main concern of ships operating on the long distance route to the Antipodes. It was felt that the adoption of twin screws on such a long voyage would demand more horsepower and therefore more coal bunkers to do the same work as a single screw. This perceived reduced mechanical efficiency acted as a check on their introduction for many years, as the owners still had to watch and account for every ton of coal. The *Gothic's* size was hitherto an advance on any ship that had previously been considered for the New Zealand route that the disadvantages of the twin screws were overcome by the extra bunker space. Indeed, the *Gothic's* tonnage of 7,755 made her the largest ship built for White Star to date, with the exception of the *Teutonic* and *Majestic* pair. In fact her passenger accommodation for 104 First class amidships and 114 Steerage aft, was almost an exact copy, albeit on a reduced scale, of the two aforementioned record breakers. Careful attention in the ship's design was paid to the long distance service which involved crossing the tropics. To this end, ventilation of the passenger accommodation and public rooms was given a priority, along with the construction of more open promenade decks. Nearly the same improvement of standards was to be found in Steerage quarters and for its day it was far ahead of its time in comfort and also that every fitting was permanent.

However, for her size she was not a large cargo carrier, her insulated space being only sufficient for 71,000 carcasses of mutton. Her refrigeration machinery was a significant advance since the early days of the frozen meat trade, consisting of two carbon anhydride compressors made by J. & E. Hall of Dartford. These processed the primary refrigerant which heat exchanged with circulating brine as the secondary refrigerant, instead of the old cold air process. Her twin triple expansion steam engines developed 4,400 ihp and gave her a sea speed of 14 knots.

Above: **The *Gothic* of 1893 was a large and well-appointed ship for the New Zealand service and jointly operated by White Star and Shaw Savill.** *World Ship Photo Library.*

She was delivered on 28 November 1893 and sailed from Belfast for Liverpool where guests were entertained on board, before sailing on to London via Cardiff for bunkers. At that time she was the largest ship to enter the pool of London or indeed in any branch of the Australasian trade. Such was the interest created when she arrived in the Thames to berth that the opportunity was taken to throw her open to the public at a shilling (5p) a head. The proceeds from this went to the Connaught Road Seamen's Hospital. The *Gothic* sailed on her maiden voyage from London on 28 December 1893, under the command of Captain Jennings arriving in Wellington three days ahead of schedule. On her third trip under Captain W. H. Kidley, she made a record passage between Plymouth and Wellington via Cape Town of 37 days 10 hours and 16 minutes at an average speed of 14.16 knots over the whole route. This bettered the record of Shaw Savill's *Arawa* which had been established 10 years previously.

The advent of the *Gothic* permitted the joint service's monthly schedule to be maintained with a ship in hand for standby. As she was much more economical than Shaw Savill's pioneering pair, *Arawa* and *Tainui*, the older *Arawa* was released for Pacific charter in 1893, until 1895. By the mid-1890s, the New Zealand trade experienced a downward movement mainly due to the competition from Argentina's flourishing meat trade. The shorter distance sailing across the South Atlantic permitted beef to be carried chilled instead of frozen. Although beef had always made up a very considerable proportion of the cargoes from New Zealand, from this point onwards it was to take a back seat partly compensated for by the rising popularity of mutton. To this

end the *Coptic* and *Doric* were withdrawn from the service in 1894-1895, leaving the *Gothic* and *Ionic* to maintain the service along with the Shaw Savill ships.

When the *Ionic* had to undergo extensive repairs during 1894, the opportunity was taken to rearrange her passenger accommodation entirely, along the lines of the *Gothic* and also to give her new refrigerating machinery capable of dealing with very much larger quantities of meat and dairy produce. By 1902, the *Gothic* was augmented on the New Zealand trade by a new trio, the *Athenic*, *Corinthic* and a second *Ionic*, all completed that year. Also, in the summer that year she was used to repatriate New Zealand troops to the Dominion following the Boer War and they were embarked at Cape Town on the *Gothic*'s regular service.

There was a scarcity of New Zealand mutton for some months at the end of 1902 and the beginning of 1903 and 120,000 carcasses of chilled mutton from North America were imported into the UK, the meat being sold from 3½d to 4¾d per lb. This setback in trade greatly affected the White Star's New Zealand service. Having left Wellington under the command of Captain Charles A. Bartlett, the *Gothic* was on the return leg home, rounding Cape Horn with calls at Montevideo, Rio and Tenerife, in early June 1906. On board were 118 First class and 97 Steerage passengers. She was also carrying a cargo of 26,633 carcasses of mutton, 44,031 of lamb, 1,446 bales of wool, 1,000 sheepskins and 1,364 bales of flax.

Following her call at Tenerife, on 3 June smoke was seen in the First class dining saloon. Its source was from smouldering bales of wool and flax which had been stowed aft in No 3 upper 'tween deck hold, which extended aft under the vicinity of the dining room. Steam hoses were used at first to put out the fire. The following morning all scorched and smouldering bales were brought up from the hold and, still burning, were thrown overboard. This might

Above: **An unusual photograph of the *Gothic* pictured at Lyttleton in New Zealand, flying both the White Star and Shaw Savill houseflags. Adjacent to her berth is the New Zealand Shipping Co.'s *Ruahine* of 1891 and *Tongariro* of 1884 to the left.** *Marine Photos, Auckland.*

have been the end of it but by 6 June as the *Gothic* was steaming in the Western Approaches off Land's End, the fire flared up again and the next day by the time she arrived off Plymouth, the fire was raging between decks. Having made it to Plymouth Sound the passengers alighted in the tender *Cheshire* whilst officers and ratings from HMS *Niobe* and personnel from Devonport Dockyard assisted the ship's company in fighting the fire. The spreading fire, fuelled by fat from the meat carcasses and 576 flasks of tallow stored beneath the flaming wool, had assumed such proportions that the ship was in danger of being entirely gutted, so she was towed to the safety of Plymouth Harbour into the Cattewater and beached. The blaze had attracted thousands of people who had gathered along the Plymouth Barbican and the Hoe to witness the struggle to save the *Gothic* from destruction. Eight hoses from attending tugs pumped more than 100 tons of water into her hold with the ship's steam lines also in operation and the ship took on a list to port with all the flooding. Captain Bartlett ordered the seacocks to be opened such that she could be settled more evenly, before the blaze was extinguished on 8 June. Although the fire was extinguished, the damage to the cargo was estimated to be around £200,000, a phenomenal sum for the day.

Extensive damage was done to the ship's First class accommodation, public rooms and holds. The decking had been burnt and stanchions had warped in the heat that major repairs and refitting were carried out by her builders over a period of eight months. In this her passenger accommodation was altered to cater for 104 Second and 250 Third class. It is thought that because she was no longer destined for her former route and role that her refrigeration plant may not have been reinstalled and some of the former insulated space may have been refitted for passenger carriage.

Returning to service after her refit she was advertised in the 1907 schedule as: 'The SS *Gothic* is a magnificent twin screw steamer: she has excellent accommodation, and carries Second and Third Class passengers only', and her Master as Captain W. Finch. Towards the end of 1907 she made her last voyage to New Zealand, her 33rd under Captain L. A. Anning, before being transferred to the North Atlantic service under IMMCo's liner reshuffle to the Red Star Line. She was given Belgian registry and renamed *Gothland*. Her former First class cabins were reclassified as Third class and she initially entered service that year between Antwerp and Philadelphia prior to operating on the Antwerp to New York route until 1911.

With a surge in emigration to Australia shortly before World War 1, the *Gothland* was transferred back to White Star for what was to be a two-year secondment. She then reverted to her original name of *Gothic* and on her first voyage on the Company's Australian trade she carried some 1,500 emigrants out to Victoria. Two years later, in 1913, she transferred back to the Red Star Line service, again as the *Gothland*, in time for the summer service between Rotterdam, Quebec and Montreal. In June 1914, the *Gothland* was stranded on Gunnars Rock, off the Scilly Isles, and her 281 passengers aboard had to be landed by the *Lyonese* of the West Cornwall Steamship Co. together with the local lifeboat. After three days aground she was towed to Southampton for repairs which took the best part of six months.

Right: **This photograph of the *Gothic* at anchor with the tug *Iona* alongside shows her hull to be in rather dilapidated condition. Could this view of her be at Plymouth on 9 June 1906 after she was raised following her fire?** *Tom Rayner Collection.*

By the time repairs were completed in February 1915, the *Gothland* was unable to enter her intended service for Red Star as Belgium had been occupied by the Germans. She was transferred to the Rotterdam to New York run which became an irregular service due to wartime activity. She made several voyages between New York, Falmouth and Rotterdam for the Belgian Relief Commission during the War, and later made several cargo-only voyages on the earlier Antwerp to New York route. Following World War 1, she was given another refit in March 1919 and during August placed on the Antwerp-New York-Baltimore service which continued on until 18 May 1921 when she sailed on a single voyage for White Star from Naples to New York still as the *Gothland*. The following year saw the *Gothland* laid up for long periods until May 1923 when she was placed on the experimental Antwerp-Vigo-Halifax-New York route. This proved too long a voyage for some Northern European travellers and the original Antwerp-Philadelphia route was reinstated.

However, this was short-lived as she made her last voyage on the Antwerp-Philadelphia run during March 1925 before being sold for scrap in November that year for £16,000. She arrived at Bo'ness on the Firth of Forth on 16 January 1926 to be broken up. Some of the *Gothic's* former Masters were Captains W. H. Kidley (1894-1906), C. A. Bartlett (1906-1907) and L. A. Anning.

GOTHIC: *Of or pertaining to the Goths, an ancient people of Teutonic stock, who under King Alaric sacked Rome. Of a style of architecture prevalent in Western Europe from the 12th to the 16th century. In more recent times, referring to a style (genre) of horror film or literature. Following the joint New Zealand service with Shaw Savill, the Gothic's name became a Shaw Savill & Albion nomenclature and was not used again by White Star.*

CEVIC

(1894-1914)
8,301 grt; 514 ft BP (532 ft OA) x 60 ft
Triple Expansion SR Engines, Twin Screw,
3,700 ihp, 13 knots
Passengers: None. Livestock Carrier.
Harland & Wolff, Belfast. Yard No. 270

The *Cevic* was launched by Harland & Wolff on 23 September 1893, primarily as a replacement for the *Naronic*. During the month she was launched, the livestock imported by White Star from New York to Liverpool was some 20,673 steers of which 13 had perished. As well as these 169 horses were imported. But in the event the *Cevic* proved to be the last of White Star's cattle boats. She was designed with a deadweight capacity of 9,800 tons and consequently

drew more water with a depth of hold of 33 ft 9 in. Upon her delivery on 6 January 1894 she was the largest livestock carrier built for White Star to date, with space for 790-1000 head of cattle. These were accommodated on the upper and bridge decks, while in the centre of the upper deck there were stalls for 20 horses.

The *Cevic* embarked on her maiden voyage six days later on 12 January from Liverpool to New York. During the loading for the return journey at New York a record cargo was carried being; 14,000 bushels of grain, 9,000 bales of cotton, 3,500 sacks of flour, 400 tons of iron, 300 tons of fresh meat, 896 steers and 8,400 packages of produce. Upon her arrival at Liverpool on 2 May 1899, the *Cevic* was the first commercial vessel to berth in the new Canada Graving Dock for her overhaul.

After settling down into her intended trade and while berthed alongside at New York on 16 October 1902, she was struck by a steam dredger and had several of her plates damaged. Moving on to 1908, when a depression in the live cattle trade, caused by the incursions of the frozen and chilled meat trade, saw the end of the New York cattle service. This also brought the curtain down on White Star's livestock carriers and the *Cevic* was transferred to the Australian run with the outward call at Cape Town. She was then routed through the Suez Canal initially as an experimental run but owing to her depth of hold, her increased draught caused her to ground regularly. Such was the case that on a return voyage from Melbourne during 1910, the *Cevic* started taking water in two of her holds after transiting the Suez Canal and arriving at Port Said on 17 March. Upon investigation it was found that there was 7 ft of water in the two holds concerned. After pumping and repairs were effected the *Cevic* resumed the voyage home and the route via Cape Town was reinstated thereafter.

Following the outbreak of World War 1, the *Cevic* was sold to the Admiralty and returned to her builders on 1 December 1914 where she was converted and disguised as a dummy battleship, HMS *Queen Mary*. Upon the completion of this transformation to a decoy she sailed from Belfast on 11 February 1915 but two days later struck a rock and holed herself and she had to put back for repairs. Again on 10 April as she was leaving Belfast she went aground in fog on Ratlin Island the next day. She was floated off on 12 April on the tide without damage and sailed on to Loch Ewe. The *Cevic's*

Above: **The *Cevic* anchored in the River Mersey. As a livestock carrier she had the capacity for 1,000 head of cattle.**
Nautical Photo Agency.

disguise as HMS *Queen Mary* appears to have been convincing to the enemy. She sailed from Loch Ewe on 13 April and took up station patrolling the North Atlantic off the Eastern Seaboard of the United States by 25 April. Apparently her appearance caused a German liner which was in the vicinity to put into New York and apply for internment!

The *Cevic* was decommissioned from her dummy battleship duty in September 1915 and refitted as her intended role by Harland & Wolff but the following year 1916 was taken up by the Royal Fleet Auxiliary and renamed *Bayol*. As such she had large cylindrical tanks fitted into her for the carriage of oil. In 1917 she moved under the Shipping Controller and was renamed the *Bayleaf*. Under the management of Lane & McAndrew she continued in the capacity as a fleet auxiliary oiler to the Royal Navy and its coastal shore establishments. She was later purchased by the Anglo-Saxon Petroleum Company (later Shell) on 9 June 1920 and renamed *Pyrula*. They used her firstly as an oil depot ship at New York from November 1921 where she was anchored in the harbour. Four years later during September she was transferred to Curacao where she was deployed as a hulk at what was to become Shellhaven. She remained there until 25 July 1933 when she was sold for scrap and towed to Genoa for demolition at the yard of Henrico Haupt.

So the *Cevic* which had experienced the demise of the live cattle trade went on to become a pioneer in the fledgling Royal Fleet Auxiliary and helped to establish the post-war tanker fleet of what would eventually become Shell Tankers.

PONTIC

(1894-1919)
395grt; 150 ft 6 in BP x 26 ft 1 in
Triple Expansion SR Engine, Single Screw,
6 rhp, 8 knots.
Passengers: None. Baggage Tender
Harland & Wolff, Belfast. Yard No. 283

The *Pontic* was built as a baggage tender to service White Star and other passenger vessels at Liverpool. She was launched on 3 February 1894 and delivered nearly two months later on 13 April. With her engines aft and plenty of deck space forward for luggage, she had the appearance of a 'Clyde Puffer'; her triple expansion machinery had cylinder bores of 13 in, 21 in and 34 in with a stroke of 24 in. She doubled up in her duties as a water carrier with a depth hold of 11 ft 1 in and had the capacity to carry 11,000 Imperial gallons.

This role proved quite successful until she was sold to the Rea Towing Co. of Liverpool on 9 October 1919 for £5,122. She was employed by them in the same role and also as a derrick barge on the River Mersey – other duties included shipping consignments of cargo to Manchester via the Canal. In this way it was more economical for smaller cargoes to be trans-shipped rather than paying the canal fees for a larger ship to sail up the canal. On 23 January 1925 she was sold to John Donaldson of Glasgow for £1,740 for scrap and this might well have been the end of her days. However, on 29 January 1925, she left Liverpool for Glasgow and collided with the Crosby Lightship. The *Pontic* then returned to Morpeth Dock at Birkenhead for repairs that took three days. Upon reaching Glasgow she was managed by Donaldson Coal Tenders Ltd and initially employed as a coal tender and later as a sand ballast carrier between Glasgow and Tail of the Bank in the ballast trade before being broken up during 1930.

PONTIC: *It is for consideration that as the French for bridge is 'Pont' that it may be of or pertaining to this, i.e. forming a bridge for the luggage from ship to shore. Of or pertaining to Pontus, a trading nation on the Northern coastline of Asia Minor in the area of Turkey's eastern Black Sea region.*

GEORGIC (I)

(1895-1916)
10,077 grt; 558 ft 8 in BP x 60 ft 4 in
Triple Expansion SR Engines, Twin Screw,
4,500 ihp, 13 knots
Passengers: None. Livestock carrier.
Harland & Wolff, Belfast. Yard No. 293

Above: **The *Georgic* of 1895 anchored in the River Mersey. She was the largest livestock carrier to be built at the time for the United States' cattle exports.** *Ensign Photo.*

The *Georgic* was launched at Belfast on 22 June 1895 as a replacement for the *Naronic* and was to be White Star's largest and last livestock carrier. In fact with a depth of hold of 36 ft which gave her a deep draught and a deadweight tonnage of over 12,000 tons, she was the largest cargo ship in the world at the time. She was completed by the builders on 8 August 1895 and while departing the shipyard, she went aground in the new harbour channel but later towed off. The *Georgic* sailed on her maiden voyage on 26 August.

The following year whilst arriving back in Liverpool from New York on 23 May 1896, she hit the entrance to the dock causing damage to her stem. She again collided with the dock some five years later on 5 August 1901. The *Georgic* was found to be too large for her particular trade and her deep draught precluded her from flexibility on other routes so she became restricted to the New York and Atlantic service for most of her operational career. During this time she became something of an accident-prone vessel, for the following year on 10 March 1902, the *Georgic* was involved in a collision at Liverpool with a barque, the *Oakhurst*, in which the latter vessel was badly damaged. The next year, whilst off Fleming Cap on 18 January 1903, the *Georgic* was again in collision with a British steamer, the *Saxon King*. Although the *Saxon King* rammed the *Georgic's* starboard side by the foremast denting her plates, it was the *Saxon King* that bore the brunt of the collision, twisting her stem and allowing the forepeak to flood! In addition some of her davit rails and bulwarks were ripped off in the brush.

On 21 March 1904, the *Georgic* collided with the British steamer *Kalabia* in the St George's Channel but the damage was minor and both vessels made Liverpool without further mishap. Again while the *Georgic* was at Liverpool on 6 January 1906, a small fire occurred on board which was extinguished with no major damage. On 26 November 1908, whilst manoeuvring at Slow Ahead in dense fog off Sandy Hook on the approaches to New York Harbour, she rammed a small 2,600 ton US flag passenger vessel, the *Finance* which was carrying 150 passengers. The *Georgic's* bows tore into the port quarter of the *Finance* causing her to take in water and develop a list of 30° to port. As the *Finance* sunk her passengers made for the rafts and lifeboats or jumped overboard into the cold water. Four lives were lost along with the *Finance's* £60,000 worth of cargo.

After the outbreak of World War 1 in August 1914, the *Georgic* was retained on her regular commercial service. As such on 3 December 1916 she left Philadelphia for Liverpool via Brest, on board were 1,200 horses, 10,000 barrels of oil and a large consignment of wheat intended for the allies. The *Georgic* cautiously hugged the eastern seaboard up into Canadian waters before heading out into the Atlantic. One week later on 10 December, and whilst 590 miles east south east of Cape Race, Newfoundland, she was intercepted by the German surface raider *Moewe*, disguised as a Swedish merchant ship. The *Georgic's* crew was taken off and once aboard the raider apparently there followed a lively discussion between the British and German officers as to the fate of the horses. Placing a prize crew aboard the *Georgic* to save the horses was not an option for the *Moewe* and in the event the *Georgic* was sunk by the *Moewe's* crew placing explosive charges below with all its cargo aboard. The extract from the *Moewe's* log kept by Count von Schlodien, the ship's commander, states: 'In lowering the boats, the steamer's (*Georgic*) crew distinguish themselves; while they are lowering a fully laden boat, the tackle breaks and 40 men are hurled down into the water - not a pleasant sight. Our boats are all quickly lowered, and we succeed in picking up all but one. Her crew of 142 come on board; it is becoming congested over here. Everything proceeds as usual; the explosive charges detonate, but the steamer sinks very slowly.' During the *Moewe's* two sorties of the War, her tally would be 40 merchant vessels and one battleship. The *Georgic* was to be the surface raider's largest victim.

GEORGIC: *One of the four books of Virgil's poetical treatise on husbandry.*

DELPHIC (I)

(1897-1917) 8,273 grt; 475 ft 11 in BP x 55 ft 3 in
Triple expansion SR Engines, Twin Screw,
3,000 ihp 11 knots
Passengers: 1,000 Third class
Harland & Wolff, Belfast. Yard No. 309

The *Delphic* was launched on 5 January 1897 for entry into the New Zealand trade in the White Star-Shaw Savill joint service. She was a smaller and slower version of the *Gothic* but without the salient features of the First class accommodation and combined Shaw Savill's ideas of a moderate-speed meat carrier with White Star's plans of a big passenger vessel. However her 'tween decks accommodation proved to be more comfortable for 1,000 emigrants. Upon her delivery on 15 May 1897 it was decided that prior to her entry on the New Zealand service, the *Delphic*'s machinery

would be 'run in' and she made two round trips on the Atlantic run. The *Delphic* sailed on her maiden voyage from Liverpool to New York on 17 June. She was then transferred to the London to New York service and sailed on her first voyage on this route on 1 August 1897. Following these, she commenced on her first White Star-Shaw Savill voyage from London to Wellington on 3 October 1897.

In 1900, the *Delphic* was chartered as a troop transport for the Boer War and on 31 March she carried 1,200 troops, which included a large part of the Imperial Yeomanry, from London to Cape Town during the outward voyage to New Zealand. The following year, on 4 April 1901, she again transported troops, this time from Queenstown to the Cape, and then sailed on to New Zealand. After the outbreak of World War 1 during August 1914, the *Delphic* was retained on her regular commercial service. Whilst off the southwest coast of Ireland in February 1917, a torpedo fired by the German submarine *U-60* just missed her. On 10 March 1917, after nearly 16 years in the New Zealand service, the *Delphic* was taken up under the Liner Requisition Scheme. Some five months later on 17 August 1917, whilst on a voyage from Cardiff to Montevideo in South America with a cargo of Welsh coal, she was torpedoed by the German submarine *U-72*. This occurred some 135 miles southwest of Bishop Rock in the Scilly Isles. Five lives were lost during the explosion, although the *Delphic* remained afloat long enough for other members of the ship's company to be saved, when the U-boat fired more torpedoes to sink her. Throughout her career the *Delphic*'s Masters had been Captains W. Sowden (1897-1901), J. Breen (1901-1911), E. J. English (1911-1913), J. J. Symons (1913-1915), J. Harries (1915-1917), and E.Davies (1917).

DELPHIC: *Of or pertaining to Delphi, an ancient Greek town famous for the Temple of Apollo.*

Below: **Another later starboard side view of the *Delphic* with the cross trees removed from her foremast. Note the White Star and Shaw Savill houseflags flying from her main and mizzen masts respectively.** *Richard de Kerbrech Collection.*

CYMRIC

(1898-1916)
13,096 grt; 585 ft 6 in BP (599 ft OA) x 64 ft 4 in
Quadruple Expansion SR Engines, Twin Screw,
6,800 ihp, 15 knots
Passengers: 258 First class, 1,160 Third class
Harland & Wolff, Belfast. Yard No. 316

After the completion of the *Georgic* in 1895 White Star laid down an even larger ship, the *Cymric*, which was originally intended to carry 830 head of cattle and with a deadweight tonnage of around 14,000. By this time the Company had already decided on a policy of moderate speed with great size and comfort for their 'express' passenger ships and around the time of the *Cymric's* launching, they had decided to run intermediate ships and to apply the same policy to them. During construction the design of the *Cymric* was altered accordingly for passenger carrying since it was becoming increasingly unpopular to carry both cattle and passengers in the same ship. Therefore a large part of the space originally intended for cattle was taken over and fitted out as Third class accommodation and the carrying of livestock on the *Cymric* was not pursued.

The *Cymric* was launched on 12 October 1897 originally with a gross tonnage of 12,552, which later increased to 13,096 tons. She had a net tonnage of 8,508 and a displacement of 23,000 tons and a depth of hold of 37 ft 11 in. She had three overall decks, a long bridge deck amidships and a boat deck over the after two thirds of it, with the usual 'island' bridge and officers' house at the fore end that had become a characteristic feature of White Star vessels. Fifteen derricks and spans on her four masts served the *Cymric's* eight hatchways. The derricks for Nos. 3 and 4 hatches (nearest the funnel) were, when in use, stepped on normal height derrick tables, but when at sea they were stowed much higher up in a horizontal position level with the navigating bridge. Ten main watertight bulkheads divided her length and a full-length double bottom gave her good sub-division.

Her twin screws were driven by quadruple expansion engines with cylinder bores of 25½, 36½, 53 and 75½ in. respectively with a stroke of 54 in. This gave a combined ihp of 6,800 which produced 14.5 to 15 knots. The *Cymric* was the first White Star vessel to be built with quadruple expansion steam machinery. She was launched on 12 October 1897 and delivered on 5 February 1898. The *Cymric* may well have been White Star's first 'intermediate' liner. However, on the North Atlantic, she could hardly be considered a pioneer as such but rather one of the earliest of a very large group of intermediates built at Belfast around the turn of the century, all around 600 ft in length and 13,000 tons deadweight, with four masts and capable of a speed of 14 to 15 knots.

Frederick Leyland took delivery of the 'Victorian' class in 1895, leading up to the *Winifredian* in 1899. Atlantic Transport Lines' 'Manitou' class developed into the *Minneapolis* sisters, slightly larger and faster than the *Cymric*. The Hamburg America Line (HAPAG) produced the four 'Pennsylvania's, which were a little shorter, deeper and bulkier than White Star's vessel but by no means as aesthetic. The Dominion Line's *Mayflower* was of almost identical dimensions whereas Cunard's *Ivernia* and *Saxonia* were a little shorter but with a larger tonnage and more accommodation. (Ironically many of these rival liners would become consorts when the International Mercantile Marine Company was established in the early Twentieth century!).

The *Cymric* sailed on her maiden voyage in White Star's secondary service from Liverpool to New York on 11 February 1898, and upon her entry into service she was then the largest cargo carrier in the world and the largest in the White Star fleet at the time. Though she only held the latter record until the following year when the new *Oceanic* entered service. The *Cymric's* profile cut a dash with observers, with four well spaced masts, single funnel, gently sheered hull to improve seakeeping and the straight Harland & Wolff stem. As mentioned, a pleasing design that would be emulated by others. She was initially designed to carry 258 First class and 1,160 Third class passengers. The accommodation was on the comfortable and homely side rather than luxurious, which attracted travellers of fairly moderate means. Although slow in passenger terms, she proved popular with the travelling public; consequently, with her high passenger carrying capacity and running economy she became a profitable ship for White Star. At first she sported the buff-coloured lower strake to her bridge deck plating which had been adopted in a good many ships at the time including White Star's other cattle boats, Atlantic Transports' liners and Cunard's *Saxonia* and *Ivernia*. However, this buff colour was later dropped in favour of the bridge deck being painted all white.

The *Cymric* maintained the Atlantic run for two years but because of her high passenger-carrying capacity she was used for two voyages as a Boer War transport from Liverpool to Cape Town on 1 January and 1 March 1900, as Transport *No. 74*. Following these, she returned to the New York service. It was whilst back on this service that on 5 August 1900 when 19 hours out of Queenstown and en route to New York, that fire was discovered in No1 hold. It raged for 36 hours before being extinguished and although the ship herself was not damaged, some £2,000 worth of cargo in the hold was destroyed or damaged by the fire. On 19 January 1901 whilst the *Cymric* was leaving Liverpool, she collided with the British steamer *Caribu Prince* in the Mersey, in which several of her plates were stove in and damage done to the deck; nevertheless she managed to depart on time for New York.

By 1903 when the new Dominion liners had been taken over by White Star and renamed, the *Cymric* was transferred to the experimental secondary Liverpool to Boston run and commenced on this route from Liverpool on 10 December 1903. Thereafter for the rest of her peacetime career she remained on the Boston run, at first running in consort with the *Canada* and then with the *Republic*. It is of interest to note that in 1905 the First class fare to Boston was £12, while

S. S. Cymric.

in 1908 after a rate war the Third class fare on the *Cymric* was five guineas (£5.25p). On 6 November 1906 whilst in a strong gale and heavy seas off the Irish coast, some of her cargo shifted causing her to list. During the same encounter, one of her derricks fell to the deck, injuring five Steerage passengers. In order to save the ship further punishment and in the interests of safety, she hove to for four hours.

In January 1909, the *Republic* (1903, ex-*Columbus*) was sunk in collision with the Italian liner *Florida* and was temporarily replaced by Red Star Line's *Zeeland* but in 1911 the *Cymric* was joined by the *Arabic* (1903, ex-*Minnewaska*). She was another unit of the aforementioned 600 ft intermediate group but slightly larger and faster than the earlier ship. This combination lasted until the outbreak of World War 1. After April 1912, and the loss of the *Titanic*, the *Cymric*'s lifeboat capacity was drastically increased. 'Collapsibles' were carried below her boat deck lifeboats and the boats on the after deck were double banked. Otherwise no outward change was made to the ship during her career, but in 1913 her accommodation was downgraded and from

Left: **The *Cymric* anchored in the River Mersey with the tender *Magnetic* alongside.**
Richard de Kerbrech Collection.

then on she carried only Second and Third class.

When the war came she continued at first on the Boston service but later on 20 December 1914 she returned to the Liverpool-New York run. On 29 April 1916 she sailed from New York under the command of Captain Frank E. Beadnell with no passengers aboard but with 110 crew and cargo only. Nine days later, at 1600 hours on 8 May, she was torpedoed three times by German submarine *U-20* commanded by Commander Walther von Schwieger, 140 miles to the west and north of Fastnet. The *Cymric* remained afloat until 0300 hours (3am) on the following day. In the sinking five lives were lost, four were killed by the explosion and a steward was drowned whilst abandoning ship. In all 105 lives were saved. Ironically the *U-20* had sunk the Cunard express liner, *Lusitania* almost to the day, the previous year on 7 May 1915.

CYMRIC: *Of or pertaining to the Welsh. Thought to be correctly pronounced 'Cum-rick' though more commonly pronounced phonetically 'Simric'. In view of the fact that Cymric is an Anglicised adjective of Cymru – the Welsh for Wales, 1953.*

Left: **Another view of the *Cymric* anchored in the River Mersey in readiness to sail for the United States.**
World Ship Photo Library.

1898-1907

Ownership, coal, stokers and wireless

In the latter part of the 19th century sail power lost favour to steam propulsion which was raised in coal-fired boilers. Coal was normally brought alongside the ship in port by coal barges. Prior to any loading into the bunkers every ventilator cowl was covered with canvas, any air vent louvres were closed and all interior spaces sealed off and where possible access doors and companionways kept shut. The coal was loaded by being transferred in large quarter-ton buckets into the coaling ports. These ports were openings in the shell plating, some 10 ft above the waterline, with bottom-hinged flaps that could take a temporary sheet iron scoop. In addition a row of simple derricks could be rigged above, the heels of which located into concave indentations in the hull, together with precarious two-man platforms adjacent to each coaling port. The coal buckets were winched up from the barge and tipped into the port which cascaded down a chute into the coal bunker space. Generally two ports served each bunker. This was a time-consuming and arduous task, which could take up to 24 hours to coal a larger liner. Before coaling, the ship's carpenter went over the ship's side to remove the eight bolts that secured each coaling port shut. Following bunkering the carpenter sealed up the ports with a buckram gasket that had been soaked in red lead, for watertightness. In addition every railing, deck, companionway and passageway had to be cleaned thoroughly, to remove the all pervading deposit of black coal dust that had seeped everywhere.

In the dark world of the engine and boiler rooms, akin to H. G. Wells' 'Morlock' world, worked the Firemen and Trimmers, known familiarly or perhaps derogatorily as the 'Black gang' or 'black feet brigade', in conditions of extreme heat, dirt, and back-breaking toil. Before sailing, firemen and trimmers signed Articles of Agreement at the shipping office when it was also customary to draw an advance note, besides which married men had a large part of their wages allotted to their wives and dependencies ashore. The Second Engineer usually set watches when those on duty went down through the boiler room by a succession of steel ladders known as the 'fidley'. In the Stokehold each watch had a leading fireman, usually an older, more experienced man who supervised the work to the satisfaction of the engineer of the watch on duty in the adjacent engine room. In passenger liners and good class vessels, probably fifty per cent of the stokehold crew would have continuous service, if not with the same ship, then with the same company. With respect to firemen, except for the few men needed for working a ship in port, they were paid off at the end of a voyage and were without pay until they signed on again for another voyage either on the same

ship or on a different ship. At the bottom of the engine-room social stratification were the trimmers who worked in the hot, airless bunkers where the gloomy atmosphere was thick with stifling coal dust. Here they filled barrows with coal which was dumped on the plates, the steel decking beneath the furnace mouths. There were on most ships other bunkers on the deck above, where the coal was tipped into 'hoppers', a chute type lift-shaft, which led down to the stokehold floor. In the main bunkers coal was cleared back towards the rear bulkheads, and the deck was always strewn with large lumps; loads were wheeled along narrow planks. Trimmers now had further to trundle their barrows and this was known as 'being on the long run'. When bunkers were full, trimmers' duties were not so demanding as when the bunkers ran down towards the end of a voyage, which involved a more laborious amount of shovelling.

The trimmer upended his coal barrow next to where the fireman worked tending the furnaces to raise the steam. Under each boiler were three or four furnaces, each with a separate door, sometimes one at each end. To conserve heat in these double-ended boilers, stoking was arranged so that their doors were never opened at the same time. The task of the firemen of keeping the furnaces at full blast demanded a good standard of physical fitness, strength and a high degree of stamina; it was not a job for the frail or faint-hearted. The routine of tending was exacting and had to be done in a specific order, at great speed and with considerable strength. The first job was to clean out one of the furnaces which had already been prepared by a process known as 'burning down'. The fire-bars were then cleared of 'clinkers', or white-hot masses of fused slag and impurities, which caused an obstruction to air for combustion, and had to be removed by dousing with water and breaking up. They were dislodged by a slice bar, known as a 'tommy' or 'jumbo', an extra-long poker over 40 lbs in weight for reaching the rear of the furnace. This tommy was thrust home four times, once along each track of the grate, showering ashes down into the ashpit and raising clinkers to the top of the coals. The next operation involved raking these out, white hot on to the plates by the rake, a 10 ft long steel implement like a garden hoe. The trimmers then shovelled the fragments and raked out ashes that littered the deck, into barrows and emptied them down the 'blower', a metal receptacle connected to the side of the ship by a pipe through which water pressure forced or blew the waste material into the sea. This was known as 'shooting the ashes'. While the trimmers were 'shooting the ashes', a fireman would be feeding a small quantity of slack to the burned-down furnace. This was known as 'coaling the bars', after which it was worked up to full capacity. In the meantime plenty of coal had been heaped onto the plates (separate from the raked clinkers), when the firemen would begin stoking up, first making sure to push over the draught lever before opening the furnace door. Failure to do this could result in a 'blowback', a searing hot flame shooting out across the stokehold. A 'pitch' of coal (about a dozen shovels full) was thrown on each fire and the door slammed tight. This stoking up required a certain degree of precision, as the furnace mouth was only just wider than the shovel or 'banjo'. If the edge of the 'banjo' struck the rim of the furnace entrance during shovelling, it could cause a nasty jar to the arm or shoulder, besides spilling the coal. To prevent burns firemen used a hand rag, which consisted of a small piece of canvas or carpet grasped in the left hand.

After the fire had burned for a while, a two-pronged rake (sometimes referred to as a 'devil') was used for levelling off the spread of coal to an effective depth of four inches. When clinkers formed they were removed by driving the heavy slice under the burning coal, then lifting several times to assist combustion. Because of the length and weight of the 'jumbo', its point was raised by leaping up and down on the handle and bearing down with the stomach muscles! When boilers were at full blast, maximum steam pressure was indicated on the brass pressure gauge above the fires with its needle pointing to a red zone on the gauge scale. This was called 'keeping her on the blood'. In addition sufficient water in the boiler was constantly monitored by a watchful eye on the water gauge glass level. In rough weather, firemen learned to stoke as the ship's bow plunged down, slamming the door shut as the ship rose again, to avoid a shower of red-hot coals on their feet. In a particularly bad gale, trimmers carried the coal in baskets rather than wheelbarrows and were usually able to keep pace with the reduced demand for steam. But slow speed carried with it a guarantee of harder work when calm seas returned.

Boots and dungarees were worn down in the stokehold, but in the bunkers the trimmers often wore their boots and 'long-johns' style drawers only and nothing else. The multi-purpose sweat-rag tied loosely around the neck was in constant use for wiping perspiration from face, brow and eyes, and clearing lips and nostrils from a sticky, clogging accumulation of sweat and coal dust. To quench their perpetual thirst the stokehold gang drank from a large can of oatmeal or honey water. If answering the call of nature became an urgent necessity, a shovel was used with the furnace as a means of disposal (a most hygienic method if nothing else, human defecation having combustible properties!). The temperature in the tropics could reach between 140°F and 150°F, and in the fierce scorching glare of the fires a man could be overcome by heat exhaustion, but soon recovered after a spell on deck. Salt sweated out on watch could be made up by taking copious amounts of salt with their meals. Burns and scalds were unavoidable at times when the skin was smeared with tannic ointment. For ablutions buckets of hot water were taken to the forecastle wash house where sweat-rags served as flannels, afterwards being wrung out for use as drying-off towels.

A fireman could deal with three, four or even five furnaces, depending upon the boiler room layout. The ratio of trimmers to firemen varied. For example, a typical mail ship of the day, having nine double-ended and two single-ended boilers, all except the single-ended boilers would be in use on the voyage, i.e. a total of 54 furnaces. The total stokehold complement could number 72, which comprised 6 leading firemen, 36 firemen, 6 firemen trimmers and 24 trimmers. One third of these men would be on duty per watch of four hours, allowing for spare men. On a typical cargo liner of the day, with three double-ended and two single-ended boilers i.e. a total of 24 furnaces, all normally in use; there would be 21 firemen and 15 trimmers. In the largest ships built for White Star, the 'Olympic' class of 1911, there were six boiler rooms, containing in all, 24 double-ended and 5 single-ended boilers. The total number of furnaces was 159. As a coal burner, and with full complement, there were 15 leading firemen, 161 firemen and 48 trimmers; a total of 224.

A common arrangement was for firemen and trimmers to be accommodated in large rooms in the forecastle, each room berthing the complete complement for a watch. On the *Olympic* the firemen were housed on four decks, D, E, F and G forward. The route to and from the boiler rooms was by way of two vertical spiral staircases which intersected the decks and the 'Firemen's passage'. Their food was fair and adequate although complaints were common on a long voyage like the New Zealand run. Condensed milk, tea, coffee, cocoa, sugar, butter, cheese and jam were available at regular intervals, while stringy meat, sausages, potatoes, haricot beans, bone-hard dry peas, and lumpy rice or tapioca pudding, were frequent dishes. In the passenger liners the black gang fared somewhat better, as trays of unconsumed food from the saloon galley were taken forward every evening by the firemen's 'peggy'. This was often referred to as 'black pan'.

As mentioned, upon arrival at their home port the black gang would go on leave, usually of short duration until their pay-offs were spent, when they would wander down through the dock gates and sign on for another voyage. On leaving port, many firemen and trimmers would be the worse for alcohol and unable to turn to and fire the boilers efficiently until they sobered up. This difficulty in steaming the boilers was augmented by the engineers themselves having to take to the shovels. The firemen and trimmers' reputation preceded them, variously described by some observers as, tough, coarse, truculent, hard-swearing, stout-hearted men of rough exterior and good-humoured and friendly. They were overseen by tactful and sometimes understanding engineers, who themselves were not considered as officers. In White Star, up until after World War 1, engineers' insignia did not bear the 'executive curl', (similar to that of the Royal Navy), as did their navigating officers.

There have been tales of stokehold fights which went beyond fisticuffs to the use of slice bars and shovels as weapons to hand. Harland & Wolff's former Technical Director, Cuthbert Coulson Pounder had a friend who was an engineer on a North Atlantic liner and had a finger bitten off during a stokehold scuffle. Whereas Charles Lightoller, one of the surviving officers of the *Titanic* of 1912, recounted about a hard-driving engineer officer who intervened in one of these rows and was never seen again. Rumour had it that he was brained with a shovel and his corpse incinerated in a furnace. Hard and tough men, who worked hard, drank hard and sometimes fought hard, nevertheless were the unseen workhorses of the stokehold. Of the original quality of coal itself, in general, Newcastle and Scotch coal burned much faster than Welsh, but did not give out such an intense local heat. However, with Welsh coal there was little or no flame, and very little smoke.

It may be of interest to note that during World War 1, the German U-boat commanders often stalked their prey and pressed home their attack round about the change of watch at 8 o'clock in the morning and at 4 o'clock in the afternoon. With all furnaces not at full blast, engines would lose their power for increasing speed at short notice, thus the ships became handicapped and easier to overhaul. The submarines were further assisted by the early morning sun or the evening light before sundown, when clear visibility was helpful. The change of the morning watch played an even more tragic role in the sinking of the *Britannic* of 1913 whilst in her guise as a hospital ship. During the changeover all the watertight doors in the Firemen's passage were open to allow access to the stokehold, during which time the German submarine let loose her torpedoes and the fate of the *Britannic* was sealed.

Moving on to Thomas Henry Ismay, as befitted a man of his standing, integrity and wisdom, he was appointed to serve on many Royal and Departmental committees, namely Lord Ravensworth's Admiralty Committee of 1884 to examine the systems of building and repairing Her Majesty's ships by contract and in the Royal Dockyards. Another was Lord Hartington's Royal Commission of 1889, to enquire into the organisations of the Army and Navy and their relations to

Below: **Firemen's quarters on the *Olympic*.**
Richard de Kerbrech Collection.

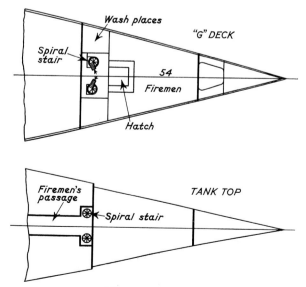

Firemen's quarters in Olympic

each other and to the Treasury. In 1889, he was Chairman of the Board of Trade Lifesaving Appliances Committee and by 1891 he was a member of the Admiralty Committee on the Royal Navy Reserve. Later in December 1891, after 40 years in business, Ismay retired from the firm of Ismay, Imrie & Co. of which he had been a founder, but continued to control the destinies of White Star as its Chairman.

He had been offered a Baronetcy but preferred to remain a great commoner instead, respected and esteemed by all across the social spectrum and one whose position in society did not depend on any title but simply his own personality and for Ismay a good name was the best title. When Ismay died at his home 'Dawpool' in Cheshire on 23 November 1899 almost 63 years of age, he left a wife, three sons and four daughters. At the time, expressions of sympathy and tributes came from every branch of the shipping world and it was recorded that he was one of the noblest characters who ever graced the commercial world. Liverpool was a city in mourning with hundreds of flags flying at half-mast such as if a member of Royalty itself had died. He was buried on 27 November in the churchyard at Thurstaston near his home of Dawpool, on the Wirral. Following his death the control of the White Star Line passed to his eldest son Joseph Bruce Ismay, who became the Chairman and Managing Director of the Company. Sir Edward Harland died in 1895 and was succeeded as Chairman by William James Pirrie.

The population of the United States of America had grown from 17,069,453 in 1840 to 75,994,575 by 1900. During this massive increase emigration from Western Europe had played a significant role, whereby some 20 million people had ventured across the North Atlantic to make a fresh start in the New World. Many of these settlers had managed to find work on the eastern seaboard of the United States. In 1840 New York had a population of a mere 391,114 which by 1900 had increased almost tenfold to 3,437,202. Other immigrants had travelled to the Mid-West to the shores of Lake Michigan where in 1840 Chicago was a small town of just under 5,000, but 60 years later had become a thriving city of 1,698,578 inhabitants. Other settlers had ventured even further across the North American continent to California. Here in 1880, Los Angeles was a township of some 11,183 but by 1900 had grown to 102,749.

Commensurate with this great influx of people had been the development of the natural riches of this vast North American continent, quite apart from the lure of gold. In 1850, the number of farms in the United States was 1,449,073 with an estimated value of £600 million that had grown to 5,737,372 by 1900 with an estimated value of £4,000 million. Concurrently, hitherto untapped mineral resources had been mined. The yearly output of iron ore in 1870 was a little over 3 million tons which by 1900 had escalated to an output of 28 million tons. From this resource the progress and the manufacture of steel had risen from 68,750 tons in 1870 to a record of 10,188,329 tons during 1900. Along with iron and steel, other domestic industries had thrived accordingly, such that by 1900 the value of the cotton crop was £92,662,000 and the tobacco crop

£10,732,500. Crude petroleum had reached an annual output of 60 million 42-gallon barrels. The fledgling automobile industry could boast production of some 4,192 motor cars. Also by 1900 the covered wagon was consigned to pioneering history. The railway network had grown from 2,818 miles in 1840 to 198,964 in 60 years, the industry itself requiring a vast pool of labour. All in all the United States was rapidly becoming one of the world's greatest markets with her overseas trade increasing by leaps and bounds. Back in 1840, the value of the United States export and import trade was an estimated £48 million which 60 years later had risen to a value of around £449 million in 1900. Somewhat ironically then over the same period, the American shipping industry had not progressed at the same rate. In fact, the reverse was the case; for a while in 1840, American sailing vessels had transported no less than eighty-six per cent of the American overseas trade. By 1900, they carried less than thirteen per cent.

The fact that British, Scandinavian, German and French steamships were carrying the lion's share of the country's trade was greatly resented by many of America's leading industrialists. They felt, and with some justification, that more efforts should be made for this lucrative trade to come under American control, and that the resultant profits should be diverted from foreign shipowners to American owners. On paper there seemed every reason to think that a system which had been successfully applied to such great industries could be applied with equal success to the shipping industry. Viewing the expanding ocean trade routes of the world and the prospect of quick and glittering profits, it seemed that the route that offered the greatest promise was the North Atlantic.

At the turn of the century, direct American shipping interests on the North Atlantic was limited to two companies; the American Line (International Navigation Company), overseen by Mr Clement A. Griscom and the Atlantic Transport Company, which under the Presidency of Mr Bernard N. Baker, had in 1893, purchased the business and goodwill of Wilson's and Furness-Leyland service to New York. It was not only in the United States that the possibilities of the formation of a great North Atlantic shipping combine had been considered. In the United Kingdom, Mr J. R. Ellerman, chairman of the Leyland Line, had given serious thought to such a project. In fact in 1898 he had sounded out the Cunard Company suggesting some form of amalgamation. The first Lord Inverclyde, then Cunard's Chairman, had replied that the company was not prepared to consider any such proposal.

Two years later on 1 March 1900, the British shipping journal *Fairplay* reported that it had been rumoured that the Leyland Line had bought the entire fleet of the Atlantic Transport Company. Further credence was given to these reports when Mr Bernard N. Baker, President of the Atlantic Transport Company left New York for Liverpool on 28 March. Negotiations however proved abortive, and on 2 May, *Fairplay* reported that the proposed merging of interests had fallen through. Meanwhile, Ellerman had not entirely given up the idea of securing control of other shipping interests on the North Atlantic. Later the same month it was announced that the Leyland Line had absorbed the British-owned West India and Pacific Steamship Company which maintained a fleet of 30 steamers operating on services between the United Kingdom, the West Indies and New Orleans.

The news created a considerable stir amongst shipping and industrial magnates on both sides of the Atlantic. Interested Americans included Mr John Pierpont Morgan, who himself had crossed to England as a fellow passenger with Mr Baker at the time of the Leyland Line-Atlantic Transport negotiations. One of the most influential and powerful figures in the United States, Pierpont Morgan, in addition to his widespread financial enterprises, virtually controlled three of the principal American railway network systems, and was completing arrangements which were to give him control of the Carnegie Steel Trust with its yearly income of £107 million. Indeed he had been an avid sailing enthusiast in his youth and later in life he was elected Commodore of the New York Yacht Club in 1897. This prompted him to donate £30,000 to buy land for a new clubhouse. It became the Beaux Arts building at 37 West 44th Street, with curved glass bay windows shaped like the stern of 18th century ships. When the opportunity arose to defend the America's Cup from a challenge by Ireland's Royal Ulster Yacht Club in 1899, Morgan formed a syndicate to defend the title.

Although on the surface he had displayed no interest in the shipping industry, it was known that he kept himself well informed about possible developments. Indeed his may well have been the influence which stopped the acquisition of the Atlantic Transport Company by the Leyland Line in that such a merger would have left the United States with only one shipping interest on the North Atlantic; that being the American Line. There is little doubt that from that time onwards Morgan began to formulate plans to acquire financial control of the Atlantic route by combining all the British and American assets into one company. As a first step he started negotiations with the Leyland Line which led to an announcement in April 1901 that J. P. Morgan and Company had purchased all the ordinary shares in the British firm.

On 2 May 1901, *Fairplay* reported: 'Mr J. Pierpont Morgan is busily engaged in forming an enormous American Atlantic Shipping Trust, and the first step taken has been to enter in negotiations with the Leyland line …This as stated above, is the initiation of a gigantic American Shipping Trust. Already I understand Mr Morgan and his friends control or are extensively interested in other steamship lines trading to America, and it is believed that these lines and others, ere long, be brought into one grand combination.' During the weeks which followed there was considerable speculation in the Press, and amongst the public, regarding the progress of the Morgan scheme. Rumour-mongers bandied about the names of half-a-dozen famous North Atlantic lines, and there was increasing disquiet and alarm over the apparent passing of British interests into American control.

Towards the end of the year the White Star Line became

the major talking point and on 16 October 1901 the *Liverpool Daily Post* stated: 'Notwithstanding the positive denials of Mr Bruce Ismay, head of the Oceanic Steam Navigation Company, the rumours that Mr Pierpont Morgan is to acquire control of the White Star Line are revived.' Matters came to a head on 4 February 1902 when a provisional agreement was reached between J. P. Morgan and Company and the White Star Line, Dominion Line, American Line, and the Atlantic Transport Company. Two months were to elapse before any official announcement regarding this agreement was published. In the meantime the Cunard Line had been keeping a close watch on these developments. Lord Inverclyde and his co-directors had not been approached regarding participation in any merger since their rejection of Mr Ellerman's proposals of 1898, but on 3 March 1900, the trustees of the first Lord Inverclyde were approached by a firm of stockbrokers, who enquired what price would be taken for a large block of Cunard shares. Ironically, the names of the principals for whom the brokers were acting, were not divulged. In reply the brokers were advised that such an offer could only be considered if similar offers were made to any other shareholders.

Five days later, on 8 March, Lord Inverclyde received word concerning the proposed Morgan combine from the Cunard agent in New York, Mr Vernon H. Brown. Realising the vastness of the issues at stake, not only insofar as the Cunard Company was concerned, but also as regards British North Atlantic shipping services, Lord Inverclyde decided to inform the Government as to what he had learned. He wrote to Lord Selborne, First Lord of the Admiralty, who was likely to be doubly interested in that the Admiralty had paid a subvention to both the Cunard and White Star Lines for the use of certain of their steamers as auxiliary cruisers in time of war or national emergency. The Admiralty were not only interested but very disturbed by the news, but as Lord Selborne, who had immediately arranged a meeting with Lord Inverclyde, pointed out, their hands were tied in that they were not privy to the Morgan negotiations. In fact the only information they had was what Lord Inverclyde had told them, and even that knowledge had not been substantiated by any documentary evidence.

In the absence of such positive proof it was extremely difficult for the government to raise any such question in the House. However Lord Selborne thought the matter so serious that he asked Lord Inverclyde to do his utmost to hold his hand and 'tender no advice to the trustees of Cunard shares to sell to the American syndicate yet awhile at all events.' At the same time he asked Lord Inverclyde if he would come to the Admiralty for a further meeting. At this meeting, which took place on 17 March 1902, Lord Selborne suggested to Lord Inverclyde that arrangements might be made for the then subsidised vessels of the Cunard Company to be placed at the disposal of the Admiralty for purchase or hire in such a way that existing or future shareholders would not be able to sell any such ships. During this interview the desirability of adding faster liners to the Company's fleet was also discussed.

Lord Inverclyde returned to Liverpool, where he reported back the Admiralty proposals to his colleagues before replying to Lord Selborne. In his reply Lord Inverclyde outlined the difficulties which might arise if the Cunard Company decided to act on the suggested proposals, and he put forward an alternative arrangement. This proved unacceptable to Lord Selborne, who explained that for the time being his immediate concern was to protect the interests of the Royal Navy in so far as they were likely to be affected by the Cunard Company joining any foreign combine. Also, that any larger issues would of necessity have to be approved by Parliament, stating, 'It is clear that even if the utmost success attends my efforts the matter cannot be settled definitely within a year.' This letter was written on 5 April. Six days later, on 11 April, the Cunard annual meeting took place in Liverpool when several shareholders enquired as to the possibility of some offers being made for the Company's property. Lord Inverclyde replied that shareholders could rest assured and that they would be advised of any proposals submitted to the directors which affected their interests.

Immediately after the meeting, Lord Inverclyde left for London, where on the following day, 12 April, he had two important appointments. The first was with Sir Christopher Furness, the prominent shipowner and shipbuilder, who at one time had been a director of the Leyland Line. Although Sir Christopher made no concrete proposals at this interview, it was evident that he was anxious to get control of the Cunard Company. The second appointment was with Mr Henry Wilding, the representative for Mr Clement A. Griscom, President of the American Line and brought forth the first definite evidence that the Morgan Combine was materially interested in the Cunard Line. It was revealed in the course of this interview that Mr Wilding had been instructed by Mr Griscom to ask whether the Cunard Company would come into the combination, or whether arrangements could be made under which the combination would obtain control of the Company.

Lord Inverclyde replied that he did not consider the first suggestion feasible and that so far as the second suggestion was concerned, if the Morgan combination were offering to control the Cunard Company they had better make an offer for its out and out purchase, but whatever offer was made it must apply to all the shareholders. On being asked for an indication of the price likely to be considered by the Cunard Company, Lord Inverclyde refused, saying that such an offer must come from the combine. One week later, on 19 April 1902, the first official public announcement was published regarding the formation of the International Mercantile Marine Company (IMMCo), as the Morgan Combine was named. The announcement closely followed the brief outlines of the Provisional Agreements of 4 February.

Under its terms J. P. Morgan and Company took over the White Star Line, the business and assets of Ismay, Imrie & Co. (managers for the White Star Line), the shares in the Dominion Line and the business and assets of Richard Mills & Co. (managers for the Dominion Line). On the American side the new syndicate took over the International Navigation

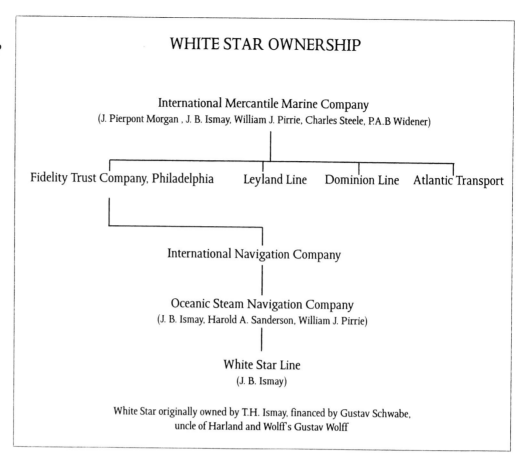

WHITE STAR OWNERSHIP

International Mercantile Marine Company
(J. Pierpont Morgan , J. B. Ismay, William J. Pirrie, Charles Steele, P.A.B Widener)

Fidelity Trust Company, Philadelphia   Leyland Line   Dominion Line   Atlantic Transport

International Navigation Company

Oceanic Steam Navigation Company
(J. B. Ismay, Harold A. Sanderson, William J. Pirrie)

White Star Line
(J. B. Ismay)

White Star originally owned by T.H. Ismay, financed by Gustav Schwabe,
uncle of Harland and Wolff's Gustav Wolff

Company (the American Line) and the Atlantic Transport Company. The Leyland Line, which had previously been purchased by Morgan, was included in the new company. By the fusion of these great shipping interests the new syndicate now controlled a fleet of 123 ships with a total gross tonnage of 1,034,884 and an aggregate book value of £15,600,000. The purchase price was estimated to be in the neighbourhood of £34,637,000 of which £10,187,000 was paid in cash and the remainder in stock. Somewhat ironically, concurrent with the merger a working alliance was affected between the newly formed IMMCo and the two major German North Atlantic companies, the North German Lloyd and the Hamburg America Line (HAPAG).

On 20 April, *The Times* published a lengthy article, in long-winded sentences, pointing out that the merger was advantageous, stating that: 'A great many rumours have been circulated during the past few months regarding the supposed purchase of various steamship lines engaged in the North Atlantic trade, and wild statements have been made that the wholesale transfer of fleets from the British flag to the United States was contemplated. We are now, however, in a position to state definitely that all these rumours have been wide of the mark, that there is no arrangement contemplated by which British ships will pass to the American flag, but that arrangements are nearly completed under which British shipping has been able to make a good bargain for itself, strengthening its present and prospective position in the North Atlantic and other trades.'

It went on to add: 'It has for some time been recognised that as a measure of self preservation it was necessary to take some steps in the common interest, and a working basis has been found between several of the leading lines, both British and American, as well as the chief Continental lines in the North Atlantic trade, on the principle of establishing a community of interest that ensures the participation of all in the improvements of trade and economies that may be effected.' The difficulties of the North Atlantic trade due to the 'rapid development of ocean travel and the high standard of excellence that the competing companies have set themselves', were dealt with, a point being made of the fact that: 'It is recognised that while a certain number of large full powered fast steamers will pay in busy seasons, and with judicious management, only a very small number can be profitably run at seasons when travel is comparatively small, and that a point was rapidly being reached which would admit of no further profitable advancement unless considerable reductions in working expenses be effected or increased rates obtained.'

The Times went on to point out that similar conditions were to be found with cargo traffic and continued: 'Under the conditions of working hitherto, each line has felt compelled to maintain its full service because its competitors did so, and the frequent spectacle has been afforded of two or more large and costly steamers making voyages to carry at a loss what one of them could readily have carried at a profit. Though all these steamers could be well and profitably employed when trade conditions are favourable, the results are simply ruinous when they are run under the conditions mentioned.' A possible way out of such difficulties would, in the opinion of *The Times*, be provided by 'a reduction in the working expenses of the different companies' and, enlarging upon this, the article suggested that such an arrangement could only be secured 'by the establishment of a community of interest amongst the various companies most directly concerned, and this is what has taken place.'

Reference was then made to the fact that the impending changes would involve 'no change of flag' and that: 'The management of all the British lines affected will be carried on by those who have been intimately connected with shipping all their lives, and they will have the advantage of working in conjunction with the ablest shipping men on the other side of the Atlantic and in Germany. Hence this arrangement is a real combination of shipping interests directed by the most experienced shipowners and shipping managers on both sides of the Atlantic, from which it is not unreasonable to expect that many advantages will accrue not only to the shareholders of the different companies by prevention of a life and death struggle, but also to travellers and shippers who will be assured more regular and better services and every development that any increase or change of trade requires, as such a combination can do many things no individual company would be justified in undertaking.'

These arguments were reiterated to a large extent in the leading article for that day, in which, after specifically naming the lines affected by the merger, *The Times* reported: 'It will be noted that the Cunard Line is not among them and that the Allan Line also maintains an independent position. Neither can well expect any diminution in the stress of competition it has to face since it is plain that the combination of its rivals relieves them of disadvantages previously common to all.'

In conclusion it was stated: 'While the interests of the shareholders seem likely to be well safeguarded, the Admiralty is relieved of the apprehension that vessels relied upon as auxiliary cruisers in case of war might be transferred to another flag. From the national point of view, therefore, the arrangement is satisfactory. There remains the general public and in particular that portion of it which patronises Atlantic liners. How will its interests be affected? The abatement of competition may be thought to involve some risk that it will not be so carefully looked after, and the matter of comfort and luxury as hitherto, and perhaps some may go far as to fear increase of fares and freights. The exacting passenger will miss some opportunities for disparaging remarks to the purser, based upon the alleged superiority of another line, but upon the whole we imagine that he will continue to get his money's worth, At all events he will not be quite helpless so long as the Cunard Company maintains its attitude of splendid isolation.'

The positive and upbeat stance taken by *The Times* was not shared by the British Government however. Five days after the IMMCo announcement had appeared in the press, Lord Selbourne wrote a letter to Lord Inverclyde in which he again reiterated that the Cunard Line should not commit itself in any way without advising the Cabinet. He wrote: - 'What I have now to complain about in respect of the other companies is that they committed themselves finally without ever giving me a chance or through me the Government. It is very possible that we could do nothing to influence the situation in a manner which the prospective parties to it might accept, but I think when such vast issues are at stake a patriotic company is bound to keep its Government informed as you have hitherto done.'

In Lord Inverclyde's reply, he repeated the difficulty of reconciling the interests of the Cunard shareholders with 'delaying tactics'; and to this Lord Selbourne further wrote: - 'I do not know why you should suppose that the position is more serious than the Government seem to realise, or that the Government are not sufficiently alive to the seriousness of the issues raised by this combination. When you first gave information on the subject the deeds were as a matter of fact already signed, and it has never at any moment been in the power of the Government to have stopped this combination. The question is, what are going to be the results of the new combinations, what can the Government do to influence these results, and what measures in respect of the future the Government should take?…I should put it thus: I fear that as a result of the combinations the Americans will gradually acquire the control of the North Atlantic shipping trade. The terms of the combination certainly give them already a large influence in it.'

Not all the British newspapers were as sanguine as *The Times*. There was a mounting opposition to the 'threat' of American control and demands for more definite action on the part of the Government. Questions were raised in the House of Commons as a result of which the Government appointed a committee to reconsider the principles on which subsidies were then being paid to British steamship companies for the possible use of certain ships as Armed Merchant Cruisers (AMC) in time of war. All these extreme activities however did not solve the domestic issues confronting the Cunard directors. These were summed up by one of the shareholders who in a letter to Lord Inverclyde wrote: 'We shareholders cannot be expected to fight single-handed, the battle of the whole nation against foreign Governments. It is quite uphill a battle enough to have to fight fair competition, but if the British people are prepared to let their trade and commerce be sacrificed by the handicap imposed by foreign subsidies it would be quixotic on the part of the shareholders of the Cunard Company to continue unprofitable competition and only for national prestige.'

This shareholder's opinion was shared by many others, and with justification. The burning question of subsidies paid to their massed competitors was indeed one of the pressing factors which made the future of the Cunard Company so uncertain. Indeed, for many years the United States Government had paid to the owners of American mail steamers engaged in the North Atlantic trade, a subsidy of £3,000 a voyage. To other American-owned steamships the US rate of carriage for mails had been 6s. 8d. (33p) per pound for letters as against the rate of 1s. 10d. (9p) per pound paid to foreign vessels. The North German Lloyd and Hamburg America Lines also received considerable assistance from the German Government either by way of mail payments, subsidies for other services which naturally helped to swell the general funds, or by the establishment of special regulations for passenger traffic passing through Germany, as instanced in the organisation of the Emigration Control Stations which were 'managed' on behalf of the German Government by the two North Atlantic lines.

As against this, payments made to the Cunard Line by the British Government in return for mail services had averaged £61,000 a year over the preceding three years, which added to the Admiralty's annual subvention of £20,000 brought the total of Cunard 'assistance' from the Government to £81,000 a year. Financially, the scales were heavily weighed against the Company. Shareholders might well feel apprehensive about the outcome of a policy of 'splendid isolation'. Meanwhile Lord Inverclyde continued his meeting in London with various negotiators. On 19 April 1902, the day of the IMMCo public announcement, he had another interview with Mr Wilding who, acting for the Morgan combine, told Lord Inverclyde that they were prepared to offer £18 per share for fifty-five per cent of the Cunard shares.

To this, Lord Inverclyde replied that such a proposal was impossible and that the Cunard board could only consider an offer based on a much higher value for the shares than that indicated. No further meeting took place and although the *New York Herald* confidently predicted that the: 'Cunard Line will soon be added to Mr Morgan's shipping combination.' No revised terms were received. At the beginning of May, Lord Inverclyde was again in touch with the Government during a meeting at the Admiralty, when Lord Selborne enquired upon what terms the Cunard Company could be kept out of the Morgan combination, and indicated that the Government were now prepared to consider something on the lines of the proposal submitted by Lord Inverclyde in March, but at that time had proved unacceptable.

It was also arranged that on the following day a meeting should be held at which, in addition to Lord Selborne, Mr Joseph Chamberlain, the Colonial Secretary, and Mr Gerald Balfour, the President of the Board of Trade should also be present. This meeting took place on 5 May when Lord Inverclyde submitted a memorandum outlining the Company's proposals. Two days later Sir Christopher Furness called upon Lord Inverclyde in London. The purpose of his visit was to enquire whether it would be possible to make some arrangement with the Cunard Company under which he would be enabled to take over control. Lord Inverclyde replied that this could not be done without consulting the shareholders. There were no discussions at this meeting regarding the possibility of the Cunard Line linking up with a British anti-combine group.

Indeed it came as a complete surprise when on 8 May, he received a letter from Lord Selborne indicating that there were serious objections to the Cunard proposals and that: 'If, as I gathered from you when I last saw you, you are in negotiation with a British capitalist with a view to the Cunard Line entering a British anti-combine in fair terms to Cunard shareholders, such an action could only facilitate the objects the Government have in view.' This letter brought a vigorous disclaimer from

Lord Inverclyde who stated: 'so far as I know there is nothing whatever being done with a view to the Cunard Company entering into a British anti-combine.' It was, however, becoming obvious that although Sir Christopher Furness had not broached the subject, it was in fact the basic idea underlying his efforts to secure control of the Cunard Line and that the Government were cognisant of the fact and, what was more, approved the proposal. This was clearly demonstrated in a further letter sent to Lord Inverclyde by Lord Selborne in which he wrote: 'Three courses are possible for the Cunard. One is that it should join the American combine. To this we strenuously object and will do all we can to assist you to justify yourself to your shareholders for not doing so. The second course is that the Cunard remain exactly as it is now, and fight the combine single-handed, only with increased assistance from the Government in some form. This is always a possible course, and the proposal you made to us was one directed to that end. The fact that we do not like the particular lines of your proposal does not mean that we should not like another proposal.

'But, as a matter of fact, we do not like the second course as well as the third which is that Cunard should enter into some form of co-operation with other British shipowners and shipping companies which for the sake of convenience I will call an anti-combine. I gather from you that that was an alternative that had been presented to you, and which you were considering, but your letter of the 8th, of course corrected that impression. Nevertheless I cannot help thinking that the possibility of such a course must exist and must enter into your calculations. If possible we should distinctly prefer it because it would seem reasonable to suppose that such a combination would possess greater strength than the aggregate of the individual companies acting separately.' This change in Lord Selborne's attitude disturbed Lord Inverclyde profoundly, and in his reply he reiterated that 'Until you first referred to the matter in your letter of the 8th instant, no such scheme had been considered by me, nor I am sure, by any of my Board.'

He then proceeded to protest against this sudden change of point and emphasised that after weeks of negotiation this impasse could scarcely be regarded as satisfactory. He concluded: 'Frankly, I think the time has come when you should say what you intend to do with regard to the Cunard Company and not continue on the present indefinite course. If you do not intend to make any arrangement with us but prefer to work with somebody else, I would much rather that you would say so and let us know where we are. In any case a time is coming when I must let my shareholders know what has been going on, so that they may judge for themselves whether their interests have been properly looked after, and moreover the directors of the Company cannot longer put off arrangements which they have had in view, but which latterly have been held in abeyance, to give you time to make up your mind whether you would do anything or not.'

It was a strongly worded letter but the circumstances warranted it. At any rate immediately he received this protest Lord Selborne replied, explaining that 'there is some misunderstanding between us which should be removed at once' and suggesting that Lord Inverclyde should meet him ' on the steps of Westminster Hall on the following day, and we will go to Mr Chamberlain's room, House of Commons.' On the same day, Lord Inverclyde received a telegram from Sir Christopher Furness asking if a meeting could be arranged in London at which in addition to Lord Inverclyde other Cunard directors could be present. On 14 May, the meeting between Lord Inverclyde, Lord Selborne and Mr Chamberlain took place when the general position was discussed in the lines of Lord Selborne's letter of 10 May. The next day Lord Inverclyde, accompanied by Mr William Watson and Mr E. H. Cunard, fellow directors and Mr A. P. Moorehouse, Cunard's General Manager, met Sir Christopher Furness and heard his proposals for a British anti-combine. Briefly, this plan involved the merging of the Cunard, Elder Dempster and Beaver Lines, the two last-named being engaged in North Atlantic services to Canada. In addition, it was proposed that the Government should exercise its right under the Admiralty subvention arrangements to buy the eight White Star vessels subsidised under this agreement and to resell them to the new British combine.

Finally it was suggested that the Government should assist the new company to build a fleet of eight new vessels; three 25-knot ships for the New York run, two 20-knot ships for the Canadian run and three 16-knot vessels for the Vancouver service. At the same time it was mentioned that an annual subvention of £350,000 rising to £850,000 should also be paid when the said ships were completed. This then was the suggested 'reply' to the American combine which Lord Selborne and his Cabinet colleagues were in favour of. It was to form the basis of the many discussions that were to take place in the weeks that followed. By the end of May negotiations had reached the stage when the Cunard Board thought it well to advise shareholders of possible changes. Accordingly on 31 May, Lord Inverclyde issued a special circular to shareholders. It read:

'At the Annual General Meeting of the Cunard Company held in April last, I stated that if anything occurred affecting the interests of the shareholders, it would be brought before them. I now therefore think it desirable to state that negotiations are in progress affecting the future position of the Cunard Company. It is not possible however to make any more definite statements at present or until proposals based on these negotiations have been submitted to His Majesty's Government. Should the negotiations result favourably the shareholders will be at once informed.'

Hence this was the position at the end of May. Throughout June while Britain celebrated the end of the South African war and looked forward with preparation to the celebrations of King Edward VII's Coronation, the negotiations continued. Hardly a day went by without an exchange of letters, and scarcely a week passed without meetings in London. Every aspect of the project was investigated and discussed. And still there were no signs of any successful conclusion being reached. Indeed it was gradually becoming obvious that the Government had changed course and could not see their way clear to supporting the ambitious project put forward by Sir Christopher Furness. At a meeting on 15 June, the

breakdown of the plan was indicated with the suggestion that an alternative scheme, omitting the inclusion of the eight White Star vessels, should be submitted. A greater setback was to follow, when on 3 July, Sir Christopher Furness advised Lord Inverclyde that after long discussions it was felt that the Canadian part of the scheme must be kept separate.

Further disappointments and setbacks were yet to be experienced. The sudden illness of King Edward which had brought about the postponement of his Coronation on 26 June had also affected official business generally. Then on 7 July, Mr Chamberlain, who had been closely involved in the negotiations, met with an accident that incapacitated him for several weeks. Consequently, it was impossible for any official meetings to be held until 30 July when Lord Inverclyde was advised that it would not be possible for the Government to reach any conclusions until October. The possibility of yet another three months being added to the months of negotiations which had already taken place was a serious matter for the Cunard Line. Since the beginning of March when Lord Inverclyde had first informed Lord Selborne about the definite formation of the Morgan combine, the Company had stayed its hand and deferred matters of urgent importance relating to a new shipbuilding programme and the general policy of the Company.

Meanwhile the IMMCo, together with the two major German shipping lines and four other foreign competitors had forged ahead with their plans in consolidating their foothold on the North Atlantic passenger traffic and routes, thereby gaining a distinct advantage over the Cunard Company. In fact for them the position had become so critical, each day lost in waiting for a decision meant a day's gain to the IMMCo. This compelled Lord Inverclyde to write to Mr Joseph Chamberlain outlining the difficulties against which the Company had to contend, and emphasising how the constant Governmental delays were prejudicing the interests of the shareholders. In addition he pointed out that the Cunard Company could not overlook the possibility of no agreement being reached with the Government in which event 'there may be no alternative for them but to face absorption or annihilation.'

This letter was sent to Mr Chamberlain on 1 August 1902, and on the same day Lord Inverclyde submitted a scheme, which in view of the failure of the previous schemes, he hoped might form the basis for direct negotiations between the Government and the Cunard Company. Three days later, on 4 August, Mr Chamberlain replied to Lord Inverclyde stating that he fully appreciated the difficulties under which the Cunard Company was labouring and regretting 'very much that I should be in part responsible for them.' He then went on to explain that his department, the Colonial Office, had been extremely busy with many urgent matters, but that he had arranged to meet Lord Selborne and Mr Gerald Balfour, the President of the Board of Trade, in the hope that they would 'be able to decide upon some suitable recommendation to be submitted to the Cabinet on Thursday.'

On 5 August, Mr Balfour informed Lord Inverclyde that the negotiations had been left in his hands and enquired if the Cunard Chairman could meet for further discussions. Lord Inverclyde agreed, the resultant negotiations proving so productive that by the end of September the Government and the Cunard Company agreed on a joint plan of action. Details of this agreement were given in a circular, dated 30 September 1902, sent by the Cunard to all the Company's shareholders. This stated:

Sir or Madam,

With reference to my circular of 31 May last, I have now the honour to inform you that I have concluded negotiations with His Majesty's Government on behalf of the Cunard Company. The following are the principal terms of the agreement.

1. The Cunard Company are to build two large steamers for the Atlantic trade of high speed. (These would emerge as the Lusitania *and* Mauretania*).*

2. The agreement is to remain in force for 20 years from the completion of the second of these vessels.

3. The Cunard Company pledges itself until the expiry of the agreement to remain a purely British undertaking, and that under no circumstances shall the management of the Company be in the hands of, or the shares or the vessels of the Company held by other than British subjects.

4. During the currency of the agreement the Cunard Company is to hold at the disposal of the Government the whole of its fleet including the two new vessels, and all other vessels built, the Government being at liberty to charter or purchase all or any such vessels at agreed rates.

5. The Cunard Company also undertakes not to unduly raise freights or to give any preferential rates to foreigners.

6. The Government are to lend the money for the construction of the two new vessels, charging interest at two and three quarters per cent per annum. The security for the loan is to be a first charge on the two new vessels, the present fleet and the general assets of the Cunard Company.

7. The Cunard Company is to repay the loan by annual payments extending over 20 years.

8. From the time the new vessels commence to run, the Government are to pay the Cunard Company at the rate of £150,000 per annum instead of the present Admiralty subvention.

A meeting of the shareholders will be convened as soon as practicable for the purpose of obtaining their approval to such alterations in the Articles of Association as will be required to enable the directors to enter into a formal agreement embodying these terms.

I am, Yours faithfully,
Inverclyde, Chairman.

The mailing of this circular to the Cunard shareholders was timed to coincide with a public announcement to be made on 1 October by Mr Gerald Balfour, President of the Board of Trade at the annual Cutler's Feast in Sheffield. In his speech, the President not only dealt with the proposed terms of the agreement between the Government and the Cunard Company, but also with the wider and in some respects more important issue of the position of the British shipping lines who had joined the new American shipping combine. At the outset Mr Balfour conceded that there had been grounds for nervousness over the transfer of a large and important section of the country's mercantile marine to the ownership and management of non-British capitalists, especially when it became known that the great German steamship companies had joined the combination under conditions of independence which the British companies did not appear to possess.

The President then went on to dispel the very real fears which had been voiced by giving details of an agreement concluded between the Government and the shipping combination which it was considered, adequately covered the situation. Under this agreement the British companies involved would remain British in constitution and management. The British ships they owned would continue to fly the British flag and would carry such a proportion of British officers and men as the British Government might require. In addition, the British ships under the control of the combination would be at the disposal of the British Government should their acquisition or temporary use be required for any public purpose. Finally, the agreement stipulated that at least half of the new ships to be built for the combination should continue to be British.

In an editorial comment *The Times*, which if it had not supported, had never strongly opposed the absorption of the British shipping companies into the Morgan combine, reported: 'These conditions dispose of nearly all the objections having any kind of validity which have been urged against the combination. They secure to the British flag a large and permanent share of the Atlantic carrying trade that will be absorbed by the carrying companies. They retain for the British Government the command in times of emergency of the fastest and best equipped liners on the seas, for the service in war or other national purpose…' And concluded, 'It will be generally felt we think that the agreements which the Government has entered into with the Atlantic shipping combination and with the Cunard Company are wise and rational. Some people will, perhaps, continue to look with a jealous eye on the power of American capital over the carrying trade of the Atlantic. Some economical purists will no doubt protest against the loan and the subsidy by which the Cunard Company is to be strengthened in its position as a purely British undertaking, though Mr Gerald Balfour explains that they only amount to what is needed to make the construction of the new fast vessels not a losing venture. But the policy of the Government will be judged by most people from a practical point-of-view.

Certain points in these agreements may be open to criticism, and as a matter of course we shall have plenty of critics in the field…With regard to the combination it is important to remember that the interest of the American capitalists in the security and freedom of the Atlantic carrying trade is a powerful guarantee for the food supplies of the United Kingdom in the event of war. A foreign enemy would think twice and thrice before attempting to intercept our food supplies as soon as it was realised that the result would be to engage in an additional quarrel with interests that are very powerful in the United States. It should be added that the agreement with the combination is to last like that with the Cunard Company for 20 years, but in the former case is to be renewable for periods of five years. If, however, the combined companies should be found to be pursuing a policy of hostility to the mercantile marine or the commerce of this country, the British Government reserve the right to terminate the agreement.'

Since the previous April when the impending formation of the International Mercantile Marine Company (IMMCo) involving the absorption of the White Star Line had been announced, the work of finalising the 'take over' had proceeded steadily. The project had caused considerable personal distress to the Ismay family, who knew full well that if Thomas Ismay, the founder of the Company, had been alive he would not have entertained the idea. But the family could not prevail against the wishes of seventy-five per cent of the Company's shareholders, and at the annual meeting of the Company in May the offer had been accepted. The purchase price exceeded £10 million, of which £3 million was to be payable in cash on 31 December 1902. It was in fact paid over at the London offices of J. P. Morgan on 1 December as recorded in an entry in the diary kept by Mrs. Margaret Ismay. In it she wrote: 'Monday 1 December. Messrs. Morgan have paid all the shareholders of the Oceanic Steam Navigation Company for their shares. This ends the White Star Line in which so much interest, thought and care was bestowed and which was my dearest one's life's work.'

The disappointment and bitterness felt by Mrs. Ismay in recording this occasion can well be understood but the White Star did not lose its identity or wither away. Far from it indeed, for it was IMMCo's flagship company and still attracted a faithful clientele. Thomas Ismay's son, Joseph Bruce Ismay, had succeeded his father as Chairman and Managing director of White Star. He was also an astute businessman and it was he who had negotiated White Star's purchase by the IMMCo and at the age of 41 was to become the head of one of the largest shipping organisations in the world. At the time of the take over Bruce Ismay and W. J. Pirrie became two of its 13 directors. Also following the take over, three of five partners in Ismay, Imrie & Co, the managing agents for the Oceanic Steam Navigation Co; William Imrie, James Ismay (Bruce's brother) and W. S. Graves, retired. This left only Bruce Ismay and Harold Sanderson, but Pirrie soon joined them as a director of the line. What was not known at the time is that between 1900 and 1914, just prior to World War 1, some 13 million people emigrated from Europe to the United States and Canada in search of a better life or a new opportunity. These travellers would generate massive profits of which IMMCo and White Star would have the lion's share.

A month after Thomas Ismay's death, a young Italian physicist, Guglielmo Marconi, had made some pioneering experiments in the field of an earth-aerial system. Marconi had moved to England from Italy in 1896 and had built a small wireless transmitting station at Alum Bay on the Isle of Wight. From 6 December 1897 until 26 May 1900, from his little wireless station, he made experimental transmissions over gradually increasing distances, starting with a tug in Alum Bay and finishing with a steamer some 40 miles away. On 15 November 1899, Marconi was returning to England from the USA aboard the American liner *St Paul* along with his wireless equipment. As the *St Paul* was steaming through the English Channel en route to Southampton some 50miles out from the Needles, the *St Paul* became the first ship to report its own arrival by wireless. On 12 December 1901, he made his first attempts at long distance communications between Poldhu Point in Cornwall and Canada using wireless telegraphy. By 1901 wireless

Below: **The *Afric* was the first of White Star's 'Colonial' class specifically designed for the Australian trade.**
Nautical Photo Agency.

Above: The *Afric* anchored in the River Mersey with what appears to be the *Pontic* moored alongside. Note the New Brighton tower by the *Afric*'s stern to the right of the picture. *Tom Rayner Collection.*

signals traversed the Atlantic, for up until this time it was believed that the curvature of the Earth's surface would be an insuperable obstacle to the transmission of wireless signals above 200 miles. In 1902, during a voyage on the American liner *Philadelphia*, he first demonstrated 'daylight effect' relative to wireless communication and in the same year Marconi patented the magnetic detector which then became the standard wireless receiver for many years. A few years later he developed and patented the horizontal directional aerial. His invention would have great influence on the North Atlantic trade at the start of the 20th century, and revolutionise communications between ships and ships and ship to shore. It was also to play a paramount role in the improvement of safety at sea.

The advent of wireless in White star Line came two years after the *Lucania* had pioneered wireless for its competitor the Cunard Line. *The Times* of 16 January 1905 reported: 'The Marconi Company has entered into an agreement with the Oceanic Steam Navigation Company (Limited) for the equipment of six of the White Star Line vessels with Marconi wireless apparatus. The names of the vessels to be fitted are: *Oceanic, Celtic, Baltic, Cedric, Majestic,* and *Teutonic*. It is hoped that the *Oceanic* may be equipped in readiness for her voyage from Liverpool on February 1. The remainder of the vessels are intended to be fitted at short intervals after that date. When these vessels have been equipped, practically all the Atlantic liners of the principal shipping companies will be carrying Marconi apparatus.'

In 1905, an attempt was made to reach a new 10-year agreement with the United States Post Office. When it appeared that everything was satisfactorily arranged, the question of the ships flying the US flag became predominant, but the Admiralty, persisting in its refusal to permit the transfer of the White Star ships under their Auxiliary Cruiser Agreement, brought about the abandonment of the scheme.

AFRIC

(1899-1917)
11,948 grt; 550 ft 2 in BP (570 ft OA) x 63 ft 3 in
Quadruple Expansion SR Engines, Twin Screw,
4,800 ihp 13.5 knots
Passengers: 320 Cabin class
Harland & Wolff, Belfast. Yard No. 322

The founding of the White Star Line was originally based on the Australian trade. Thomas Ismay had purchased the name and houseflag of Pilkington & Wilson's White Star Line of clipper ships which had made such a big name for itself during the gold rush years of the 1850s. So, not surprisingly, it was not until the late years of the 19th century were the early intentions of the Company revived and fulfilled with an order of five 12,000 grt steamers for a service to Australia via the Cape. The ships had an accommodation for 320 'Cabin' Class passengers and a huge deadweight cargo capacity of 15,000 tons, including 240,000 ft³ of refrigerated space for loading Australian meat. The five ships were built and delivered in two groups.

The *Afric* was launched at Belfast on 16 November 1898 as the first of three sisters, sometimes referred to as the 'Jubilee' Class (as their introduction coincided with Queen Victoria's Diamond Jubilee, 1897-1899). The three vessels were intended to provide a monthly service from the UK to Australia on White Star's newly reintroduced 'Colonial service'. The *Afric*, along with her sisters the *Medic* and *Persic* were all twin screw, four-masted, schooner-rigged steamers; apparently plans had been drawn up during their design stage for sail. Their hulls, which were of three-island type, had three continuous decks and seven holds which were served by 25 derricks. Four of these derricks were mounted on what had been termed 'crane posts' which were stepped abreast of the funnel. Passenger accommodation was situated aft of amidships, mainly on the upper 'tween deck. The *Afric* carried 320 single class passengers designated as Cabin and when on voyage they had the unrivalled run of the ship.

The *Afric* was delivered on 2 February 1899 and sailed on her maiden voyage from Liverpool to New York on 8 February on what was essentially a 'shakedown run'. Upon her return, she put back to Belfast from Liverpool on 23 March 1899, for seven months worth of improvements, to meet the demands of the Australian route, as she would return back along the 'clipper way' against wind and current. The *Afric* made her first voyage to Sydney via Cape Town on 9 September 1899. The itinerary was from Liverpool, Las Palmas (Tenerife) and Cape Town to Australian ports, Albany, Adelaide, Melbourne and Sydney. The return voyage was by the same way via Durban, Cape Town, Tenerife, Plymouth and London, before sailing for Liverpool for loading once more.

During the Boer War period between 1900-02, the *Afric* transported troops and horses to South Africa on the outward leg of her scheduled voyages to Australia; returning them to the UK at a later date on the homeward voyages back from Australia via South Africa. As such she was designated as troop transport *A19*. This schedule was interrupted when she made one voyage on 11 August 1900, from Liverpool to New York before reverting to the Australian run. It is of interest to note that during 1907, White Star fares that year were £19 from Liverpool to Australian ports and 15 guineas (£15·75p) from Liverpool to Cape Town. These vessels were in fact the precursors of the many one-class liners that were to eventually flourish on the Australian route.

During World War 1, the *Afric* continued on her commercial service, for many years without incident. However on the leg of another voyage from Liverpool to Sydney and whilst en route to Plymouth she was torpedoed on 12 February 1917 by German submarine *UC-66*, 12 miles South-south-west of the Eddystone Lighthouse. Five persons were killed by the explosion and 17 others drowned, but 145 of her complement, including the Master, survived.

AFRIC: *Of or pertaining to Africa, i.e. African. Afric's name was not used again by White Star but eventually adopted as Shaw Savill & Albion nomenclature.*

MEDIC
(1899-1928)
11,985 grt; 550 ft 2 in BP (570 ft OA) x 63 ft 3 in
Quadruple Expansion SR Engines, Twin Screw,
4,800 ihp, 13.5 knots
Passengers: 320 Cabin Class
Harland & Wolff, Belfast. Yard No. 323

The *Medic* was launched at Belfast on 15 December1898, but her completion was delayed until 6 July 1899 so that improvements that were made to the *Afric* could be incorporated as updated modifications into her construction. One of these was the provision of a large bunker capacity, in order that she could make the outward or homeward voyage without additional coal bunkers. Also the *Medic* could carry 100,000 frozen meat carcasses in her refrigerated spaces. The *Medic* sailed on her maiden voyage from Liverpool on 3 August 1899, via Cape Town to Australia thus inaugurating the new Australian service. She was welcomed there with tremendous enthusiasm and excitement.

On that inaugural trip and on his first White Star appointment as Fourth Mate was Charles Herbert Lightoller, who was later to be the only surviving senior officer of the *Titanic* disaster of 1912. He wrote of the *Medic*'s arrival in Sydney: 'She was a show ship, the biggest that had ever been out there, and the people in Australia gave us the time of our lives. Everything and everywhere it was *Medic*.' As she was the first ship on the route, on her homeward voyage to the UK she carried Australian troops and horses to South Africa as the Boer War had started on 12 October that year. In 1914 when World War 1 began, the *Medic* was retained on her scheduled commercial service because of her large refrigeration and meat carrying capacity up until 27 October

Below: **The *Medic* anchored in the River Mersey, dressed overall and ready to sail for Australia**.
Richard de Kerbrech Collection.

1917, when she was commandeered under the Liner Requisition Scheme until after the War. During this time one such trooping duty was in the Gallipoli campaign.

On 26 March 1919, the *Medic* was relinquished from war service and returned to White Star. She continued on the Australian service in consort with the *Persic*, *Runic* and *Suevic* until December 1927 when she made her last voyage on this run and was laid up. She was sold for around £35,000, to A/S Hektor (N. Bugge) of Tonsberg, Norway in June 1928, and converted to a whale factory ship by H. C. Grayson of Birkenhead and renamed *Hektoria*. The conversion included the construction and fitting of a stern ramp whereby whale carcasses could be hauled up on deck and 'flensed' instead of being laid alongside the ship after injecting with air and flensed, as had been the normal practice. She was refitted with 18 huge cargo tanks for the storage of 8,000 tons of whale oil, whilst at the same time

Above: **A stern quarter view photographed minutes later, possibly on the day of the *Medic*'s maiden voyage**. *John Clarkson.*

her coalbunkers were increased to take 4,960 tons. Altogether her alterations had increased her gross tonnage to 13,834 and she was ready in time for the 1928-1929 whaling season off South Georgia.

During the autumn of 1932, the *Hektoria* reverted to British registry having been transferred to Hektoria Ltd. of London, later to become Hektor Whaling, but employed in the same trade. As such, she was taken up as an oil tanker for the Ministry of War Transport during World War 2; and on 11 September 1942 whilst in convoy on the North Atlantic, was torpedoed and sunk by German submarine *U-608*, in position 48°55′ North, 33°38′ West.

MEDIC: *Of or pertaining to Media, an ancient country of Western Asia in Persia. Pronounced 'meedick', the ship's name was not used again by White Star but eventually adopted as Shaw Savill & Albion nomenclature.*

Below: **A rather rare photograph of the *Medic* just getting underway with her mizzen and after mast derricks 'topped off'**. *Richard de Kerbrech Collection.*

OCEANIC (II)

(1899-1914)
17,274 grt; 685 ft 8 in BP (704 ft OA) x 68 ft 4 in
Triple Expansion SR Engines, Twin Screw,
28,000 ihp, 19.5 knots
Passengers: 410 First class 300 Second class, 1,000
Third class.
Harland & Wolff, Belfast. Yard No. 317

A significant milestone was reached by White Star during 1899 when their second *Oceanic* entered service. With the withdrawal of the Company's first *Oceanic* from service in 1896, events and vast improvements in the field of marine engineering, naval architecture and the safety and comfort of passengers had moved on since she inaugurated the Oceanic Steam Navigation Co's transatlantic service. The North German Lloyd had embarked on a new series of liners for their New York service starting with the *Kaiser Wilhelm der Grosse* in 1897. In addition to this, White Star's record-breaking pair, the *Majestic* and *Teutonic* had become outmoded by Cunard's 12,900 ton sisters, the *Campania* and *Lucania*.

The second *Oceanic* owed much of her design innovation to White Star's Marine Superintendent, Captain John G. Cameron. But before work could even start on her a massive 500 ton overhead gantry had to be constructed at Harland & Wolff's yard. This formed a moving bridge over the ship whilst under construction, which travelled on rails carrying riveting machines, electric lamps and cranes. In fact it was the first time that hydraulic riveting was used in the shipyard and in all some 1,500 men were employed on *Oceanic*'s construction. And so it was that her keel was laid in 1897 on what was to be a busy time at Harland & Wolff's for the next

three years. The *Cymric* was still under construction and the yard would also be building and completing the 'jubilee class' concurrently, namely the *Afric*, *Medic*, *Persic*, *Runic* and *Suevic*. All in all it was a boom time for Belfast and Ireland as a whole.

The *Oceanic* was built under Admiralty supervision for possible use as an auxiliary cruiser, at a cost of nearly £1 million and launched on 14 January 1899. On that winter's day more than 50,000 people watched the launch, many cramming the banks of the river to see it. A stand for 5,000 visitors had been erected and both seagoing and land based White Star staff were among the honoured guests. As had been the custom laid down by Thomas Ismay, there was no launching ceremony as such as the ship and the White Star Line rather than any individual would take centre stage. On that day the *Oceanic* was the largest and last British transatlantic liner to be launched in the 19th century, and as such was the first vessel to exceed the length of the PS *Great Eastern* which had been launched 41 years earlier.

A radical departure of design based on the Company's operational procedure and safety influenced the *Oceanic*'s construction. The hull was divided by 13 transverse watertight bulkheads about 49 ft apart, while a longitudinal bulkhead, 97 ft long, divided port and starboard engine rooms. There was a cellular double bottom which extended the whole length of the ship, and included nine longitudinal girders. This double bottom was 5 ft 1 in deep, except in the vicinity of the engines, where its depth was increased by 2 ft. The frames, for about two-thirds of the length amidships, were of channel

Below: **Launch of the *Oceanic* at Belfast on 14 January 1899.**
Richard de Kerbrech Collection.

LAUNCH OF A VESSEL AT BELFAST

section bar 9 in x 4½ in x 4 in, spaced 31½ in apart; but towards the ends, these were replaced by frames of angle and reverse angle bar riveted to each other. The steel plating used varied from 1 in to 1.4 in. There were seven plated decks, five of which were continuous from stem to stern.

The _Oceanic_ was propelled by two sets of 4-cylinder, triple expansion engines. Each engine's high pressure cylinder was 47½ in diameter, intermediate pressure cylinder 79 in diameter and the two low pressure cylinders 93 in diameter. All had a common stroke of 6 ft. The reversing process was effected by combined steam and hydraulic power. Steam was supplied by 15 return-tube Scotch boilers, 12 double-ended and 3 single-ended, which consumed 480 tons of coal per day and produced steam at a pressure of 192 psi enabling the engines to develop a total of 28,000 ihp at 77 rev/min which could give her a service speed of 21 knots.

When completed, the ship's two sets of reciprocating engines were the largest in the world. The double-ended Scotch boilers were constructed of special tensile steel plate 1½ in thick. Opposite furnaces were riveted to a common combustion chamber. The boilers were 16 ft 6 in diameter with a total weight of 1,100 tons. The _Oceanic_'s twin propellers were of 22 ft 2½in diameter built up from gun metal bosses with three manganese bronze blades bolted on. The propellers were installed very close together, and an aperture in the stern frame allowed for this feature. Their drive via the engines was through large multicollar thrust blocks.

The _Oceanic_ had a bunker capacity for 3,700 tons of coal, sufficient to enable her to steam 24,000 miles at a speed of 12 knots in accordance with her requirement for an auxiliary cruiser in times of need. She had a displacement of 28,500 tons at load draught and a depth of hull of 49 ft 6 in. She was built on the 'long ship' principle with a length/beam ratio of 10:1 which would later affect her performance. Her four continuous decks gave her a most striking profile which was dominated by two oval sectioned funnels with a height 64 ft above the deck houses, and like the earlier _Majestic_, spaced widely apart. As had been their intent, White Star had previously announced that for their future tonnage for the express service, they would concentrate on size and comfort rather than high speed; and so it was for the _Oceanic_. Capitalising on their experience gained with the _Cymric_, it would maintain a 'slow and sea steady' service for the new liner. Ismay had sensed that travellers were

Above: **During 1907, the *Oceanic,* along with the *Majestic, Teutonic* and the *Adriatic,* was switched to Southampton. This undated photograph shows the *Oceanic* departing Southampton for New York being aided by one of the port's Red Funnel tugs.** *Tom Rayner Collection.*

becoming less concerned with saving a few hours on an Atlantic crossing, rather than making the voyage in luxury.

Another factor for this decision may lay with the fact of the economy of fuel consumption. Essentially the amount of coal burned in ships of the day varied as the cube of the speed attained. For example, if the consumption of 100 tons gave a steady speed of, say, 10 knots throughout the day, a consumption of 200 tons will increase the speed by only three knots. Burn four times as much, and even then the speed will barely reach 16 knots! Horse power, i.e. the rate of doing work, is closely linked with a ship's speed and therefore with its fuel consumption, and the following figures will give some idea of how the latter shoots up as the speed is increased. To emphasise this point, if a ship is steaming at 21 knots when developing a horse power of 22,000; to steam at 22 knots she would need to develop 25,000, or an increase in 3,000 for an extra knot. For 23 knots she would need to develop 30,000, an increase in 5,000; at 24 knots, 40,000, an increase of 10,000; at 25 knots, an increase of 12,000. As can be seen the increase is itself increasing, and at high speeds the running costs rapidly escalate for only a trifling gain in speed.

The *Oceanic* was designed to carry 410 First class, 300 Second class and 1,000 Third class and a crew of 394. Her accommodation was exceptionally well spaced, the dining saloon being positioned between the funnel uptakes. Public rooms were sumptuous with oak panelling washed with gold; massive carved doorposts and walls covered with highly embossed leather gilt. Saloons were domed and staterooms large and lofty. Many of the First class light fittings were gold plated and lavatories were of marble and throughout the ship many fine carvings, statues and paintings were featured. The architect Richard Norman Shaw acted as consultant for much of the interior design, including the dome and richly decorated panels of the First class dining saloon. The specialist contractor G. Trollope & Sons undertook the work in the saloon, which by 1 June 1899 was near its completion. Thomas Ismay's rigid policy of 'nothing but the very finest' was strictly adhered to.

After having attained a speed of more than 20 knots on trials, she left Belfast for Liverpool on 26 August 1899 and later on 30 August was open to the public and the press and she was received with great fanfare. It was a defining period for White Star for it had been 30 years since the founding of the Oceanic Steam Navigation Co. Amid all the hyperbole, the *Oceanic* departed on her maiden voyage from Liverpool to New York on 6 September under the command of Captain John G. Cameron. Thomas Ismay had planned to be aboard for the trip but was not well enough to do so. The voyage took 6 days 2 hours 37 minutes and she made the 2,780 mile crossing at an average speed of 19.57 knots, and apparently never rolled more than 6° throughout the entire crossing! Again, the *Oceanic* was received with a rapturous welcome upon her arrival in New York.

The long narrow design upon which the *Oceanic* was based had caused a major problem to manifest itself, excessive vibration at full speed. Although this was a disappointment; she in fact averaged over 20 knots on a number of crossings and was capable of higher speeds; it was

Above: **This early photograph of the *Oceanic* shows her size compared to previous Harland & Wolff-built passengers ships.** *Real Photographs Co.*

found necessary to operate her at around 19-19.5 knots. In this way she was never required to develop more than 20,000 of her available 28,000 ihp. The *Oceanic's* early years on the Atlantic were not without incident. During 1900 she was struck by lightning whilst at anchor and lost the top of her mainmast, and on 4 August whilst berthed at New York, adjacent to the *Bovic*, a fire in the *Bovic's* No 3 hold was in danger of getting out of hand with flames threatening the safety of the *Oceanic.* Fortunately the *Bovic's* crew mustered to fight the fire together with the New York Fire Department and brought the blaze under control. 1901 was also a fraught one for the *Oceanic,* for on 6 June she returned to Liverpool having lost a blade off one of the propellers, on this occasion the decision was made to sail again at once and arrive two days behind schedule. Later on 7 August 1901 while in fog off the Tuskar Rock near Rosslare in South East Ireland, she collided with and sank the Waterford Steam Navigation Co's *Kincora.* The seven crew aboard, half the *Kincora's* complement were killed but only the *Oceanic's* bows were damaged.

On 18 November 1904 and four days out from New York, the *Oceanic* encountered heavy gales, high seas and snow. The ensuing battering carried away part of her bulwarks and stove in two portholes, which allowed considerable water to flood the ship. Nine months later on 23 August 1905, whilst the *Oceanic* was berthed at Liverpool, a fire broke out which damaged the woodwork in the Third class compartment number four. It was put out by the ship's crew and did not interrupt her sailing schedule. During 1905, some of the *Oceanic's* 45 firemen 'mutinied' because they were fed up with working in the dark, hot and filthy conditions of the boiler rooms. Thirty-three were charged with mutiny under the Merchant Shipping Act of 1894 and jailed. A stark contrast to the unabashed luxury of the First class travellers!

The *Oceanic* proved a popular vessel and she went on to earn the title the 'Queen of the Seas', and it was rumoured that because of her reliable schedule, the port officials in New York and Liverpool used to set their watches by her arrival.

White Star's decision to move their main express service to Southampton meant that the *Oceanic* made her last sailing from Liverpool to New York on 22 May 1907. Whilst berthed at Pier 48 in New York and in the midst of a dock workers' strike and ready for the return journey on 3 June, arson was suspected. A fire, thought to have been started on purpose, broke out in the *Oceanic's* after hold, destroying among other cargo, the scenery of the actor Forbes Robertson. In addition, all bedding and fittings in the women's after Steerage quarters were ruined. The fire was brought under control after two hours, having caused around £1,000 worth of damage. The *Oceanic's* return voyage was delayed and she left New York on 5 June for Plymouth, Cherbourg and Southampton. Following this, along with other major units of White Star, the *Majestic, Teutonic* and the newly-introduced *Adriatic,* the *Oceanic* transferred her UK terminal to Southampton and made her first voyage from that port to New York on 19 June 1907. This permitted a call at Cherbourg that had proved particularly popular with the American Line passengers and it also enabled White Star to have an 'express' steamer leaving Southampton every week.

On 11 September 1909, a small fire broke out in the *Oceanic's* after hold while she was berthed at Southampton but it was soon extinguished. A year later whilst leaving New York on 23 November 1910 she collided with a coal barge *Red Star No. 19.* During the impact the barge's elderly captain and his wife were thrown into the water but soon rescued by a passing tug. On 29 February 1912, whilst on a voyage from Southampton to New York, the *Oceanic* shed one of her propeller blades. The voyage was completed but the out-of-balance forces or 'whip' due to the continuous rotating shaft, had set up excess vibration and put extra load on the shaft bearings. Temporary repairs were carried out in New York.

Two months later whilst berthed at Southampton during the coal strike, coal supplies were transferred from the *Oceanic* to the new flagship *Titanic.* On 10 April, with the *Titanic's* maiden voyage getting under way from the White Star Dock, the 44,460 ton vessel passed No38 berth where the *Oceanic* and the American Line's *New York* were moored abreast of one another, the latter vessel outboard. The effect of the *Titanic's* greater displacement, gave rise to 'canal effect' or 'shallow water effect', which drew the *New York* towards her and caused the ropes that moored her to the *Oceanic* to part. The *New York*'s bow was still moored but her stern swung outwards into the path of the *Titanic*. The Southampton tugs *Hector* and *Neptune* guided the *Titanic* away form the impending collision and the *New York* was pushed back to be re-moored alongside the *Oceanic* once more. Later the same year on 5 August, the *Oceanic* was delayed on her departure from Southampton to New York when her port engine broke down. The repairs, which delayed her schedule by six hours, were carried out at sea.

She encountered some typical North Atlantic winter weather on 13 January 1914 whilst crossing to New York into the teeth of a gale. In this the bridge port glasses were smashed in and the bridge supports were bent or carried away. The *Oceanic*'s commercial career drew to a close when she made her last voyage to New York from Southampton on 22 July 1914. Following the outbreak of World War 1, the *Oceanic* was commandeered by the Royal Navy on 8 August 1914 and fitted with sixteen 4.7 in guns in accordance with the agreement under which she was constructed. As HMS *Oceanic* she was allocated to the 10th Cruiser Squadron on the northern patrol as an Armed Merchant Cruiser. As such her mission was to maintain the blockade of the North Sea, with a patrol area extending from the Norwegian coast far out into the Atlantic to cover all approaches to the European continent from a northerly direction. The 10th Cruiser Squadron was made up predominantly of Armed Merchant Cruisers, and throughout its period of existence, no fewer than 41 different passenger ships served with the Squadron for some length of time, some armed with guns up to 6 in calibre.

One of the peculiarities of manning a former merchant ship as a warship manifested itself during this period. The *Oceanic*'s current Master, Captain Henry Smith, along with many of his officers who were in the Royal Naval Reserve were detailed to remain with the ship under the overall command of a naval officer, Captain William Slayter RN, along with other naval officers. The crew was an amalgam of naval ratings and merchant seamen, and some of the latter had never seen or manned a gun before. The resulting rivalry between the men of the two services in addition to a covert antagonism between Captain Smith and Captain Slayter set the scene and ethos aboard the *Oceanic* prior to her taking up station for combat duties.

The *Oceanic* departed Southampton on 27 August and sailed up the west coast of Britain with a brief call at Scapa Flow in Orkney. Her task on the northern patrol was to guard the waters between the North of Scotland and the Faroes, stopping and searching every ship that was suspect, and monitoring shipping movements, along with the look out for German U-boats. A ship as large as the *Oceanic* would have been particularly vulnerable to submarine attack around dusk and daybreak. Accordingly, the ship's company had to 'stand to' at these times. As a result it happened that one of the normal ship's watches would finish, go below for rest, and have to come up again only 40 minutes later. Captain Slayter ordered the ship's clock to be altered by 40 minutes so that the watch change and general standby

occurred at the same time. Because of the threat of enemy submarines, the *Oceanic* maintained a zig-zag course procedure in accordance with admiralty instructions, which led to some confusion among the *Oceanic*'s navigators.

On the evening of 7 September 1914, the *Oceanic* was thought to be in a position west of the Island of Foula, itself some 20 miles West of the main group of the Shetland Islands. Notwithstanding the fact that seemingly accurate land fixes were taken on the North and South ends of the island, the following morning the *Oceanic* grounded on the Shaalds of Foula, an unbuoyed underwater reef, two miles East of Foula; at high water in flat calm and clear weather! The *Oceanic* had been reckoned to be 14 miles to the south west, this was certainly a large navigational error or possibly an error of judgement! A ship with two captains (but one commanding officer). Captain Slayter was on the bridge throughout the night and Captain Smith took over whenever Captain Slayter rested during daylight hours. On the morning of 8 September, Slayter went below after dawn broke, with the visibility of seven miles, leaving orders to steer north east in the direction of Foula Island.

Captain Smith had strongly disagreed with the policy of navigating a ship as large as the *Oceanic* with its deep draught anywhere near the outlying islands, because of the possibility of local reefs in the vicinity. After steaming for a while with their position thought to be well south of the island, Smith ordered a change of course; due west to the open sea, away from any hidden dangers like outlying reefs. They had unwittingly travelled 14 miles further than previously calculated, and instead of being south of the island they were in reality, east of it. Instead the westerly course was taking them straight for the Island and on to the reefs lying two miles off it! In the calmness of the situation, and because visibility was still around seven miles, an extra watch on the starboard beam was detailed where the Island was expected to appear when the mist lifted. Even if their calculations were slightly in error, they still expected to see Foula Island long before they were in the locality of any reefs.

When the Island did appear it was off the starboard bow. Then Captain Slayter returned to the bridge and both he and Captain Smith estimated that their position was some five miles off south of the island and therefore in no real danger. However, their true position was barely two miles away! Captain Smith had given an order which was immediately countermanded by Captain Slayter upon his arrival on the bridge and his full but incorrect assessment of the situation. So the *Oceanic* which had been in fact steering between the reef and the island, changed course and drove onto the Shaalds. Although aground in calm weather, by 11 September, the efforts of two Royal Navy tugs *Forward* and *Alsatian* to pull her free from the reef were in vain and even an attempt by the battleship HMS *Hannibal* which had put a 6 in hawser aboard failed. In the meantime the trawler *Glenogil* safely rescued the ship's company of 400.

For two weeks the *Oceanic* remained impaled on the rocks and in this time, during which the weather had deteriorated, the 573 ton Royal Navy salvage vessel *Lyons*, under the

Above: **The *Persic* anchored in the River Mersey, ready to sail and dressed overall. This could be on the occasion of her maiden voyage to Australia.** *B&A Feilden.*

command of Lieutenant Gardiner, was dispatched to salvage what it could. All the 4. 7 in guns were removed along with its ammunition, also all but one of the gunshields was taken off, but the *Oceanic* remained firm swept by tides running up to 12 knots. The rough weather eventually culminated into a severe northwesterly gale which pounded and rocked the stricken hull until several plates were stove in and rivets sheared. This caused the *Oceanic* to ship water and she slid into deeper water of five fathoms. At a subsequent court martial hearing no blame was apportioned to either Captains with the ship's navigator Davy Blair being given a reprimand. However it came to light that there were certain differences in operational procedures between the Royal Navy and Merchant Navy practice which had not been resolved. Bearing in mind it was still early in the war these included the inconsistencies in watchkeeping practice and the way in which the engine room log was recorded. Quite apart from this, Captain Smith, the *Oceanic's* original Master had in effect been usurped in his role having been subordinated to a Naval Officer.

As a result the Admiralty instructed that the procedures for ships taken up from trade as Armed Merchant Cruisers would in future be commanded by their regular Masters with their crew, and the Royal Navy would be responsible for Northern Patrol action. The wreck of the *Oceanic* was sold during the 1920s by the Admiralty to one of the Scapa Flow salvage companies for £200, and by March 1924 only parts visible were cut down to the water line. Strong tides proved too difficult for underwater salvage operations and these were abandoned. Nearly 60 years later, two Scuba divers, Simon

Martin and Alec Crawford, went to salvage the *Oceanic's* wreck with more up-to-date equipment. Between 1973 and 1979, they salvaged many artefacts along with over 200 tons of pre-nuclear age, non-ferrous metals from the ship's engine room and its two 29-ton propellers. Although White Star always ordered ships in pairs, it was proposed that a sister for the *Oceanic* be ordered to be named *Olympic* but following Thomas Ismay's death on 23 November 1899, the construction of this proposed liner was postponed.

PERSIC

(1899-1927)
11,973 grt; 550 ft 2 in BP (570 ft OA) x 63 ft 3 in
Quadruple Expansion SR Engines, Twin Screw,
4,800 ihp, 13.5 knots
Passengers: 320 Cabin class
Harland & Wolff, Belfast. Yard No. 325

The *Persic* was launched by Harland & Wolff on 7 September 1899 and completed two months later on 16 November to become the third of the class to enter service on the Colonial run. The *Persic* sailed on her maiden voyage from Liverpool to Sydney via Cape Town on 7 December 1899 and during this trip transported some 500 troops to South Africa for the Boer War campaign. On the outward voyage cracks in the rudder stock casting culminated in it breaking by the time she reached Cape Town. Rather than carrying on with limited manoeuvrability on two screws the *Persic* remained at Cape Town until a replacement, supplied by Harland & Wolff,

Above: **The *Persic* being towed by a tug into the lock for discharging. Note all her derricks 'topped off' for cargo handling. Like others of her class she had the refrigerated capacity to take 100,000 carcases of frozen mutton.** *Nautical Photo Agency.*

could be shipped out and fitted. Early the following year 1900 when the voyage resumed, sick and wounded Australian troops were repatriated in her. Later that year on 26 October, the *Persic* stood by and rescued the crew of the burning schooner *Madura*. Like the *Medic,* at the outbreak of World War 1, the *Persic* maintained her scheduled regular service, but along with her sisters was taken up for war service on 9 November 1917 under the Liner Requisition Scheme. On 12 September 1918, whilst carrying 2,800 United States troops, she was torpedoed by the German submarine *UB-87* off the Scilly Isles but managed to reach port where she was beached. All on board were rescued. On completion of her war service she was released from duties on 11 July 1919 and returned to White Star and subsequently overhauled and modernised. The *Persic*

Below: **The *Persic* was the only vessel of the 'colonial' class to end her days at the breakers, her four sisters were sunk during the two world wars. She is seen here anchored in the River Mersey.** *Richard de Kerbrech Collection.*

returned to her post-war service to Cape Town, Freemantle, Adelaide, Sydney and Brisbane but calling at Southampton in place of Plymouth on the homeward run. However a fall back in trade in the early years of the 1920s caused some uneasiness for White Star. As a cautious measure they made arrangements for a joint service with the Blue Funnel Line. Shortly after this the Aberdeen Line was phased in, but things did not improve. By 1926, the *Persic* was refitted by Harland & Wolff's Govan yard where her main engines were found to be suffering from advanced wear and tear, with limited service life. So the *Persic* made one last voyage to Australia, departing Liverpool on 26 September 1926 and laid up in the River Mersey upon her return. In June 1927, she was sold for £25,000 to Hendrik Ido Ambacht and on 7 July she left the Mersey for the Netherlands to be scrapped.

PERSIC: *Of or pertaining to Persia. The nomenclature ceased to be used by White Star but was taken up by Shaw Savill.*

RUNIC (II)

(1900-1930)
12,482 grt; 550 ft 2 in BP (565 ft OA) x 63 ft 4 in
Quadruple Expansion SR Engines, Twin Screw,
5,000 ihp, 14 knots
Passengers: 400 Third class.
Harland & Wolff, Belfast. Yard No. 332

The *Runic* was launched by Harland & Wolff on 25 October 1900 and delivered two months later on 22 December. The *Runic* was the 39th vessel launched by them for White Star, the total aggregating some 86,501 gross tons. Upon her completion, along with her sister the *Suevic*, she made up the five-ship service to provide a monthly itinerary to Australia. The *Runic*'s dimensions, machinery and layout of a single funnel and four masts was similar to the earlier

Above: **The *Runic* was the fourth sister of the 'colonial' class. Careful study of this photograph shows that she has an awning rigged over her poop deck, indicating that she may be in hotter climes.** *A. Duncan.*

group of the *Medic, Afric* and *Persic*, but certain improvements had been incorporated into the design of the *Runic* and her sister ship. She had three decks and seven holds served by 21 derricks and a forecastle deck 55 ft long. The ship's bridge and deck officers' accommodation was placed well forward. The after well deck was enclosed, hence this gave a combined bridge deck (107 ft) and poop (57 ft) which provided increased passenger carrying space. Originally the *Runic* and *Suevic* could carry over 400 passengers in Third class but later, due to a change in trade requirements, this was reduced to 260 in Cabin class. For the carriage of cargo on the Australia trade, the *Runic* had a very large refrigerated cargo capacity for the stowage of 100,000 carcasses of mutton. There was also a special hold set apart for the carriage of 20,000 bales of wool from Merino sheep. She had a bunker capacity of 3,000 tons to cater for coal consumption of 80 tons per day.

Following her handing over on 22 December that year, the *Runic* sailed on her maiden voyage from Liverpool to Sydney on 19 January 1901. The *Runic* soon proved extremely popular with settlers and travellers alike and later that year on 25 November she went to the assistance of the Union-Castle liner *Dunottar Castle* which had broken down, and towed the disabled liner into the port of Dakar in West Africa. The *Runic*'s schedule was rarely interrupted but during World War 1 on 21 January 1915, she was taken up as an Australian transport with the designated number *A54*. Whilst in the English Channel on 1 May that year she collided with and sank a smaller transport, the 946 grt *Horst Martini*; no lives were lost in this encounter. Later during the war she was commandeered under the Liner Requisition Scheme from 28 November 1917 until 10 April 1919.

Following her release back to commercial service, she returned to the Australian run but by October 1921 she went back to Harland & Wolff for reconditioning and reconstruction of her passenger accommodation. Until late

Right: **When the *Runic* was launched by Harland & Wolff on 25 October 1900, she was the thirty-ninth ship launched by the builders for White Star, with a total aggregate tonnage of some 230,000 tons.** *The Sphere.*

1928 White Star was contributing three vessels to the Australian service, the *Runic*, *Medic* and the *Ceramic* of 1913. Up until this time White Star often experimented on extending their service itinerary to take in more ports to serve and whilst the *Runic* was operating on its extended itinerary to Glasgow, she was in collision with HMS *London* at Gourock Pier on 3 November 1928. She suffered minor damage to her stern.

The *Runic* made her last voyage to Australia in December 1929 for White Star and upon her return was laid up for disposal after nearly 30 years service, albeit interrupted by the War, for the Company. She was sold in July 1930 for further trading to the Sevilla Whaling Co. of London (a subsidiary of A/S Sevilla of Norway). Like her former consorts, the *Medic* and *Suevic*, sold two years previously,

the *Runic* was converted to a whale factory ship. She was rebuilt at the Germania shipyard in Kiel, and was renamed the *New Sevilla* with an increased gross tonnage of 13,801 and registered in Dublin. Not long after she entered service in this capacity, A/S Sevilla was taken over by Christian Salvesen during April 1931.

Nine years later, during World War 2, the *New Sevilla* was en route from Liverpool to Antarctica when she was torpedoed on 20 October 1940. She was hit 30 miles off Malin Head, Galway in position 55° 48′ N, 07° 22′ W, by torpedoes from the German submarine *U-138*. Although she remained afloat for 20 more hours and 412 crew were saved, two lives were lost.

RUNIC: *The name became a Shaw Savill & Albion nomenclature and was not used again by White Star.*

Below: **This full broadside view is what the photograph identifies as 'Transport *Runic*', photographed in Sydney as an Australian troopship. Note her troop transport number *A54* at the bow and stern has been obliterated by the censor (and vandalised for posterity!).** *Richard de Kerbrech Collection.*

Above: **The *Runic* anchored in the River Mersey, ready to sail. Note the separate bridge island with accommodation for the ship's deck officers.** *World Ship Photo Library.*

SUEVIC

(1900-1928)
12,531 grt; 550 ft 2 in BP (565 ft OA) x 63 ft 4 in
Quadruple Expansion SR Engines, Twin Screw,
5,000 ihp. 13.5 Knots
Passengers: 400 Cabin class.
Harland & Wolff, Belfast. Yard No. 333

When Harland & Wolff launched the *Suevic* on 8 December 1900, she was the last of five ships intended for the Colonial service and slightly larger than her earlier sisters. Following her completion on 9 March, she sailed on her maiden voyage from Liverpool to Sydney on 23 March 1901. On this trip and subsequent early voyages, she carried British troops and stores out to Cape Town for the Boer War during the outward voyages and Australian units to the Cape on the homeward voyages. The trooping duties upset the new route previously established for the *Suevic* and her

sisters, (but was a great earner of revenue), and it was not until 1902 that the actual scheduled monthly service was settled. Outward bound ships called at Las Palmas, Cape Town, Albany, Adelaide, Melbourne and Sydney. On the homeward voyage a call at Durban was added. Following the end of the Boer War, the *Suevic* sailed almost without incident on her intended route.

It wasn't long before the *Suevic* was to carve her name in maritime history by becoming 'the ship that would not die', when she was involved in one of the most unique salvage operations of the 20th century. On 17 March 1907, under the command of Captain Thomas Johnson Jones, whilst in the western approaches to Plymouth, carrying 382 passengers, 141 crew and a near full load of cargo, she grounded on the Stag Rock near the Lizard Point in Cornwall. Inbound from Australia at full speed in the drizzle and fog, her arrival at Plymouth had been estimated when she was thought to have been 138 miles from Lizard Point. When thought to have been approximately 122 miles off the Cornish coast, the Lizard light should have been sighted dead ahead but amidst the gloom due to the weather and as a result of some miscalculations, the Lizard light suddenly appeared to the *Suevic*'s port. In fact she was 16 miles ahead of where she had been reckoned; it was felt that it was too early for lead soundings to be taken, and she went aground at full speed on the Stag Rock. The Cadgwith and Coverack lifeboats went to the *Suevic*'s aid and rescued all the 382 passengers that were aboard. The following day, attempts were made to refloat her by reversing the engines, without success. On 20 March, an effort was made to lighten the impaled bow when her forward cargo was unloaded into small coasters; again this attempt was in vain. The bow section which held her fast was leaking badly whereas her stern section with the engine and boiler room was floating free and was undamaged. The weather worsened and by 27 March, exposed to gale force winds and the Atlantic swell, the *Suevic* was driven on to the Cornish coast. Unless she could be removed from the rocks, the entire ship was at risk

of total loss. Many experienced salvage men believed that the best course of action was to abandon the *Suevic* to her fate, even then the traditional course of action in such situations, in order to save further unnecessary cost. This was not the view of the Liverpool & Glasgow Salvage Association. Acting on behalf of the White Star Line, they recommended that the bow section be severed by detonating explosive charges just aft of the stricken section, thus liberating the stern section for salvage.

The move was almost unprecedented, for a short while previously the Elder Dempster steamship *Milwaukee* had been recovered in a similar fashion, but whereas her reconstruction had been a technical success, it had been done at an extremely high cost. Similarly, another steamship, the *Highland Fling* had also been rebuilt following a stranding but hers too had been an unprofitable exercise. In spite of the fact that the operation to rebuild the *Suevic*'s bow section and join it to the existing stern section was an ambitious project way ahead of its time, the Salvage Association believed it was a worthwhile risk and financially viable. The underwriters were only interested in the cargo and were not concerned with the recovery of the ship as the hull insurance was borne by White Star! Replacement costs were therefore the owner's responsibility, for even at 1907 prices the cost of a replacement vessel would have been quite high. As far as the crippled ship was concerned, some 400 ft of her length was sound and it was this portion that contained the boilers, engine room and passenger accommodation, all of which were undamaged. Salvage therefore was a worthwhile option to explore, for, if successful, it was cheaper to rebuild the ship rather than to scrap her and write the cost off against the insurance fund.

Below: **An early photograph of the *Suevic* taken whilst at anchor in the River Mersey. Looking in pristine condition and dressed overall this could well be the occasion of her maiden voyage.** *John Clarkson.*

Towards the end of March the *Suevic* had been stripped of all the cargo worth saving, valued at around £400,000 and included a large consignment of frozen mutton and rabbit carcasses which had been loaded into numerous barges and coasters. Having been adequately lightened, all was ready for the critical stage of the operation to commence. Under the water, the lower part of the bows was a tangled mass of steelwork at the point where the swell had ground it on to the rocky pinnacle. The cargo holds in the forward part of the ship were also open to the sea with considerable damage to the hull plating. It was important to select the most suitable point at which the hull should be severed so that any areas of structural weakness that might complicate the rebuilding, would be avoided, and at the same time to retrieve as much of the ship that was intact as possible. It was finally decided that the *Suevic* should be cut in two immediately abaft the bridge island. This was effected by the placing and detonation of explosive charges strategically around the hull. This took place over several days and had to be undertaken in stages. First the keel girder, then the port side garboard and bottom, starboard side garboard and bottom, bilge to keel port side, bilge to keel starboard side, and so on. Finally, the separation was completed with the cutting of the side plating from the bilge keels to the water line. All in an era before the Oxyacetylene flame cutting process!

The work was drawn out and laborious, by necessity, because the divers were only permitted to work on the sea bottom at high and low water when there was little or no tidal movement. Successful completion of each stage required very careful calculations to determine the size and precise placement of each charge. In the event the operation

went off without too much complication. Finally, with the tugs *Ranger*, *Herculaneum* and *Blazer* taking the strain on steel hawsers attached to the stern, ably assisted by the *Suevic*'s own engines steaming 'full astern' and following the last detonations, at 08.36am on 2 April 1907, the *Suevic* was successfully divided. Aided by the swell, the buoyant stern lifted and parted from the bow and floated free on an even keel.

Once afloat, the tugs *Linnet*, *Herculaneum* and *Blazer* with the *Blazer* alongside, swiftly secured the after section of the *Suevic* to prevent it running aground again on other rocks in the reef. The damaged bow section was abandoned where it lay and was eventually broken up by the pounding of the waves during the night of 9/10 May. The stern section then made its way to Southampton stern first, largely under its own steam, employing its still sound engines and boilers. The accompanying tugs provided assistance with steering but played no major part in towing the *Suevic* to her destination. There was little alternative to steaming astern as it also minimised the strain on the exposed watertight bulkhead. This was a matter of some importance and later, it was necessary to treat the newly built bow section in the same way when it was launched.

Meanwhile as the strange convoy made its way along the South coast, they encountered some quite severe weather which led to the *Ranger* running aground. To render further assistance, two additional tugs were dispatched from Southampton. The *Suevic*'s stern section eventually docked at Southampton's Test Quay at 09.30am on 4 April 1907.

Above: **Assisted by the tugs *Blazer, Ranger* and *Herculaneum*, the freshly separated stern section of the *Suevic* is pulled clear of her stranded bow.** *Gibsons.*

Two days later, the remains of the *Suevic* were drydocked for preliminary repairs in the Trafalgar drydock which was owned and operated by Harland & Wolff. Work commenced with tidying up the plating, the damaged pipework of the refrigerating system and other fixtures and fittings that ran across the expanse of the exposed end to which a new bow section was to be joined. The damaged side plating was removed for some distance aft of the bulkhead, temporarily revealing eight of the ship's ribs and frames, before replacement steel sheets were riveted in place. Simultaneously, the decking was shored up with heavy timbers to prevent collapse or distortion prior to assembly with the new bow section. Men from the Southampton shipbuilders John I. Thornycroft were also employed to augment the Harland & Wolff workforce in an attempt to get the *Suevic* back in service as soon as possible.

Soon after the parting of the wrecked ship had been accomplished, a new bow section was ordered from Harland & Wolff's at Belfast. It was constructed to the ship's original plans and was 212 ft in length, but marginally longer than the severed bow, so that it would slightly overlap the salvaged stern end just beyond the after bulkhead of No 3 hold. Some wags of the day claimed that the *Suevic* was the longest passenger ship in the world, extending from her stern in Southampton to her bow in Belfast. Following its launch, stem first to avoid unnecessary stresses on the bulkhead, on 5 October 1907 at Queen's Island, the bow section was completely fitted out in all respects in readiness for sea. All masts and rigging were in place as was the bridge island structure, fully equipped with navigational equipment, wheel and engine room telegraphs. On either side of the bridge the lifeboats were installed in their davits. Prior to its departure for Southampton it was ballasted with a quantity of machinery destined for the Harland & Wolff repair shops there; in addition a number of heavy pumps were also installed in case of leaks. The new bow left Belfast under tow on 19 October 1907, sailing via the Irish Sea and around the Cornish coast, past the place where its abandoned predecessor had succumbed to the elements. The twin-funnelled paddle steamer tug *Pathfinder* led the way, pulling the forward section along bulkhead first, somewhat surprisingly, in view of

previous precautions. The tug *Blazer*, secured astern controlled the steering of the naked bow structure.

Six days later, at 10.45am on 25 October, after a temporary stop at Carrickfergus because of bad weather experienced off the Tuskar Rock, the bow arrived at Southampton and was at first secured alongside the docks. The Trafalgar Dock was flooded at low tide so that the after section should not be disturbed from her shorings although the exposed fore part flooded where the frames had been exposed. The new bow section was floated in gently by being nudged by the tugs and married up such that the extended plates slid over the exposed frames, prior to the caisson being shut and the dock pumped dry. Final adjustments for alignment were effected by hydraulic rams installed in the bottom of the dock. The workmen then set about joining the ship together again, riveting the overlapping plates to the ribs and frames, connecting together the metal frames, decks and deckheads, installing new bulkheads and linking up all the cables and pipework that extended from one end of the ship to the other through the fracture joint. Where any weakness might have occurred during her motion in a seaway, extra doubling plates and girders were riveted for additional strength. This was no mean feat, both in terms of the extent of the work and its technical complexity, but everything was completed within three months. Ironically such was the faith of the Company in the effort and skill of the workforce to complete the repair on time that they advertised the *Suevic*'s scheduled sailing for January 1908, even before the forward section was completed!

With the reconstruction under way, the *Suevic*'s Master, Captain Jones was found liable for her stranding and had his Master's Certificate of Competency suspended for three months; ironically it was his last trip prior to retirement. In addition White Star were found liable for the numerous mutton and rabbit carcasses that were washed up around the Cornish coast and were required to pay £50 to reimburse the local County authorities for the cleaning up operation.

Above: **The *Suevic*'s after portion arrives at Southampton revealing the extent of the damage.** *Nautical Photo Agency.*

She left the drydock and sailed for Liverpool on 10 January 1908, fully restored in readiness to resume her commercial service. Whilst there she was visited by Lord Pirrie who gave the ship the once over. Her first sailing was on 14 January 1908, as scheduled, under the command of Captain Mathias. On this outward voyage she carried a cargo of live animals and horses bound for Australia.

The *Suevic*'s reconstruction was not only a pioneering feat but had been achieved in a remarkably short time. But how did the quality of the major surgery endure in service during that pre-welding era? It appears that the *Suevic*'s subsequent career from this point was of an unusually long duration and of a quite strenuous character, thus demonstrating that in her salvaged and rebuilt form she was as good as new, and vindicated the decision to do so. She sailed for six more years on her scheduled Liverpool – Australia route and when World War 1 broke out, she was at first retained on commercial service with White Star because of her ability to carry a large quantity of frozen meat. However, the *Suevic* was soon taken up by the Australian Expeditionary Force and during May 1915 she made one trooping voyage to Mudros for the Dardanelles campaign. Between 10 September 1917 and 11 June 1919 she was transferred to the Shipping Controller under the Liner Requisition Scheme which maintained her on the Australian meat trade with the passenger accommodation being used for trooping. It wasn't until January 1920 that the *Suevic* was

released from Government service during which she had sailed some 250,000 miles through her wartime service.

She made a return to commercial service sailing from Liverpool to Australia on 2 February 1920 but towards the end of that year she went for an extensive refit and refurbishment to Portsmouth Dockyard, in which her passenger accommodation was altered to provide for 266 Second class only. On 14 March 1924, the *Suevic* arrived back in the UK after completing her 50th voyage on the Australian route. Four years later in October 1928 she was sold to Yngar Hvistendahl's Finnvahl A/S of Tonsberg for £35,000 who converted her to a whale factory ship at Fruppe's Germaniawerft, Kiel. She was renamed *Skytteren* and employed in the Antarctic among the whaling fleet. By 1939, she was laid up at Gothenburg in Sweden at the

Right: **The *Suevic*'s stern section is initially drydocked in the No6 Trafalgar Dock showing the inside of the No2 hold with its insulation exposed.** *FGO Stuart.*

Above: **Taken out of the drydock and work begins in removing buckled plating and the mainmast. The skeletal ribs and frames are exposed and shored up with timber props.**
Richard de Kerbrech Collection.

outbreak of World War 2 and following the invasion of Norway by the Germans in April 1940, along with several other Norwegian ships, she was interned at that port.

As the Norwegian Government in exile and the King were in London, occupied Norway under the Quisling Government claimed the 15 ships in Gothenburg but plans were afoot in Britain to mount an operation, codenamed 'Operation Performance' to spring these ships and bring them to the UK. In this, once in international waters they would be escorted and protected by Allied forces. The operation proved disastrous, for on 31 March 1942, escorted by Swedish warships they were hoping to make a dash for freedom. Instead they were guided into the paths of well informed German warships when they entered Norwegian waters. Only two ships, Tschudi & Eitzen's *B. P. Newton* and J. O. Odzell's *Lind*, made it to safety. Six ships were sunk by enemy action and three returned to Gothenburg where they were arrested, while two other whale catchers were captured by German armed trawlers in Swedish waters. On 1 April,

the German Navy intercepted the *Skytteren* together with the *Buccaneer* and *A. O. Andersen* just outside Swedish territorial waters, the crew scuttled the *Skytteren* off Maseskjaer on the west coast of Sweden. The incident was played down as it proved an embarrassment for neutral Sweden and their occupying neighbours. Some 35 years after major ship surgery the 'ship that would not die' was sunk at the hands of its own crew.

SUEVIC: *Of or pertaining to the Suevi, a North European people who finally settled in Sweden. The nomenclature ceased to be used by White Star but was taken up by Shaw Savill & Albion. More correctly pronounced 'sweevic'.*

Below: **Returned once more to drydock, the fully supported and shored up stern section awaits the arrival of the new bow.**
Nautical Photo Agency.

CELTIC (II)

(1901-1928)
20,904 grt; 680 ft 11 in BP (700 ft OA) x 75 ft 4 in
Quadruple Expansion SR Engines, Twin Screw,
14,000 ihp, 16 knots
Passengers: 347 First class, 160 Second class, 2,350
Third class
Harland & Wolff, Belfast. Yard No. 335

When the *Celtic* was launched by her builders, Harland & Wolff, on 4 April 1901, she marked the end of an era; for she was the last ship to be ordered by Thomas Ismay, the Company's founder, before his death in November 1899. She was the largest ship in the world at the time and the first to exceed the tonnage of Brunel's *Great Eastern* of 1860.

Above: **They had the technology. They did rebuild her. A feat of remarkable salvage and repair for its day, the rejoined and lengthened** *Suevic.* *Ensign Photo.*

Below: **The** *Suevic* **after returning to service. This photograph of her taken around 1911 shows her alongside at Durban Docks. It clearly shows her longer bow with her name in gold on the black hull. She spent another 34 years in service ending her career as a whale oil factory ship.**
Richard de Kerbrech Collection.

The Docks, Durban

The *Celtic* was the first vessel of a quartet of sisters which became known as the 'Big Four', the others would be the *Cedric, Baltic* and *Adriatic*. As with the *Oceanic* of 1899 the emphasis of the Company culture had shifted from building ships not for speed but for comfort, safety and reliability. Although capable of an average speed of 17 knots, the *Celtic* operated more economically at a service speed of 16 knots with a coal consumption of 280 tons per day. Following her handing over on 11 July 1901, it was apparent that there was another design feature which made a complete break from White Star's tradition of 'narrow ships'. Her breadth of 75 ft 4 in made her one of the 'beamiest' vessels of her day. In addition she had a large draught of 36 ft 5 in, which necessitated the approach channels to Liverpool being dredged to accommodate her in the fully loaded condition.

The *Celtic* sailed on her maiden voyage from Liverpool to New York on 26 July 1901. With her larger passenger-carrying accommodation and large cargo carrying capacity of 17,450 tons, her turnaround time in Liverpool and New York was extended to a week for unloading, disembarking and embarking passengers and their baggage, coaling and re-provisioning. Fast Atlantic crossings were henceforth left to Cunard and North German Lloyd. As something of an experiment, during February 1902, she made a five-week cruise from New York to the Mediterranean which attracted some 800 passengers. A year later whilst on the Atlantic service, on 15 April 1903, the *Celtic* collided with the British steamer *Heathmore* in the Mersey. The *Celtic* had to return to port for repairs to a small hole in her port side amidships, caused during the collision. In September 1904, the *Celtic* had the distinction of carrying the record number of passengers for the Company in peacetime, some 2,957 on a westbound Atlantic crossing, ironically exceeding her full carrying capacity!

A well known idiom which states that 'imitation is the highest form of flattery' complimented White Star when in October 1905 the German HAPAG Line took delivery of their new liner *Amerika* from Harland & Wolff. In all respects she was a slightly faster more luxurious version of the *Celtic*, even to the same rig of four masts and two funnels. Whilst in the midst of a rough Atlantic crossing on

Above: **The *Celtic* was the first ship to exceed 20,000 gross tons. Together with her three sisters they became known as the 'Big Four'. She is seen here in the River Mersey about to sail for the United States.** *Nautical Photo Agency.*

25 December 1905, the *Celtic* encountered a large wave during the Christmas dinner festivities which struck the Second class accommodation and the Engineers' quarters; some of the deck stanchions were snapped and two large plate glass windows of the Second class Smoking room were smashed, alarming all the passengers aboard. As the motion attenuated from this point calm ensued.

On 6 April 1907, the *Celtic* sailed on the first of two round voyages from New York to Southampton via Cherbourg on charter to the American Line as a replacement for their *St Paul*, the last crossing under this charter was from Southampton to New York via Cherbourg on 18 May. In the summer of 1907 when White Star moved their major operations to Southampton the *Celtic* remained at Liverpool along with the *Baltic* (1904), *Cedric* (1903) and *Arabic* (1903), thereby inaugurating a new Thursday service from Liverpool to New York. It may be of interest at to look at some fares to New York White Star offered during 1908. The Second class fare on the Southampton run had been £9 10s (£9. 50p) in the *Oceanic* and £9 in the *Adriatic, Majestic* and *Teutonic*, while the Third class fare had been £6 15s (£6.75p) in the first two vessels and £6 15s in the others. Under a new arrangement for that year whereby there would be an adjustment for rates for travelling in older steamers, for Second and Third class only. Accordingly the *Oceanic's* fares were reduced to £8 and £6, the *Adriatic's* to £7 10s (£7.50p) and £6, and in the older ships £7 10s (£7.50p) and £5 15s (£5.75p).

On the Liverpool run the rate in the *Celtic, Baltic* and *Cedric* had been £9 and £6 15s (£6.75p) which were reduced to £7 10s (£7.50p) and £6, and when the *Adriatic* operated out of this port, hers were reduced from £8 10s (£8.50p) and £6 10s (£6.50p) to £7 and £5 5s (£5.25p) respectively. The *Cymric*, on the Boston route, had her Third class fare reduced from £6 to £5 5s (£5.25p). The Cunard and

American Lines soon followed all these revised fares started by White Star. On 9 December 1908, whilst en route to New York the *Celtic* was struck bow on by a large wave; in this encounter the steel bridge support girders were buckled and the heavy wooden railing wrenched from the bridge. A year later, having returned from New York and whilst unloading at Liverpool on 28 December 1909, cotton in the *Celtic*'s No6 hold smouldered and burned for two days but was eventually extinguished by fire crews.

The New York terminals were preparing for the longer *Olympic* and her sister in 1911. To this end the New York Harbour authorities extended Pier 59 by some 90 ft in order to protect and accommodate the stern of the *Olympic*. On 11 June 1911, the *Celtic* collided with the newly extended pier, thereby necessitating repairs to it. The following year, on 28 December 1912, the *Celtic* was battling through some heavy Atlantic sea conditions whilst crossing to New York and the table racks (fiddles) were used for the first time since 1910. One large wave caused the ship to pitch so deeply that her stern port propeller lifted out of the water and raced. The steam governor failed to cut in and caused the steam shuttle valve to collapse with the additional demand. Repairs were effected while the *Celtic* steamed at 'Dead Slow Ahead', corkscrewing in the heavy Atlantic swell.

Following the outbreak of World War 1, the *Celtic* was requisitioned for war service on 4 August 1914, and on 20 October commissioned as an Armed Merchant Cruiser (AMC) and fitted with eight 6 in guns. As such she joined the 10th Cruiser Squadron in Cruiser Force 'B'(which at one time comprised up to some 21 liners) on 4 December 1914 under a naval captain with her former Master Captain Hambleton as navigator. Just over a year later in January 1916 she was decommissioned from this role, the Admiralty having conceded that converted large liners did not match their purpose built cruisers of the day. The *Celtic* was then hastily converted to a troopship, operating between Liverpool and Egypt until 7 March that year when she

resumed her normal commercial service between Liverpool and New York, hostilities permitting. Whilst outward bound from Liverpool on 15 February 1917, the *Celtic* struck a mine (which had been laid by German submarine *U-80*) off the Isle of Man. In the explosion 17 lives were lost and she sustained a 30 ft gash in the side of No1 hold. The London & North Western Railway Co.'s ferry *Slieve Bawn* took the passengers off and landed them at Holyhead, while the *Celtic* was towed to nearby Peel Bay on the Isle of Man. The Isle of Man Steam Packet Co's *Tynwald* carried repair equipment and divers from Liverpool and temporary repairs were undertaken to enable her to return to Liverpool where more permanent repairs could be made.

Upon the completion of these repairs she was taken up under the Liner Requisition Scheme from 17 April 1917 for the next two years. One of the facilities that the *Celtic* and her sisters could offer was that she had deep tanks capable for carrying 700 tons of high-grade oil. This was usually pumped into barges before docking at Liverpool. In this manner each of the 'Big Four' sisters could supply 1,400 tons of much-needed oil per week for the Royal Navy. A month later on 19 May 1917, the German submarine *U-57* failed to press home an attack on the *Celtic* when off South West Ireland, but on 31 March 1918, she was torpedoed again in the Irish Sea by *UB-77* with a loss of six lives. She was initially beached then towed back to Harland & Wolff's in Belfast for repairs. She was eventually released from the Liner Requisition Scheme on 17 May 1919 and handed back to White Star for refit and refurbishment of the accumulated war damage that had to be put right.

During January 1920, the reconditioned *Celtic* resumed her Liverpool to New York service establishing White Star's regular Liverpool schedule, but her passenger

Below: **Another early photograph of the *Celtic* in the River Mersey about to depart for New York. When built she was the largest ship in the World.** *John Clarkson.*

Above: **A later view of the *Celtic* without the crosstrees on her mainmast, anchored in the River Mersey with her derricks 'topped off' ready for cargo handling.** *Real Photographs Co Ltd.*

accommodation had been reduced to 350 First, 250 Second and 1,000 Third class. She had a collision on 21 April 1925 in the Irish Sea with Coast Line's *Hampshire Coast*, the *Celtic* suffering only superficial damage but the coaster was badly damaged and managed to reach port. Almost two years later on 29 January 1927, she was in collision again, this time with the United States Shipping Board's *Anaconda* whilst off Long Island, this time only minor damage was sustained by both vessels. Also in 1927, with more newer ships being introduced into the Company, and her relatively slower crossing by comparison, the *Celtic* was converted and re-designated Cabin class and her accommodation altered for 2,500 passengers.

The following year on 1 December 1928, the *Celtic* had left New York with 300

Right: **The *Celtic* moored alongside the Prince's Landing Stage at Liverpool, with the tender *Magnetic* alongside.** *Tom Rayner Collection.*

passengers and 350 crew aboard under the command of Captain Gilbert Berry. Among the passengers were 30 survivors of Lamport & Holt liner *Vestris* that had foundered in high seas on 12 November 1928 off the Maryland coast. Sailing eastbound with a call at Boston she made a good uneventful eight day crossing but upon approaching Cobh (Queenstown), the weather deteriorated and strong winds prevailed. Early on the morning of 10 December she arrived off Daunt Rock lightship near Roche's Point by which time she was in the thick of a south-westerly gale and sleeting rain. The Master decided it was too rough to pick up the pilot and decided to abandon tendering for Cobh and steam on to

Liverpool but as he sailed on another sea change saw the storm abate and calm seas return. In the meantime the pilot, who had been waiting an hour for the *Celtic* to arrive, on hearing that the liner had steamed past returned to port. In the meantime Captain Berry felt that because the weather had quelled and that because he had 70 passengers and 750 mailbags destined for Ireland, that a call at Cobh would be prudent after all. He gave the order to come about and head for Cobh but he headed back into rough weather again and had to heave to outside Cobh waiting for the pilot and the tender once more. When the pilot arrived he was unable to board and as dawn approached Captain Berry took the *Celtic* in closer to the harbour entrance. Gusting winds and heavy swells drove her aground at Roche's Point, her engines were put to 'Full Astern' and in the ensuing manoeuvre the swell lifted her off but she grounded once more on Cow and Calf Rock. The *Celtic*'s whistle sounded and alerted the Roche's Point lighthouse keeper to notify the rescue services and local lifeboats.

The *Celtic* had been holed amidships with one of her holds flooded but was firmly aground on the rocks. At early light the Cork tug *Morsecock* and the Dutch tug *Gelezee* arrived to put lines aboard the *Celtic* and tow her off, without success. The Cobh tender *Failte* arrived to take the passengers off but the ship's list to port and strong tides sweeping the same side initially hampered this. Eventually they were safely disembarked and were able to be put on the mail train to Dublin; in the meantime the *Celtic* had shipped much water into No3 hold and her stokehold. The following morning the two tugs were joined by a German salvage tug, the *Seefalke* and Liverpool and Glasgow Salvage Association's tug *Restorer* and they were joined two days later by the tug *Ranger*. No doubt the Salvage Company was seeking to repeat its success gained on the *Suevic*. The *Celtic* was by now 27 years old and with an insurance value of £230,000. Both salvers and the Company felt that recovery and repair were out of the question and the *Celtic* was declared a total constructive loss. All items that could be salvaged were. Crockery, cutlery, linen and furniture and fittings were saved and even 200 tons of fruit and four cars that had been loaded in New York. Because the *Celtic*'s tall funnels and masts were obstructing the Roche's Point Lighthouse they were cut down to deck level just days after being declared a total loss, as she was in danger of becoming a navigational hazard. At the same time a bridge was constructed between the ship and the shore in order to unload her and everything was removed by this route. The wreck was later sold to the Danish salvers, Petersen & Albeck of Copenhagen, who took until 1933 to cut up the hull where she lay with the oxy-acetylene blow torches and provide much needed work for local Irish labour. A sad end for an innovative liner of the Edwardian era.

ATHENIC
(1902-1928)
12,234 grt; 500 ft 4 in BP (516 ft OA) x 63 ft 4 in
Quadruple Expansion SR Engines, Twin Screw,
4,800 ihp, 13 knots
Passengers: 120 First class, 120 Second class, 450
Third class
Harland & Wolff, Belfast. Yard No. 341

The *Athenic* was the first of three new sister ships built for the joint White Star-Shaw Savill service to New Zealand and replaced the earlier *Coptic*, *Ionic* and *Doric* on that route. She was launched by Harland & Wolff on 17 August 1901 and delivered five months later on 23 January 1902. The *Athenic* and her sisters *Corinthic* and *Ionic* were only 9 ft longer than the *Gothic* of 1893 but were constructed with 10 ft extra beam than the earlier ship. She had a under deck tonnage of 11,395 and a net of 7,833 and was constructed with four decks. This enabled the *Athenic* to be fitted out with an extensive passenger accommodation for the route. In addition she had a large deadweight capacity of 13,300 tons with a depth of hold of 45 ft and being specifically designed for refrigerated cargoes, had an insulated capacity of 300,000 ft^3 in ten chambers, (possibly making her and sister ships among the largest refrigerated carriers of the day). Her quadruple expansion engines each had cylinder bores of 22, 31½, 46 and 68 in diameter and a stroke of 48 in and were rated at 4,800 ihp. Steam was supplied by three double-ended and three single-ended boilers. The three sisters revolutionised the New Zealand service.

The passenger accommodation was particularly comfortable with careful attention being paid to the lighting and ventilation of the passengers' quarters. The First and Second class accommodation were amidships with the First class dining saloon on the awning deck under the bridge and the Second class at the after end of the superstructure. The Third class quarters were on the main deck abaft the No5 'tween decks hold. The Smoking Room was in a deckhouse between the mizzen and jigger masts, while the Third class Dining room was right aft. Owing to its length the *Athenic* had a far greater amount of deck space available to passengers than before. One of the disadvantages of these enhanced dimensions meant limited facilities on her route, especially when docking and drydocking the ship.

The *Athenic* sailed on her maiden voyage from London on 14 February 1902 under the command of Captain C. H. Kempson who was to be her Master for another 26 voyages, until 1913. She arrived at Wellington on 2 April. The route was the same as previously, London, via Plymouth, Tenerife, Cape Town and Hobart, terminating at Wellington. The homeward journey to London was via Cape Horn, Montevideo, Rio di Janeiro, Tenerife and Plymouth. During a call at Tenerife on 20 January 1905, the *Athenic* rammed one of the rival steamers of the New Zealand Shipping Co. (NZSCo). The 5,715 ton *Whakatane* had put into the port the previous day with disabled steering gear. By 1907, fares

Above: **An early photograph of the *Athenic* anchored in the River Thames off Gravesend. The White Star and Shaw Savill houseflags may be seen on the main and mizzen masts respectively. Judging by the freshly painted condition, this photo was taken not long after she entered service.**
Richard de Kerbrech Collection.

to New Zealand from the UK were £64 First; £38 Second and £17 Third class.

As an endorsement of the service, Miss Mildred Savill, of Chelmsford, Essex, whose antecedents had founded Shaw Savill, together with her Mother and Father, embarked on a round voyage, (a World cruise by today's standards), on the *Athenic*. She departed on her voyage in the December of 1910 and returned on 4 April 1911. She and her parents travelled First class and during the voyage rumours abounded romantically linking the Purser and Miss Savill. Her photographic log of the 25,281 mile journey, which must have been the experience of a lifetime, was recorded in two scrapbooks. Dock labour troubles at Wellington during 1912 affected the *Athenic* when the stevedores ('wharfies') went on strike and refused to load frozen cargo onto her. The New Zealand farmers came down to the docks to load their own produce so that it would not spoil on the dockside. Striking dockers tried to entice the *Athenic*'s crew to come out in sympathy but without success.

By 1914 just before World War 1, it was decided to abandon Plymouth as a port of call for the landing of homeward bound passengers and mails in favour of Southampton, used by White Star's Atlantic liners since 1907. In fact when the war broke out in August that year, the *Athenic* was in New Zealand waters and for a time she

was kept on commercial service because of her large meat carrying capacity. On 28 February 1916, whilst homeward bound and calling at Santa Cruz in Tenerife, she embarked British prisoners captured by the German surface raider *Moewe*. They had arrived there in J. Westoll's ship *Westburn* which had been taken as a war prize and later scuttled. Later during December 1916 she carried the 20th Reinforcements from New Zealand to the UK to augment the ANZAC troops, as such she was designated HMNZT *No11*. From 16 March 1917 until 3 July 1919 the *Athenic* was taken up under the Liner Requisition Scheme and carried frozen meat from Australia and New Zealand, homeward via the newly-opened Panama Canal which made a significant saving in distance, time, coal and turnaround time in London. During the latter stages of the war and in order to make more efficient use of her refrigerated carrying capacity, all the sheep carcasses in New Zealand were ordered to be 'telescoped' to save space, and all rabbits were 'hook skinned' to save about thirty per cent of their bulk!

When the United States entered the war in 1917, the *Athenic* was re-routed homeward to call in to the East Coast ports to embark regiments of 'doughboys' and transport them across the Atlantic to their new war theatre. Following the war and whilst homeward bound after transiting the Panama Canal, on 3 May 1920, the *Athenic* rescued 80 passengers and crew of the Munsen's Line *Munamar*, which had grounded on Little San Salvador Island in the Bahamas. The rescued were disembarked at Newport News in Virginia. In 1926, the White Star Line was returned to British owners from the IMMCo empire and the New Zealand interests went under the control of Lord Kylsant's Royal Mail Steam Packet Company combine. The Shaw

Savill & Albion Co. Ltd also came under the Kylsant control in 1928, which resulted in two planned 20,000 ton liners being abandoned in favour of four large refrigerated motor cargo ships which were built instead.

As the 1930s approached and the ships like the *Athenic* and her sisters grew outdated, the general tempo of the New Zealand trade increased. General cargo liners, faster than the White Star liners, were placed in regular service and Shaw Savill introduced the Aberdeen sister ships *Mataroa* and *Tamaroa* in the service on a charter arrangement. At the same time the New Zealand Shipping Co. (NZSCo) also had under construction three new 16,000 grt 'Rangi' class liners. The once spectacular accommodation of the *Athenic* was now very much second rate and dated. Apart from making a single round voyage to Sydney from Liverpool during April 1927, she made her last voyage from London to Wellington in October 1927. In May 1928 the *Athenic* was sold for what was to be an even longer career under the Norwegian flag.

She was purchased for £33,000 by Hvalfangerselskapet Pelagos A/S Svend Foyn Brunn to be managed by Brunn & Von der Lippe of Tonsberg. She was drastically altered to convert her to a whale factory ship by Smith's Dock Co., South Bank-on-Tees and emerged in her new guise as the *Pelagos*, with her original coal-fired boilers having been converted to oil fuel; however her former First class accommodation was retained intact! During World War 2 and whilst on her twelfth voyage to the Antarctic, the *Pelagos* together with another factory ship, a supply ship and 11 whaling vessels was captured on 15 January 1941 by the German surface raider, the *Pinguin* and taken to Bordeaux. As a war prize, she was commandeered and operated by the German whaling company Erste Deutsche Walfang Ges as a depot oiler to the Kriegsmarine's 24th Submarine Flotilla, based in Norway. She was sunk at Kirkenes on 24 October 1944 during German naval experiments. Following liberation she was raised in 1945 and put back into service with the Norwegians for further whaling and continued as a whale oil factory ship with a much modified superstructure, with Svend Brunn of Tonsberg.

On 25 June 1962, she was sold to Eckardt & Co. of Hamburg and arrived there on 28 June for scrapping. A long career for a Harland & Wolff ship and a testament to its structural integrity. Her former masters included Captains C. H. Kempson (1901-1913), J. E. Crossland (1913-1918) and C. E. Starck (1918 and after World War 1).

ATHENIC: *Of or pertaining to Athens, the leading city of ancient and the capital of modern Greece. Following its withdrawal the name became a Shaw Savill & Albion nomenclature and was not used again by White Star.*

Below: **Another photograph of the *Athenic* anchored in the River Thames. On the reverse the correspondent wrote from Tenerife on 12 September 1910: "I presume this is the 'Ark' you travelled to New Zealand on" and "We have had a breakdown with one of the engines; so have had only one propeller going this past 18 hours till it was put right consequently we arrived here some hours late." It is not clear if he was writing about the *Athenic*, but such were the problems on the ships' engines encountered on the New Zealand route.** *Richard de Kerbrech Collection.*

Above: The *Athenic* as a troopship during World War 1 designated as HMNZT *No11.* *World ship Photo Library.*

Right: A postwar photograph of the *Athenic* moored off Gravesend. One of her lifeboats is in the river whilst another boat appears to be lowered. *Richard de Kerbrech Collection.*

Below: Although London was her main terminus, here is a photograph of the *Athenic* being towed from the River Mersey into Liverpool Docks. *John Clarkson.*

CORINTHIC

(1902-1931)
12,231 grt; 500 ft 4 in BP (516 ft OA) x 63 ft 4 in
Quadruple Expansion SR Engines, Twin Screw,
4,800 ihp, 13 knots
Passengers: 120 First class, 120 Second class,
450 Third class
Harland & Wolff, Belfast. Yard No. 343

The second sister, the *Corinthic*, was launched by Harland & Wolff on 10 April 1902 and delivered three months later on 14 July 1902. Like the *Athenic*, her depth of hold was 45 ft with a net tonnage of 7,646. On 20 November 1902 she sailed from London on her maiden voyage under the command of Captain Inman Sealby and arrived at Wellington on 6 January 1903. Like the *Athenic* before her, the *Corinthic* offered excellent accommodation in the three classes and she became popular both with travellers and on the New Zealand coast when she called.

One passenger wrote on a card back to England, when nearing Port Wellington on 24 April 1907: 'Well I have nearly reached my destination (13,200 miles) away from you. I leave this ship tomorrow and tranship to another on which I go 300 miles. Have had splendid passage and am now anxious to see Mrs Cunningham and farm who will be my future companion and home.' On the outbreak of World War 1, she remained on her normal London to Wellington service due to her large meat carrying capacity. On one of her return trips via the Panama Canal she called at New York (presumably to discharge frozen meat) on 27 April 1916. Whilst berthed at Pier 59 a fire broke out in her forecastle causing an estimated £100 worth of damage.

The *Corinthic* was taken up under the Liner Requisition Scheme from 23 June 1917 until 23 July 1919 and was still used for her frozen meat carriage. Just prior to this during April 1917, whilst under the command of Captain F. Hart, she embarked the 23rd Reinforcements of the New Zealand Expeditionary Force. They were billeted in the Third class accommodation. Later in the October that year she carried the 30th Reinforcements in company with Shaw Savill's *Arawa*. In the same year she escaped from a shadowing submarine in

the English Channel. The *Corinthic* returned to commercial service in 1920, for by this time the New Zealand service was returning to normal. As with other Company and Shaw Savill steamers returning to the UK via the Panama Canal they were scheduled to call at Port Royal in Jamaica for coal bunkers; this was an added attraction to the passenger service.

The post-war service was up to full strength when the *Corinthic* was joined by the *Athenic* and *Ionic* along with two Shaw Savill ships. Homewards the ships began calling at Southampton instead of Plymouth and in July 1921, Southampton was substituted for Plymouth for embarkation, but Plymouth was still occasionally used. Whilst homeward bound in the North Atlantic in February 1923, she rescued the crew from the sinking Newfoundland schooner *Marguerite Ryan*. In 1926, the *Corinthic* raced outward bound to New Zealand against NZSCo's *Remuera* and both ships remained in sight of each other all the way. (No doubt the race was suspended during the Panama Canal transit!).

On 3 March 1928 when calling at Plymouth, the *Corinthic* rammed the Royal Navy battleship HMS *Queen Elizabeth*. For the Royal Navy this was just one more incident that brought them into conflict with White Star. There had been the collision between the *Olympic* and HMS *Hawke* in 1911 and the anomaly in command and navigation that led to the loss of the *Oceanic* during September 1914, it's a wonder that White Star officers were still able to continue serving in the Royal Naval Reserve (RNR), but they did. As Shaw Savill's *Mataroa* and *Tamaroa* were introduced into the service during 1926 and with the imminent entry into service of NZSCo's three new 16,000 grt fast motorships, the *Athenic* was sold in 1928. This left the two remaining liners, the *Corinthic* together with the *Ionic* with the two Shaw Savill vessels, to maintain the four-weekly run from Southampton to New Zealand via Panama in 32 days. In 1929 the *Corinthic*'s accommodation was

Below: **The *Corinthic* anchored in the River Thames off Gravesend. This picture was taken by that town's photographer, W. T. Munns, and may possibly have been photographed during her first visit to London.**
Richard de Kerbrech Collection.

Above: **A post-war photograph of the *Corinthic* probably in New Zealand waters. On the reverse is written: 'RMS *Corinthic* at Sea 28/7/23' starting with: 'The *Ionic* is taking letters tomorrow…' and franked by the Southampton Paquet .** *Richard de Kerbrech Collection.*

converted to Cabin and Third class only and she made her last voyage from London to Wellington during August 1931.

Following the completion of her 71st voyage she was sold to Hughes, Bolckow for £10,250. Upon her return to London the High Commissioner for New Zealand, Sir Thomas Wilford, conducted a ceremony at the Royal Albert Dock. In this her houseflags were symbolically hauled down to mark the end of her service after 29 years dedicated to the New Zealand trade. The High Commissioner paid tribute to the *Corinthic*'s long association with the New Zealand trade and the valuable contribution that White Star and Shaw Savill had made in bringing it about. She arrived at Blyth on 16 December 1931 for demolition, but because of the depression and the low price of scrap metal at the time, the demolition was completed by Swan, Hunter & Wigham Richardson of Wallsend from 14 April 1932. The *Corinthic*'s past Masters included Captains I. Sealby (1902-1904), H. F. David (1904-1909), F. Hart (1909-1917 and later) and J. E. Crossland (1917 until after the war).

CORINTHIC: *Of or pertaining to Corinth, an ancient Greek city. Following its withdrawal the name became a Shaw Savill & Albion nomenclature and was not used again by White Star.*

Below: **The *Corinthic* being broken up by Swan Hunter's yard on 30 January 1933 to help alleviate unemployment in the area.** *Ian Rae.*

IONIC (II)

(1902-1934)
12,352 grt; 500 ft 4 in BP (516 ft OA) x 63 ft 4 in
Quadruple Expansion SR Engines, Twin Screw,
4,800 ihp, 13 knots
Passengers: 120 First class, 120 Second class,
450 Third class
Harland & Wolff, Belfast. Yard No. 346

The *Ionic* was launched by Harland & Wolff on 22 May 1902 and was completed some seven months later on 15 December 1902. Her twin screws were driven by two sets of quadruple expansion engines with cylinder bores of: HP 22 in, IP 31½in and LP 68 in at a stroke of 48 in. These developed 641 nhp and a maximum ihp of 4,800 which was intended to give her a service speed of 14 knots. She soon followed the *Corinthic* into service and departed on her maiden voyage from London on 16 January 1903 under the command of Captain J. B. Ranson, with general cargo and passengers and arrived at Wellington on 5 March.

The Engine Room log was meticulously recorded by the *Ionic's* Chief Engineer, Mr G. McLellan. It recorded that on the outward passage by way of Plymouth, Tenerife, Cape Town and Hobart, that the *Ionic* steamed 13,235 miles at an average speed of 12.1 knots and consumed 3,660 tons of coal, an average of 79.1 tons a day. On the homeward passage of 12,177 miles via Cape Horn, Rio de Janeiro and Tenerife was made at an average speed of 11.8 knots, the ship being in a deep loaded condition. As such she burned 3,870 tons of coal, an average of 89.1 tons a day. For her 17th voyage in 1909, the *Ionic* had the distinction of being the first ship trading to New Zealand to be fitted with Wireless telegraphy. It was an experimental set that could receive signals only, and it was designed by Lieutenant J. Holland RNR, the Second Officer of the *Ionic*.

It was decided by Shaw Savill to abandon Plymouth as a port of call for the disembarkation of homeward bound passengers and mails in favour of Southampton. The first ship to make the new call was the *Ionic* on her homeward bound passage in August 1914. Following the start of World War 1, the *Ionic* was requisitioned in August 1914 as a troopship for the New Zealand Expeditionary Force and a year later on 31 December 1915, she was missed by a torpedo whilst operating in the Mediterranean. Between 5 July 1917 and 13 August 1919, she operated under the Liner Requisition Scheme and in this capacity she carried outward the 37th Reinforcements of the New Zealand Expeditionary Forces in May 1918 when Captain V. W. Hickson was her Master. On 31 January 1919, having been derequisitioned earlier than expected from government service, she resumed commercial service to New Zealand via the Panama Canal. Apart from the obvious fuel saving benefits of the new route, it saved an appreciable distance on the voyage to New Zealand; was particularly scenic and interesting to transit for the passengers and avoided the intense heat and discomfort of a possible Suez Canal and Red Sea route.

Although a single voyage was made by the *Ionic* after the war had ended, it was not until January 1920 that the New Zealand service returned to normal, with firstly the *Athenic* returning, then the *Corinthic* and then the *Ionic* followed by the two Shaw Savill vessels. As previously stated, the liners called at Southampton instead of Plymouth for landing passengers and in July 1921, Southampton was substituted for Plymouth for embarkation. In 1927, the *Ionic* rescued the crew of the French fishing vessel *Daisy* off the Grand Banks. The *Daisy*, a 246 grt wooden three-masted schooner, built in 1908, sank but with no loss of life. By 1928 when the *Athenic* was sold for further trading as a whale oil factory ship, the *Ionic* along with the *Corinthic* and the two Shaw Savill ships maintained the New Zealand service.

In 1929, the *Ionic's* accommodation was converted to Cabin and Third class only and as such the ship was quite successful in this role in spite of her age. The completion of the Tilbury Landing Stage caused various London interests

Below: **The *Ionic* anchored in the River Thames off Gravesend preparing to sail. The Tilbury-Gravesend ferry *Carlotta* is moored alongside.** *Tom Rayner Collection.*

to do their best to persuade White Star and Shaw Savill to land their passengers there, but on ordinary voyages the *Ionic* remained faithful to Southampton in order to avoid carrying its passengers up the Channel, where there was more possibility of delay than in any other part of the voyage. By the end of 1931, the *Corinthic* was sold for breaking up leaving the *Ionic* to soldier on in the New Zealand service.

Again in 1932, the *Ionic* was altered to carry 280 Tourist class passengers only which enabled her to compete with the new modern liners on the route. In 1931, Lord Kylsant's Royal Mail Steam Packet Co. group, who had purchased the White Star interests from the IMMCo during 1927, crashed. Consequently in 1933 Shaw Savill & Albion came under the control of Furness, Withy & Co. The following year 1934 saw the amalgamation of the Cunard and White Star lines and as a result all White Star's interests in the New Zealand trade were transferred to the Shaw Savill & Albion Company. So it was that the *Ionic* transferred to Shaw Savill under this arrangement. She continued on the London to Wellington service, calling at Southampton, in consort with the *Mataroa* and *Tamaroa*. The only change to her livery was the White Star Line gold band around the hull being replaced by a white band.

By 1936, the *Ionic*'s engines were still remarkably sound and she was still able to maintain a good sea speed for her age. But her cargo-carrying capacity as compared to her registered tonnage, her economy and her passenger accommodation had fallen below the expected passenger standards of the day. Despite having established herself on the New Zealand coast since the turn of the century, Shaw Savill could not afford to continue to run her for sentimental reasons. On 9 September 1936, the *Ionic* sailed on her 79th and final voyage to New Zealand and upon her return to London in December that year she was laid up, pending disposal.

In her long career of 33 years under the White Star and Shaw Savill houseflags, the *Ionic* had steamed a total of 2,008,055 miles. She had had made 78 voyages from London to New Zealand as well as a trooping voyage to Egypt in 1935. In the course of the voyages to New Zealand she had rounded Cape Horn 35 times and carried many thousands of tons of general cargo out and refrigerated cargo home, without a single significant mishap. In this time her Masters included Captains J. B. Ransom (1902-1905), J. O. Carter (1905-1909), E. Roberts (1909-1913), C. E. Starck (1913-1915), Davis (1915-1916), H. T. Rowlands (1916-1917), V. W. Hickson (1917-1920), and A. H. Summers (1920). The *Ionic* was sold to Japanese shipbreakers for £31,500 and on 6 January 1937 she left Liverpool for Osaka for scrapping. At the request of the Mayor of Auckland at the time, the ship's bell was sent out to the Auckland War Memorial Museum for preservation.

CEDRIC

(1903-1931)
21,035 grt; 680 ft 9 in BP (700 ft OA) x 75 ft 4 in
Quadruple Expansion SR Engines, Twin Screw,
14,000 ihp, 16 knots
Passengers: 365 First class, 160 Second class,
2,352 Third class
Harland & Wolff, Belfast. Yard No. 337

The *Cedric*, the second of White Star's 'Big Four', was launched on 21 August 1902 and delivered on 31 January 1903. Like her precursor, the *Celtic*, she had a large passenger and cargo-carrying capacity, but unlike others of the class, the *Cedric* was the only one (and possibly the first liner) fitted with Welin gravity davits instead of the earlier quadrant or radial davits. Her depth of hold was 44 ft 1 in with a load draught of 36 ft 9 in and she had a deadweight capacity of 17,700 tons.

The *Cedric* sailed on her maiden voyage from Liverpool to New York on 11 February 1903, and upon her entry into service, White Star's *Britannic* of 1874, was sold in the July that year for scrapping after almost 30 years in service. With the new *Cedric* White Star felt it was in a position to improve their Friday sailings from Liverpool which up until her entry into service had been a glorified cargo service. The Cunard Line felt that this was against the spirit of a prior contract agreement between companies operating across the Atlantic and made it one of the reasons for their withdrawal from the pool. From now on the *Cedric* sailed as a large unit of the newly formed IMMCo Combine.

On 26 November 1903, the *Cedric* docked in New York after having been somewhat delayed by her arrival at that port. It was rumoured that she had been sunk in collision with Lamport & Holt's *Titian* in mid-Atlantic. This rumour, caused by her being overdue, had not a vestige of truth in it. Some 16 months later, whilst at sea in a storm on 15 March 1905, and with some 21 confirmed cases of measles aboard, the *Cedric* was struck broadside on by heavy seas on her port side. During the impact the forecastle's side was buckled and

Above: **The *Ionic* on a rare visit to Liverpool under tow to enter the docks complex. Note all her derricks are 'topped off' in readiness for cargo handling.** *B&A Feilden.*

the No1 hatch cover badly damaged. Several ports were smashed and the ship's bell carried away. Internally some of her woodwork splintered and among the distressed passengers a baby boy was born in Steerage.

From 1906 until 1911, the *Cedric* made a special cruise from New York to the Mediterranean during the winter and occasionally two in the spring, generally between January and March. While in port at Liverpool on 30 august 1910, a small fire broke out on board the *Cedric*, fortunately the damage was negligible. A year later on 22 June 1911 while docking at New York she hit a temporary pier extension of the new Chelsea pier, which was badly damaged; the *Cedric*, however, was not. Following the *Titanic* disaster of April 1912 the *Cedric* was already berthed in New York ready to sail. Her departure was delayed until the *Carpathia* arrived with the survivors from the foundering, so that any survivors or crewmembers not required for the impending Court of Inquiry who wished to could travel back to Liverpool.

Below: **By 1935, the *Ionic* had transferred to Shaw Savill's ownership. This view shows her manoeuvring astern from her berth at Southampton, still on the New Zealand trade but with her best years behind her.** *Peter Roberts.*

The following year on 18 December 1913, during a departure from the Liverpool Landing Stage, the *Cedric* struck the Post Office's overhead gangway with her stern, considerably damaging the gangway. Following the outbreak of World War 1, the *Cedric*, along with the *Celtic* was requisitioned in November 1914 as an Armed Merchant Cruiser and fitted with 6 in guns. In this role she was allocated to the 10th Cruiser Squadron, operating on 'A' patrol along with the *Teutonic*. However the *Cedric's* great size made her unsuitable in the AMC role and she was decommissioned in 1916 and converted to a troopship, initially for trooping to Egypt and Palestine and later when the United States entered the War, to New York. From 20 April 1917 to 18 March 1919 the *Cedric* was operated under the domain of the Liner Requisition Scheme and for a time she carried between 2,500 and 3,500 tons of fuel oil in her deep tanks for Royal Naval vessels.

In the last year of the war, on 29 January 1918, whilst in Convoy HG 27, the *Cedric* rammed Canadian Pacific's liner *Montreal* whilst off Morecambe Bay. The following day the *Montreal* was taken under tow but later sank when 14 miles from the Mersey Bar lightship. On 24 July 1919, whilst

Above: **A good broadside photograph of the *Cedric* showing her Edwardian-era style of two funnels and four masts.** *Richard de Kerbrech Collection.*

berthed in New York, fire broke out in No6 hold and rapidly spread. The fire was such that two city fireboats were in attendance along with city's West 20th Street police and the New York Hospital ambulance. In the blaze 20 firemen became trapped in No6 hold, some overcome by smoke. Police, firemen and the *Cedric's* crew risked their own personal safety to drag the stricken firemen to safety. The blaze was extinguished after one and a half-hours, having caused £5,000 damage to the ship's hold.

The *Cedric* was relinquished from her duties with the Liner Requisition Scheme and returned to her owners in September 1919. Following a refit at Harland & Wolff she

Below: **The *Cedric* well underway to the United States via Queenstown. Note the early feature of the crosstrees on her mainmast.** *Nautical Photo Agency.*

Above: **The *Cedric* manoeuvring in the River Mersey preparing to dock at Liverpool.** *B&A Feilden.*

was returned to service and sailed from Southampton between 1919 and 1922 before reverting to Liverpool. Whilst on the return leg from New York on 30 September 1923 the *Cedric* collided with Cunard's *Scythia* in dense fog near the Tuskar Rock Light in the St. George's Channel, off the Irish coast. During the impact three passengers and one crewman of the *Scythia* were hurt when they fell. The *Cedric* sustained only minor damage but the *Scythia* had received a large hole in her starboard side forward above the water line, necessitating her to return to Liverpool for repairs.

Again, whilst at New York on 26 December 1924, fire broke out in one of the *Cedric's* holds in which 102 bales of Peruvian cotton had been previously been loaded. The ship remained undamaged but the cargo of cotton was condemned. Under the IMMCo she was placed on the Boston route and during a call there on 12 September 1926, she was about to dock when she started to drift colliding

Below: **The *Cedric* photographed leaving Liverpool for the breakers on 11 January 1932. Note that the open promenades on the boat and promenade decks have been rigged with storm tarpaulins for the voyage to Japan.** *B&A Feilden.*

with a river steamer, the *Van*, moored at its berth. During this brush the riverboat's starboard side planking was broken and a guardrail smashed.

By 1928, the *Cedric's* passenger accommodation was converted to Cabin class only, in keeping with some of the newer liners coming into service. As such she made her last sailing from Liverpool to New York on 5 September 1931, her place on the Liverpool to New York service being taken by the new 27,000 grt motor liner *Britannic*. Later that year the *Cedric* was sold to Thos. W. Ward for £22,150 and she left Liverpool on 11 January 1932 for Inverkeithing to be scrapped.

CEDRIC: *Was an early Anglo-Saxon Chieftain.*

VICTORIAN

(1903-1916) 8,825 grt; 512 ft 6 in BP x 59 ft 3 in
Triple Expansion SR Engine, Single Screw,
4,500 ihp, 13 knots
Passengers: 60 Second class (Saloon)
Harland & Wolff, Belfast. Yard No. 291

Of the large fleet owned by the Liverpool firm of Frederick Leyland & Co, the main consisted of cargo ships. Apart from their Mediterranean interests which were later disposed of, the Company maintained various services across the North Atlantic, principally on the Boston trade. After the Company became part of the IMMCo in 1902 there was much flexibility and interchange of tonnage between the ships that came under the Group's sphere of interest.

The *Victorian* was built for Frederick Leyland during 1895 and launched by Harland & Wolff at Belfast on 7 July 1895. Like the White Star ships of the late Victorian era, she had four masts and the hull was of three-island type, the illusion of a flush weather deck being caused by the

Above: **This photograph shows the *Victorian* in her Leyland Line livery in 1899 as a Boer War Transport *No 66*. In 1903, she was chartered by White Star for six voyages.**
Nautical Photo Agency.

fitting of full height bulwarks in the wells. There were four hatches forward and three aft of the machinery space. Much of the 'tween deck space was fitted out for the carriage of cattle which formed the mainstay of Leyland's business, apart from passenger accommodation. Large for a cargo ship with a depth of hold of 35 ft and a displacement tonnage of 17,200 tons, she was the first Leyland ship to be certificated to carry more than the statutory 12 passengers. Her single triple expansion engine was supplied with steam at 190 psi by two double-ended and two single-ended boilers.

The *Victorian* sailed on her maiden voyage from Liverpool to Boston on 7 September 1895. From November 1899 she was requisitioned as a transport for the Boer War, in which capacity she transported mainly horses and supplies to South Africa. She was used almost exclusively in this role until November 1902, designated as Transport No 66. With effect from 28 February 1903 she was transferred within the IMMCo group to White Star management but without a change of ownership, and on 24 April she joined other cattle ships on the Liverpool-New York service for six round voyages. In 1904 the *Victorian* remained in Leyland ownership but was operated by White Star having been repainted in White Star livery. This continued until 1910 when she reinstated her Leyland livery.

Whilst in her new White Star colours, on 31 October 1904, the *Victorian* docked at Liverpool following a small fire in the hold stowed with cotton when still at sea; as a result, 254 bales were condemned. Following the start of World War 1, she was called up as an Armed Merchant Cruiser in August 1914 and renamed *Russian*, at the request of the Admiralty. This name change was possibly to avoid her being confused with Allan Line's *Victorian* of 1905. Just two years later on 14 December 1916, whilst in the Mediterranean, in ballast on a voyage from Thessalonica to Newport in South Wales, she was torpedoed and sunk by German submarine *UB-43* some 210 miles east of Malta, with the loss of 28 lives.

ARMENIAN

(1903-1915) 8,825 grt; 512 ft 6 in BP x 59 ft 3 in
Triple Expansion SR Engine, Single Screw,
4,500 ihp, 13 knots
Passengers: 60 Second class (Saloon)
Harland & Wolff, Belfast. Yard No. 292

The *Armenian* was built as a sister to the *Victorian* by Harland & Wolff for Frederick Leyland's cattle and cargo service from Liverpool to Boston. She was launched on 25 July 1895 and delivered two months later. She sailed on her maiden voyage from Liverpool to Boston on 28 September 1895. Along with her sister the *Victorian*, she was taken up for Boer War transport from November 1899 until 1902 in which role she completed six round voyages to Cape Town, carrying horses and munitions.

Following the take-over by IMMCo the prestige of White Star increased enormously by its association with the Group. However the reverse was the case with the Leyland and Dominion Lines. Leyland withdrew from the Liverpool-New York service in February 1903 in deference to White Star, which took over the Dominion Lines Liverpool to Boston service and fleet later in the year. From 20 March 1903, the *Armenian* transferred to White Star management but not ownership and joined the cattle and cargo service between Liverpool and New York along with the *Victorian*, *Georgic* (1895), *Bovic* (1892) and *Cevic* (1894). Along with the *Victorian* she carried Second class passengers; they were rated as 'Saloon' passengers, which in effect was an early attempt at re-grading of First class accommodation to what would eventually become known as 'Cabin class'. However on 17 December 1903 both ships carried their last passengers and they ceased carrying any forthwith.

During one such voyage on 5 October 1903 while 145 miles east of Sandy Hook on the approach to New York Harbour, the *Armenian* suffered engine failure and had to heave to, to effect repairs. The passing liner *Finland*, on seeing the 'Not under command' signal, offered assistance but the *Armenian* refused and made good repairs. On 20 May 1907, while at New York's Pier 40, there was a Longshoremen's strike. Strikebreaking labour was brought in to unload the *Armenian*'s cargo which in No1 hold consisted

Above: **This photograph shows the *Armenian* in her Frederick Leyland livery, she was used for transporting horses to South Africa during the Boer War. She served White Star's cargo service between Liverpool and New York for nearly seven years.** *ScanpixTR.*

of cork and bleaching powder. A fire mysteriously broke out in this hold but was put out after half an hour.

Later that same year on 25 November, having arrived at Liverpool from New York, she was being manoeuvred into the lock basin of Sandon Dock by the tender *Magnetic* when the towrope snapped. The *Armenian* was carried by the tide against the wall of the lock, this buckling a number of the plates on the ship's port quarter and starboard side. When a tow was once more gained she was berthed in Canada Dock for survey. During 1908, there was a serious slump on the North Atlantic and White Star's cargo service was withdrawn between the beginning of June and the end of October. Subsequently the Company lost its reputation for strict regularity, and there were several occasions when it was suspended again for months on end.

During 1910, she reverted to the Leyland Line pink funnel livery and sailed on her last voyage for them on 3 March 1914 before being laid up. Following the outbreak of World War 1, the *Armenian* was commandeered as a transport for horses to France, but later on 28 June 1915 she became Leyland's first casualty of the war. She was first fired on by German submarine *U-24* some 40 miles off the Cornish coast after the crew had abandoned ship and later torpedoed and sunk in approximate position 50°40′N; 06°24′W. She had been carrying 1,400 mules from Newport News to Avonmouth destined for use by the army in France. Nine of her crew and 29 mule handlers were killed.

ARABIC (II)

(1903-1915)
15,801 grt; 600 ft 8 in BP (616 ft OA) x 65 ft 6 in
Quadruple Expansion SR Engines, Twin screw,
9,800 ihp, 16 knots
Passengers: 200 First class; 200 Second class;
1,000 Third class
Harland & Wolff, Belfast. Yard No. 340

The first and largest of the several passenger liners transferred to White Star after their acquisition by the IMMCo. She had originally been laid down at Harland & Wolff as Atlantic Transport Line's *Minnewaska*, but due to the internal transfer was launched on 18 December 1902 as the *Arabic* for White Star. The *Arabic* was a typical example of what was classified as an intermediate ship and she was completed on lines very different to those originally specified. In her intended configuration, the requirement was originally for a very large cargo capacity and rather limited passenger accommodation for First class only. Instead, she was completed on 21 June 1903, with a greater passenger space for First, Second and Third classes. If built as the *Minnewaska*, she would have been constructed with only one midship block of superstructure, this with a 170 ft continuous bridge deck as its base with only a small deckhouse aft. In her completed state the *Arabic*'s superstructure remained the same length but was given an open base, while there was a separate island bridgehouse block with the officers' accommodation forward with two other short blocks aft. The final state had a considerable affect on the *Arabic*'s gross tonnage. The masts and funnel positions and height of the funnel remained unchanged.

With the acquisition of the Dominion Line ships, White Star had a fleet of 10 passenger liners on the New York and Boston service. It was originally planned that the *Arabic* would enter the Liverpool to Boston trade but in the event

Above: **The *Arabic* of 1903. She later became a war loss when she was sunk off the Old Head of Kinsale in August 1915 with a loss of 44 lives. Here she is seen departing Liverpool for the United States.** *World Ship Photo Library.*

she was switched from this schedule and sailed on her maiden voyage from Liverpool to New York on 26 June 1903, instead. On this route her consorts were initially the *Celtic*, *Cedric* and *Cymric*, but within a few months the *Cymric* was transferred to the Boston route. Nearly two years later on 14 April 1905, the *Arabic* joined her, having been released by the newly built *Baltic*; but alternated with New York as the United States terminus as the passenger trade demanded. In the early part of the 20th century the cruising type of voyage had gained popularity and during 1905 the *Arabic* made the first of several annual spring cruises to the Mediterranean.

In 1907, so as to capture some of the Continental passenger traffic, White Star Line transferred its main New York service from Liverpool to Southampton. Their four large liners, the *Oceanic* (1899), *Majestic* (1890), *Teutonic* (1889) and the *Adriatic* (1907), the last of the 'Big Four' made the Hampshire port their terminus. Concurrently, a new Thursday service from Liverpool was started with the *Baltic*, *Celtic*, *Cedric* and the *Arabic*. As such the *Arabic* departed on the new schedule for New York on 20 June 1907. Whilst docked at Liverpool on 30 June 1911 fires

broke out five times during the day in different cabins and store rooms around the ship. They were thought to have been caused by planted incendiary devices and were put out after causing minor damage.

Following the *Olympic*'s entry into service and her maiden voyage from Southampton on 22 June 1911, the *Adriatic* switched to the Liverpool to New York service in August that year. This released the *Arabic* from the New York run and she returned to the Boston route resuming her sailing on 1 August 1911. During 1913, the *Arabic*'s passenger accommodation was re-graded, First class was discontinued and she became designated a Cabin class ship. At the same time extra lifeboats were added in accordance with the new Board of Trade (BoT) regulations following the loss of the *Titanic* in 1912. On 16 September 1914, the *Arabic* arrived at Liverpool from Boston under the command of Captain Finch. Fires were under way in Nos 1 and 2 holds as she docked. The *Arabic*'s crew together with the Liverpool Fire Brigade brought the blazes under control and extinguished them.

After the start of World War 1 in August 1914, White Star's 'Big Four' were requisitioned as AMCs, in order to fill the commercial vacuum this created, the *Arabic* was transferred to the New York service on 23 December 1914 and retained her peacetime livery. Eight months later on 19 August 1915, whilst outward bound from Liverpool for New York with 434 passengers and crew on board, the *Arabic* was off the Old Head of Kinsale outside Queenstown, when German Submarine *U-24* under the command of Lieutenant Commander Schneider torpedoed her. The torpedo which struck the *Arabic*'s starboard side aft, effectively severed the ship in two and she sank within seven minutes in position 50° 50′ N, 08° 32′ W. Prompt action

Below: **A three-quarter stern view of the *Arabic* taken some time after 1912. Note the plethora of nested collapsible lifeboats; these were carried following recommendations of safety at sea after the *Titanic* disaster.** *Eric Johnson.*

and a disciplined evacuation in so short a time enabled 390 people to be taken off safely but 44 lives were lost including some Americans. The action was contrary to a German Government announcement that passenger ships would be given sufficient warning to allow passengers to disembark, especially since the Cunarder *Lusitania* had been sunk 3 months earlier in the same locality by *U-20*!

The United States Government exchanged diplomatic notes with Germany over the incident, demanding an explanation for the attack apparently without warning. In response the Germans claimed that the Commander had attacked in self-defence believing that the *Arabic* was about to ram his U-boat. Assurances that such an attack would not be repeated proved sufficient to appease growing public concern in the United States, albeit temporarily. In May 1996, the *Arabic's* wreck was located in 361 ft of water but much further out in the Western Approaches than was originally supposed. White Star Historian Paul Louden-Brown was Project Historian on the subsequent dive that took place on the wreck in an attempt to locate a consignment of gold bullion. It was thought that the *Arabic* was carrying a cargo of gold bars, £4.7 million at 1915 prices (£200 million at 1990s prices) bound for the United States in payment for munitions being sent to Britain. No gold was found but many artefacts such as company crockery were recovered from the wreck's stern section.

ROMANIC

(1903-1912)
11,394 grt; 550 ft 4 in BP (566 ft OA) x 59 ft 4 in
Triple Expansion SR Engines, Twin Screw,
8,700 ihp, 14 knots
Passengers: 200 First class, 200 Second class, 800 Third class
Harland & Wolff, Belfast. Yard No. 315

The Dominion Line in the summer seasons of the 1890s was running a service from Liverpool to Quebec and Montreal and in winter to Halifax and Portland, Maine. A new liner, the *Canada*, had made a name for herself on the Canadian run, then inaugurated a winter service to Boston. This proved so successful for the company that she was retained on this route during the summer season. New tonnage was then purposely built for the Boston trade. The first of these was launched on 7 April 1898 as the *New England*; the others being the *Commonwealth*, *Mayflower* and *Columbus*. The *New England* was originally built for the Dominion Line's profitable Liverpool to Boston and Boston to the Mediterranean trade. Her net tonnage was 7,416, with a deadweight capacity of 9,800 tons. There were three overall decks with promenade and boat decks above and six holds and six hatchways. Like the rest of the four ships completed, she had the appearance of being a flushed-deck ship, although Lloyd's Register listed her as 'Forecastle 70 ft, bridge 318 ft, poop 92 ft'. This would leave 'wells' in way of

Nos 1 and 5 hatchways which could have been decked over and enclosed by bulkheads. However with these wells having open scuppers this was a means of reducing gross tonnage.

The *New England* was a twin screw ship and her Harland & Wolff built engines were 4-cylinder, triple expansion steam reciprocating type with cylinders of 30½ in, 50¼ in, 58 in and 58 in bore, with a stroke of 54 in. They produced an ihp of 8,700 which could give a maximum speed of 15 knots. There were three double-ended and three single single-ended boilers consuming 160 tons of coal per day; her bunker capacity was for 3,680 tons. The *New England* departed on her maiden voyage from Liverpool to Boston on 30 June 1898. After the IMMCo take-over of the White Star and Dominion Lines in 1902, the combine shuffled ships from one company to another in order to maximise on IMMCo profits and streamline operational efficiency throughout the combine. Almost immediately from the take-over, White Star assumed the Dominion Line's profitable routes.

Subsequently the *New England* departed Liverpool on her last trip for Dominion on 17 September 1903 and two months later in November the she was sold internally along with her three consorts and renamed the *Romanic*. She was retained on the Liverpool to Boston route but it was to be the first sailing by White Star service to Boston and the *Romanic* departed on this on 19 November 1903. An opportunity was identified in the lucrative market for emigrants leaving Italy and Sicily bound for a new life in the United States as there was a dearth of Italian-flag passenger vessels at the time. White Star seized this opportunity to fill this vacuum by placing a fleet of its ships on this route. To this end the *Romanic* (appropriately named), along with other units, was switched to the United States to the Mediterranean service. She commenced on this route sailing from Boston on 5 December 1903 to Naples and Genoa with calls at the Azores and Gibraltar. The westbound sailing would be in the reverse order, with the call at Naples to pick up Sicilian passengers that had crossed the Messina Straits to join the ship.

On 12 July 1907, whilst in thick fog off the Nantucket Shoals lightship, the *Romanic* collided with a 66-ton fishing schooner, the *Natalie B. Nickerson*. The schooner with a crew of 18 sunk with a loss of three lives and the survivors were picked up by the *Romanic* and landed at Boston. The *Romanic* was a regular and reliable ship on the route for some eight years and in that time she became well established and liked by the travellers; the ship's name had been well chosen! The growth of Italy's own merchant fleet began to displace the British-flag White Star vessels on the Mediterranean route and on 22 November 1911 the *Romanic* arrived in Boston on her last westbound crossing returning to Genoa to await disposal. She made a positioning voyage sailing from Genoa to Glasgow on 3 January 1912 and later that month was sold to the Glasgow based Allan Line. She was renamed *Scandinavian* and her accommodation refitted to carry 400 Second and 800 Third class passengers, in this time her gross tonnage rose to

Above: **The *Romanic*, formerly Dominion Line's *New England*. This was White Star's initiative to capitalise on the passenger traffic between Italy, Sicily and the United States. She is seen here in Mediterranean waters.**
Richard de Kerbrech Collection.

12,099 tons. She commenced on her service for Allan on 23 March 1912 between Glasgow to Halifax and Boston on their winter itinerary. Nearly two months later on 4 May, she switched to the Glasgow to Quebec and Montreal, Canadian summer service.

Following the outbreak of World War 1, she carried troops of the Canadian Expeditionary Force to Glasgow on 22 August 1914. With effect from 1 October 1915 the Allan Line interests and fleet were bought by Canadian Pacific Ocean Services but the *Scandinavian* continued on their service. Between 1917 and 1918 she was operated under the Liner Requisition Scheme and on 22 August 1918 made her first voyage for her owners between Liverpool and New York and three months later on 19 November switched to the Liverpool to St John, New Brunswick route.

In an attempt to fill the vacuum left by Belgian ships following the War, she was placed on the Antwerp-Southampton-Quebec-Montreal; route departing from the continental terminal on 18 May 1920. This she maintained regularly for two years but by 1922 there was a surplus of ships plying this route. She made her last westbound voyage on 24 May that year and was laid up the following July at Falmouth, awaiting disposal. In January 1923 she was moved up to the Gareloch and on 9 July 1923 she was sold for breaking up to F. Rijsdik of Rotterdam. One week later on 16 July she was resold to Klasmann & Lentze of Emden and during October that year she was moved to Hamburg for scrapping.

ROMANIC: *Of or pertaining to the Romans.*

CRETIC

(1903-1923)
13,518 grt; 582 ft BP (601 ft OA) x 60 ft 4 in
Triple Expansion SR Engines, Twin Screw,
8,500 ihp, 15 knots
Passengers: 260 First class, 250 Second class,
1,000 Third class

R. & W. Hawthorn, Leslie & Co, Hebburn-on-Tyne
Yard No. 381

Built in 1902 by Hawthorn, Leslie & Co. at Hebburn-on-Tyne for Frederick Leyland & Co. She was launched on 25 February 1902 as the *Hanoverian* and as such was Leyland's largest ship at the time, catering for 260 First class passengers only. She departed on her maiden voyage from Liverpool to Boston on 19 July 1902. After completing only three round voyages Frederick Leyland was absorbed into the IMMCo combine and the *Hanoverian* was transferred to the Dominion Line, also within the group, and her accommodation was extended to take Second and Third class passengers also. She was renamed *Mayflower* and made her first voyage under this new name from Liverpool to Boston on 9 April 1903. Later that year, after having made seven round voyages, she was sold within the group to White Star, along with the other liners owned by the Dominion Line, namely, *New England* (1898), *Commonwealth* (1900), and the *Columbus* (1903). The *Mayflower* was again renamed and became the *Cretic*, and went on to give White Star 20 years service; these as we shall see, were not without incident.

The *Cretic* made her first voyage as a White Star liner from Liverpool to Boston on 19 November 1903. After 10 round trips she was transferred to the Mediterranean service to capture the lucrative emigrant market of Italians and Sicilians travelling to the United States. She inaugurated this service during November 1904, sailing from Boston to Naples and Genoa then back to New York via Naples and Boston, arriving at New York on 7 December. On 25 November 1907, whilst en route from New York to Genoa, the *Cretic*'s main steam pipe burst as she was steaming

Above: **The *Romanic* was probably the first liner with two masts in White Star service.** *Nautical Photo Agency.*

through the Mediterranean. She put into the nearest port, Algiers, for repairs to enable her to complete the journey. Fifteen months later, on 23 February 1909, with nearly a full complement of 1,100 passengers aboard, the *Cretic* was inbound to Boston from the Azores when she grounded on the Centurion Ledge inside Boston harbour. She was refloated after half-an-hour but failed to answer her helm and went aground again. Red distress rockets were fired to summon help and with the aid of Boston harbour tugs the *Cretic* was refloated the following day.

A month after this untimely delay another more frightening incident occurred on 26 March while she was crossing to New York. Straw in the mattress of a Steerage class passenger had caught fire (was this as a result of smoking in the bunk?). A minor panic ensued and several Steerage passengers stormed the Cabin accommodation in a threatening manner. They were placated and sent back and the fire extinguished immediately. On 2 May 1910, whilst on a voyage from New York to Genoa via Naples, the *Cretic* badly damaged one of her propellers. She was drydocked at Naples for repairs before the return leg of the voyage. On 21 November 1911, she made her last trip from Genoa to New York as her terminus switching to Boston during March 1912.

A major breakdown occurred again on 18 September 1913, the *Cretic* limped into Gibraltar harbour after one of her main engine crankshafts had broken during the Atlantic crossing. Her scheduled sailing itinerary was cancelled and she was drydocked at Naples where repairs were carried out. Whilst berthed at New York on 26 September 1914, fire broke out in *Cretic*'s No3 hold. Two New York fireboats attended to help tackle the fire with a minor loss to the cargo carried in that hold. After the outbreak of World War 1, in August 1914, the *Cretic* along with the *Canopic* continued on the Mediterranean service. She left Genoa on 17 March 1915 on the Naples-Boston-New York itinerary. Later she operated on the Liner Requisition Scheme between 13 May 1917 until 22 February 1919.

One documented incident during this time occurred on 26 October 1917 when shortly after leaving a Mediterranean port. Fire was discovered in her No1 hold which was loaded with a consignment of Turkish tobacco. In an attempt to extinguish the fire the hold was flooded causing the *Cretic* to trim by the bow, without success. Upon reaching the Azores, fire appliances there pumped in more water and brought the fire under control, albeit temporarily. The fire reignited after she resumed her voyage and it was only when she eventually docked at Liverpool that the fire was fully extinguished. By January 1918, she made her last crossing from Genoa to Boston where she arrived on 31st of that month, hereafter the eastbound voyage terminated at Liverpool. Between April 1918 and 5 September 1919 she was deployed on the Liverpool to New York service. On one of these she left Liverpool on 13 March 1919 for New York via Halifax where she disembarked 2,000 Canadian troops returning from the war in Europe. After her release from wartime duties the *Cretic*'s accommodation was re-graded to carry 300 First class, 210 Second class and 800 Third class and following this she was reinstated on White Star's Mediterranean service along with the *Canopic* departing New York on 24 September 1919.

Whilst berthed at Genoa on 14 August 1920 and raising steam, the main steam stop valve on one of the *Cretic*'s boilers blew out severely scalding six and killing one of those working nearby. By 1922, the *Cretic* had become surplus to requirements on the route having been largely displaced by the growth of Italian passenger liners and she made her last westbound crossing from Genoa on 18 October that year. In June 1923, she was sold back to her original owners Frederick Leyland & Co. and renamed *Devonian.* As such she reverted to their Liverpool to Boston service but this time with an accommodation for 250 Cabin class passengers only.

In April 1926, the Cabin was re-graded as 'Tourist Third cabin' and from 10 December 1927 until 9 March 1928 the *Devonian* completed three round voyages for the Red Star Line sailing New York-Plymouth-Antwerp Eastbound and Antwerp-Southampton-New York Westbound. Following these, which terminated at New York, she then repositioned to Philadelphia and then completed two and a half round voyages, leaving Boston for the last time on 15 September 1928, before being laid up. The following January she was sold for breaking up to P. & W. McLellan, Bo'ness on the Firth of Forth.

So a passenger ship which rolled among the companies of the IMMCo and seemed to have been notorious for a string of engine failures, managed to give the combine a creditable life span of 27 years.

CRETIC: *Of or pertaining to Crete, the island in the Eastern Mediterranean.*

REPUBLIC (II)

(1903-1909)
15,378 grt; 570 ft BP (585 ft OA) x 67 ft 8 in
Quadruple Expansion SR Engines, Twin Screw,
10,500 ihp, 16 knots
Passengers: 1,200
Harland & Wolff, Belfast. Yard No. 345

Harland & Wolff originally built the *Republic* as the *Columbus* in 1903 for the Dominion Line. She was launched as such on 26 February 1903 and handed over on 12 September that year. The *Columbus* sailed on her maiden voyage for Dominion from Liverpool to Boston on 1 October 1903. After the Dominion Line became part of the IMMCo and having completed only two round voyages, she was transferred to White Star that same year and renamed *Republic*. She made her first voyage for White Star from Liverpool to Boston on 17 December 1903.

From 2 January until 27 April 1904, the *Republic* was switched to the Boston-Naples-Genoa Mediterranean service along with her consorts *Canopic*, *Cretic* and *Romanic* to capitalise on the Italian and Sicilian emigrant trade to the United States. However, from May until 22 September that year she was returned to the Liverpool to Boston service. During one of her turnarounds at Boston, on 3 June 1904, the *Republic* was in collision with the Canadian Atlantic & Plant Steamship Co's steamer *Halifax*, which forced the latter ashore. Although neither ship was seriously damaged,

Above: **An early photograph of the *Cretic* at anchor in the River Mersey ready to sail.** *Nautical Photo Agency.*

the *Halifax*'s owners brought a court action against White Star, claiming that the *Republic*'s officers were negligent. During that October she was again switched back to the Boston-Naples-Genoa-Naples-New York route; in fact during subsequent voyages, the *Republic* was employed on the New York to Mediterranean run in autumn and winter and the Liverpool-Boston service during spring and summer.

Some three years later on 16 February 1907, as the *Republic* was entering Naples harbour, she was in collision with the Italian steamer *Centro America*, in which both ships sustained some damage. On 28 December 1908, whilst the *Republic* was berthed at Genoa being victualled, an earthquake struck at Messina in Sicily, claiming the lives of some 85,000 people. Many of the survivors decided to emigrate to the United States. The *Republic* departed on schedule from Genoa on 30 December and left Naples on 2 January 1909 with several earthquake survivors bound for New York, where she arrived on 14 January. In the meantime on 10 January, the Lloyd Italiano's liner *Florida*, which was fully booked as a result of the earthquake, departed Naples for New York. On board were 18 Cabin class passengers and 824 Steerage, many rendered homeless by the Messina earthquake, along with a cargo of macaroni. The *Florida* and the *Republic*'s eventual paths were to bring them into a collision course. The *Republic*, which had recently been fitted with Marconi's latest wireless telegraphy equipment, was under the command of Captain William Inman Sealby. The *Republic* loaded 650 tons worth of food and provisions for Rear Admiral Sperry's fleet and, it was rumoured, some £50,000 in gold bound for the United States Navy at Gibraltar. Along with these were the first relief supplies for the Messina earthquake victims bound for Naples. In addition to all this valuable frozen and perishable cargo there were 525 passengers and 297 crew on board.

Above: **The *Cretic* was originally built for Frederick Leyland as their *Hanoverian* before being transferred to White Star. This post-1912 photograph of her at sea shows her with rows of nested lifeboats, following the *Titanic* disaster.** *Eric Johnson.*

As a possible portent of what was to come, at 1500 hours (3pm) on 22 January 1909 as the *Republic* manoeuvred astern from her New York pier she clipped the steamer *Bermudian*, before getting underway and clearing New York harbour bound for the Mediterranean. In the meantime the *Florida* was in the final 36 hours of her westbound crossing. Into the early hours of 23 January, the *Republic* and *Florida* were about 175 miles east of the Ambrose Lightship in the approaches to New York harbour and groping their way through thick fog in the vicinity of the Nantucket Lightship The *Florida*, unlike the *Republic*, had not been fitted with wireless telegraphy. (This seems somewhat ironical that an Italian ship had not taken up an invention by an Italian aristocrat!).

At 5.40 am, the *Florida*'s lookout suddenly saw the *Republic* looming out of the fog. Both ships were on collision course and no evasive action was possible and the *Florida*'s stem drove into the *Republic*'s port side, just aft of amidships, gashing her all the way down and laying her engine room open to the sea. Apart from her bow compartments being stove in, the *Florida* suffered little damage and was protected by her collision bulkhead from sinking; therefore was able to manoeuvre astern from the collision. Things were more serious on the *Republic*, for her engine room was quickly flooded and she started to list to port. The ship's generator failed and she was plunged into darkness. Although the wireless office was slightly damaged the Wireless Officer, Jack Binns, was able to transmit the distress call CQD (in reality 'CQ' meant 'Attention all Stations' and 'D' indicated a distress call) at 6 am. This is believed to be the first radio distress message in the history of sea travel!

The signal was picked up by Marconi's own land station at Siasconsett, who relayed the message on to the White Star's *Baltic* which was then nearing New York. She promptly turned back and began a long search for the *Republic*. French Line's *La Lorraine* also answered the distress call with 'I am coming', as she was about 120 miles from the scene. Her captain, Commandant Tournier relayed the message to Cunard Line's *Lucania* as he believed her to be nearer, and he also advised Captain Sealby to 'Make all the noise you can.' Other ships alerted were Anchor Line's *Furnessia* and American Line's *New York*. Sounding the *Republic*'s siren could have proved confusing for a ship attempting the rescue, for the Nantucket Lightship was somewhere in the vicinity also sounding her foghorn and ringing her bell. Nevertheless the *Florida*, guided by the ship's siren, had returned to the *Republic* and taken on board all her passengers and crew who had evacuated their stricken ship without panic. All but 47 stayed aboard in the hopes of salvage.

Owing to the thick fog the *Baltic* did not arrive on the scene until later in the day at 7 pm. When she did she transferred all the passengers from both the *Florida* and the *Republic*, some 1,700 people in all. This was carried out in the early hours of the next morning, using the *Baltic*'s, *Republic*'s and the *Florida*'s lifeboats, under the glare of the *Baltic*'s searchlight, and over a period of seven hours. The *Florida* was able to return to New York under her own steam but the *Republic* was starting to founder. Attempts by attending US Revenue cutters *Senaca* and *Gresham* and the *Furnessia* to tow the *Republic* proved fruitless and by 4pm Captain Sealby ordered the skeleton crew to Abandon Ship. She sank by the stern at 8.30pm in 34 fathoms of water off Martha's Vineyard; her Master was rescued from the sea. In all four lives were lost as a result of the collision. On 24 January, the *Florida* was escorted into New York by the US Revenue cutter *Senaca*. The *Baltic* returned to New York with the survivors aboard. Captain Sealby and Wireless Officer Binns were hailed as heroes and a newspaper of the day carried in its editorial a tribute to: 'The men of steady nerves and courageous hearts who, patiently and skilfully, directed the splendid rescue - and who are willingly sharing

the thankfulness and gratitude of the country with Mr Marconi, whose wireless telegraphy made it possible.'

Indeed, this successful rescue aroused great interest in wireless communication and there was an immediate call for the necessary apparatus to be fitted to all large ships. This marked an immense improvement in the safety of life at sea; ironically, no such revision was made to the BoT lifeboat capacity regulations accordingly. Following the collision, the White Star Line sued Lloyd Italiano for negligence to the tune of £400,000 through the United States' courts. They were successful and were compensated after the *Florida* had been sold for around £40,000. The *Republic* was supposedly carrying some £50,000 in gold along with a shipment of newly minted Golden Eagle dollar coins; however when her wreck was located in 1987 by a United States salvage expedition, no gold was found.

As a more fitting tribute to the *Republic* and its rescue, a silver medal was struck later in 1909 called the CQD Medal. Its reverse read: 'From the Saloon Passengers of the RMS *Baltic* and RMS *Republic*,' and cited: 'To the officers and crews of the SS *Republic*, *Baltic* and *Florida* for Gallantry. Commemorating the rescue of over 1,700 souls Jan 24th 1909.' A fitting tribute to a rescue that was undertaken with minimum loss of life and one in which wireless telegraphy had played its first major role in rescue at sea.

CANOPIC

(1904-1924)
12,097grt; 578 ft 4 in BP (594 ft OA) x 59 ft 4 in
Triple Expansion SR Engines, Twin Screw,
8,700 ihp, 16 knots
Passengers: 275 First class, 232 Second class,
770 Third class
Harland & Wolff, Belfast. Yard No. 330

As with other Dominion Line liners of the day the *Commonwealth* was designed primarily for their Liverpool-Boston service. She was built by Harland & Wolff at Belfast and launched on 31 May 1900 with a net tonnage of 7,717 and a large deadweight capacity of 11,380 tons and a displacement of 21,780 tons on a load draught of 30 ft 5 in. Her length/beam ratio made her on the narrow lines as with earlier Harland & Wolff ships and her depth was 35 ft 10 in. She had three overall decks and nine main bulkheads with a full-length double bottom. Six holds and hatchways were served by derricks on the masts and on two pairs of derrick posts, during cargo handling great use was made of spans.

The *Commonwealth*'s outward appearance was that of a 'flush decker' but she was really a three-island type with the well decks plated over and large doors fitted abreast them, two forward and one aft. Promenade and boat decks extended over about 193 ft amidships. Her propelling machinery consisted of two sets of 4-cylinder, triple expansion engines, each with cylinder bores of 29½, 50, 50, and 58 in diameter with a stroke of 54 in. There were three double-ended and three single-ended cylindrical boilers with all the uptakes being led to a single large oval-sectioned funnel. The machinery, all built by Harland & Wolff, gave the ship a speed of 16 knots and in fact it is recorded that she made an occasional voyage at an average of 16.5 knots.

The *Commonwealth*'s original passenger accommodation catered for 275 First, 232 Second, and 770 Third or Steerage but these numbers often varied to some extent. Upon her delivery on 22 September 1900 her appearance was one of a pleasing but simple design, with a single imposing funnel midway between her two masts. The hull had a graceful sheer with narrow lines and the typical Harland & Wolff features of a straight stem and counter stern. She was registered at Liverpool under the ownership of the British & North Atlantic Steam Navigation Co. Ltd and sailed on her maiden voyage from Liverpool to Boston on 4 October 1900. During her first few crossings the *Commonwealth* was found to be rather large for the winter service so she completed the last of her initial voyages to Boston on 16 November 1901 and transferred to the Boston-Naples-Genoa-service. She commenced on these that November for three round voyages trial service before returning to the Liverpool-Boston route on 10 April 1902.

By this time the Dominion Line as with White Star were being targeted by the IMMCo Combine, who were not so much interested in Dominion's Canadian services, but felt there was a strong potential on the established Boston route that Dominion had forged. This was a success that singled them out as an obvious concern to include in the general take over. At the end of 1902 the Dominion Line was absorbed into IMMCo's control. White Star was by far the largest and most influential company in the new combine and was soon to be favoured, for towards the end of 1903 they took over the Boston services of the Dominion Line and its four latest ships. To this end the *Commonwealth* completed her last voyage as a Dominion liner from Liverpool to Boston on 5 November 1903 before being transferred to White Star and renamed *Canopic*. The other three involved in the transfer were the *New England*, *Columbus* and *Mayflower*, which were renamed *Romanic*, *Republic* and *Cretic* respectively. As a form of 'compensation' the cattle and cargo ships *Nomadic* and *Tauric* were transferred to the Dominion Line and two years later the ageing *Germanic* was altered to suit her for the Canadian service and handed over to them as the *Ottawa*. In some small way this sought to redress the imbalance on this route.

The *Canopic* made her first voyage under White Star, from Liverpool to Boston on 14 January 1904 before returning from Boston to Naples and Genoa on the successful Italian and Sicilian emigrant trade and settling into this route for the next 10 years. This itinerary took in

Above: **On 9 January 1909, the *Republic* collided with the Italian liner *Florida* off Nantucket and sank.** *World Ship Photo Library.*

Boston to the Azores, Gibraltar, Naples, Genoa and back in consort with the *Romanic* and *Cretic*. Later on, New York became the North American terminal in place of Boston. The three liners proved very popular with their Mediterranean clientele but by 1908 competition was mounting from some home-grown Italian shipping companies introducing their own passenger ships on the lucrative route.

On 23 November 1910, a day after leaving Naples, a fire broke out in a hold beneath the *Canopic*'s Steerage accommodation. Both officers and crew fought the blaze while over 1,000 passengers slept, unaware of the turmoil going on under them. After four hours the fire was extinguished and the debris washed away. By 1912, the competition had gained such momentum that the *Romanic* was sold to the Allan Line and renamed *Scandinavian*. The *Canopic* and *Cretic* remained to carry on the service on their own. The *Canopic* had remained much the same in appearance from her time with the Dominion Line, but at some time, possibly following the *Titanic* disaster that year, her appearance was slightly changed by the extension of her promenade deck forward to join up with the short deck abreast the foremast. An additional set of boats and davits was fitted on each side on this extension. The following year, on 14 October 1913, she was manoeuvring in Naples harbour when she collided with and sunk a lighter. During the collision one of the *Canopic*'s propeller blades was sheared off and the other two bent. This required docking and repair.

When World War 1 broke out in 1914, the *Canopic* continued on the Mediterranean service making her first voyage departing New York on 23 August to Naples, Genoa and return. During a particularly strong gale on 27 February 1915, the *Canopic* was berthed at Naples when she broke free from her moorings and fouled three steamers also in port. She damaged all the *Gianicolo*, *Tellus* and *St Ninian* above their waterlines. Between 26 March 1917 and 21 February 1919, she operated under the Liner Requisition Scheme during which time she was involved to some extent in trooping. By March 1918, she resumed Boston as her terminal arriving there on 30 March and following the end of the war she was switched to the Liverpool-Boston-New York route for a single trooping voyage helping return the 'doughboys'. This she undertook from 6 February 1919 after which she was released from Government service and returned to White Star. From 27 February she resumed the New York to the Mediterranean route and was joined seven months later by the *Cretic*, she was once again offering accommodation in three classes. The *Canopic* remained on this route for another two years but in 1921 was replaced by the larger and more modern *Arabic* (ex-*Berlin*). During October 1921 she made her last westbound crossing from Genoa before being transferred to Liverpool.

Following a short refit in which she was converted to cater for 524 Cabin and 656 Third class only. As such she departed Liverpool on 13 April 1922 for Halifax and Boston, for two voyages before being placed on the White Star-Dominion's Liverpool-Canada service for the 1922 summer season. She commenced this itinerary on 13 May making six round voyages from Liverpool-Quebec-Montreal. That same year, White Star saw an opportunity to step in where the practical extinction of the large German companies had left a vacuum, in particular an emigrant service between Bremen and Canada, calling at Cherbourg and crossing to Quebec and Montreal in the summer. To this end, during spring 1922 the Company seized this opportunity and placed the *Vedic* and *Poland* on this route. This soon led to an even larger service between Germany and America and in the November the *Canopic* together with the newer *Pittsburgh* took the places of the earlier pair. The *Canopic* inaugurated this now extended route on 10 November 1922 from Bremen-Southampton-Halifax-New York, however the following year, in November 1923, the German terminal was changed to Hamburg (Cuxhaven).

The *Canopic* along with the *Pittsburgh* had included Southampton in their calls as an opportunity stop and even made an occasional call at Danzig for emigrants, but this service operated by these two vessels only lasted some 18 months or so, for by this time, the emasculated German lines had managed to build up their fleets to operate on their old routes. On 4 May 1924, the *Canopic* made her last westbound crossing from Hamburg to New York, before returning to Liverpool. During September that year she made a single round voyage from Liverpool to Philadelphia before returning to partial layup. She made a final crossing from Liverpool to Portland, Maine on 20 March 1925 and returned to be disposed of. In October 1925 the *Canopic* was sold for scrapping and she was broken up at Briton Ferry in South Wales.

The *Canopic* had proved an asset to White Star with 22 out of her 25 years having been spent in their service, 13 of them on the Mediterranean run. In this time she had proved herself to be a steady, reliable and competent ship. Her appearances in the Mersey and in the UK waters in general were few and far between and she was much better known in Italy and Sicily than in England and it is this clientele with whom she established her goodwill and popularity.

CANOPIC: *Of or pertaining to Canopus, an ancient Egyptian town near Alexandria.*

CUFIC (II)
(1904-1923)
8,249 grt; 475 ft 10 in BP x 55 ft 2 in
Triple Expansion SR Engines, Twin Screw,
2,170 ihp, 11 knots
Passengers: 60 Second class
Harland & Wolff, Belfast. Yard No. 294

During 1895 and 1896, Harland & Wolff launched two cargo ships for the West India & Pacific Steamship Co. of Liverpool, the *American* and the *European*, together the two sisters would follow identical career paths during their operational lives. The *American* was launched on 8 August 1895 and entered service with the West India & Pacific Steamship Co. on 8 October 1895. She sailed on her maiden voyage from Liverpool to New Orleans on 9 October and upon her arrival at the Gulf port loaded a consignment of

Below: **An early photograph of the *Canopic* which had originally been built as the *Columbus*. She was placed on White Star's Mediterranean route.** *Nautical Photo Agency.*

Above: **The *Canopic* in the River Mersey prior to sailing, with the Royal Liver Building in the background**. *B&A Feilden.*

cotton. During 1898, she was chartered by the Atlantic Transport Line and placed on their New Orleans and Baltimore cargo services. However, this service was short-lived for on 1 January 1900, Frederick Leyland & Company bought the entire fleet of West India & Pacific Steamship Co's 20 ships, which was then under the Chairmanship of John Ellerman. The same year the *American* was taken up as a war transport for the Boer War. In 1901 Frederick Leyland was taken over by J. Pierpont Morgan and later incorporated into his IMMCo group in 1902.

The *American* was deployed on White Star's Liverpool to New York service for the best part of 1903 and during the following year she was sold within the group to White Star and renamed *Cufic*. As such, along with her sister, which had been renamed the *Tropic*, she was allocated to White Star's Australian service and sailed on her first voyage from Liverpool to Sydney on 21 May 1904. She maintained this route for cargo only but with berths for Steerage emigrants was also an option, along with the *Afric* (1899), *Medic* (1899), *Persic* (1899), *Runic* (1900) and *Suevic* (1901). With the *Cufic* and *Tropic* now deployed in the trade, the earlier cargo steamers *Nomadic* (1891) and *Tauric* (1891) were transferred by White Star to the Dominion Line. Following the outbreak of World War 1 in August 1914, the *Cufic* was commandeered as a war transport and as such was fitted with two 4.7 in guns, but later during the war she was taken up under the Liner Requisition Scheme between 6 March 1917 and 9 September 1919.

Following the war the *Cufic* returned to the Australian run for four years. A fall back in trade on this route during the early 1920s caused her to be withdrawn and laid up in Liverpool on 24 August 1923. Later in December that year she was sold to G. B. A. Lombardo of Genoa for scrapping and sailed on 13 December 1923 for that port. Upon her arrival at Genoa, on 25 January 1924, she was resold to Soc. Anon. Ligure di Nav. a Vapore (managed by E. Cesano) of

Genoa and renamed *Antartico*. They operated her until 1927 when she was once again sold within Italy to E. Bozzo & L. Mortola and renamed *Maria Giulia*. They operated her in service until 2 April 1930 when she was laid up at Genoa pending disposal. In November 1932 she was scrapped at Genoa. Surprisingly, the *Cufic*, which had remained in White star ownership for 19 years, had a continuous operational career of 35 years prior to being laid up.

TROPIC (II)

(1904-1923) 8,262 grt; 475 ft 10 in BP x 55 ft 2 in
Triple Expansion SR Engines, Twin Screw,
2,170 ihp, 11 knots
Passengers: 60 Second class
Harland & Wolff, Belfast. Yard No. 303

Launched on 9 July 1896, the *European*, along with her sister ship the *American*, was built primarily as a cargo ship by Harland & Wolff for the West India & Pacific Steamship Co. Ltd of Liverpool. Following her completion on 3 December 1896, the *European* sailed on her maiden voyage on 9 January 1897 from Liverpool to New Orleans. She continued in this trade for 3½ years until on 1 January 1900, the Liverpool based Frederick Leyland & Co, under the Chairmanship of John Ellerman, purchased the West India & Pacific Steamship Co.'s entire fleet of 20 ships. Along with her sister the *European* was taken up as a war transport for the Boer War.

In 1901, Frederick Leyland was taken over by J. Pierpont Morgan and later incorporated into the IMMCo group in 1902. During 1904 the *European* was sold within the group to White Star and renamed *Tropic*. As such along with her sister, now the *Cufic*, she was allocated to White Star's Australian service on the meat trade, making her first voyage for them from Liverpool to Sydney in July 1904. It is of interest to note that a source reported that for 29 June 1905: 'The *Tropic* suffered severe damage after going ashore 15 miles north of Constitucion, Chile. Her Second Officer and

BALTIC (II)

(1904-1933)
23,884 grt; 709 ft 2 in BP (725 ft 9 in OA) x 75 ft 7 in
Quadruple Expansion SR Engines, Twin screw,
 14,000 ihp, 16 knots
Passengers: 420 First class, 500 Second class,
 1,800 Third class
Harland & Wolff, Belfast. Yard No. 352

purser reportedly drowned. After being refloated five days later, it was found that decking beneath the engines had buckled, boiler stays had broken, the bottom had been pushed up under the boilers and machinery deranged.' Why the *Tropic* was in this area is not known but it could be that she may have discharged general cargo in Australia, then sailed to New Zealand and loaded for the UK and hence steamed across the Pacific via Cape Horn. On 12 December 1908, she was in collision with the Argonaut Steam Navigation Co's coaster *Wyoming*, off the Skerries.

Following the outbreak of World War 1 in August 1914, the *Tropic* at first remained on the Australian meat run but later was taken up under the Liner Requisition Scheme between 30 June 1917 to 10 July 1919. Upon her release the *Tropic* returned to the Australian service for four years. However, a fall back in trade on that route during the early 1920s expedited her sale in December 1923 to Ditta L. Pittaluga of Genoa, who retained the name. In January 1924, she was sold along with the *Cufic*, to Soc. Anon. Ligure di Nav. a Vapore (E. Cesano) and renamed *Artico*. After three years she was sold back to Pittaluga and renamed *Transilvania*, and operated by them until 2 February 1930 when she was laid up at Genoa for disposal. During 1933 she was scrapped at Genoa. Like her sister the *Cufic*, the *Tropic* had until being laid up, an operational career of 35 years, and 19 of them with White Star.

Following the launch of the *Cedric* on 21 August 1902, the keel and frames of the *Baltic* were already in place at Harland & Wolff's and progress under way when work was suspended on the instructions of White Star. They had advised the builders at this early stage in her construction that they wished to have her launched as the largest ship in the world at the time. This proved to be not such an easy matter for the hull was at an advanced stage, however the centre girder and keel plates were parted amidships and the after portion moved (probably by hydraulic jacks) 27 feet. The gap was framed and plated before the modified sections were joined. (Possibly a portent of what was to come with the new bow section of the *Suevic* in 1907). The inserted length increased her tonnage over the *Cedric* and *Celtic* by 2,840 gross tons, made her 28 feet longer and 3 inches wider in the beam. The extra length made possible considerable improvements in her accommodation and perhaps had a bearing on the *Baltic*'s eventual popularity over her earlier sisters.

Below: **The *Cufic* photographed in the River Mersey outward bound for Australia with her derricks 'topped off' after cargo handling.** *Nautical Photo Agency.*

Above: **The *Tropic*, White Star's last purpose-built cargo ship is seen here anchored in the River Thames off Tilbury, with her derricks ready for cargo handling.** *Nautical Photo Agency.*

The *Baltic* had a net tonnage of 15,119, a displacement of around 39,800 tons and a deadweight capacity of 19,880 tons on a load draught of 37 ft 3 in. She had four full-length decks; shelter, main and lower, with an orlop deck outside machinery spaces and three tiers of superstructure above the weather deck, namely promenade, boat and sun decks, split to make way for the after hatchways. The bridge and officers' accommodation was isolated forward, a common practice with White Star. There were eight holds and hatchways and, for her time, the ship could carry enormous cargoes. The derricks for working the holds seemed sparse but great use of spans was made when handling cargo in Liverpool and New York.

The *Baltic* had 11 main bulkheads and a full-length double bottom 5 ft 1 in deep which increased to 5 ft 10 in under the engine room. A standard compass platform, nearly 12 ft high, was situated on top of the sun deck, this was an installation in all four sisters intended to reduce deviation. Fourteen lifeboats and two emergency boats were originally carried. The *Baltic* had twin screws, four-bladed bronze propellers, driven by quadruple expansion steam engines with cylinders of 33, 47½, 68½, and 98 in bore and a stroke of 63 in. Together they could produce 14,000-15,000 ihp to give an average speed of 16 knots. Steam was supplied by eight double-ended Scotch boilers at a pressure of 210 psi. At full speed these boilers would consume coal at the rate of 280 tons per day.

The *Baltic* was installed with the same machinery as the earlier *Celtic* and *Cedric*; therefore at the time of her alteration in length and displacement her steam plant was so near to completion. Hence any significant change was impossible and when commissioned she was unable to maintain the schedule of her slightly shorter sisters. The original accommodation was for 425 First, 450 Second and 2,000 Third class passengers. The First class rooms were well appointed, solidly furnished, spacious and homely. Situated over the midships half-length they had a Smoke Room and library forward under the sun deck, Lounge and Drawing Room on the promenade deck, while the Saloon was on the upper deck and this extended the full width of the ship and was surmounted by a large dome. It could seat 370 at small tables for small parties, no longer the fore and aft 'baronial' type tables for the full length of the room. There were a few First class suites and a number of single-berth cabins. The Second class were well provided for abaft of the mizzenmast and on the decks below. Third class were aft of them again, and also forward, on the upper and main decks, with a large number of 2, 3 and 4-berth cabins, with the remainder in dormitories.

The White Star Line had a particularly good reputation for Third and Steerage on the North Atlantic. The *Baltic*'s crew numbered around 350, so that when full to capacity, there could be as many as 3,170 people on board. These together with the ability to carry some 15,000 tons of cargo made for a very large 'payload'. She was launched on 21 November 1903 and it was reported in the *Illustrated London News* at the time '*Baltic*, which is the largest vessel afloat, was launched on Saturday, Miss Julia Neilson, who has been appearing in *Sweet Nell of Old Drury*, performing the christening ceremony.' A break from the apparent non-high profile namings so favoured by White Star. Upon completion she was handed over to White Star on 23 June 1904 and at that time she was hailed as the world's largest liner, albeit for almost a year. She sailed on 29 June 1904 on her maiden voyage from Liverpool to New York, however owing to the modifications that were made while the ship

Southampton was effected during 1907. With the entry into service of *Baltic's* new sister, the *Adriatic*, the latter was moved to Southampton along with the older *Oceanic*, *Majestic* and *Teutonic*. Concurrently the *Baltic* in consort with the *Celtic*, *Cedric* and *Arabic*

was on the slipway, with no increase in power for her Quadruple engine sets, the *Baltic's* service speed was lower than anticipated. After entering service these were modified. Alterations in her valve gear and cylinders of the main engines were made and an additional 1,000 ihp was made available, which gave her sufficient speed.

Concerning the carriage of mail by sea, efforts were being made to speed up the process. A procedure which had been trialled on the German liners of the day, whereby the mails were sorted to ongoing destinations at sea, was extended to British liners. Commencing with the *Baltic*, which on 14 May 1905 was delayed by some six hours due to machinery problems, but sailed later that day. The arrangements for the co-operation of the Royal Mail and US Mail officials was very similar to that already arrived at with the German Post Office, and there was no difficulty in finding volunteers who were willing to take up the ocean service. In return for their ordinary Post Office wages, officials were offered along with their rations and quarters on board ship, an extra £6 per round voyage and in addition to half a guinea (52½p) for every day spent ashore in New York. The British Government's share in this arrangement came to about £6,000 a year, but they regarded it as being well worth it. The following year, on 3 November 1906, after completing an eastbound crossing and whilst berthed at Liverpool, fire broke out in No5 hold while she was alongside. The fire was eventually extinguished and flooded with hose water; however some 640 bales of cotton were subsequently damaged by the blaze and flooding.

Whilst at the end of her westbound crossing on 8 March 1907, and on the approaches to New York Harbour, the *Baltic* ran aground 1½ miles outside Sandy Hook. There she remained for several hours before refloating. Another incident a month later on 13 April added to her misfortune. Following the turnaround in New York and whilst embarking on her next eastbound voyage, the *Baltic* was in collision with a loaded coal barge under tow off Jersey City, New Jersey. The barge sunk. White Star's decision to move the express passenger service from Liverpool to

inaugurated a new Thursday service from Liverpool. Whilst operating on this new itinerary, on 29 August 1907, the *Baltic* was damaged by fire whilst alongside at New York. Although extinguished by the ship's firefighters and the New York Fire Department, fire and water damage totalled some £2,000.

As has already been mentioned, on 23 January 1909, the *Baltic* received the CQD distress signal via her wireless telegraphy set from the stricken liner *Republic* that had been in collision with Italian Lloyd's *Florida* in thick fog some 180 miles east of the Ambrose Light Vessel. At about 6 am, Wireless Officer Tattersall on board the *Baltic* picked up the signal. The *Baltic*, bound for New York and already past the Nantucket Light vessel, turned to go to the help of the two stricken ships. Although the *Baltic* was only about 64 miles from the ships there was no direction-finding system or GPS in those days and it was not until 7 pm, after groping her way through thick fog, that she found them. At the collision point itself the *Republic* was very severely damaged with her engine room flooded and all power gone. The *Florida's* bows were crumpled back but she was not found to be in danger of sinking. Backing off from the impact, she lost the *Republic* in the fog at first but eventually found her again.

Captain Sealby of the *Republic*, upon seeing that the foundering of the ship was imminent, transferred all his 641 passengers to the *Florida* and then he and his crew abandoned ship as well. On board the *Florida* there had been some panic as many of her passengers were refugees from the Messina earthquake which had occurred before their departure from Sicily; this under those circumstances was understandable. From the *Florida* it appeared that the *Republic* might remain afloat so its Captain returned to her with a skeleton crew. When the *Baltic* arrived around 7pm her Captain started transferring all the passengers of both stricken ships to his own and during the night all 1,260 of these were taken aboard without loss. This simple statement cannot begin to describe how the ferrying of so many men, women and children at night, in fog and in ship's lifeboats rowed by oars was no mean feat.

Other ships had arrived on the scene and eventually: two United States Revenue cutters took the *Republic* in tow. However by 8pm on Sunday evening she sank, her Captain and small crew that re-boarded being picked up from the sea. The *Baltic* took her load of survivors to New York and the *Florida* reached the same port under her own steam. This was the first time that wireless had demonstrated its value in saving life and instituting rescue and salvage services at sea. The wireless officers, Binns in the *Republic* and Tattersall in the *Baltic*, had made history and both had remained at their primitive sets until the very end of the rescue operation. Some 18 months later on 30 June 1910, the *Baltic* was herself in collision, albeit a minor one, when she brushed with German-American Petroleum Company's tanker *Standard*, about 1,100 miles East of the Ambrose Light vessel. Although no serious damage was caused to the tanker which was loaded with one million tons of petroleum, one of her crewmen received internal injuries as well as breaking three ribs. He was transferred to the *Baltic* for surgery. Damage sustained by the *Baltic* was more significant as two holes were torn in her bows, one causing the flooding of her forward hold.

By 1911, it is of interest to note that Second class fares to New York from Liverpool in the *Baltic* was £9 and Third Class £6 10s (£6.50)! In 1912, the *Baltic* played a small part in the *Titanic* disaster. On 14 April whilst negotiating the Atlantic, the *Baltic* received warning of icebergs from a passing steamer. At 1.42pm she sent the following signal: 'Captain *Titanic*. Have had moderate variable winds and clear, fine weather since leaving. Greek steamer *Athenai* reports passing icebergs and large quantities of field ice today in lat. 41° 51′ N, 49° 52′ W … Wish you and *Titanic* all success. Commander'. The message was acknowledged by the *Titanic*'s Captain Smith who took the Marconigram and handed it to J. Bruce Ismay who was travelling on the ship's maiden voyage. Mr Ismay in turn put it into his pocket where apparently it remained for six hours until it was returned to the Captain.

That same day, following the *Titanic*'s collision with the iceberg, the *Baltic* received a SOS distress call from the *Titanic*, relayed via the

Above: **RMS *Baltic* leaving Liverpool for Japan on 17 February 1933.** *John Clarkson.*

Cunarder *Caronia*. She steamed towards the *Titanic*'s reported position for nine hours and then later heard from the *Carpathia* that the *Titanic* had sunk; following this message she stood down from the rescue. The loss of the *Titanic* resulted in the recommendations that there should be 'boats for all' and all Atlantic liners started doubling their complement of lifeboats. The *Baltic* was fitted with three boats under davits on each side of her sun deck, 'decked' boats under all those already carried on the boat deck and short after decks and an extra pair right aft; a total of 22 more boats than previously installed. The others of the 'Big Four' were similarly fitted. Ironically, during a lifeboat drill at New York on 26 July 1914, the *Baltic*'s No13 lifeboat fell from its davits, killing one occupant and injuring nine others.

Following the outbreak of World War 1 in August 1914, the *Baltic* was at first retained along with the *Adriatic* on the New York run until 1915. It was in the early months of the

Right: **The *Baltic* (left) and the *Laurentic* (right) together in the Gladstone Dock.** *Tom Rayner Collection.*

Above: **Another 'doctored' photograph of the *Baltic* about to sail. She appears to be at speed under her own power but was probably under tow when the picture was taken.** *John Clarkson.*

war, on 19 November 1914, whilst departing New York's Ambrose Channel for Liverpool, that the *Baltic* collided with the steamer *Comal* which was en route to Galveston, Texas. The *Comal* was damaged with port side bow plates stove in, necessitating drydocking. The *Baltic* was undamaged and as the *Comal* sailed away from the scene, the *Baltic's* passengers shouted well wishes. From 1915 onwards, she was taken up under the Liner Requisition Scheme as a troopship and whilst employed in this role, on 26 April 1917, she was attacked unsuccessfully by German submarine *UC-66* over two days pursuit. A month later in May she carried the first contingent and the Headquarters Staff of the United States Expeditionary Force to Liverpool. She was presented with a plaque commemorating this. Other duties during the war were to carry much needed oil fuel for the Royal Navy in her double bottom and deep tanks. During the first 10 months of 1918 she carried over 32,000 Canadian and US troops across to France and on 12 December that year the *Baltic* resumed the Liverpool to New York passenger service.

On 30 March 1921 whilst the *Baltic* was in tow of the tug *Blue Ridge* at New York's Robin's Drydock, she sustained propeller damage, and a week later suffered a minor fire at Fletcher's Drydock. It was also during this year that the *Baltic's* Third and Steerage accommodation was rebuilt for 1,166 Third class and the following year when the *Adriatic* returned to Liverpool for the next six years the 'Big Four' were together again on the weekly service. Every fortnight one of them also called at Boston. One of the *Baltic's* unsung praises was that her crew's football team won the Atlantic Soccer Club Tournament during 1926, being the first British ship to do so. In June 1923, the *Baltic* had to return to Liverpool after striking a submerged object off Ireland's Southern coast. Her sailings were delayed

for three days whilst repairs were in progress. In 1924, the *Baltic* was reboilered and later that year, whilst berthed at New York, on 8 October, nearby tugs failed to control the docking of Red Star's *Finland*, and wind and tide forced her to drift into the *Baltic* which was already moored. Both vessels sustained only minor damage.

In an attempt to keep up with the new trends attracting passengers, on 29 October 1927 the *Baltic* was reclassified as a 'Cabin class' ship with revised accommodation for 393 Cabin, 339 Tourist and 1,150 Third class passengers. Her other three sisters were likewise reclassified the following year, 1928, the same year as the *Celtic* ran aground off Queenstown and became a total loss. On 6 December 1929, the *Baltic* rescued the crew of the sinking schooner *Northern Lights*, off Newfoundland. The following month, on 18 January 1930, just before her departure for New York via Boston, a sudden tidal surge on the Mersey caused the *Baltic* to be thrown against her pier at Liverpool. The impact damaged her propeller blades. It took divers nine hours to repair the damage before she was able to sail.

The world slump of the 1930s was beginning to make inroads into the number of passengers and cargoes carried across the North Atlantic. Coupled with this the advent of the Company's large motor liner *Britannic* in 1930, heralded the end of the remaining three four-masters' careers. The *Georgic* entered service in 1932, and together with her sister they operated the Liverpool service between them. The *Cedric* had been sold in 1931 and the *Baltic* commenced on her last voyage from Liverpool to New York on 17 September 1932, finally departing the latter port on 1 October for her last eastbound crossing. Following this she was placed in reserve pending disposal, her place on the service having been filled by the new motor ship *Georgic*. In January 1933, she was sold to Japanese shipbreakers for £33,000 along with her consort, the *Megantic* and she sailed from Liverpool on 17 February 1933 under the command of Captain J. S. Corfe, bound for Osaka for scrapping.

GALLIC (I)

(1907-1913)
461 grt; 150 ft 2 in x 28 ft 2 in
Compound Expansion SR Engines, Paddle, 9 knots
Passengers: No information available
John Scott & Co. Kinghorn, Fife Yard No. 87

She was originally launched on 7 June 1894 and completed that month as the last paddle steamer *Birkenhead* for the Birkenhead Ferries Department of the Corporation of Birkenhead. As such she operated on their cross-Mersey service between Woodside and Liverpool and later between Rock Ferry and Liverpool. A need was identified by White Star to establish a tender service at Cherbourg for their vessels calling there following their move to Southampton and including the French port in their new schedule. White Star acquired the *Birkenhead* in March 1907 and renamed her *Gallic* then sent her across to Cherbourg. This was only a stopgap measure as by 1911 two new twin screw tenders, the *Nomadic* and the *Traffic,* were completed by Harland & Wolff, and sent to Cherbourg to replace the *Gallic.* Following their entry into service the *Gallic* returned to Liverpool where she was occasionally used as a baggage boat. In 1914, after a relatively short career she was broken up at Garston on the River Mersey.

GALLIC: *Of or pertaining to the Gauls, Gaulish or French.*

ADRIATIC (II)

(1907-1934)
24,541 grt ; 709 ft 3 in BP (729 ft OA) x 75 ft 6 in
Quadruple Expansion SR Engines, Twin Screw,
16,000 ihp, 17 knots
Passengers: 425 First class, 500 Second class,
2,000 Third class
Harland & Wolff, Belfast. Yard No. 358

The *Adriatic* was the last of White Star Line's 'Big Four' and was ordered in December 1903. She was launched on 20 September 1906, the same day as Cunard's *Mauretania,* and delivered to her owners on 25 April 1907. Speculation abounded as to why she took four years to build. Rumour has it that her original hull became the Hamburg America liner *Amerika* which entered service in 1905 as the German liner's Yard number was 357. This could not have been the case as the *Adriatic* was nearly 40 ft longer and 1ft 9 in more in beam than the *Amerika* and if any confusion did arise it would probably have been very early on such as the appropriation of the shipbuilding berth rather than the ship.

The *Celtic* of 1901 had been the first of the White Star quartet, the Company's example being quickly followed by the Hamburg America Line and then by Germany's North German Lloyd. As each ship entered service she exceeded her predecessor slightly so that each became the largest ship in the world for a short time. The *Celtic* and the *Cedric* had the same dimensions but the *Baltic* was given 28 more feet in length and a few inches in beam, with exactly the same machinery, which apparently resulted in her keeping a little tight to her operating schedule. In order to counter this and to make her better suited to run in consort with the *Oceanic,* the *Adriatic* was given the same dimensions as the *Baltic* but with more powerful machinery and increased boiler power.

In addition to the *Adriatic's* gross tonnage of 24,541, she had a net tonnage of 15,638 and a displacement of 40,790 tons together with an enormous deadweight of 19,710 tons on a draught of 37 ft 3 in. Her depth was 52 ft 8 in. Her hull, flush-decked and with the weather deck as the shelter deck had a total of 9 steel decks, five of them overall, and 11 main bulkheads with watertight doors in them, able to be operated from the bridge. There was a double bottom 5 ft 1 in in depth which extended the full length between the peak bulkheads and eight holds and hatchways.

Her twin, 3-bladed manganese bronze propellers were driven by quadruple expansion engines with cylinders of 35½, 51, 73½ and 104 in bore, with a stroke of 63 in. Between them they developed some 16,000-17,000 ihp which gave her a maximum sea speed of 17.5 knots. The crank pins were 21 in in diameter. The boilers, eight double-ended, worked at a pressure of 210 psi consuming coal at the average rate of 290 tons per day. When she entered service in April 1907 it was in marked contrast to that of Cunard's *Lusitania* and *Mauretania* which entered service in September and November that year also. They were installed with the innovative Parsons turbines of 70,000 shp, the way ahead for marine propulsion, the *Mauretania* having achieved a mean speed of 27.4 knots during her trials! Notwithstanding this, White Star preferred the tried and tested reliability of the reciprocating machinery supplied by Harland & Wolff.

Passengers catered for originally were 425 First, 500 Second and 1,900 Third class, which together with a crew of 557 made a total of 3,382 people carried. But because the *Adriatic* was very large and her decks spacious, and though perhaps the accommodation was not so luxurious as some of the express ships of the day, she was nevertheless exceptionally comfortable throughout. The *Adriatic* proved to be one of the most popular liners on the North Atlantic. Her passenger numbers were reduced after World War 1 to 400, 460 and 1,320. Among her public rooms was the innovation of the first indoor swimming pool and Turkish bath.

Although very similar in appearance to the *Baltic,* she could be easily distinguished by a pair of derrick posts on her fore deck and the double-tiered short deck between her mizzen and jigger masts. The *Adriatic's* funnels were a little larger than those of the *Baltic* and later in her career she alone of the four ships had the fore end of her promenade deck glassed in with large windows. The *Adriatic* sailed on her maiden voyage from Liverpool to New York on 8 May 1907 under the command of Captain Edward J. Smith, later Master of the *Titanic.* Upon her arrival at New York Captain Smith proudly commented to the press about his brand new liner: 'I cannot imagine any condition which would cause a ship to founder. I cannot conceive of any vital disaster happening to this vessel. Modern shipbuilding has gone beyond that.'

Ideally she was intended to join the other three of her type to inaugurate a luxury intermediate service between Liverpool and New York but White Star had decided to move their express mail service operation to Southampton in advance of the three projected 'Olympic' trio for that route. They decided in the meantime to open up the service with the ships that were already in operation and so the *Adriatic* left New York on 22 May, not for Liverpool but for Southampton, calling at Plymouth and Cherbourg en route. She was given a much deserved Hampshire welcome when she entered the port for British transatlantic liners had until then hardly used it at all. This was followed by a great send off on 5 June 1907 when she left for New York and inaugurated the new mail run via Cherbourg and Queenstown.

Her consorts on the Southampton route were the *Teutonic, Majestic* and *Oceanic* and although the *Adriatic* was slower than any of them she was considerably bigger and she soon built up a high reputation for solid comfort, reliability and steadiness which made up for the extra time on passage. It is interesting to note that her Second and Third class fares at this time were £7. 10s (£7.50) and £6. An unfortunate

incident occurred on 10 October 1908 when four of her crewmen were accused of looting passengers' baggage. Their 'takings' to the value of nearly £4,000 was found stashed in hiding places throughout the ship. During the following year on 4 November 1909, whilst inbound to New York she grounded at the entrance to Ambrose Channel for some five hours. Another incident happened at Southampton on 8 August 1910 when Firemen aboard her mutinied.

Once established the *Adriatic* only served the Southampton route regularly for four years. The *Olympic* made her maiden voyage in June 1911 with the *Titanic* due to enter service the following year and with the big ship's arrival the *Teutonic* was taken off and switched to the Canadian service. The *Adriatic* made her last voyage from Southampton on 26 July that year and went up to Liverpool during August to join her three sisters. She resumed the Liverpool to New York route on 26 August 1911 and together with her intended consorts she maintained that service up until the advent of World War 1. Apparently during the winter of 1911 she undertook one or two Mediterranean to New York voyages.

The loss of the *Titanic* in April 1912 had tremendous consequences on maritime safety which encompassed tighter safety regulations, enhanced design requirements, constant wireless watch and the initiation of an ice patrol not to mention watertight compartmentalisation and structural integrity. Outwardly the only visual change in the *Adriatic*, as with almost all other liners of that period, was a considerable increase in the number of her lifeboats. Decked boats were placed under all those already carried and three extra sets of davits and boats were fitted on each side of her sun deck. On 5 May 1912, Bruce Ismay travelled back to Liverpool on her after he had attended the Court of Enquiry

Below: **The *Adriatic* being made ready for launching at Harland & Wolff's yard. Her drag anchors are rigged in readiness and the fore poppet of her cradle has been constructed.** *Real Photographs Co Ltd.*

Above: **An old company postcard showing the *Adriatic*'s Reading and Writing room.** *Richard de Kerbrech Collection.*

following the loss of the *Titanic*, together with other members of the ship's crew who had been required to attend the inquiry. Somewhat ironically on 1 December 1912 whilst the *Adriatic* was berthed at Funchal in Madeira, one crewman was killed and three others injured during a lifeboat drill being carried out.

When World War 1 broke out in August 1914, the Southampton service was discontinued at once and the White Star fleet was largely dispersed on a variety of war work. However the *Adriatic* and *Baltic* were retained on the Liverpool to New York route to maintain as good a service as they could under the wartime conditions; they were augmented by the *Lapland* for a time. The *Adriatic*'s large cargo capacity was of enormous benefit to the country in the importation of stores and foodstuffs. In her wartime role she had drawn suspicion to the US authorities of her defensive armament that had been fitted and also that she might have been calling at Halifax to embark Canadian troops thereby flaunting the United States' neutral integrity. She continued throughout the war on the transatlantic run until the United States joined the Allies in 1917 and then carried US troops to the European war theatre. She also earned a reputation for herself as being the largest and most regular of the big munitions carriers and the storage of high grade oil in her double bottom tanks.

From 12 April 1917 onwards she came under the Liner Requisition Scheme but it made little affect on her schedule. Whilst tied up at Pier 60 in New York on 26 January 1918, a fire was discovered among several barrels of oil stowed on the *Adriatic*'s deck. The New York City firefighters flushed the deck with their hoses thereby sweeping any burning oil into the North River and minimising damage to the ship. (Nowadays, blanketing foam would be used to smother an oil-based fire). Following the war's end in 1918, the *Adriatic* continued on the Liverpool-New York run making her last voyage on 28 July 1918. She was released form Government duties on 28 February 1919 and was given a full reconditioning. In this her accommodation was upgraded to cater for 400 First, 465 Second and 1,300 Third class passengers. It is believed that at the same time windows were fitted at the fore end of her promenade deck.

On 3 September 1919, the *Adriatic* sailed from Southampton to New York via Cherbourg thereby re-opening the Southampton service, in consort with the *Lapland*, to be joined the following year by the *Olympic* which had distinguished herself throughout the War. The following year whilst returning from New York en route to Cherbourg, the *Adriatic* encountered heavy seas on 24 October 1920 which carried away lifeboat No 20. By 1922, the *Olympic* would be joined by the ex-German liners *Homeric* and *Majestic* which essentially completed the big ship trio and thereby making the *Adriatic* redundant on the Channel run; she made her last trip from Southampton to New York on 14 December 1921.

She was withdrawn and sent back to Belfast for a refit, and following this re-entered the Liverpool service on 13

May 1922 along with the *Baltic*, *Cedric* and *Celtic*. Three months later on 11 August 1922, five men were killed by an explosion in the *Adriatic*'s No3 hold which was being utilised as a reserve coal bunker at the time. The explosion happened at 2am as she was preparing to sail from Queenstown for New York. Apart from the fatalities, some £250 worth of cargo was damaged and the hatch doors on three decks were shattered. The resulting fire could have been far more serious had not the crew dealt with it very promptly, despite the loss of their shipmates.

During 1923 a call at Boston was inaugurated and for five years the service continued regularly but on 14 November 1924, whilst en route from Southampton to New York she sailed into a hurricane and had three lifeboats smashed and one carried away. In 1925, the *Adriatic* was chartered for one voyage by Welsh Americans travelling to the National Eisteddfod and also that year, when some 18 years old, made her fastest eastbound crossing of 7 days and 6 minutes. From around 1926 onwards she was placed on winter cruising in the off-season periods. The take-over of the White Star Line by the Royal Mail Group in January 1927 made no difference to the ship's service and on 10 July 1927 she was the first ship to enter the new Gladstone Dock at Liverpool shortly after its official opening by King George V. By 1928, the slackening of world trade and the impending world slump was being distinctly felt and shipping companies were trying out new means of filling their ships. Upon her return from a Mediterranean cruise she was converted to a Cabin class ship with accommodation for 506 First, 560 Tourist and 404 Third class passengers. On 28 April 1928 she left Liverpool on her first voyage in this new role and proved a tremendous success, and later in the year her accommodation was again improved. In December that year the *Celtic* was wrecked off the South coast of Ireland and the gradual break-up of the famous quartet had begun.

Whilst manoeuvring in New York on 8 September 1929, the *Adriatic* was in collision with the *Suffolk*, a small coastal steamer. The *Suffolk*'s bows were stove in while the *Adriatic* sustained damage to her port quarter in which three plates, five frames and six beams were buckled. Although it seemed that offering winter cruises to help fill empty passenger berths might be the answer, the *Adriatic* was laid up for the winter at Liverpool in 1929 and only undertook voyages in the summer from thereon. The new motor liner *Britannic* joined the Liverpool service during 1930 followed by the *Georgic* two years later. By this time there was little chance of filling such large ships to their capacity. However during 1931 the *Adriatic* tried out an experimental weekend cruise of 2½ days at the Bank Holiday weekend, with the fares as low as £5 for Cabin and £3 for Tourist. Notwithstanding this she was laid up at Liverpool again on 30 August 1931 after her September cruise was cancelled.

Her former consorts had now come to the end of their useful lives, for the *Cedric* was scrapped in 1932 and the *Baltic* went to Japanese breakers the following year but the decision was made to place the *Adriatic* on full time cruising and as reserve ship, for by now the British economy seemed to be picking up after the Depression; even so she was laid up during August 1932. In the summer of 1933, she cruised out of Liverpool on a 'Seven Days for £7' cruise calling at Corunna, Lisbon, Madeira, and back to Liverpool. This itinerary continued until 31 August when she was laid up for the off season. In February 1934, the merger between Cunard and White Star took place and the *Adriatic* was transferred to the new Company; on the 24th of that month she made her last voyage to New York via Cobh, Halifax and Boston before being placed on full-time cruising.

The progress of one of these cruises was described by Peter Roberts of Brighton who as a young 13-year-old schoolboy set down his experiences and impressions on a charter cruise from Liverpool which commenced on 29 March 1934 at a cost of 19 guineas (£19.95p) for the 17-day cruise:

'This was a Scouters and Guiders cruise, to visit and hold international Scout and Guide Rallies at Gibraltar, Villefranche (for Nice), Malta, Algiers, and Lisbon, accompanied by the Chief Scout and Guide,

Lord and Lady Baden-Powell. Lord Baden-Powell was convalescing from an illness, and was sometimes to be seen in a deck chair in the privacy of the deck by the 'island' bridge Officers' quarters. On the afternoon of departure, the *Adriatic* was lying in midstream in the Mersey as the *Doric* was alongside the Prince's Landing Stage and sailed at 4pm on a 14-day Scholars' Easter Cruise. As the *Adriatic* approached the Landing Stage, I was impressed by her smart appearance, dressed overall in cruise bunting, and a new coat of paint ready for the first cruise of the season. She was indeed the most elegant and graceful of the 'Big Four'; her extra length, slightly wider funnels, and part enclosed promenade deck gave her a more 'modern' impressive appearance. We sailed from Liverpool about 8pm and the following day (30 March) we were in the great sweeping seas from the Atlantic, approaching the Bay of Biscay. In the distance, I could see the *Berengaria* outward bound for New York. Later in the day, the sea moderated to a heavy swell and we overtook the *Doric* with storm tarpaulins on her promenade deck. However there was no sign of life or the 'scholars' watching the spectacle of the *Adriatic* passing, perhaps they had not yet found their 'sea legs'!

'Captain C. P. Freeman had been in command of the *Adriatic* for some years. He seemed quite elderly and lame, with rather a 'Churchillian' face, and must have been due for retirement. He was in the RNR and he signed my souvenir, 'Charles P. Freeman'. The ship's orchestra repertoire included the latest Noel Coward melodies, selections from CAVALCADE

Above: **The *Adriatic* passes an anchored dredger whilst inbound possibly for Liverpool. She was the last and largest of the 'Big Four' and the only one to have the forward end of her promenade deck windows covered over.** *B&A Feilden.*

and BITTER SWEET, also 'Hillbilly' songs such as 'I'm headin' for the Last Round Up'. At Villefranche, near Nice, the Duke of Connaught, who was resident there, came out on the tender to pay a visit. By the time we reached Algiers and Lisbon, I noticed the *Adriatic* was on a higher draught. After more than a fortnight's consumption of coal, and being built for a large cargo capacity, perhaps she did not have quite sufficient ballast, as she tended to have a long slow roll as she encountered following seas once out again into the Atlantic. Nevertheless, this did not detract from her reputation as a steady ship.

'It was at about this point that after passing Gibraltar and homeward bound off Portugal that I had the opportunity to visit the engine room and stokeholds, which was an unforgettable and awe-inspiring experience. It was a memory of seeing probably the world's largest marine reciprocating engines and the conditions under which the stokehold crew had to work in the days of big coal-fired liners. The engines seemed huge; it was like being in the

Right: **All is not what it seems, for the *Adriatic* is at the Prince's Landing Stage ready to *sail* for New York. She reinstated the Liverpool-New York service during 1922. The Post Office covered gangway for the use of mail only has been retracted after loading.** *Richard de Kerbrech Collection.*

Above: **The *Adriatic* outward bound from Southampton for Cherbourg. Note the addition of the crosstrees on her mainmast.** *Tom Rayner Collection.*

presence of a steam-breathing monster with the great hissing pistons and crankshafts. I also went along to the end of one of the propeller shaft tunnels. The last night of the cruise we slowly moved through fog in the Irish Sea with the steam whistle siren mournfully blaring. On deck next morning in the River Mersey, I was approached at the deckrail by one of the lamptrimmers, a cheerful, humorous wiry little man called Joe, who had often remarked on my being on deck in all weathers, or in the foredeck watching the sea and wash 'with my raincoat buttons nearly blown off'. He lived in Liverpool, and it was a sign of the depression days of poverty that he asked me to write,

Below: **Dressed overall the *Adriatic* is towed into the Gladstone Dock to inaugurate its use following its opening by King George V on 10 July 1927.** *B&A Feilden.*

and if possible, send any old spare clothing which families badly needed.'

Of the accommodation, Peter Roberts recalls:

'The Drawing Room off the First class entrance hall was the former 'Ladies Room', of medium size with pale pink décor, and was used for lectures and as a cinema for silent films. Opposite the door led into the larger Smoking Room, now modernised and more attractive than the former dark toned wood, leather upholstery and stained glass. The Lounge forward was a pale avocado green in a style that was to be developed in the *Olympic*. As the cruise was all one class, the Second class rooms were used for entertainment, children's games and Scout meetings. My cabin was on 'B' Deck and I remember in the long corridors and the sound of creaking of the great ship's structure in a seaway. The Bath Steward would announce, 'Gentlemen's bath ready!' and so down a corridor to a hot seawater bath and saltwater soap!'

In July that year, the *Adriatic* transferred to Cunard White Star operations and immediately became redundant along with the short-lived Canadian service liners *Albertic* and *Calgaric*, under the new regime. She made her final cruise out of Liverpool in the September and was laid-up pending disposal in the October. She was sold during November to Japanese breakers for £48,000, and on 19 December 1934 she sailed out of the Mersey for the last time bound for Osaka, where she arrived on 5 March 1935 for demolition. So the last of White Star's four-masters had passed into history. With the exception of winter cruises and layups in her later years she had given almost 27 years of continuous Atlantic service and her spacious decks, steadiness and homely comfort had made her a popular favourite among regular travellers and cruise clientele alike.

LAURENTIC (I)

(1909-1917)
14,892 grt; 550 ft 4 in BP (565 ft OA) x 67 ft 4 in
Triple Expansion SR Engines + LP Turbine,
Triple Screw, 12,000 ihp, 16 knots
Passengers: 230 First class, 430 Second class,
1,000 Third class.
Harland & Wolff, Belfast. Yard No. 394

Perhaps of all the shipping companies absorbed into J. P. Morgan's IMMCo the Dominion Line 'drew the short straw'. Bought out at the peak of its prosperity, it was asset-stripped of its best ships on the main Liverpool to Boston service namely the *Commonwealth*, *New England*, *Mayflower* and *Columbus*. All these were transferred internally to White Star and renamed *Canopic*, *Romanic*, *Cretic* and *Republic*, respectively. By way of replacement, two ships were ordered from Harland & Wolff for the Dominion Line's Canadian

service and provisionally named *Alberta* and *Albany*. They were laid down in 1907 but as events transpired, these vessels were ceded to White Star and the two were completed as the *Laurentic* and *Megantic*. The *Laurentic* was launched on 10 September 1908 and unlike the trend of the Cunard Line in adopting steam turbines as the main propulsion, White Star remained cautious. The *Laurentic* was to be a triple screw vessel with each of the outer screws driven by a 4-cylinder, triple expansion, steam reciprocating engine. The exhaust steam from these was then used to drive a large low pressure turbine directly driving the centre screw, since there was no astern turbine she had to be manoeuvred as a twin screw ship. The LP turbine was built by John Brown as Harland & Wolff had no turbine expertise at that time. This was known as 'combination machinery' and would be the type of propulsion later selected in White Star's 'Big Three' – the *Olympic*, *Titanic* and *Britannic*.

The sister ship *Megantic* had a conventional machinery installation, consisting of two 4-cylinder, quadruple expansion engines developing the same power on twin screws. Later operational experience revealed that for the same steam consumption, on a lower machinery weight, triple screw machinery showed a twenty per cent power increase compared with the twin screw, quadruple expansion engines. Also, for the same power, the coal consumption of the *Laurentic* was about twelve to fifteen per cent less than that of the *Megantic*! The *Laurentic* was handed over on 15 April 1909, and in addition to her accommodation for some 1,660 passengers, she carried cargo, some of it refrigerated, which could be stowed in six holds.

The *Laurentic* inaugurated 'The White Star-Dominion Joint Service' and sailed on her maiden voyage on 29 April 1909 from Liverpool to Quebec and Montreal. Sharing with her sister, the *Megantic*, and together with the Dominion liners *Canada* and *Dominion*, a weekly service on this route was established. The *Laurentic* was the largest but not the fastest ship on this route to date. She was equipped with a First class reading room and a smoking room with a partly glassed ceiling for the sun to shine through. So if one had not got the money to travel in the prestige liners but still wanted luxury, the *Laurentic* would be an ideal choice. Early the following year on 22 January 1910, whilst on a westbound crossing, she encountered a particularly heavy storm. In this the large bridge ports were smashed and a bridge telegraph put out of action temporarily. The Deck Officers' accommodation was flooded and a 20-foot length of railing wrenched from the deck.

Later in 1910, after murdering his unfaithful wife, Dr. Peter Harvey Crippen (a US citizen), and his lover Ethel le Neve fled from England to Antwerp. Here they boarded the Canadian Pacific liner *Montrose* which sailed on 18 July 1910 for Canada under the command of Captain Henry Kendall. Two days earlier on 16 July, Chief Inspector Walter Dew attended Bow Street Police Court and obtained a Warrant for the arrest of Crippen and le Neve, not knowing where they were. Crippen, who was under the assumed name of Robinson, had shaved off his moustache, and le Neve was disguised as a teenage boy whilst on board. Their story was that she was Crippen's invalid son and that they intended to start a new life in California. However, le Neve's feminine voice and mannerisms became obvious to many aboard. The Master, Captain Kendall, saw a report about the wanted pair in a foreign newspaper, and became suspicious of the two passengers who had boarded at Antwerp. He ordered the couple to be watched more closely. As a result of the crew's observations, a woman's corset was discovered in their cabin, and Crippen was found to be in possession of a revolver. Kendall's suspicions were further confirmed on reading a description and seeing photographs of the fugitives in the *Daily Mail.*

Pandering to Crippen's vanity, he invited the pair to dine with him at the Captain's table, where he plied them with drinks and proceeded to entertain them with a series of bawdy jokes. As Crippen laughed, Kendall could see the distinctive gold fillings with which he had been fitted. On 22 July, swearing Llewellyn Jones, the Marconi wireless operator, to secrecy, Kendall instructed him to send a Morse message to the nearest coastguard station which read: 'Have strong suspicion that Crippen London Cellar murderer and accomplice are amongst saloon passengers. Moustache shaved off, growing a beard. Accomplice dressed as a boy, voice, manner and build undoubtedly a girl.'

This message was relayed by telegraph and telephone, and reached Chief Inspector Dew at Scotland Yard just in time for him to travel to Liverpool on 23 July to catch the faster *Laurentic*. With the *Montrose* slowing her speed, the *Laurentic* overhauled her at sea. This enabled Dew to come aboard with the navigation pilot for the St Lawrence River at Farther Point, Quebec and arrest Crippen before the ship docked on 31 July. All three returned on the *Megantic* and Crippen was subsequently hanged for his crimes. This was the first documented case of wireless technology being used to apprehend a criminal.

The *Laurentic* along with the *Megantic* at one time were the largest, though not the fastest, liners on the Canadian route; during the winter months both were sometime visitors to New York. In 1911 the *Laurentic* set a bit of a record for the Canadian run with a round trip time of 13 days 4 hours. Quite extraordinary for its day given normal North Atlantic conditions and a steady speed of 16 knots! Whilst at Montreal on 13 September 1914, she was commandeered as a troop transport for 1,800 men of the Canadian Expeditionary Force. She departed Montreal on 26 September and formed part of a 32-troopship convoy which carried 35,000 Canadian troops to Europe and sailed from Gaspé Bay on 3 October. The *Laurentic* sailed in convoy with 'Blue Squadron' which comprised the *Royal George, Lapland, Virginian* and *Tunisian* which arrived and anchored off Plymouth on 14 October.

During 1915, the *Laurentic* was converted into an Armed Merchant Cruiser and fitted with seven 5.5 in and three 4 in deck guns. Under the command of Captain Reginald A.

Norton, the *Laurentic* was engaged to carry a cargo of £5 million comprising 3,211 bars of gold bullion, to Halifax, Nova Scotia to pay for Canadian munitions supplied to the British forces. She left Liverpool on 21 January 1917 and landed a contingent of naval ratings at the Buncrana base HMS *Hecla* in the North of Ireland. She sailed at 5pm from Buncrana on 23 January, in fine cold weather. At the entrance to Lough Swilley off County Donegal, she struck two mines that had earlier been laid by German submarine *U-80.* As the explosions occurred in the vicinity of the engine room many of the engineering staff were killed, the ship's lights went out and she flooded rapidly. She capsized and sank in under an hour in 125 feet of water, position 55°18′ N, 7° 35′ W, with a loss of life of 354 lives of a total complement of 475. Although 15 lifeboats managed to get clear, many of these died of exposure and hypothermia in the bitterly cold sea. Her Master was among those saved. Of all the wartime losses attributed to mine explosions, the sinking of the *Laurentic* was the worst.

The following month on 9 February, the *Laurentic's* wreck was located by Commander Guybon C. Damant and a team of 12 divers led by Ernest 'Dusty' Miller. The task was designated a Class 'A' Security salvage job. She lay in 60 fathoms of water listing 60° to port. Although recovery of the gold was commenced during May with the lighter *Volunteer* in attendance, two months later in July it had to be curtailed due to bad weather. Strong gales and rough seas broke up the hull and the gold bars plunged further into the bowels of the wreck. Due to war requirements the salvage operations were suspended and the £836,000 worth that had already been recovered was all that could be reached easily.

Salvage operations were resumed in 1919 and during the five summers to 1924, working from their salvage ship *Racer* Commander Damant and his team recovered 3,186 bars of gold valued at £4,958,000 (each bar weighed approximately 10½ lb). At this stage only 25 bars worth £41,292 had not been located. The distorted shape of the gold bars was as a result of the immense pressure the divers had to undergo to effect the salvage. Amazingly, over 5000 dives were made to the *Laurentic* at a cost of £128,000, a truly remarkable feat of salvage given the diving and decompression technology for its day. For their services Damant was promoted to Captain and awarded the DSO and each diver received £6,739 and an OBE. Not until August 1952 were further salvage operations made to locate the remaining 25 gold bars.

The memorial to those lost on the *Laurentic* is in a small churchyard at Fahan less than a mile south of Buncrana. It is a magnificent Celtic cross surmounting a granite base. The *Laurentic's* bell survives in the belfry of a small Church of Ireland Church at Port Salon in Donegal.

LAURENTIC: *Pertaining to the Laurentian Mountains, north of the St. Lawrence River. (A Canadian connection).*

1907-1920

Men of Vision and the advent of the 'Olympic' class

Since White Star had declared a policy of placing supreme comfort and size before speed with the introduction of the *Oceanic* of 1899; this gained the Company a considerable following with the travelling public and a reputation for excellence. One of the original founders of the White Star Line, William Imrie, who had set up the partnership of Ismay, Imrie & Co., died in 1906 aged 62. By 1907, their rival, the Cunard Line, had introduced two 32,000 ton record breakers, the *Lusitania* and *Mauretania* into service. Cunard had refused to join the IMMCo combine and had won a £2.6 million, low interest, Government loan to build these two luxury liners which were gradually gaining their own following on the North Atlantic.

Also in 1907, White Star transferred its main New York service from Liverpool to Southampton, leaving their secondary route from the Mersey maintained by three of the 'Celtic' class, which were unaffected. Those operating from Southampton were the new 24,541 grt *Adriatic*, the 17,272 grt *Oceanic* and at 9,984grt, the elderly *Teutonic* and *Majestic*. The latter three made a poor showing compared with the newer, faster tonnage that Cunard offered. By 1908, an emigrant could travel to the United States for just £2 and J. P. Morgan foresaw fixed ticket prices in the hope of eliminating competition. However, for J. Bruce Ismay, one of the answers to the stiff competition from Cunard and other players from the continent was to build larger and finer ships with greater carrying capacity.

Thus it was that one midsummer night in 1907, J. Bruce Ismay, Chairman of both White Star and of IMMCo, dined at the Belgravia house of Lord Pirrie, the Chairman of Harland & Wolff. Lord Pirric, who himself as William Pirrie, spent four years serving a 'gentleman apprenticeship' in the drawing office, learning how to design and build ships, rose through the early days at Harland & Wolff, to be made a partner in 1876. Following the death of Sir Edward Harland in December1895 he became Chairman the following year.

At the time of this meeting the *Lusitania* had entered service with the *Mauretania* nearing completion. The conversation between the two men and their wives turned to the ships that might be built to counter Cunard's lead. From the informal discussions came a proposal to build a class of three large vessels of immense size, which would later become the *Olympic, Titanic* and *Britannic* (originally proposed as the *Gigantic*). That agreed, the remaining problems were that there were no slipways, drydock or even a pier that could accommodate their proposed size. These liners would make the Atlantic crossing in under a week; however the emphasis would be on safety and comfort. Comfort on a scale so magnificent that the few additional hours at sea on these 'floating palaces' would be savoured.

Cash would become readily available because of White Star's pre-eminent position in the IMMCo and its owner J. Pierpont Morgan stipulated that he would underwrite 'the finest vessels afloat'. This may have been said with a little trepidation for it was White Star's first innovation of such a large class of liner on the North Atlantic, since the American owners had acquired it. For the IMMCo this might possibly be a 'leap in the dark'! A fixed price contract of £3 million for the *Olympic* and *Titanic* was agreed, but this did not preclude Harland & Wolff from submitting a larger account for 'extras to contract', which was known as cost-plus basis.

Prior to the ships of the *Olympic* class being constructed, new slipways had to be built and extended. So in order to accommodate the large vessels, Harland & Wolff demolished three existing slipways including the one vacated by the *Laurentic*, in their Queen's Island shipyard and built two much larger ones in their place, namely slipways No2 and No3. The ground in way of the new slips was piled throughout and covered with concrete up to 4½ feet deep. To facilitate the economical erection and hydraulic

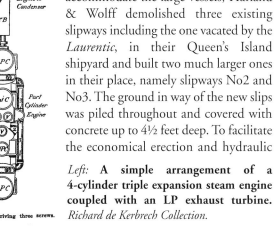

Left: **A simple arrangement of a 4-cylinder triple expansion steam engine coupled with an LP exhaust turbine.** *Richard de Kerbrech Collection.*

riveting of the two ships, two enormous gantries were constructed over the slips and equipped with a system of moving cranes travelling on overhead rails, and with four large electric lifts. The Glasgow firm of Sir William Arrol & Co. Ltd erected these and they covered an area of 840 x 240 feet. The height of the travelling cranes was 214 feet. In addition to modifications to the joiners' shop and others, the platers' shed was remodelled and equipped with machinery to handle the steel platework for the two liners. As well as these, a 200 ton floating crane was purchased from Deutsche Maschinenfabrik AG of Duisburg in Germany, to lift the propelling machinery and boilers on board during their fitting out stage after launching.

Above: **An unusual photograph of the *Laurentic* of 1909, possibly taken following her hand over to the Company from Harland & Wolff.** *Richard de Kerbrech Collection.*

Preparations were not confined to Harland & Wolff, for it was necessary that adequate berthing and drydocking facilities would be available for the new vessels upon their completion. In concert with Harland & Wolff, Belfast Harbour Commissioners had begun the construction of a new graving (dry) dock during 1903. Designed to be the largest in the world, it was completed in 1911 in time to permit the drydocking of the *Olympic* on 1 April. In the meantime, across in the United States, IMMCo prevailed upon the New York Harbour Board to extend the White Star piers a further 100 feet into the North River. Such was the influence of J. P. Morgan that the work was carried out at the City's expense, despite many taxpayers' objections.

So the foundations were laid for White Star's and Harland & Wolff's most ambitious and costliest project to date. By the end of 1910, however, White Star's financial position was far from strong. They had only raised half of the budget in the bank for building the *Olympic* and *Titanic*. The amount of £1,198,583 had still to be raised. The whole amount had been achieved by mortgaging their entire fleet as collateral. Another factor that had to be addressed was that there had been some bad business figures on the North Atlantic since 1908 due to rivalry between the steamship companies. This forced the major companies to work together through the Atlantic Conference by making some urgent decisions. At the Conference of 1911 it revealed that passenger carrying figures for the first half of that year were down by over 140,000 on the previous year. In particular, the number of continental passengers had shrunk which resulted in compensation from British to continental companies to the tune of £55,140.

By the time these gloomy issues were being deliberated the *Olympic* would be in service and attracting passengers. By contrast, in 1911 Harland & Wolff were experiencing a boom time with a full order book and full employment. At the time of the construction of the *Olympic* and *Titanic*, Harland & Wolff had a workforce of around 14,000 men, with between 3,000 and 4,000 men being allocated to the completion of the *Olympic*. During the same period the shipbuilders were also completing the tenders *Nomadic* and *Traffic* for White Star (both delivered 27 May 1911); the *Patriotic* for the Belfast Steamship Company (delivered 28 March 1912); the P&O liner *Maloja* (delivered 7 September 1911); Aberdeen Line's *Demosthenes* (delivered 5 August 1911); Union-Castle's intermediate liner *Galway Castle* (delivered 9 October 1911); White Star's *Zealandic* (delivered 12 October 1911); Royal Mail's *Arlanza* (delivered 8 June 1912) and *Deseado* (delivered 27 June 1912). In addition to these, between 6 October and 30 November 1911, the *Olympic* had returned to Belfast for major hull and propeller repairs, following her collision with HMS *Hawke*.

Turning to White Star's other joint service on the New Zealand run, by 1909 they had increased their shareholding capital in Shaw Savill & Albion to £22,000 made up of 100 preference shares of £5 each and 4,300 ordinary shares of £5 each. Subsequent vessels built for this route were owned jointly by the two companies.

Below: **A port side view of the *Laurentic* at anchor in the River Mersey.** *Nautical Photo Agency.*

MEGANTIC

(1909-1933)
14,878 grt; 559 ft 4 in BP (565 ft OA) x 67 ft 4 in
Quadruple Expansion SR Engines, Twin Screw,
11,000 ihp, 16 knots
Passengers: 260 First class, 430 Second class,
1,000 Third class
Harland & Wolff, Belfast. Yard No. 399

In order to help fill the vacuum on the Canadian route to rival their competitors Allan Line and Canadian Pacific, the Dominion Line originally ordered two liners which were laid down in 1907 as the *Albany* and *Alberta*. These in turn were transferred to White Star whilst on the stocks and with them the White Star Line itself entered the Canadian passenger trade under the name of White Star-Dominion Line, a new competitor which greatly angered the old-established Allan Line. The transfer of these two vessels so soon after the removal of the Dominion fleet from the Boston route seems rather ironic but made good business sense. At the time White Star's prestige was very high and was likely to attract good patronage to the renewed service, and so it was that the *Alberta* became the *Laurentic* and the *Albany* was renamed *Megantic*.

As such the *Megantic* was launched 10 December 1908. Together with her sister, the *Laurentic*, the *Megantic* was a little larger than Canadian Pacific's 'Empresses' and Allan Line's 'Vs', and together they were the biggest ships yet built for the Canadian service. They were used in a similar fashion to Cunard's *Carmania* and *Caronia* as a form of full-scale experiment to decide on the machinery for the planned *Olympic* and her sisters. The *Megantic* was designed for more conventional machinery of quadruple expansion engines driving twin screws, while the *Laurentic*, with the same hull

form and boiler power, was installed with the new 'combination' machinery of reciprocating engines on wing shafts and spent steam exhausting into a low pressure turbine driving three screws.

The *Megantic*'s twin screws were driven by twin 4-cylinder, quadruple expansion steam engines having cylinders of 29, 42, 61 and 87 in in diameter with a stroke of 60 in. They were supplied by six double-ended boilers supplying steam at 190 psi and produced 11,000 ihp which gave the ship a service speed of 16.5 knots. She had a net tonnage of 9,183 and a deadweight tonnage of 8,790, but her load displacement on a draught of 27 ft 6 in was 20,470 tons. Her moulded depth was 41 ft 2 in. The *Megantic* had three overall decks with orlops in the end holds and two open decks above the long bridge deck, a total of seven in all. Her hull was subdivided by 10 watertight bulkheads and there were six holds and hatchways; No3 separating the 'island' bridge and Mates' accommodation from the rest of the superstructure.

The *Megantic*'s total passenger capacity varied considerably during her career but at the time of her completion on 3 June 1909, it was 260 First, 430 Second and over 1,000 Third class. The First class accommodation which occupied the midships portion of the ship was extremely comfortable. The Second class were accommodated on the two short decks in way of the mainmast and in the bridge deck space below, while the Third class passengers were berthed on the lower decks both forward and aft. The *Megantic* sailed on her maiden voyage from Liverpool to Quebec and Montreal on 17 June 1909 and her entry into service completed the requirement for the four-ship service on the weekly White Star-Dominion Line Joint Service, together with the

Below: **The *Megantic* photographed here and the *Laurentic* were the first two liners built for White Star with a single funnel and two masts.** *Richard de Kerbrech Collection.*

Laurentic, Canada and *Dominion*. Although the *Megantic* was around 30 ft longer and 7 ft more in beam than Allan Line's turbine-driven *Victorian* and *Virginian* on the same route, they were capable of 18 knots!

The following year on 27 May 1910, whilst preparing to sail from Montreal, a small lake steamer, the *J. H. Plummer*, collided with the *Megantic*, thereby delaying her departure by a day. Later during August 1910, the *Megantic* departed Montreal with the murderer Dr Crippen and his girlfriend le Neve together with their arresting officer, Chief Inspector Dew, on board. The Canadian service prospered and was strengthened in 1911 by the substitution of the *Teutonic*, which was switched from the New York service and slightly altered, for the *Dominion*. The *Megantic* ran steadily on the Canadian service and during this time her operational performance was compared with that of the *Laurentic* (q.v.). The latter's 'combination' machinery with the central low pressure turbine proved more efficient and effective in service, however the cost of re-engining the *Megantic* was prohibitive, and her power plant, which could give her a steady speed of 16-17 knots was considered adequate for service demands.

Following the outbreak of World War 1, the *Megantic* was requisitioned for trooping duties. Like her sister *Laurentic*, the *Megantic* also sailed from Gaspé Bay on 3 October 1914 as part of a large 32-ship convoy carrying a total of 35,000 Canadian troops to Europe. The warships HMSs *Charybdis*, *Diana*, *Eclipse*, *Glory* and *Talbot* accompanied them. As the convoy neared the western approaches to the UK it split into squadrons depending on their intended ports of destination. The *Megantic* was allocated to the White Squadron in company with the liners *Bermudian*, *Royal Edward* and *Franconia*. They sailed on to Plymouth and arrived there ahead of the Blue Squadron, which included the *Laurentic*,

and proceeded to Devonport where they anchored on 14 October. Between 30 November 1914 and 21 April 1915 she was operated on the Liverpool to New York run and following this she was again used as a troopship with a capacity for 1,800 men.

A near miss occurred on 24 February 1917 when she was attacked by German submarine *UB-43* but sustained no damage. Between 6 April 1917 and 21 February 1919 the *Megantic* operated under the Liner Requisition Scheme and from April 1918 was again placed on the Liverpool-New York route. On 11 December that year she made her first post-war sailing from Liverpool to New York and remained on this run until her last trip on 1 April 1919. The *Megantic* was given a brief refurbishment at Belfast, with an accommodation for 325 First, 260 Second and 550 Third class prior to returning to the Canadian service during May 1919. In this she operated alongside the ageing *Canada*, which was brought in to replace the lost *Laurentic*, with the new emigrant ship *Vedic* joining them in 1920. During the winter season she operated cruises between New York and the West Indies.

Commencing 9 January 1920 she made a single voyage on the White Star-Shaw Savill & Albion joint service carrying Government staff from Liverpool to Sydney; returning via Wellington, Panama and New York and following this she resumed the Liverpool-Canada service. This route was greatly strengthened in 1922 with the completion as a passenger ship of the last Dominion liner *Regina*. Subsequently the *Vedic* was taken off the run and the following year replaced by the new *Doric*. In May 1924, the *Megantic* was converted to a Cabin class ship which proved popular with the travelling public, and she continued on the Liverpool service. The elderly Dominion liner *Canada* was withdrawn, after 30 years service, during 1926 and around this time the *Regina* was painted in White Star colours while still retaining her Dominion name. With effect from 1 January 1927, the ownership of White Star passed from IMMCo control to that of the Royal Mail Steam Packet Co. Group (RMSP Group) and the Canadian service was renamed White Star (Canadian Services).

Concurrent with this change marked the end of Royal Mail's New York service and the transference of their ships that had operated on it. The *Ohio* became the *Albertic*, and the *Orca* was renamed the *Calgaric*, both scheduled for the Canadian run. When in the same year the new *Laurentic* entered service, the *Megantic* was redundant. She was withdrawn and chartered by the Government for a trooping voyage to Shanghai to protect British interests and citizens there from the rising tide of Chinese Nationalism and the seizure of foreign assets by them.

In March 1928, she again had her accommodation reshuffled to cater for 452 Cabin, 260 Second (Designated Tourist) and 550 Third class passengers and on 22 March she was transferred to the London-Le Havre-Southampton-Halifax-New York route when the St. Lawrence was icebound. From 19 April the service was further extended to Quebec and Montreal for the summer months, in consort with the *Albertic*. This became her regular annual schedule against the backdrop of the depression. During 1930-31 she operated on economy cruises together with the *Adriatic*, *Calgaric* and *Laurentic* (*II*), before returning briefly to the London-Canada route for a few voyages. Notwithstanding the efforts of the Company to make their ships pay, she was becoming one of the shipping victims of the Great Depression. On 16 May 1931, she made her last voyage on the Southampton-Quebec-Montreal route and was subsequently laid up in July at Rothesay Bay. She sailed in February 1933 from Rothesay to Osaka to be broken up.

MEGANTIC: *Thought to originate from the Greek word 'Mega' which signifies very large.*

ZEELAND/NORTHLAND

(1910-1911; 1914-1920)
11,905 grt; 561 ft 7 in BP (580 ft OA) x 60 ft 2 in
Quadruple Expansion SR Engines, Twin Screw,
10,000 ihp, 15 knots
Passengers: 342 First class, 194 Second class,
626 Third class
John Brown & Co, Clydebank. Yard No. 342

The *Zeeland* was built during 1900 by John Brown as part of a pair for the Red Star Line. The Red Star Line or more correctly Societe Anonyme de Navigation Belge Americaine was essentially a Belgian American concern operating passenger vessels from Antwerp to the East Coast ports of the United States. After 1893 its funnel colours were black with a white band, similar to those of the American Line, with whom it was closely allied. Its ships ran variously under the Belgian, United States and British flags and were registered in different groups under various company names. Those of its liners that flew the Red Ensign were operated by the International Navigation Company of Liverpool. The ships were frequently interchanged, so creating a rather labyrinthine structure. For the purposes of simplicity all such vessels may be regarded as Red Star liners.

By 1899, directors of the Red Star Line decided to initiate a major building programme which could win back its share of the Atlantic First class traffic in addition to that of the emigrant trade. A group of four ships, two to be built at John Brown & Co. Clydebank and two in the USA from W. Cramp's yard. The *Vaderland* was launched on 12 July 1900 into the Clyde and this was followed by the *Zeeland* on 24 November 1900. The *Zeeland* was a steel ship of 7,511 net tons, designed as a good-paying proposition with a large passenger carrying capacity and a deadweight tonnage of 10,000. She was intended to have a maximum speed of 16

Below: **An unusual photograph of the *Zeeland* in White Star livery showing her at speed. John Brown of Clydebank had originally built her for the Red Star Line.**
World Ship Photo Library.

knots so that she and her sisters could maintain 15 knots at sea and between them operate the weekly Antwerp to New York service.

The *Zeeland* had a depth of 38 ft 2 in and a loaded draught of 30 ft 1 in. There were three principal decks, two of them overall. The hull was subdivided with the installation of 11 watertight bulkheads, and during construction the builders had taken the unprecedented step in strengthening the stem and the forward run of the ship's hull in case of encountering ice at high speeds on the Atlantic! Her twin screws were driven by quadruple expansion steam engines each having cylinder bores of 31, 44, 62 and 88 in in diameter, with a stroke of 54 in. Steam at 200 psi was supplied by eight single-ended cylindrical boilers which consumed some 100 tons of coal a day when steaming at full speed. To cater for this she had a bunker capacity for 3,000 tons of coal. The *Zeeland's* First class accommodation for 342 was to a high standard without being in the luxury range. The fore part of her long bridge deck was given over to First class cabins and the after part to 194 in Second class. The whole main deck was devoted to passengers, the spaces from forward to aft being: Three spaces for 626 Third class, then the remainder of the First class, the First class saloon (between the funnels), galley, Second class saloon, and then Second class cabins.

The *Zeeland* appears to have been a well proportioned ship of the forecastle, bridge and poop variety with a sheer, counter stern and the popular two-funnelled four-masted rig so common at the turn of the century. Her funnels were of flat-sided oval section, and the four masts were single poles only and not equipped to carry yards. With a single boat deck above the bridge deck, and with no houses above that, the superstructure was low for a ship of her size and gave her the appearance of being long and sleek. As built she had a short double tier of deckhouses and open decks in the after well deck. Her hull was black with a red line at upper deck level. This feature was indefinable at a distance and in most black and white photographs. However later in the *Zeeland's* career she had her forecastle, bridge and poop strakes painted white along with her sisters. The engine and boiler room ventilation cowls were of the vertical trunk type with a hinged lid or cover that opened forward; similar to those fitted in the *Lusitania*. These were later changed for the more normal style of cowl.

During her trials on 4/5 April 1901, the *Zeeland* achieved an average speed of 17.4 knots over the measured mile and 17.3 knots during a 12 hour sea trial. She then left the Clyde for Antwerp and sailed on her maiden voyage on 13 April from that port to New York. She flew the red ensign and officially was owned by the International Navigation Company of Liverpool. On this crossing she averaged a speed of 17.1 knots, a creditable speed for its day which was marred a bit by losing an anchor upon her arrival at New York. She later undertook some sailings for the American Line while their *New York* was undergoing alterations. In 1902 Red Star's *Finland* and *Kroonland* joined the fleet and the ships were then able to offer a weekly service from Antwerp. They were able to depart Antwerp on a Saturday and arrive in New York on the morning of the following Monday week; a regular schedule that was maintained up until 1910.

Also during February 1902, the IMMCo combine was formed which then took ownership and control of White Star, Dominion, Leyland, Atlantic Transport, American and Red Star as well as influencing control over the major German companies and the Holland America Line. From this point Red Star became even more labyrinthine in nature and with the transference and the swapping of vessels and services, even more difficult to follow. From August 1904 the Red Star ships initiated a call at Dover both outwards and homewards and this became a regular port of call up until the outbreak of World War 1. The former White Star liner *Gothic* became Red Star's *Gothland* during 1907 and was employed under the Belgian flag on the Philadelphia service. They were joined in 1909 by the new *Lapland* on the New York run which meant that Red Star had a surplus ship. That same year the *Zeeland* was involved in a serious collision in the Straits of Dover with Ropner's steamship *Hartlepool*. Both ships sustained considerable damage and both were held by a court as equally to blame.

White Star's *Republic* had been sunk in a collision a few weeks before the *Lapland* entered service, and as the *Zeeland* was surplus to requirements she was transferred to White Star and steamed to Liverpool to replace the lost *Republic*. She sailed on her first voyage for her new owners on 19 April 1910 on the Liverpool to Boston route in consort with the *Cymric* and as such was repainted in White Star livery. The *Zeeland* once again reverted to Red Star on 14 September 1911 under the British flag and the following year in wake of the *Titanic* disaster, her poop deck was extended aft to take another set of davits on each side and further lifeboats stowed beneath the original boats. In addition her bridge was enlarged and fitted with 'cabs'. Later in the autumn of 1912 she transferred to Belgian registry and placed under the Belgian flag.

In July 1914, she arrived in New York following a collision in mid-Atlantic with Atlantic Transport Line's *Missouri*. This had left a hole in her bow extending from the deck almost down to the waterline. The following month World War 1 broke out with the invasion of Belgium putting an end to the Antwerp route. The headquarters of Red Star were switched to Liverpool and all its ships placed under the British flag. On 11 September, the *Zeeland* returned to White Star to replace their ships requisitioned for Government service. During that September she became a Canadian transport and took part in the first convoy of Canadian troops to sail for the UK. In November 1914 she returned to commercial service making her first voyage from Liverpool to Quebec and Montreal for the White Star-Dominion Joint service and a month later when winter had set in her East Coast ports were Halifax, Nova Scotia and Portland, Maine. The following year she once more reverted to the International Navigation Co. of Liverpool and in February 1915 was renamed *Northland* (probably to avoid confusion with White Star's *Zealandic* which had entered service in 1911). From March that year she remained on the same route as previously but in June she made her last voyage from Liverpool to Quebec and Montreal before the *Northland* was again engaged on Canadian trooping duties until July 1916. From the following August when she reverted to the White Star-Dominion for seven round voyages after which she was taken over by the Shipping Controller under the Liner Requisition Scheme.

From April 1917, she was used on the Atlantic run carrying Government cargoes, munitions and ferrying Canadian and American troops back home. Overcrowding and food messing arrangements prompted complaints about the ship from some units but she continued on this work until well after the Armistice. The *Northland* was decommissioned in September 1919 and after paying off was sent round to Harland & Wolff's at Belfast for reconditioning and conversion to oil fuel. The yard was so congested following the war that the refit took over a year and she had to go to Antwerp to be finished off. In Belgium her former name *Zeeland* was reinstated and she was able to accommodate 228 First, 268 Second and 1,040 Third class passengers. She was returned to Red Star ownership and was still under the British flag. She commenced her post-war commercial service form Antwerp on 18 August 1920, calling at Southampton before crossing to New York.

Below: **The *Olympic* on her purpose-built slipway in readiness for launching. She was painted white and the fore poppet of her launching cradle has been completed. The vastness of the gantry surrounding the hull gives an idea of the sheer size of the undertaking.** *William J. Nelson.*

On this service she was joined by her former sisters *Finland* and *Kroonland* and also the *Lapland*. Later during April 1923 her passenger accommodation was reconstructed to Tourist class only in which her gross tonnage increased to 11,667.

Also in 1923, the *Zeeland* operated temporarily in consort with the old American Line's *St Paul* and she successfully operated on her route for the following three years. At one stage she was in collision with a Danish schooner at Antwerp in which 12 men were overcome by smoke during a fire in one of the schooner's holds. On another occasion she was seriously delayed from sailing during a Belgian railway strike. By late 1926, the ripples of the depression were beginning to be felt and in January 1927 the *Zeeland* was transferred to the diminishing fleet of the Atlantic Transport Line to run on a Tourist class service between London and New York with the *Minnekahda*.

Prior to the transfer taking place the Government hurriedly requisitioned her to rush 1,000 Royal Marines out to Shanghai to protect British interests and citizens there from the rising tide of Chinese Nationalism and the seizure of foreign assets. The *Zeeland* joined the *Megantic* on this deployment and it is rumoured that she made what might be considered to be a record run between London and China! Upon her return she was painted in Atlantic Transport's colours of red funnels with black tops and renamed *Minnesota*. The service lasted from 30 April 1927 until 21 September 1929 with a period of layup in between. In October that year she arrived in London at the end of her last crossing from New York and a few days later left under her own steam for Thos. W. Ward's yard at Inverkeithing. She was broken up during 1930.

OLYMPIC

(1911-1935)
45,324 grt; 852 ft 6 in BP (882 ft 9 in OA) x 92 ft 6 in
Triple Expansion SR Engines + LP Turbine,
Triple Screw, 35,000 ihp + 16,000 shp
21 knots
Passengers: 735 First class, 675 Second class,
1,030 Third class
Harland & Wolff, Belfast. Yard No. 400

The *Olympic* was designed by a team at Harland & Wolff comprising Lord Pirrie, Thomas Andrews, the managing director of the design department, and Lord Pirrie's nephew, Edward Wilding, deputy to Andrews and responsible for the design calculations, stability and trim and finally the shipyard manager, Mr Alexander M. Carlisle. Bruce Ismay was kept involved in the early stages of the design concepts and later in the final project specification. They had originally envisaged that the new ship should have three funnels and two masts but the most prestigious liners in service at that time had four funnels so it was felt that the *Olympic* and her sisters should follow the trend. Her keel was laid on 16 December 1908.

The *Olympic* and later the *Titanic* were constructed of mild steel (which will be referred to later), with cellular double bottoms 5 ft 3 in deep. The bottom plating was hydraulically riveted; the strakes were arranged clincher fashion and the underside of the framing was joggled to avoid the use of tapered packing pieces. In order to reduce the number of butts and overlaps to a minimum, plates of a large size for their day were adopted. The shell plates were from 30 to 36 ft long and 6 ft wide; the largest plates weighed some 4¼ tons. The hull was subdivided by 15 transverse watertight bulkheads, the doors of which were electrically controlled from the bridge. Should any two of the largest compartments become flooded, the vessel could remain afloat indefinitely. These safeguards led White Star to believe that the ship was practically unsinkable.

There were eight steel decks amidships: A, the boat or promenade deck; B, the bridge deck; C, the shelter deck; D, the saloon deck; E, the upper deck; F, the middle deck; and G, the lower deck. At the ends an orlop deck was fitted, which made nine decks in all. Accommodation was provided for 735 First class, 675 Second class and 1,030 Third class passengers. In addition the *Olympic* had a crew of about 860 and was capable of carrying some 3,300 persons in total. The *Olympic* had triple screws, and was propelled by a combination of reciprocating engines and an exhaust, low pressure, steam turbine. The two 3-bladed wing propellers 23 ft 6 in in diameter were driven at 75 rev/min, each by a set of inverted direct-acting triple expansion steam reciprocating engines of 15,000 ihp with 4-cylinders of 54, 84, 97 and 97 in bore, all with a common stroke of 75 in. The steam for these engines was supplied at 215 psi by 24 coal-fired, double-ended and 5 single-ended Scotch boilers.

The boilers were arranged in six entirely independent and isolated boiler rooms and the uptakes from these six boiler rooms ran into three funnels, the aftermost fourth funnel being a dummy. The centre 4-bladed, cast manganese bronze propeller of 16 ft 6 in diameter was driven at 165 rev/min by a massive Parsons turbine of 16,000 shp which took exhaust steam from the reciprocating engines at 9 psi absolute (i.e. sub atmospheric). The *Olympic*'s massive bulk would be steered by a solid cast steel 'plate' rudder made up of six sections bolted together, with an overall length of 78 ft 8 in and 15 ft 3 in wide, its total weight being just over 101 tons.

The huge structure rose in the gantry against the Belfast skyline and as she neared completion her hull was originally painted black. However, before her launch it was decided that she be painted white to ensure that this new challenger for clientele on the North Atlantic would make a good view and show up for attending photographers and show the *Olympic* to her maximum possible advantage. At the day of the launch on 20 October 1910, those attending the list of VIPs such as Lord Pirrie, J. Pierpont Morgan, Bruce Ismay and the Lord Lieutenant of Ireland were present, but it was not such a grand affair as one might suppose. Instead the *Olympic* followed White Star policy of not being named or sent on its way with Champagne; merely the trigger was released at the appointed time of 11am and she took 62 seconds to glide down the slipway and into the waters of the River Lagan.

After a further seven months of fitting out and engining, and having her propellers fitted in the Thompson Graving dock, she undertook her trials on 28 May 1911 with the White Star tenders *Nomadic* and *Traffic* in attendance. Over the measured mile runs the *Olympic* averaged 21.75 knots. Following these she was handed over and sailed from Belfast on 31 May, (the same day as the *Titanic* was launched), and arrived at Liverpool on 1 June, with guests aboard, where

Below: **Machinery arrangement of the *Olympic*.**
Harland & Wolff.

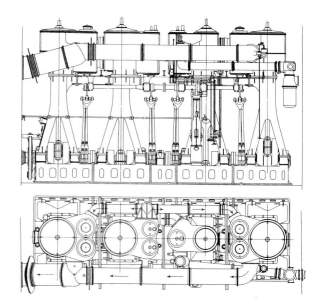

she was open to members of the public. White Star's senior master, Captain Edward J. Smith was appointed as Master for their new masterpiece. For First class passengers the *Olympic* boasted a squash racquet court, a Turkish bath, a fully equipped gymnasium, swimming bath, plunge pool, Parisian-style cafes and libraries staffed by librarians. Indeed some suites offered on the *Olympic* had private promenade space at a cost of £870 during the high season. For First class passengers, free meals were served in the Jacobean-style dinning room; however, to dine in the a la carte Louis XVI restaurant, panelled in French walnut, was extra.

Upon her arrival at Southampton, the *Olympic* was again open for the public to look around and proceeds from the small fee charged went to local hospitals and other charities. After much publicity she sailed on her maiden voyage form Southampton on 14 June 1911 via Cherbourg and Queenstown. For most of the voyage she was accompanied by rather adverse weather conditions but the *Olympic* rode these to prove her seakeeping qualities. During the outward passage she averaged 21.17 knots, completing the journey from Queenstown to New York in 5 days 16 hours 42 minutes, and on the eastbound return trip averaged 22.32 knots. Considering when new in 1907, Cunard's *Mauretania* record eastbound crossing averaged 23.69 knots with her turbines generating 70,000 shp, the *Olympic*'s speed is very laudable for a non-challenger.

Following her maiden voyage Bruce Ismay, who made the crossing, wrote to Lord Pirrie, saying: '*Olympic* is a marvel, and has given unbounded satisfaction.' The *Olympic* made a considerably better crossing speed a little later when on passage from Queenstown to the Ambrose Light Vessel, in which she crossed in 5 days 7 hours and 29 minutes at an average speed of 21.8 knots. On the return passage it was again 22.32 knots. Moving on to the *Olympic*'s fifth voyage from Southampton on 20 September 1911, again Captain Smith was Master in which he was joined by Mr Henry F. Wilde as Chief Officer, and Mr William McMaster Murdoch as First Officer. Ironically, in less than seven months all these same navigators would perish on the *Titanic*. Also aboard for the local-waters knowledge was the pilot Captain George W. Bowyer, who would be giving the helm orders; he was White Star's preferred pilot. After her departure from Southampton, the *Olympic* steamed down Southampton Water and had turned to starboard around the Calshot Spit buoy. From here it was in the approaches to the West Bramble buoy and the ship had to steer a 'Z' bend manoeuvre in the confined channel to avoid the shallows and the Bramble Bank.

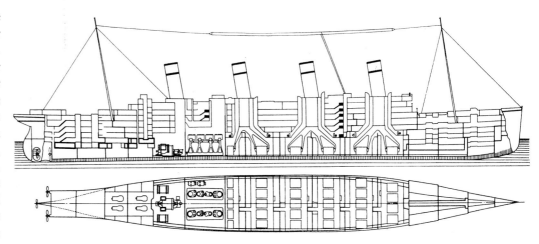

Above: **The *Olympic*'s main side view and plan.** *Harland & Wolff.*

The *Olympic* started to execute her 110° turn to port to round the West Bramble Buoy to bring her into the main channel that would take her down past Cowes Roads and into Spithead. At about 12.40 pm, the *Olympic* was passing the Thorn Knoll Buoy when a warship was sighted about two miles away steaming up The Solent from the West. The warship turned out to be the cruiser HMS *Hawke* of 7,350 tons displacement, a warship with 5 in thick side armour and an underwater ram bow, a steel casting packed with concrete, built in 1891. She was returning to Portsmouth after engine trials in the Western Solent. The *Olympic* gave two short blasts on her whistle to indicate an impending turn to port to take the eastern channel at 11 knots. HMS *Hawke* under the command of Commander William Blunt was passing Egypt Point at Cowes and was closing on the turning *Olympic* at 15.5 knots, with the full broadside of the *Olympic* in their path, a path that was now converging. Regulations stipulated that if HMS *Hawke* was the 'stand on' ship (i.e. that vessel which may proceed on its intended course unhindered), then she should have right of way. If however the *Hawke* was an overtaking vessel, it would have been her duty to keep out the way of the overtaken *Olympic*.

Below: **A contemporary photograph from *The Sphere* of 8 April 1911, showing the *Olympic* entering the new Thompson Graving Dock.** *The Sphere.*

When the *Olympic* had completed her turn and steadied up with increasing speed on her new course, the *Hawke* was observed to be 400 or 500 yards astern on the starboard quarter. Gradually the *Hawke* started to overhaul the *Olympic* and was abreast of her being on a parallel course 300 yards away, when, at the same time the *Olympic*'s central, turbine driven, propeller was engaged giving her a significant increase in speed. As she moved through the waters of The Solent just North of East Cowes, the *Olympic*'s massive hull set up changes in pressure and velocity well ahead of her bow and on either beam as well as astern. These changes are accentuated in restricted waterways. The *Hawke*, being of a much smaller displacement, and significantly less than 3½ times the length of the *Olympic* away, was drawn in towards the *Olympic* by what is now known as 'canal' or 'shallow water effect'. This may sometimes be avoided by helm action, if the effect is recognised in time. Thus the *Hawke* sheered to port toward the *Olympic* overcoming the action on the part of the *Hawke*'s helmsman, and collided bow on with *Olympic*'s starboard quarter, 80 ft forward of the stern abreast the mainmast.

The 45 ft high triangular opening penetrated between 6 ft 8 in and 8 ft into the hull. The hole was mainly above the waterline with a smaller puncture nearer the waterline caused by the *Hawke*'s ram bow. Later detailed examination of the damage revealed that plate tears in the area of the impact exhibited a clean break with very little distortion of the plates, being more of a cleavage type fracture. There were also some failures in the riveted joints and plate ripping adjacent to the hole made by the *Hawke*. Many of the plate tears were unusually sharp and manifested 'brittle' type fracture. Evasive action on the part of the *Hawke* to go astern of the *Olympic* proved fruitless when the cruiser's helm jammed. The impact caused the *Hawke* to heel over to starboard and be swung away in the water like a top as the *Olympic* went past. On seeing the *Hawke*'s manoeuvre, the pilot ordered the *Olympic*'s engines stopped. What was not

Below: **The *Olympic* anchored in the River Mersey during her visit to Liverpool on 1 June 1911.** *Tom Rayner Collection.*

Above: **Resplendent in her new paintwork, the *Olympic* arrives at Southampton.** *Nautical Photo Agency.*

known at the time was that the *Olympic*'s starboard propeller had been badly damaged in the collision with one of the blades, having had chunks broken from it when it was struck by the *Hawke*'s ram bow.

The *Olympic*'s watertight doors were shut as a precaution and while her two aftmost watertight compartments were flooded there was no immediate danger of her sinking. As luck would have it passengers were in the dining room and the Second class cabins in the vicinity of the collision were vacant at the time. Having missed the tide the *Olympic* anchored in Osborne Bay, off East Cowes, for the night. The Red Funnel tug *Vulcan* was sent to stand by. An inspection of the damage meant that the *Olympic* could not continue her voyage, which was promptly cancelled. Passengers were taken off by tender and transferred to other vessels to complete their passage. The following day, Thursday 21 September, the *Olympic* was towed back into Southampton. Here an assessment of the damage by Company officials required her to be drydocked back at her Belfast builders, who had the only facility for a liner so long. Prior to this, shipwrights and carpenters from Harland & Wolff's Southampton yard shored up the hole in her hull with large wooden patches above the waterline and steel plates below which took 10 days to complete.

Finally in a light loaded condition, the *Olympic* left Southampton on 4 October for Belfast at 10 knots under her own steam, and completed the 570 mile voyage in two days. Once drydocked, work on the repairs to the propeller and hull were commenced. Spares intended for the *Titanic*, which was being fitted out, were used. The construction of the sister ships outboard propellers were three cast bronze blades attached at their root by a series of bronze studs and nuts to the cast steel boss. In this way experience showed that a damaged blade could be replaced at a minimum cost because of the expensive nature of bronze. (With the combination of the two dissimilar metals in contact it must surely have been a recipe for galvanic/electrolytic corrosion; the cast steel hub became a huge sacrificial anode! In the era before welding, small chunks lost from a propeller blade or edges could be replaced either by 'dressing off' or casting in which molten bronze would be poured into a box to make up the tip. This was then 'dressed off'. Another alternative method called 'hammer welding', was used on smaller propellers, and may well have been used.)

This period was the penultimate time these two sisters would be together, and indeed a photograph captured the occasion showing that the two were identical, except that the *Titanic* did not have the forward part of her promenade deck enclosed. Following the collision, HMS *Hawke*, with her bows stove in by the impact, proceeded direct to Portsmouth, constant pumping being necessary to keep her afloat. Repairs took several months, as it was necessary to rebuild more than 20 ft of her bow section. Repairs to the *Olympic* cost more than £103,000 and she did not return to service until 30 November that year. As a result the three subsequent round trips that were cancelled cost the Company more than £150,000 in lost earnings. In the ensuing litigation and appeal which followed, White Star sued the Admiralty and Commander Blunt for damage, which in turn resulted in the Admiralty bringing a counter claim against White Star for the damage caused to HMS *Hawke*. At the Court of Inquiry evidence was conflicting as the Admiralty claimed that they were the 'stand on' ship with the right of way, and that the *Olympic* crowded the *Hawke* out of the channel, and that the latter's helm jammed during an evasive manoeuvre. The *Olympic*'s owners claimed that she was being overhauled by the *Hawke*, and that it was the liner that was the 'stand on' ship and therefore had right of way. Later model tests showed that the warship was pulled in towards the *Olympic* by the suction set up due to the disparity of the displacements of the two ships moving through a seaway so close together.

The Court found the *Olympic* to blame, although White Star itself was exonerated as their ship was under compulsory pilot with Captain Bowyer in charge at the time. A final Appeal was brought before the House of Lords on 9 November 1914 in which the original finding was upheld. The deliberation was that HMS *Hawke* was a *crossing* ship and not an *overtaking* ship; as such it was the *Olympic*'s duty to keep out of the way, whilst it was the *Hawke*'s duty to maintain her course and speed. Early the following year on 21 February 1912, the *Olympic* left New York on an

Below: **The *Olympic* steams down through Spithead outward bound for New York. She is seen following her major rebuild of 1914 with extra lifeboats. She is moving though the line of warships that are anchored at the Fleet Review of 16 July 1914 and is blowing in salute.** *Marilyn Averis.*

Eastbound crossing that was to prove eventful. Three days later on Saturday 24 February, whilst some 750 miles east of Newfoundland, it was thought that she struck what may have been a submerged wreck, and shed a blade from her port propeller. The ship experienced a slight shudder but her passengers did not panic. The *Olympic* completed her voyage, calling at Plymouth and Cherbourg before arriving at Southampton on 28 February. Following the disembarkation of passengers she sailed for Belfast to be drydocked. It was hoped that the drydocking and replacement blade could be turned around in a full day, but missing the tide and prolonged stormy weather further compounded delays. It was not for a full week that the repairs were completed and the *Olympic* sailed from Belfast

on 7 March, and eventually resumed her sailing schedule from Southampton on 14 March.

A month later and *Olympic*'s sister *Titanic* had stolen the limelight and bathed in the publicity as White Star's new 'darling', with Captain E. Smith in command of her. On Saturday 13 April 1912, the *Olympic* left New York bound for Southampton via Plymouth and Cherbourg, under the command of Captain Herbert J. Haddock. Two days later she received the *Titanic*'s distress call at 1.00am on 15 April when she was approximately 505 miles south of the *Titanic*'s reported position. Upon receipt of the *Titanic*'s SOS the *Olympic*'s Master immediately altered course and ordered full power from the engine room to speed to her sister's rescue. Wireless communication between the *Olympic* and the *Carpathia* and other vessels in the vicinity of the disaster caused the Master to stand down from the rescue attempt. Ironically *Carpathia*'s Captain Rostron had advised him that it was Bruce Ismay's wish that any survivors from *Titanic* not see her identical sister ship! For her part *Olympic*'s wireless transmitted news of the disaster and known survivors' names via the wireless station at Cape Race.

Whilst at Southampton in August 1912, the *Olympic* was bunkered with 4,000 tons of coal in 14½ hours, the previous time taken having been 18 hours. This set something of a world record for the coaling of a liner for its day. As a result of the disaster, and the ensuing loss of confidence by prospective passengers travelling in a ship resembling the *Titanic*, the *Olympic* made only five more round voyages. She was then sent to Belfast for a major refit and additional safety improvements from 10 October 1912 until 22 March 1913. These were also retrofitted to the third sister of the ordered trio which was under construction on No. 2 slipway, and was to be named *Gigantic*. Although originally designed to remain afloat with two compartments flooded, a complete inner skin was fitted as well as the double bottom being extended around the turn of bilge and up the sides as wing walls to between the middle and upper decks in the area of the engine and boiler rooms. Extra bulkheads were built and others raised to the strength deck height at the top of the hull. The modifications, with her side bunkers re-sited amidships, improved her watertight integrity such that she could remain afloat with six watertight compartments flooded. In addition, her lifeboats were increased from 20 to 68 in total, with a total capacity for 3,700 persons.

All this work required the removal of funnels and boilers to gain access to the double bottom, as well as all the piping and much of the electrical wiring. Not surprising, the work took five months at a cost of £250,000, the price towards the cost of a new intermediate liner. During her absence from the service, the American Line had stepped in to maintain her sailing schedule. Upon completion, the *Olympic*'s First class capacity had been reduced to 750 and her gross tonnage increased to 46,439. All White Star ships were similarly treated as indeed were other British liners which did not have sufficient lifeboat passenger carrying capacity.

She returned to service on 2 April 1913 from Southampton and soon resumed her steady three-weekly round trip schedule between Southampton and New York, in consort with the elderly *Majestic* (1889) and the *Oceanic* (1899). Now a safer ship on the route, up until World War 1 her popularity returned as public confidence increased. The *Olympic* soon established herself as a favourite among the travelling public, especially in light of all the newer and much larger competition from Cunard's *Aquitania* and

Below: **The *Olympic*'s first class dining saloon.** *C. R. Hoffmann.*

Above: **The *Olympic*'s first class smoking room.** *C. R. Hoffmann.*

HAPAG's *Imperator*. When World War 1 broke out on 4 August 1914, the *Olympic* was en route to New York and for a while stayed on commercial service. Between August and October she made three Atlantic crossings carrying some 6,000 US citizens returning from Europe to avoid the war. During this time her UK terminus was switched to Liverpool from Southampton and then later on, to Greenock on the Clyde, to avoid German patrol boats and submarines.

On one of these eastbound crossings which had started from New York on 21 October 1914 bound for Greenock with 1,600 passengers on board, she reached the approaches to Northwest Ireland on 27 October and received a wireless warning of recently laid mines in the vicinity. Meanwhile not far away, some 20 miles northeast of Tory Island, the 23,000 ton displacement battleship HMS *Audacious* had struck a mine at 8.30 am, laid by the German AMC *Berlin* (later to become White Star's *Arabic III*). She had been holed in her port quarter and attempted to steam for the shelter of nearby Lough Swilly. At 10 am, the *Olympic* received the *Audacious*'s distress call and made her way gingerly to the area, finding the warship down by the stern in a heavy swell. A tow was attempted with one of the *Olympic*'s lifeboats taking a 6 in wire cable aboard. Other vessels in attendance were HMS *Exmouth* and the fleet collier *Thornhill*. When the towline took up the tension it snapped. A 9 in wire cable then replaced this but the battleship's crew was unable to secure it. 250 of the 900 men of *Audacious*'s crew were taken off by 14 of the *Olympic*'s lifeboats operating a shuttle service. The attending naval vessels evacuated others. High winds and choppy seas prevented the *Olympic* shipping her lifeboats when she was ordered to proceed to Lough Swilly at 1900 hours (7 pm); the *Audacious* sank at 2100 (9pm).

A virtual news blackout was imposed about the warship's loss and passengers were advised not to reveal what they had seen. The *Olympic* anchored in Lough Swilly from 27 October to 2 November while the minefield laid by North German Lloyd's *Berlin* was swept for safer navigation. Following this delay she sailed for Belfast where her passengers disembarked, and whilst there she was requisitioned as a troopship. Here, all her fittings and furniture were removed and placed into storage. She was fitted forward with a 12-pounder, and a 4.7 in gun aft. The full conversion took 10 months and during September 1915

Above: **The *Olympic*'s first class lounge.** *C. R. Hoffmann.*

she emerged with a capacity to carry 6,000 troops, and placed under the White Ensign.

An eventful war lay ahead for the HMT *Olympic*, and the following month she made the first of a series of trooping voyages to Mudros Island for the Dardanelles and Gallipoli campaigns, under the command of Captain Bertram Hayes. During November 1915, whilst off Cape Matapan in Greece, she was pursued by a German submarine but the *Olympic*'s high speed (she could make 23 knots with all of her boilers fired up) and manoeuvrability outpaced her pursuer. Early the following year on 23 and 26 February 1916, whilst again near Mudros Island, two torpedoes narrowly missed her. A month later on 23 March, the *Olympic* commenced on a series of ten round trips from Liverpool to Halifax, to transport Canadian troops to the European war theatre. These crossings to Canada were without incident, and were carried out unescorted and at high speed. Her record of regular safe voyages across the Atlantic earned her the title of 'Old Reliable' in naval and military circles, and her reputation and value to the war effort could not be understated.

On 12 January 1917, the *Olympic* returned to Belfast for the fitting of six additional 6 in guns to defend her against submarine attacks and other surface raiders. This increase in her weaponry was in addition to the routine maintenance that was required. On 5 April 1917 she sailed once again under her blue ensign with a British diplomatic mission on board headed by Mr A. J. Balfour, bound for Halifax. The mission went on to the United States and finally sailed back to the UK on the *Olympic* at the conclusion of the conference. By late summer she was painted to a new 'dazzle' specification; a paint scheme intended to confuse potential attacking submarines by distorting the ship's perspective in daylight. The artist Norman Wilkinson, then a Lieutenant in the RNR, designed the 'dazzle' paint scheme. Following this she sailed for New York and arrived there on Christmas Day 1917 to embark her first contingent of US troops, following the United States entry into the war. She departed on her eastbound crossing with the 'doughboys' on 11 January 1918.

The following spring, the *Olympic* sailed on her 22nd trooping voyage from Southampton to New York on 24 April 1918. Following her turnaround at New York where she embarked a full complement of US troops, a US Navy destroyer escorted her on the return leg of her voyage as far as the western approaches to the English Channel. Here she was to rendezvous with RN destroyers to take over the escort. As dawn broke on the 12 May and the *Olympic* approached the Lizard in Cornwall, a German submarine

Below: **The *Olympic*'s restaurant.** *C. R. Hoffmann.*

Above: **The *Olympic*'s first class veranda café.** *C. R. Hoffmann.*

was spotted hove to on the surface, on the *Olympic*'s starboard bow, apparently quite oblivious to the great liner's presence. Captain Hayes decided to try and ram the U-boat. A shot from *Olympic*'s 6 in gun failed to hit but alerted the submarine. The U-boat tried to evade the *Olympic* by turning at full speed inside the *Olympic*'s arc of turn, and with a hard to starboard the submarine ran under the liner's bow, was damaged and sank. A US destroyer picked up survivors, and later confirmed that the sunken German submarine was *U-103*. At the time, although not feeling the impact of collision, it was later discovered during drydocking, that the *Olympic*'s stem was twisted some eight feet to port with several adjacent plates being buckled.

Following the war's end on 11 November 1918, the *Olympic* was again chartered on 8 December by the Canadian Government and carried some 5,000 troops home to Halifax. The repatriation of military personnel continued for 10 months, along with the return of US troops from the UK and France to Halifax. One of the high points was when 6,148 Canadian troops, a record number carried, were disembarked at Halifax during April 1919. As her war service came to an end the final tally could reveal that she had carried some 41,334 civilian passengers, 80,088 Canadian and 42,835 US troops as well as 24,600 troops on the Mediterranean. In addition, she had transported 12,000 men of a Chinese labour battalion of 'Coolies' who were employed behind the lines on the Western Front; without so much as a casualty. She had steamed some 184,000 miles and consumed 347,000 tons of coal, her main engines performing without defect. Indeed, she had well earned the title 'Old Reliable'!

Her ramming of the *U-103* was the only recorded instance of a merchant ship sinking a submarine in World War 1, by taking the attack to the U-boat threat! It also earned for her Master, Captain Bertram Hayes, the DSO. Emerging from the conflict, the

Olympic was the only one of the intended three sisters to survive, as the *Britannic* had become a war loss when she struck a mine in the Aegean Sea on 21 November 1916, and sunk. Apart from the New York service, the *Arabic (II)* and *Laurentic* on the Halifax run had been sunk, along with the *Cymric*, *Georgic*, *Afric* and *Delphic (II)*, which normally traded to Oceania. Under the Treaty of Versailles, former German liners were ceded to Great Britain and those such as the *Majestic (II)* (ex-*Bismarck*), *Homeric* (ex-*Columbus*) and *Arabic (III)* (ex-*Berlin*), were purchased by White Star. The two former would maintain the envisaged three-ship service along with the *Olympic*. Upon the completion of her repatriation duties, the *Olympic* returned to Belfast for an extensive refit and refurbishment, to restore her to her former glory and incorporate some updated features to meet the demands of the post-war traveller.

On 12 August 1919, after shipping into the Thompson Drydock at Belfast, it was discovered that the *Olympic* might possibly have been struck by a torpedo which did not explode. This was thought to have happened in the closing stages of the war. The torpedo's impact against the hull had caused a large indentation to the plating and flooding had resulted from small fissures and failed rivets in the plates outside her wing wall. The flooding was not detected until the drydocking, for once the drydock had been pumped dry, water was found to be pouring from a large buckled area of hull plating that also manifested tears and failed rivets! The main task in hand was to convert the *Olympic*'s boilers from coal-fired to the more modern oil-fired. Gone would be the days of coaling ship and its attendant filth. Bunkers were made 'watertight' and lined with steam pipes for heating the thick heavy boiler oil to make it less viscous for pumping. Pumps and piping would convey the oil from the bunkers via filters to the boiler burners and valves. Gone would be the backbreaking task of shovelling coal; instead, a hand-controlled valve on the burner atomiser. Stokers and

Below: **The *Olympic* is photographed here on 14 July 1924, high and dry in Southampton's floating dock**. *Mick Lindsay.*

Trimmers now had to 'jump through hoops' to qualify as Firemen. There were to be 33 boiler room attendants, 12 cleaners and 9 greasers; a total of 54 compared with a total of 224 that were required when she burned coal. As such the *Olympic*'s engine-room staff was drastically cut by 170; an ensuing saving in labour costs that was not welcomed in the shipping pool circles. The accommodation space vacated by the axed personnel was rearranged for Third class passengers.

Olympic's peacetime fittings and furniture, stored since 1915, were renovated and reinstalled to bring her back to the luxury liner she had been, with a revised accommodation for 750 First, 500 Second and 1150 Third. The total cost of the refit was a little under £500,000 but proved well justified as she would carry the houseflag for a further 15 years and survive the White Star Line itself! Whilst she was out of action for nearly a year, her place on the North Atlantic run was taken by the *Lapland*, on which many of the *Titanic*'s survivors had returned to the UK in 1912. On 25 June 1920, the *Olympic* returned to the Southampton to New York service in consort with the *Adriatic*. Later in the year she made the eastbound crossing from Ambrose Light to Cherbourg in 5 days, 13 hours, 10 minutes at an average speed of 22.53 knots. In 1921, the *Olympic* made her fastest crossing in 5 days, 12 hours, 39 minutes. The faster turnaround time in ports because of oil refuelling meant an increase in scheduled crossings, and between June 1920 and the end of 1923 she made 49 Atlantic round trips in between her regular servicing schedule. In fact, during October 1923, the eastbound crossing from New York to Southampton was made in 5 days, 20 hours, 21 minutes and later in December she made the westbound crossing in 5 days, 21 hours, 8 minutes!

By 1922, the *Olympic* had now been joined by the *Homeric* and *Majestic* on the Southampton to New York run,

On October 20, 1910, was launched the White Star liner *Olympic*, a ship which marked a notable advance in ocean transport. She was over 882 feet in length, and 46,000 tons gross tonnage. Her sister ship was the *Titanic*.

Above: **In this unusual photograph the *Olympic* shows off her lines. Judging by the pristine condition of her paintwork it may have been taken early in the 1930s prior to the Cunard and White Star merger.** *Fox.*

to maintain the fortnightly three-ship service, which had originally been planned for the *Olympic* and her two sisters. As such, from 1924 to 1928, the *Olympic* averaged 15 round trips per annum on this schedule. On 22 March 1924, after having slipped her moorings, the *Olympic* was manoeuvring astern from Pier 59 into the North River, with her stern swinging out upstream into the River. At the same time the Furness-Bermuda liner *Fort St George* was gradually gaining speed towards the Manhattan side of the river. The *Fort St George* sought to turn to starboard towards the New Jersey shore to pass around the *Olympic*'s stern which was still underway astern prior to steaming slow ahead towards the

Below: **Another photograph of the *Olympic* taken in The Solent. Cracks appeared in her port crankshaft at the end of 1932, which caused her to be withdrawn from service for 3½ months.** *Tom Rayner Collection.*

Above: **The *Olympic* on one of her last voyages from Southampton. This photograph was taken in 1934 following White Star's merger with Cunard and she is flying both houseflags.** *P. A. Vicary.*

Narrows. The two ships collided; the *Fort St George*'s port quarter was struck by the *Olympic*'s towering stern. The Furness liner sustained 150 ft of buckled decking, her mainmast was sheared off at its base and two derricks were damaged, as well as lifeboat davits and rails twisted by the impact costing £35,000 worth of damage. This made her put back into Pier 95, while the *Olympic* hove to for a while, whilst the stern damage was inspected by divers. It was discovered not too serious as she could still answer her helm and continued on her voyage. Fortunately there were no casualties.

Also during 1924, Southampton's new Tyne-built Floating Dock arrived in the port. It was able to accommodate the *Olympic* and her consorts, which meant no more expensive and time-consuming trips back to Belfast for drydocking and maintenance. By 1927, White Star returned to British control when it became part of Lord Kylsant's Royal Mail Steam Packet Group of companies. For Royal Mail it was a financial risk but there were many in the shipping industry who welcomed the Oceanic Steam Navigation Co. back from United States financial interests. In 1928, her accommodation was revised to 675 First, 560 Tourist (a new class recently introduced which combined the old Second class and the best of Third), and in addition to 830 Third class. To cater for this restructured clientele, the sanitation facilities were updated with new baths being installed.

Following the Wall Street crash and the Depression that resulted, 1929 affected White Star like other shipping companies by the drop in passenger receipts. Indeed, during 1930 over 1 million passengers had crossed the North Atlantic, and by 1935 this would plummet to less than ½ million! In 1930, partly as an attempt to capture some dollars and take advantage of the United States liquor laws, the *Olympic* ran 2, 3, 4 and 5-day short trips (usually referred to as 'booze cruises' or 'Four day Whoopee Cruises'). They became quite an institution on the Eastern Seaboard of the United States as a cheap and fun weekend

at sea, at least for those who could afford them. Calls were made between New York and Halifax in order to exploit a legal 'loophole' in compliance with US Navigation Laws, which forbade foreign ships from trading directly between United States' ports. In these the *Olympic* operated along with the *Majestic*. Between each their stay in New York lasted a week. The loss of revenue on the North Atlantic service became painfully apparent for during one eastbound crossing in April 1930, the *Olympic* carried only 185 passengers in total! The small amount of passengers crossing the Atlantic could not sustain the number of passenger liners and shipping companies all vying for this shrinking market.

Strangely, 1932 was a boom year for cruising with more than 100,000 Britons spending their holidays at sea. During that period more than 200 cruises were operated from British ports. It was not surprising that both Cunard and White Star joined in the competition and the *Olympic* sailed on Whitsun and August Bank Holiday cruises from Southampton with fares as low as £3 per head. In October of the same year the *Olympic* developed a small fracture in the crankshaft journal of her port engine, during a homeward bound voyage. Following this her subsequent sailings were cancelled and her machinery surveyed. The rumour spread that the *Olympic* was about to be withdrawn from service and scrapped. Instead she was given a 3½ month overhaul at Southampton by Harland & Wolff. In the course of this her accommodation was again updated to take 618 First, 447 Second and 382 Third class passengers. While the *Olympic* was out of service, the newly-introduced motorship *Georgic* was switched from Liverpool to operate from Southampton in her place. The *Olympic* resumed her service on 1 March 1933; however White Star's losses for the year 1932 amounted to £152,045.

Although the *Olympic* had been more than 20 years in service and probably to some her Edwardian décor and dated fittings may have seemed a little passé, she was still a very popular vessel and proved more attractive to passengers than her two 'adopted' consorts, the *Majestic* and *Homeric*. In fact by 1933 only five ships were on the North Atlantic trade, The *Majestic* and *Olympic* from Southampton; the two new motorships *Britannic* and *Georgic* from Liverpool and the *Laurentic* to Canada from Liverpool. As a result of the depression and the Cunard Line wishing to seek Government finance for their new superliner 534, for the Atlantic ferry, Cunard and White Star merged, as survival replaced rivalry. So on 10 May 1934, the *Olympic* passed to joint ownership. Almost a week later, on the morning of 16 May 1934, whilst nearly at the end of her westbound passage, the *Olympic*, under the command of Captain John W. Binks, was entering the final leg of her journey and in the vicinity of the Nantucket Shoals. Entering thick fog, the *Olympic*'s Master reduced her speed to 12 knots. In addition her bow and crow's nest lookouts were doubled as well as regularly sounding the ship's whistle, for they were in the vicinity of the Nantucket Lightship, the Eastern outpost light of the American Continent; (with a modest candle power of 3,000 and a visibility distance of 13 miles in clear weather!).

Although the *Olympic* had picked up the Lightship's radio beam signal, it indicated that it was on the liner's starboard bow. Shortly after 11am the *Olympic* steered to port in an attempt to put some distance between the two vessels, but looming out of the fog low down was the Lightship's port beam. The *Olympic*, too late to take evasive action, rammed and sunk the Lightship. She immediately hove to and launched her lifeboats to pick up survivors, but seven of the Lightship's 11-man crew had perished, with only three bodies being recovered. Damage to the *Olympic*'s stem was minimal. The United States Government Bureau of Lighthouses held the *Olympic* responsible for the loss and sued White Star for £100,000; the writ was served on the *Olympic* whilst berthed at New York, which delayed her sailing. Although Cunard White Star accepted liability, they later appealed and contested the sum and eventually forfeited an agreed £70,000.

By 1935, rationalisation was the watchword of the day and Cunard White Star was seeking to dispose of older tonnage, and the *Olympic*'s name was in the frame. On 27 March 1935, she departed Southampton on her last round trip to New York and upon her return was laid up on 12 April at Southampton. Later on 20 August, after she had been laid up for five months, she was opened for inspection to prospective buyers and at the time she was the largest vessel ever to be offered for scrap value. On 10 September, Sir John Jarvis bought her for £100,000 only to resell her to Thos. W. Ward & Co. Ltd (Metal Industries), for the same amount with the proviso that she be broken up at Jarrow, to alleviate the chronic unemployment in the North East of England. On 11 October 1935, the *Olympic*, which had 257 round crossings of the Atlantic to its credit, had steamed a total of 1½ million miles, had earned in World War 1 her sobriquet of 'Old Reliable' and herself outlived the existence of the White Star Line, sailed from Southampton for the Tyne, arriving there on 13 October. After nearly two years of dismantling after which her hull had been cut down to the waterline level, on 19 September 1937, the remains of her hull were towed to Thos. W. Ward's Inverkeithing yard in Scotland, for final demolition.

OLYMPIC: *Of or pertaining to Olympia in Greece.*

Below: **A stern view photograph taken on the same day. In less than a year she would be sold out of the new company for scrap.** *P. A. Vicary.*

NOMADIC (II)

(1911-1927)
1,273 grt; 220 ft 8 in BP x 37 ft 1 in
Compound Expansion SR Engines, Twin Screw,
12 knots
Passengers: 1,000 (First and Second).
Harland & Wolff, Belfast. Yard No. 422

After her keel was laid on 22 December 1910, the *Nomadic* was built alongside the smaller *Traffic* and launched on 25 April 1911 for use as a tender to White Star and other liners, and based at Cherbourg. She was initially built to attend the needs of the Company's *Olympic* and *Titanic* and she was completed on 27 May 1911 (as was the *Traffic*), so that she could begin her duties and be present at the *Olympic*'s trials before she left Belfast. Indeed, the *Nomadic* accompanied the *Olympic* to Liverpool on 31 May and thence to Southampton before sailing on to Cherbourg to take up station there on 3 June, and replace the earlier *Gallic*. As such she was registered there and placed under the ownership of George Auguste Laniece, under the French flag. The *Nomadic*'s plush interiors included bars, elaborate pillars and sweeping staircases. These were meant to give the First and Second class an entrée of what they could expect on the two luxury sisters, even before they boarded; in addition to their baggage.

On 13 November 1911, after nearly six months in service, the *Nomadic* was coming alongside the liner *Philadelphia*, in the Cherbourg roads, when she collided bow on with the liner. The impact crushed the tender's bow and twisted her stem, necessitating repairs. At 7pm on 10 April 1912, the *Nomadic* was tender to the *Titanic* for the first and last time. In this capacity she carried 172 First and Second class passengers out to the vessel and returned with 24 disembarking passengers, in the course of 90 minutes. When World War 1 broke out in August 1914, the transatlantic traffic to the United States all but stopped, and the *Nomadic* was transferred to Brest in Brittany where she served as a naval tender and later the transportation of US soldiers. Originally built without a wheelhouse, one was later added.

In 1927, it was decided that the *Nomadic*, together with the *Traffic*, was not being utilised to her fullest capacity serving only as she did, ships of the IMMCo Group. So, White Star sold her to the Compagnie Cherbourgeoise de Transbordement of Paris. For their part of the deal the French company signed an agreement with White Star concerning the transfer of their passengers and eliminated operating problems. Following the Cunard White Star merger in 1934, the *Nomadic* (along with the *Traffic*), was taken over by the local towage company Societe Cherbourgeoise de Remorquage et de Sauvetage, Les Abeilles of Le Havre. She was renamed *Ingenieur Minard* and her funnel was painted black with a red band. She remained at Cherbourg along with the *Traffic*, which had been renamed *Ingenieur Reibell*, and both vessels continued to tender the liners up until World War 2, when they parted company.

During the invasion of France in 1940, the *Ingenieur Minard* was utilised again as a troop carrier and took part in the evacuation of British soldiers from Le Havre. She sought refuge in the United Kingdom and during World War 2 operated mainly along the South coast of England in the role of a coastal patrol vessel and minelayer. She returned to

Below: **White Star's tender *Nomadic* based at the Bassin du Commerce in Cherbourg.** *Richard de Kerbrech Collection.*

Cherbourg after the war in 1945 and for a much-needed refit. In this her mast was repositioned abaft the wheelhouse, part of her bulwarks were replaced by open rails and her passenger capacity was reduced to 500; following which she resumed her normal service of tendering the liners. She continued in this role until November 1968 when she was sold to Somairec for demolition at Le Havre.

The *Ingenieur Minard* was resold to Mr Yvon Vincent who reinstated her original name. She sailed from Conflans Sainte Honorine up the River Seine to Paris and to become a floating restaurant. Prior to this her funnel was shortened and the mast removed so that she could pass under the bridges of Paris and was moored at Quai Debilly in the shadow of the Eiffel Tower. She traded as a restaurant under the name *Nomadic* from 1974 onwards. However, the restaurant closed in 1999 and the ship was seized by the Port of Paris Authority for the non-payment of mooring fees. The *Nomadic*'s built-up superstructure and stanchions were removed again to lower her height to remove her from her Paris berth, and in 2003 she was towed to Le Havre pending her fate.

The Paris authority put the *Nomadic* up for auction at Paris on 26 January 2006. She was auctioned off to the Department of Social Development of the Northern Ireland Government for Euro 250,001 (£171,000) for a euro more than the reserve price; which was a sole bid. The *Nomadic* was shipped aboard a submersible barge and secured with large steel posts buttresses before being towed back to Belfast. She arrived there on 17 July 2006 for restoration.

TRAFFIC (II)

(1911-1927)
675 grt; 175 ft 7 in BP x 35 ft 1 in
Compound Expansion SR Engines, Twin Screw,
12 knots
Passengers: 500 Third class only
Harland & Wolff, Belfast. Yard No. 423

The *Traffic* was launched two days after the *Nomadic* on 27 April 1911 although she was completed at the same time on 27 May. She was essentially a back-up vessel and one of her roles was that of carrying the Third class passengers to the liners; ironically the smaller vessel for the largest complement of passengers. She was powered by the two twin-cylinder compound engines of 12 in and 24 in bore with a stroke of 15 in. Her net tonnage was 420. Her main function was that of a baggage tender and to facilitate this, she was fitted with electric conveyors, one at each end of the superstructure, which could reach to the liner's upper deck. Along with the *Nomadic*, she attended the sea trials of the *Olympic*, but on the following day proceeded to Cherbourg to take up her IMMCo tender duties, where she arrived on 3 June.

As with the *Nomadic*, the *Traffic* was registered at Cherbourg under the French flag and although a White Star ship she was in the ownership of George Auguste Laniece. On 10 April 1912, she was a tender for the 102 Third class

passengers that boarded the *Titanic* during that liner's only call at Cherbourg, they occupied only a fifth of the *Traffic*'s capacity. When World War 1 broke out, she served with the *Nomadic* at Brest as a naval tender, returning to Cherbourg during October 1919. During 1927, the *Traffic* was sold with the *Nomadic*, to the newly-formed Compagnie Cherbourgeoise de Transbordement of Paris, there being an agreement in the sale concerning the transfer of White Star passengers during tendering. On 5 June 1929, the *Traffic* was damaged in a collision with the *Homeric* and she sustained damage to her starboard rails and plates necessitating repairs. Later in October that year, she was fitted with new propellers to enhance her manoeuvrability. Whilst tendering the Atlantic Transport liner *Minnewaska* on a particularly stormy day on 9 December 1929, the impact caused by the *Traffic* coming alongside damaged plates in her bulwark, sheer strake and stringer on the starboard bow. The aforementioned arrangement negotiated with White Star worked quite smoothly until White Star merged with Cunard in 1934 and with it came the inevitable economic cuts. The *Traffic* (along with the *Nomadic*) was taken over by the local towage firm of Societe Cherbourgeoise de Remorquage et de Sauvetage Les Abeilles of Le Havre and renamed *Ingenieur Reibell*. Under new management and livery she remained at Cherbourg and tendered the liners up until World War 2.

When this did come in September 1939, the *Ingenieur Reibell* was taken over by the French Navy initially as a minelayer X23. Following the invasion of France she was scuttled on 17 June 1940 at Cherbourg. She was later raised by the Germans and apparently put back into service with them as a coastal convoy armed escort. Whilst serving with the Kriegsmarine she was sunk during an action in the English Channel on 17 January 1941.

BELGIC (III)

(1911-1913)
10,151grt; 490 ft 5 in BP (510 ft OA) x 58 ft 2 in
Triple Expansion SR Engines, Twin Screw,
6,000 ihp, 14 knots
Passengers: 1,800 Third class only.
New York Shipbuilding Corporation, Camden,
New Jersey, USA Yard No. 8

The New York Shipbuilding Corporation of Camden, New Jersey originally completed this vessel as the 7,913 gross ton *Mississippi* in April 1903, for the Atlantic Transport Line. Owing to Harland & Wolff's order books being full, due to the spate of orders from the partners of the IMMCo, the *Mississippi*, along with her sister the *Massachusetts* were built in the United States. As such they were the first American flag ships to sail under the Atlantic Transport houseflag. The *Mississippi* was launched on 15 December 1902 and initially designed and constructed to transport cattle eastbound to the UK. Three years later, in 1906; she was transferred within the IMMCo Group to the Red Star Line under the Belgian flag. Her accommodation was altered so that she could carry 1,800 Third class passengers, and she was renamed *Samland*. She was then employed on the Antwerp to New York run carrying cattle, cargo and passengers, making her first voyage on that route on 7 July 1906. She later switched her itinerary to the Antwerp to Philadelphia service but was replaced on this route by the *Gothland* (ex-*Gothic*).

On 30 August 1911, she was transferred once more within the Group to White Star's ownership and renamed *Belgic* as such her gross tonnage was rerated to 10,151. The *Belgic* was placed on the Liverpool to Australia service. This she continued in until White Star took delivery of the *Ceramic* in 1913. The *Belgic* then became surplus to requirements and she reverted back to the Red Star Line and her former name of *Samland*, and was transferred to the Belgian flag once more. She re-entered the Antwerp-New York service on 27 December 1913. When World War 1 broke out, she was employed on the London to New York service from 2 October 1914, but as soon as hostilities ceased, went back to the Antwerp run from March 1919. Moving on to May 1926, the *Samland* was involved in a salvage feat when she went to the assistance of the British steamer *Emlynian*, which had lost a propeller in mid-Atlantic, and was in danger of foundering in the heavy seas. With great difficulty the *Samland* eventually put a line aboard the *Emlynian* and towed her as far as the Azores. The salvage award for members of the crew amounted to £4,800. In 1930, the *Samland* was laid up, and finally went to Van Huyghen Freres of Ghent, in 1931, for demolition.

Below: **A rather unusual if not poor photograph of White Star's third *Belgic*, originally built as the Atlantic Transport Line's *Mississippi*.** *Scanpix TR.*

ZEALANDIC
(1911-1926)
10,898 grt; 447 ft 6 in BP (494 ft OA) x 63 ft 1 in
Quadruple Expansion SR Engines, Twin Screw,
4,700 ihp, 13 knots
Passengers: 6 First class; 1,000 Third class
Harland & Wolff, Belfast. Yard No. 421

1909 to 1914 were boom years for the emigrant traffic to Australia and New Zealand. At that time White Star and Shaw Savill & Albion were maintaining a joint service to New Zealand from the UK. The passenger and cargo service was monthly from London by White Star's *Athenic*, *Corinthic* and *Ionic* in conjunction with Shaw Savill's new *Tainui* and *Arawa*. Concurrent with this was a frequent cargo service that operated from Liverpool or London around the Cape of Good Hope, employing a number of Shaw Savill ships and the solitary White Star ship *Delphic*.

It was not uncommon for these cargo ships to be utilised to help out the passenger vessels with the increasing number of emigrants, by carrying large numbers in temporary accommodation in their 'tween decks. To increase and improve this capacity, a new and larger type of cargo liner was introduced and between 1909-1911, four twin screw ships of over 10,000 gross tons were brought out. All were closed shelter deckers, had a speed of 13.5 knots, and had a large refrigerated and general cargo space and semi-permanent accommodation for 1,000 emigrants. All four were built in Belfast, the first two, Shaw Savill's *Rangatira* and *Waimana* by Workman Clark & Co. Ltd, and the other two, *Pakeha* and *Zealandic* by Harland & Wolff. All four were 'near sisters' but the *Zealandic* had several basic variations made to her which made her the largest of the group.

Above: **This photograph of the *Zealandic* at an unidentified port shows her hull in a rust-streaked and unpainted condition. She has a Jacob's ladder down her side and her derricks are 'topped off' for cargo handling. The wind scoops protruding from her forecastle portholes indicate that it could be somewhere hot.** *Nautical Photo Agency.*

The *Zealandic* was launched at Harland & Wolff's on 29 June 1911 and would be the last White Star addition to the joint service. She was designed as a closed shelter decker of 10,898 gross tons but was recalculated at 8,090 with the shelter deck 'open' and 5,172 net tons. These latter tonnages were later reduced to 7,924 and 5,058 respectively. Deadweight capacity was 10,560 tons and her displacement 18,230 tons, while her load draught was 28 ft 6 ½ in., increasing to 30 ft 3 in when a closed shelter decker. The *Zealandic* had two full-length decks below the shelter deck and a long forecastle and bridge deck above, with a short poop. Her boat deck had three boats either side, further boats were stowed inboard of the after ones. Her six holds, 'tween decks and hatchways were served by numerous derricks on the masts and on two sets of derrick posts, three abreast, operated by steam winches, a feature on all four 'sisters'. A very

large refrigerated space was provided, and on homeward voyages, cargo could be carried in the temporary steerage accommodation.

The *Zealandic*'s twin screw machinery consisted of two quadruple expansion steam engines with cylinders of 22, 31½, 46 and 65½ in bore and a 48 in stroke. Steam at 215 psi was provided by two single-ended and two double-ended cylindrical boilers, burning coal, of which 1,890 tons could be bunkered. The engines produced between 4,700 and 5,960 ihp and gave her a speed of 13 knots with a maximum of up to 14 knots. Her semi-permanent accommodation provided for 1,000 Third class with 6 berths for First class and improved standards of comfort introduced for female emigrants. The *Zealandic* was delivered on the 12 October 1911 and was distinguishable from the Shaw Savill trio in that she had a slight rake to her masts and funnel and a longer forecastle and bridge deck, in addition to her well deck bulwarks. She sailed on her maiden voyage from Liverpool on 30 October to Wellington via the Cape; her homeward leg would be across the Pacific and around Cape Horn, with a call at Rio or Montevideo.

Departing Wellington on 22 January 1913, the *Zealandic* carried what was then a record cargo of wool. Later that year she was chartered by the Western Australian Government to

Below: **The *Zealandic* was built to augment the company's earlier ships on the New Zealand route. She was designed with a large capacity for frozen mutton.** *Tom Rayner Collection.*

convey emigrants to that state; accordingly her passenger accommodation was remodelled for this role. Following the outbreak of World War 1, because of her valuable refrigeration capacity, she was retained on the New Zealand run with occasional calls at Australian ports. Nearly a year later, on 2 July 1915, she was in the English Channel and was chased by the German submarine *U-39* but even at 13 knots she managed to outrun her pursuer. Two years further on she was taken up under the Liner Requisition Scheme on 27 July 1917. In this capacity, although it is not known why, whilst outward bound to the Cape, she called at the island of Tristan da Cunha on 20 April 1918. It is thought that she was routed there by the Government to check that all was well (after all the nearest land was German South West Africa), or simply to deal with mail and/or passengers.

The *Zealandic* remained on the New Zealand service whilst under the Requisition Scheme until 15 June 1919 when she was released from Government service and returned to White Star ownership. During her war and immediate post-war career it is thought that the *Zealandic* did not carry any emigrants to Australia. By 1920, a new cargo service was inaugurated from Liverpool to Auckland, Wellington, Lyttleton, Port Chalmers and Dunedin via the Panama Canal. The *Zealandic* and her Shaw Savill consorts were placed on this service. Together with the *Waimana* and *Pakeha* she was once again fitted for 1,000 Third class passengers on account of the new boom in New Zealand immigration brought about by 'assisted passages'.

On 3 April 1923, the *Zealandic* was steaming in the vicinity of Cape Howe, Southeast Australia where she went to the rescue of a disabled steel barque, the *Garthsnaid*, owned by the Marine Navigation Co. of Canada. She towed the stricken sailing vessel into Melbourne for which her crew were awarded the salvage fee of £6,350. During 1926, Lord Kylsant, head of the Royal Mail group of shipping companies, bought the control of White Star which carried with it a big shareholding in the Shaw Savill & Albion Company. Soon afterwards the Australian Commonwealth Line (formerly Geo. Thompson's Aberdeen Line), was acquired by White Star. Two of the Aberdeen Line (White Star) liners, the *Sophocles* and *Diogenes* were chartered by Shaw Savill and in return, the *Zealandic* together with the *Waimana* were chartered to the Aberdeen Line in June that year. The *Zealandic* was renamed *Mamilius*, and the *Waimana*, *Herminius*.

Lord Kylsant's takeover of White Star's and Shaw Savill's interests became officially effective from 1 January 1927, and in her new role as the *Mamilius*, she spent six years on the London to Australia service, up until 1932, when the Royal Mail Group crashed. The White Star Line was in financial difficulties also, and so it was that the Australian service which was relinquished by the Royal Mail Steam Packet Co. Ltd (RMSP), passed to the ownership of Shaw Savill, as did the *Mamilius*, who then renamed her *Mamari*. The following year Shaw Savill itself was absorbed into the Furness Withy Group. The *Mamari* served Shaw Savill for seven years, but in September 1939, following the outbreak

of World War 2, she was sold to the Admiralty. In her new wartime role, the *Mamari* was converted and camouflaged by Harland & Wolff as a decoy vessel to represent the aircraft carrier HMS *Hermes* and anchored in the Firth of Forth. It seems that she proved effective as a decoy for a time she was successful in deceiving enemy intelligence. However, the genuine HMS *Hermes* was later sunk on 9 April 1942 off Trincomalee by Japanese aircraft.

When the decoy role's purpose had been served, it was decided that she would be more valuable as a refrigerated cargo ship once again. On 2 June 1941, whilst proceeding to Chatham Dockyard to be reconverted to a refrigerated carrier, she struck the wreck of the tanker *Ahamo*, about 30 miles North of Wells in Norfolk, and was beached at Cromer following a German air raid. On 4 June 1941, she was torpedoed whilst aground by a German E-boat and abandoned as a total loss. So the 30-year-old former *Zealandic* ended her days in wartime livery as the Acting HMS *Hermes* (temporarily). During her White Star career her Masters included Captains J. Breen (1911-1917), A. E. Jackson (1917-1919), A. Brocklebank (1919-1920) and V. W. Hickson (1920).

ZEALANDIC: *Of or pertaining to Zealand, a province in the Netherlands.*

TITANIC
(1912)
46,328 grt; 852 ft 6 in BP (882 ft 9 in OA) x 92 ft 6 in
Triple Expansion SR Engines + L P Turbine,
Triple Screw, 35,000 ihp + 16,000 shp, 21 knots
Passengers: 905 First class, 564 Second class,
1,134 Third class
Harland & Wolff, Belfast. Yard No. 401

The *Titanic*, sister to the *Olympic*, was launched at noon on 31 May 1911 at Harland & Wolff's yard shortly before the newly completed *Olympic* sailed from Belfast. The *Titanic* was the second of Bruce Ismay's 'big three' and being slightly larger than the *Olympic* was the world's largest liner. Like the *Olympic*, Alexander M. Carlisle, Harland & Wolff's Chief Naval Architect, who had retired from the builders in 1911, had designed her. It was subsequently revealed that it was he who made provision for the *Titanic* to carry 64 lifeboats although at one stage in the design 48 boats were considered. However, this was not implemented as others thought that their installation would clutter the decks and spoil the general spaciousness and aesthetics of the new ship. Instead she was completed with 20 lifeboats which included four Engelhardt collapsible lifeboats with altogether a total capacity for 1,178 passengers.

The *Titanic*'s machinery was the same as her sister's but some of the staterooms were more luxurious. Her entry into service and its attendant publicity eclipsed that of the *Olympic* a year before. Following her trials on the previous

day the *Titanic* was handed over to White Star on 2 April 1912. Captain Edward J. Smith, White Star's most senior and experienced Master, was due to retire but he was persuaded to stay on and command the *Titanic* on her maiden voyage. Captain Smith was at the time the highest-paid man at sea, earning £1,250 a year plus an extra bonus of £1,000 if he returned his ships in good order! The *Titanic* sailed from Belfast on 3 April with a skeleton crew of 120. Coincidental with her entry into service, and a potential threat to the *Titanic*'s sailing schedule, was the latter stages of a protracted coal miners' strike. With coal in very short supply, the *Titanic* had about 1,880 tons of her total capacity of 8,000 tons when she arrived at Southampton. During the 570-mile trip from Belfast to Southampton, she underwent further trials and machinery adjustment, and at one stage achieved a high speed of 23.25 knots.

The lack of coal was further aggravated by a smouldering fire in No10 bunker on the starboard side of boiler room No 6, which ignited when she left Belfast. Often coal sluices down through which the coal passed to the bunkers caused combustion, a conflagration easily extinguished by hoses. Notwithstanding this, Southampton's Board of Trade nautical surveyor, Maurice Harvey Clarke, granted her a Certificate of seaworthiness. It was probably the largest ship he had to survey during his career to that date and he carried out three inspections. Even so the unchecked fire smouldered on unabated for a further 10 days throughout her maiden voyage. Whilst at Southampton for the week the *Titanic* burned some 415 tons of coal to run the steam-driven generators and the domestic hot water and heating facilities. All that week in order that the *Titanic* should sail on her scheduled maiden voyage, coal was commandeered from other IMMCo ships, which included the *New York* and *Philadelphia*. More coal was gleaned from other Southampton inbound White Star liners such as the *Oceanic* and *Majestic*, which had bunkered extra coal in the United States. In all, some 4,427 tons were gathered from these vessels. In addition to Captain Smith, the *Titanic*'s Chief

Officer was Henry Wilde, transferred from the *Olympic*. This last minute appointment displaced William McMaster Murdoch to First Officer and Charles Herbert Lightoller to the position of Second Officer. The *Titanic* was installed with the latest Marconi Marine Wireless Telegraphy equipment and the Marconi Marine Radio Officers were Jack Phillips and Harold Bride.

The rumour that the *Titanic* was 'unsinkable' may have spread from the ship's publicity. The description of the 15 watertight doors, which divided her hull into 16 watertight compartments, read: '… is held in the open position by a suitable friction clutch, which can be instantly released by means of a powerful electro-magnet controlled from the Captain's bridge, so that in the event of an accident, or at any time when it may be considered advisable, the Captain can, by simply moving an electric switch, instantly close the doors throughout and make the vessel practically unsinkable.' Or perhaps Captain Smith's earlier confident remarks when he commanded the *Adriatic* on her maiden voyage five years previously, which were: 'I cannot imagine any condition which would cause a ship to founder. I cannot conceive of any vital disaster happening to this vessel. Modern shipbuilding has gone beyond that.' He was now in command of a liner built at the zenith of shipbuilding technology and twice the size of the *Adriatic*, he had no reason to doubt the structural integrity of the *Titanic*. J. Bruce Ismay, the Chairman and Managing Director of White Star represented the Company on her maiden voyage and Thomas Andrews, Harland & Wolff's Managing Director, was sailing as the builder's guarantee representative

Right: **A set of the *Titanic*'s engines under construction in the shipyard during 1911.** *Harland & Wolff.*

along with seven other Harland & Wolff employees.

914 passengers embarked at Southampton which included 180 First, 240 Second class and 494 Third class. Quite a few passengers had been switched from other liners which lay idle in the port due to the coal strike. Some had even been transferred from the French Liner *France*, also likewise affected. Other passengers joined at Cherbourg and Queenstown which made a total of 1,308; 599 in First and Second and 709 in Third Class or Steerage. Fares ranged from special suites for a single fare of £500 (there were two of these, one of which was occupied by Bruce Ismay). An average First class one-way fare was around £30; a Second class passage about £12 and a Third class passage about £8. This has to be taken in context that the skilled craftsman who worked on *Titanic* earned about £2 a week while an unskilled labourer earned about £1. In contrast it was estimated that the millionaires on board the *Titanic* represented a total capital of at least £120 million. The total crew signed on articles were 898 which made a total capacity of 2,206 persons. The *Titanic* carried 16 lifeboats; the maximum required for a vessel over 10,000 gross tons under 1894 BoT Regulations at the time. In addition she carried four collapsibles, previously referred to, stowed on top of the bridge. They provided a total capacity for 1,178 persons.

During the week's stay at Southampton, the *Titanic* had been busy coaling ship from its donors and loading supplies, as well as signing on crew who were largely seafarers from that port. Such was the nature of her preparing to sail that she was not open for inspection to members of the public. At noon on 10 April 1912, the *Titanic* eased away from 44 berth in the White Star Dock and the same phenomenon that had drawn the *Hawke* to the *Olympic* a year before, began to manifest itself again! The shallow water effect or 'canal effect', caused by the movement of the *Titanic*'s large displacement as she was under way, caused the nearby *New York*, moored outboard of the *Oceanic*, to be dragged away from her moorings towards the *Titanic* as she was passing the strikebound liner. As the *New York* strained at her moorings, the 3 in. steel cable snapped and whipped through the air, fortunately not hitting anyone. Prompt action on behalf of Captain Smith by reversing the port propeller and attendant tugs averted a collision. The slight delay caused by this incident made the *Titanic* late at Cherbourg where a number of wealthy American passengers, including John Jacob Astor, inconvenienced by the delay, embarked. The following day the *Titanic* anchored off

Above: **The black-painted hull of the *Titanic* in the Arrol Gantry before her launch.** *William J. Nelson/Harland & Wolff.*

Queenstown where two tenders brought the last passengers and mails aboard, before heading out into the Atlantic. The *Titanic*'s route followed the Southern (arc) track across the Atlantic to avoid icebergs that were normally prevalent in the Northern track.

The *Titanic* was Captain Smith's fourteenth White Star command and he was due to retire after this trip. He held a commission as a Commander in the Royal Naval Reserve (RNR), and as other officers of the crew were also in the RNR, the *Titanic* was entitled to fly the Blue Ensign (which also enhanced White Star's status). In a lifetime at sea Captain Smith had met most situations and he was very much respected as a navigator and a seaman, and also popular with regular White Star passengers. As this was a smooth crossing for the time of year, Captain Smith had the *Titanic*'s speed brought up to 21.5 knots. Through his experience it was 'custom and practice' to push a vessel at full speed if weather conditions permitted. Most Atlantic Masters frequently did in order to maintain the regular advertised sailing schedules. There was no need not to steam at full speed; after all, not many liners collided with icebergs and the chances of meeting a small one (a 'growler') in the vast Atlantic was remote. Passing other liners was much more common!

The South track should have been safe but the winter of 1912 had been particularly mild in the Arctic and the ice flow had drifted south on the Labrador Current, futher South than anyone could remember. By 12 April the bunker fire was eventually extinguished.

Safe navigation and the avoidance of collision relied upon deduced (dead) reckoning, the ship's chronometer and extra vigilance from the lookouts; in fog 'pebble splash and dog bark' would be the other instincts to draw on. So on the night of 14 April the *Titanic* was South East of Newfoundland pushing through the cold waters of the Atlantic, which were at -2°C, at full speed.

Around 12.00 on 14 April, while steaming westerly at a little over 21.5 knots, Captain Smith altered course further South based on ice reports being radioed in. Later in the evening of that day a further nine ice warning messages were received from other vessels. The *Titanic* received a signal from the steamer *Mesaba* which radioed in a position in the *Titanic*'s track, that it had encountered heavy field ice and several large icebergs. Apparently the message was not delivered to the navigational personnel nor posted on the bridge, as was the protocol. Another steamer, the *Rappahannock*, signalled at 22.30 hrs that she had passed several large icebergs and heavy field ice and she had also sustained damage to her rudder. The Radio Officer acknowledged this signal.

The crow's-nest lookouts, Frederick Fleet and Reginald Lee, were told to keep a sharp lookout for ice.

At 22.55, the Leyland Line's cargo-passenger ship *Californian* had stopped due to a heavy field surrounding it. The *Californian* was in the vicinity of the *Titanic*'s position as her wireless signal, informing all ships that she was at a standstill, was strongly received and interrupted the *Titanic*'s routine radio transmissions. The *Titanic*'s Radio Officer acknowledged the *Californian*'s signal, replying: 'Keep out! Shut up! You're jamming my signal, I'm working Cape Race.'

At 23.35 Cyril Evans, the *Californian*'s Radio Officer shut down his radio set for the night; this was standard operating procedure for its day.

The sea conditions being cold and calm with a new moon, the *Titanic* powered on at 21.5 knots, with no reduction in speed as it was not custom and practice, towards the ice field that surrounded her.

By 23.30 most of the *Titanic*'s passengers had turned in for the night but there would always be a few revellers and card players who remained.

A little after 23.40 Fleet spotted a dark object looming some 500 yards in the distance on the *Titanic*'s path. He rang the bell three times and phoned the bridge to report: 'Iceberg right ahead.' First Officer William

Above: **The last time the two sisters were in port together in March 1912. The *Titanic* (left) has vacated the Thompson Graving dock to allow the *Olympic* (right) access following the loss of a propeller blade at sea.** *Harland & Wolff.*

Murdoch moved the bridge telegraph to 'Stop', then 'Full Astern', ordering 'hard a starboard!', to evade the iceberg. This was the tiller order such that the helm and heading should be brought round to the port. Although the *Titanic* veered around some 20° to port, it took some 30 seconds to answer her helm over a quarter of a mile. Murdoch also pressed the button to shut all the watertight doors.

The *Titanic*'s momentum carried her underway through the water and impacted with the iceberg on the starboard side of her hull. Beneath the water from near the bow to 300 feet further aft, a protruding 'spur' of ice from the berg 'pecked' at the hull exerting a very high concentrated pressure as it made contact. Thus, a series of glancing impacts, which caused the rivets to fail and fracture ('pop') under sudden increased loading, which in turn led to torn seams, and in addition the plate caulking was broken below the waterline. All this happened intermittently as the hull scraped past the spur. The area laid open to the sea was later estimated by Mr. Edward Wilding, at the enquiry, to be 12 ft². Through the gap in the plates the seawater entered and flooded the watertight compartments at a rate of 400 tons a minute.

Below: **An unusual photograph of the *Titanic* at Belfast as she makes ready to sail for Southampton.** *Nautical Photo Agency.*

Subsequent forensic analysis on wreckage recovered from the site pinpointed the wrought-iron rivets, which had been formed with slag in them and were succeptable to "brittle fracture". In other words, at sustained lower temperatures they had a low resistance to sudden impact, or, from being fairly tough at normal sea temperatures had become brittle at freezing temperatures. Also, the nature of rivets is that they are designed to resist failure in a shear mode. During impact with the iceberg, they would have been submitted to a sudden load in tension (i.e. a tensile mode). The *Titanic* had been steaming through seawater temperatures as low as -2° C (28°-30° F), sometime prior to the impact.

Above: **The *Titanic* leaving Southampton on her maiden voyage on 10 April 1912.** *Richard de Kerbrech Collection*

The *Titanic's* hull, like that of the *Olympic*, was divided by 15 transverse bulkheads, extending well above the waterline, into 16 watertight compartments. She had been designed to float with any two of the first four compartments from the bow flooded. In addition, she had a cellular double bottom, but the collision and subsequent gashes occurred above this. The damage sustained by the iceberg caused the first five watertight compartments to be exposed to flooding. The compartments extended from the cellular double bottom of the ship to five decks above, fore and aft. But from the third bulkhead to the ninth, they extended up to the fourth deck above. As each compartment, working aft from the bow, filled, the bow sunk deeper, and seawater flowed over the top of the bulkheads. With five compartments flooded, the ship could not survive. Indeed, Thomas Andrews's snap appraisal of the situation, along with that of the ship's carpenter John Hutchinson, estimated that the liner had just over an hour before foundering.

Below: **Another view across Southampton docks with the *Titanic* sailing. The *New York* has been returned to her berth by tugs.** *Richard de Kerbrech Collection.*

Captain Smith ordered the Radio Officers to send out the Regular International distress call for help, CQD at 00.10 (12.10am) on 15 April, whilst passengers were roused to muster at their lifeboats, not long after Phillips and Bride decided to send the new SOS call and alternate it with CQD. Although the *Titanic's* position was thought to be some 19½ miles from the *Californian*, it was Captain Arthur Rostron of Cunard's *Carpathia* whose radio picked up the distress call. He turned the *Carpathia* about and ordered 'Full Steam Ahead', a maximum of 17 knots, to the *Titanic's* last reported position. He radioed back that he estimated he would be there in four hours time. So the little *Carpathia* went crashing through the same dark night and calm sea, icebergs or no icebergs, on a mission of mercy.

When the first lifeboat was lowered it contained 27 passengers and crew, less than half its capacity of 65 (perhaps 10 more at a squeeze in a calm sea). Between 00.45 (12.45am) and 2.05 am, the officers and crew managed to lower 18 of the *Titanic's* 20 lifeboats. By 2.10 am, the stern of the *Titanic* rose out of the sea to an angle of 80°, but the generators were still running to light the ship. Below decks order became chaos, anything not fixed or fastened in place moving towards the bow. From later reports, high stresses

Above: **Her first and last time after leaving Southampton, the *Titanic* is photographed in The Solent on 10 April 1912 as she sails off into history.** *Tom Rayner Collection.*

experienced by the main deck caused the hull to split in two, just forward of the fourth funnel. The forward section quickly sank as the stern settled back for a few seconds, before it again rose to the vertical position; at first remaining motionless before it began its plunge to the Atlantic floor 2½ miles below.

Of the 1,308 passengers and 898 crew, 703 survivors were rescued by the *Carpathia*. Only 320 bodies were recovered from the sea. The sinking had claimed the lives of Captain Smith and Thomas Andrews; J. Bruce Ismay was more fortunate; he managed to get into Engelhardt collapsible C, but did not look back at the sinking liner he owned. For surviving he was vilified in the press, especially in the United States, particularly in the papers owned by the newspaper magnate William Randolph Hearst. White Star's reputation was almost in tatters and the ramifications were grave. Not only was there a large loss of life but insufficient life-saving apparatus for all aboard. If the largest, most modern, 'unsinkable' ship was lost on her maiden voyage, what hope was there for others? The travelling public lost confidence in the Company and its ships – even regular clientele were shocked. Never was there a display of loss of confidence in international travel until that experienced by air travel following the attack on the World Trade Center's Twin Towers in New York on 11 September 2001, in which the airlines and aircraft industry suffered as a result. But business and travel on the North Atlantic by sea had to go on as it was the only way to cross. The *Olympic*, as *Titanic's* sister ship, would be shunned at first but gradually would win back regular passengers for White Star and (unknown at the time) would become the 'standard bearer' for the Company, until her demise in 1936.

Communities both sides of the Atlantic in Southampton, Liverpool, Belfast and New York were at first devastated and the shockwaves of the disaster gradually permeated around the world. Emigrants' homesteads in Eastern Europe mourned and the English-speaking empire, which naturally depended on sea trade, also felt a sense of great loss. As a mark of respect to Thomas Andrews and the seven guarantee team of workmen who had lost their lives in the disaster,

Harland & Wolff closed the shipyard on Saturday 20 April 1912.

At the subsequent Board of Trade enquiry into the loss of the *Titanic*, Mr Edward Wilding, Thomas Andrews's deputy, was called to represent the builders, Harland & Wolff. Mr Wilding presented his evidence in a clear and concise manner after being lambasted by hours of questions regarding the technical and theoretical detail of the ship. They mainly concerned as to what had happened during the sinking and the *Titanic's* perceivable survivability following its collision with the iceberg. Wilding's stability and trim calculations were based on empirical formulae and the sequence of the events that resulted in the loss of the *Titanic* could not have been foreseen at the time. The degree of damage sustained and the manner in which it occurred was unimaginable, and therefore could not have been anticipated or allowed for. Shortly after, the enquiry was concluded, Harland & Wolff being exonerated of any blame for the loss of the vessel.

Following the loss of the *Titanic*, the BoT Regulations were changed to improve the safety of life at sea such that sufficient life-saving apparatus should be available for all passengers and crew. This then was interpreted to mean that all those aboard a ship could be accommodated in half the lifeboats carried. In addition was the setting up in 1913 of the International Ice Patrol Service managed by the United States of which the UK contributed thirty per cent of the total outlay. Its function consisted of locating all ice threatening the steamship tracks, such as drifting icebergs in the sea lanes and placing that information in the hands of every steamship Master by means of wireless telegraphy. Together with a Gulf of St Lawrence Ice Patrol Service, they broadcast regular bulletins on ice conditions together with recommendations as to the route to be followed. The transatlantic shipping lanes were routed further south during winter and spring months. Every vessel was required to be installed with Wireless Telegraphy to be manned continuously over a 24-hour period by competent Radio Officers or Marconi's own officers. Lloyds of London paid out £1 million insurance for the loss of the *Titanic*'s hull.

There were winners and losers. Captain Arthur Rostron of the *Carpathia* was lauded; he was awarded not only the Liverpool Shipwreck & Humane Society Medal, but also the United States Congressional Medal of Honour, the highest award that country could bestow on a person. All the *Carpathia*'s crew received a special medal commissioned by Molly Brown of Denver. Gold was awarded to Captain Rostron and his senior officers, silver to the junior officers and bronze for the rest of the crew. Captain Stanley Lord of the *Californian*, by comparison, was castigated. Seemingly he was in the wrong place at the wrong time, and did nothing when the standby watchkeeper reported seeing rockets that had been fired during the *Titanic*'s sinking. Edward Wilding went on to become Managing Director of Harland & Wolff in January 1914 and left the firm in 1924. The *Olympic*'s watertight bulkheads were extended up to the main strength deck as was the cellular double bottom. Similar modifications were made to the *Britannic* whilst under construction on the stocks.

In June 1913, Bruce Ismay retired from the Presidency of IMMCo and was retired as a Director of White Star. That same year saw record profits announced by the Company as a surge of emigrants travelled on their liners. In 1914, the world would have to come to terms with another tragedy of global proportions, so perhaps the *Titanic* disaster caused the lamps across Europe to dim momentarily.

TITANIC: *Of or pertaining to the Titans; gigantic, colossal.*

CERAMIC

(1913-1942)
18,481 grt; 655 ft 1 in BP (675 ft OA) x 69 ft 5 in
Triple Expansion SR Engines + LP Turbine,
Triple Screw, 7,750 ihp, 15 knots.
Passengers: 600 (820 maximum) Third class
Harland & Wolff, Belfast. Yard No. 432

During 1899, White Star had inaugurated their 'Colonial' service to Australia via the Cape with their new vessels *Afric*, *Medic* and *Persic* of around 12,000 tons. By 1901, these were followed by the *Runic* and *Suevic*, which were slightly larger vessels of the same class. At the time these five ships were among the largest ships on the Australian run and their emigrant accommodation was more spacious and better appointed than their rivals on this route. Their closest competitors serving Australia were the Aberdeen Line and Lund's Blue Anchor Line since 1880, which mainly catered for First class clientele. In tandem White Star also operated the New Zealand service jointly with Shaw Savill & Albion since 1883.

By 1911, the Colonial service had prospered considerably and had made a good reputation for itself in safety, regularity and punctuality. The size of ships introduced by the Aberdeen Line had risen to 11,000 tons in the form of the *Themistocles* and *Demosthenes*, while by 1910 the Blue Anchor Line had been absorbed into the P&O branch service. The period from then up until the outbreak of World War 1 was one of rapid expansion on the Australian run. Aberdeen Line introduced the *Euripides*, Blue Funnel entered with their *Aeneas*, *Ascanius*, *Anchises*, *Nestor* and *Ulysses*, and P&O had five ships built for the route. White Star's riposte was to order the largest ship for the route to date, the *Ceramic*, fifty per cent larger in tonnage than the earlier Colonial consorts and she was launched on 11 December 1912. She was the last White Star liner to be ordered by J. Bruce Ismay as the following year when she entered service, he retired from the Company.

The *Ceramic* displaced 34,520 tons, and had a net and deadweight tonnage of 11,729 and 19,590 respectively, a draught of 34 ft 9 in and a depth of 43 ft 10 in. She was built with seven decks; the bridge deck was 395 ft long with a 210 ft boat deck above that. Below were four overall decks and an orlop deck at the ends outside the machinery spaces. Her great overall length of 675 ft, which was not exceeded

Below: **The *Ceramic*, resplendent in her new paintwork, lies anchored in the River Mersey, ready to sail.**
Richard de Kerbrech Collection.

Above: **Another view taken as the photographer's boat moves around the vessel shows the *Ceramic*'s fine sheer and her counter stern. Note the crewmember scaling the rigging to the foremast.** *Tom Rayner Collection.*

covers on the after deck; an eerie peacetime addition.

Combination machinery, successfully trialled in the 'Olympic' trio, was selected for the *Ceramic*. This consisted of triple expansion, 4-cylinder steam reciprocating engines coupled to the wing propeller shafts, with exhaust steam passing to a low pressure turbine on the centre shaft. All three prime movers were in the same engine room with the turbine abaft the wing engines. The reciprocating machinery had cylinders of 26½ in, 42 in, 47½ in and 47½ in bore with a stroke of 51 in. The total horsepower developed on all three shafts was 7,750, which gave her a speed of 15 knots. Steam at 220 psi was supplied by six double-ended boilers, with 36 furnaces, situated in two boiler rooms. The coal for them was stored in cross-bunkers at each end and side bunkers.

on the route for twenty-six years by Shaw Savill's *Dominion Monarch*, which was only 7 ft longer. Her wide beam was designed such that she could enter the old lock at Tilbury with just a foot to spare. Her hull was subdivided by 12 main watertight bulkheads, dividing the ship into two end compartments, two boiler rooms, an engine room, seven main holds and a large bunker hold forward of the bridge which could be used either for reserve fuel or dry cargo. The *Ceramic* had a very large cargo capacity of 836,000 ft³ of which 321,000 ft³ were refrigerated. The Nos 2, 5 and 6 lower holds were insulated as were the 'tween deck spaces in Nos 2, 3, 4, 5 and 6. Her eight hatchways were served by 22 8-ton and one 15-ton derrick mounted to her four masts and the coaling hatchways on her boat deck by four small derricks on samson posts. Eighteen sets of lifeboat davits were fitted with double-banked lifeboats stowed under most of them. She had also been fitted with two 4.7 in rapid-firing guns, culled from an 1887 Japanese cruiser, installed under

Originally designed to cater for 600 Third class passengers, this however could be extended to a maximum of 820 in times of greater demand on the emigrant trade. They were accommodated in mainly two and four-berth cabins on the middle and upper decks with the public rooms on the bridge deck. The main dining saloon was situated on the middle deck over the reserve bunker space, which was probably very noisy for staff during coaling! Instead of being a separate 'island' as had been the traditional practice by the builders, the navigating bridge was at the forward end of the boat deck, integral with the superstructure and this gave the *Ceramic* a rather sleek, uncluttered appearance. With four well-spaced lofty masts and a single large funnel, she gave a

Below: **Entering service just before World War 1, the *Ceramic* survived but became a major loss during World War 2 whilst in service with Shaw Savill.** *John Clarkson.*

balanced profile. Built at a cost of £436,000, her entry made a transition for she was the last vessel built for White Star with four masts and their first large cargo carrier.

She was completed on 5 July 1913 and on 11 July arrived at Liverpool to be present at the Mersey Pageant, staged in honour of the opening of the Gladstone Graving Dock by King George V. She hosted some 600 guests and was third in a line of ships behind two warships at the event. At night, she was illuminated with an electrically lit white star on each side of the hull, amidships. The hyperbole of the events surrounding the *Ceramic*'s entry into service must have been somewhat of a fillip for White Star as they were still reeling from the tragic events of the previous year and the loss of confidence by the travelling public. On 24 July 1913 she sailed on her maiden voyage to Australia via Cape Town and as such was the largest liner to sail to the Southern Hemisphere and the largest liner on the Cape run up until 1921. The *Ceramic* soon established herself on the route and became a popular ship with passengers. She had barely got into her stride when a year later in August 1914 World War 1 broke out. Because of her large size and cargo capacity she was retained on the Australian run and for the first few months of hostilities was used as a troopship for the Australian Expeditionary Force with the pennant number *A40*. In May 1916 whilst in the Mediterranean with 2,500 servicemen on board, she was narrowly missed by a torpedo fired by an unidentified vessel although thought to have been a surfaced submarine. The after 4.7 in gun jammed after two or three rounds and the engine room staff stoked her hard to give her a speed in excess of 15 knots to outrun her pursuer. Again on 9 June 1917 a torpedo missed her when steaming in the English Channel.

The *Ceramic* was used for both commercial and trooping work and she was taken up under the Liner Requisition Scheme from 10 July 1917 when she was returned to the regular Australian service where her large holds and great refrigeration space proved an asset to the war effort. On 21 July 1917, whilst carrying a large consignment of bullion to South Africa, she was attacked by a surfaced German submarine off the Canary Islands. The track of a torpedo was seen to starboard but the ship's helm was put hard over and it shot past 20 feet under her stern. The *Ceramic* then worked her speed up to 16.5 knots to escape her assailant. She was released from the Liner Scheme on 1 April 1919 and sent back to her builders for refurbishment before embarking on her first post-war voyage from Liverpool on 18 November 1920 re-establishing the Cape-Australia route which had been suspended in 1914. She ran in consort with the four remaining ships of the 'colonial' service, the *Afric* having

Above: **The *Ceramic* under tow, escorted by a tug, ready to sail from Liverpool.** *Richard de Kerbrech Collection.*

been sunk in 1917, their accommodation having been re-graded as 'Cabin class'. In addition other ships running in loose alliance were those of Blue Funnel, Aberdeen Line, Shaw Savill & Albion but the popularity of the *Ceramic* earned her the sobriquet 'Queen of the Southern Seas'. The newer *Sophocles* and *Diogenes* joined them in 1922. By 1 January 1927, the White Star Line was purchased by Lord Kylsant's Royal Mail Steam Packet Company for £7 million, along with the Aberdeen and Shaw Savill interests. Although this would mean a massive upheaval for White Star, it made little difference to the *Ceramic*'s continued and regular service to Australia. Around the same time of the takeover, the *Persic* was scrapped in 1927, and the *Runic*, *Suevic* and *Medic* were all disposed of in 1929.

On 18 December 1930, whilst inbound from Fremantle, the *Ceramic* collided with PSNC's motorship *Laguna* off Gravesend. Both vessels sustained only slight damage. In this year only the *Ceramic* remained as last of the big White Star ships serving that route and she ran in consort with the Aberdeen liners under the title of the White Star-Aberdeen Line, jointly with Blue Funnel. In 1932, Shaw Savill acquired the Aberdeen interests and following White Star's merger with the Cunard Line in 1934, the *Ceramic* together with the *Ionic* and the Aberdeen fleet, passed into full Shaw

Below: **This photograph shows the *Ceramic* in her later years, possibly sailing for South Africa judging by the courtesy flag on her foremast.** *A. Duncan.*

Savill ownership. She made her first sailing for Shaw Savill from Liverpool to Brisbane on 25 August 1934 with accommodation for 411 passengers only. Shaw Savill decided to update and modernise the *Ceramic* at their earliest possible opportunity which occurred in June 1936. She was sent to Harland & Wolff's Govan yard for extensive refurbishment which lasted two and a half months and occupied 1,000 of the workforce. In this all her accommodation was stripped out and renewed in the period's modern style, with a large proportion of single-berth rooms, some with private bathroom, all with hot and cold running water. Most of them were rebuilt on the Bibby tandem cabin system, with outside ports.

Public rooms were redecorated and a veranda café was constructed at the after end of the boat deck. The forward end of the bridge deck below the boat deck was glassed in. The number of passengers was reduced to 336 and the number of lifeboats reduced accordingly, the two after boats on each side of the boat deck were fitted with luffing davits. The crew's accommodation was repositioned on the middle deck, sailors and firemen aft and stewards forward. A considerable amount of work was carried out in the engine room, the boiler water feed heating system was improved and her condensers converted to the two-flow regenerative system, to improve the overall thermal efficiency. New bronze propellers and a streamlined rudder were also fitted. Ironically, the opportunity was not taken to convert her to oil burning, the company seeming content to continue to use coal. All this improvement work was the sole responsibility of Captain R. J. Noal, Shaw Savill's Marine Superintendent. The result was that her gross tonnage increased to 18,750 and her speed increased by one knot on trials to 16 knots, a real renaissance for a ship 23 years old. Externally, the *Ceramic* looked much the same, except for the conspicuous veranda café and the enclosed bridge deck forward. White Star's gold riband was repainted white for Shaw Savill's livery. Work was completed in Glasgow by 15 August and she sailed for Liverpool to resume her normal service. She sailed from Liverpool on 22 August 1936 for Australia via Cape Town and Durban, joining the *Themistocles, Nestor, Ulysses, Anchises* and *Ascanius* on the service. During the next three years she ran as regularly as usual and the new accommodation made her one of the most popular, comfortable and tastefully appointed ships on the run. In 1939, she and her consorts were joined by the new 20 knot motor liner *Dominion Monarch*, whose entry would signal the demise of some of the older ships' careers.

Following the outbreak of World War 2 in September that year, the *Ceramic* was not taken up for trooping but was left to maintain a cargo and passenger service to Australia until February 1940 when she came under general requisition. On 20 July 1940, she left Liverpool with 280 passengers on board in a convoy of some 56 ships bound for Australia via Cape Town. Whilst steaming south off towards the Equator on the morning of 11 August she was in collision with Andrew Weir's *Testbank*, in the same convoy. The *Testbank* had her bows stove in while the *Ceramic*

suffered a large hole at the forward end of No1 hatch which shipped water. Her passengers were transferred firstly to HMS *Cumberland* then to P&O's *Viceroy of India*. The *Ceramic* steamed on in heavy seas to the safety of Walvis Bay where she arrived four days later. There she remained for five weeks while temporary repairs were carried out. Reaching Cape Town on 27 September where further limited repairs were effected she was unable to be drydocked there but later sailed on to Durban where she arrived on 14 December for drydocking. Leaving Durban on 23 December eventually making landfall at Fremantle on 5 January 1941. The *Ceramic* sailed around the Australian coast calling at Albany, Adelaide, Melbourne, Sydney and eventually coal bunkering at Newcastle. She returned to Sydney for drydocking at Cockatoo Naval Dockyard. She then embarked naval ratings, a number of Free French forces and members of ships' crews that had been mined or attacked off the Australian coast, all bound for the UK. In addition she loaded a large quantity of refrigerated meat, much needed back home in the UK. She left Fremantle independently on 4 April, sailing westwards in more southerly latitudes calling at Cape Town and then on to the West Indies where she joined a convoy bound for Liverpool. She eventually reached Liverpool without further incident on 28 May 1941 after some 10 months and 13 days away.

In the autumn of 1942 after continuous wartime voyaging, largely without incident, she underwent an extensive refit at Liverpool. Following this on 23 November 1942, she sailed from Liverpool for Australia, independently routed with 378 passengers and 278 crew on board. On the night of 6 December whilst west of the Azores en route to St Helena, in the position 40º 30′ N, 40º 20′ W she was torpedoed by the German submarine *U-515* under the command of Captain Lieutenant W. Henke. The *Ceramic* sunk before distress signals could be sent out. With the general censorship of shipping information during the war the Admiralty assumed that she had been sunk without survivors. In fact there was one survivor, a 20-year-old Royal Engineer Eric Munday, who was picked up by the *U-515* which returned later to the scene of the sinking. Overnight storms had apparently wiped out the lifeboats and claimed 655 lives. This however was not revealed for several months until the survivor was able to write his testament from his POW camp at Marlag-Milag-Nord near Hamburg.

So it was that the *Ceramic* that had been launched in the wake of the *Titanic* tragedy, the last of White Star's four-masted cargo and passenger liners, went on to become the 'Queen of the Southern Seas' and establish the Company's reputation on the Australian route. She had survived World War 1, the Royal Mail takeover and a change of ownership only to disappear behind a cloak of mystery in the Atlantic.

CERAMIC: *Derived from the Greek word keramos, meaning Potters Earth. The name was not used again by White Star but passed to Shaw Savill & Albion nomenclature.*

LAPLAND

(1914-1920)
17,540 grt; 605 ft 8 in BP (620 ft OA) x 70 ft 3 in
Quadruple Expansion SR Engines, Twin Screw,
14,500 ihp, 17 knots
Passengers: 450 First class, 400 Second class,
1,500 Third class
Harland & Wolff, Belfast. Yard No. 393

The *Lapland* was launched by Harland & Wolff on 27 June 1908 for the Red Star Line's Antwerp to New York service. The Red Star Line was the popular name for the Societe Anonyme de Navigation Belge-Americaine which was owned by the International Navigation Co. which in turn was part of the IMMCo group. The *Lapland* had been engined by Harland & Wolff in that her twin quadruple expansion engines were arranged on the 'balanced' system supplied by steam at 215 psi supplied by eight double-ended boilers. In service they would consume about 240 tons of coal per day with a bunker capacity of 3,876 tons. She was built with nine decks, six holds and her hull divided into 10 watertight compartments. Her deadweight tonnage was 13,360 with a depth of hold of 37 ft 5 in.

Accommodation for the passengers, including 60 First class staterooms was on the uppermost two decks. Although she was a single ship order without any sisters planned, with her two tall funnels and masts she bore a striking resemblance to White Star's *Celtic* and HAPAG's *Amerika*, albeit a bit smaller in tonnage and shorter in length. Apart from the fact she had two funnels and a raised forecastle, her appearance was more akin to Holland America's *Nieuw Amsterdam* of 1907. On 27 March 1909, the *Lapland* was completed and left Belfast for trials before sailing on to Southampton for drydocking. In mid-April she sailed from Antwerp to New York with a call at Dover en route. Upon her entry into service she was the largest ship to fly the Belgian flag. Following the *Titanic* disaster of 1912 one of the *Lapland*'s more unpleasant voyages was the repatriation of surviving crew members from the *Titanic*, following their attendance at the subsequent Court of Enquiry held in the United States. They were messed in Third class accommodation to protect them from prying journalists.

Upon the outbreak of World War 1 in August 1914, the *Lapland* was transferred to the Red Ensign and registered at Liverpool under the ownership of the International Navigation Co. Two months later, on 3 October, she sailed from Halifax, Nova Scotia in convoy with 31 other ships

Below: **This photograph shows the *Lapland* in Red Star livery under tow from a tug in Southampton Water sailing for New York.** *World Ship Photo Library.*

Above: **The *Vaderland* in Red Star livery.**
Richard de Kerbrech Collection.

which transported the First Canadian Expeditionary Force to England. Upon her arrival in the UK she was transferred to White Star Line's Liverpool to New York service in place of the *Cedric* which had become an Armed Merchant Cruiser. On 29 October 1914, she augmented her consorts, the *Zeeland* and *Vaderland* on this route. For the most part of the war she sailed from Liverpool and in April 1917 was mined off the Mersey Bar lightship, but reached port safely. In June 1917, the *Lapland* was taken up for troopship duties, with a capacity for 3,000 troops, under the Liner Requisition Scheme and as such she sailed mainly from Southampton.

On 23 November 1918 following the Armistice she was placed on the Liverpool to New York run once more and completed six round voyages, the last one being on the 2 August 1919. Following this she sailed from Southampton on 16 September 1919 to New York via Cherbourg and augmented the *Adriatic* on this service. This was short-lived however, for she made only three more round voyages for White Star, the last one departing Southampton on 26 November 1919. Following this she was given a minor refit in which she was converted to carry 389 First, 448 Second and 1,200 Third class passengers, and her gross tonnage increased to 18,565, before reverting to Red Star ownership. On 3 January 1920, after being painted in Red Star livery, she reopened Red Star's Antwerp to New York service, under the Belgian flag, calling at Southampton outwards and at Plymouth and Cherbourg homewards. For the benefit of large numbers of Canadians then travelling to and from Europe, Halifax was often included in her itinerary. She was replaced at Southampton by the *Olympic* in January 1920.

In December 1924 whilst manoeuvring in the River Scheldt, the *Lapland* was in collision with Nederland Line's *Java*, but this incident caused no damage to either liner. By 1926, her Third class accommodation was reduced to 540 passengers and she was used mainly on cruises from New York to the Mediterranean. In 1929, the *Lapland* was one of four ships that were transferred to Frederick Leyland & Co, within the IMMCo, following the disbanding of the International Navigation Co. This was done without a change of livery or route. Although primarily used on cruises, in the face of high operational costs, she was withdrawn from these and made her last Atlantic crossing on 11 June 1932, before being laid up at Antwerp. During October the following year she was sold to Japanese shipbreakers for £30,000. She left Antwerp on 19 November 1933 on a long voyage via the Cape to Osaka, where she was scrapped during 1934.

VADERLAND/SOUTHLAND

(1914-1917)
11,899 grt ;560 ft 8 in BP(580 ft OA) x 60 ft 2 in
Quadruple Expansion SR Engines, Twin Screw,
10,000 ihp, 15 knots
Passengers: 342 First class, 194 Second class,
626 Third class.
John Brown & Co. Ltd, Clydebank. Yard No. 341

Built by John Brown & Co. at Clydebank as a sister to the *Zeeland* for the International Navigation Co, the *Vaderland* was launched on 12 July 1900. She was allocated to the Red Star Line flying the Red Ensign and delivered to her owners on 29 November 1900. Owing to a mishap during May 1899 in which American Line's *Paris* went aground on the Manacles in Cornwall, the *Vaderland* undertook the stricken vessel's itinerary. So the maiden voyage of the *Vaderland* took place on 8 December 1900 form Southampton to New York via Cherbourg, under the auspices of the American Line. But she returned from New York on 26 December to Southampton and Antwerp and this is probably when she commenced her career with Red Star. Subsequently she made several more voyages under joint or American Line auspices before eventually passing to Red Star at the end of 1901. During 1903 she transferred to the Societe Anonyme de Navigation Belge-Americaine under the Belgian flag and was registered at Antwerp. Other changes that occurred were that Dover was often substituted for Southampton. Prior to World War 1, she made her last pre-war sailing on 25 July 1914 and when the Germans invaded Belgium in August 1914, the *Vaderland* was berthed at New York. She was immediately transferred to White Star and made her first voyage on her rescheduled itinerary from New York to Southampton on 3 September that year. In December 1914 she was switched to the White Star-Dominion Line service and made three round voyages from Liverpool to Halifax and Portland, Maine, owing to the closure of the St Lawrence River to navigation.

In the spring of 1915, the *Vaderland* was renamed *Southland*, because her original name bore a similarity to HAPAG's *Vaterland*. Following this she was requisitioned as a troopship and used for trooping in the Salonika/Dardenelles campaign. In this capacity she transported troops to Mudros from where the soldiers were disembarked and mustered into early types of landing craft ('K barges'), to be disembarked at the Dardenelles. On one of her voyages between Alexandria and Mudros she was transporting some 1,400 troops of the 2nd Australian Division of the ANZACs, when on 2 September 1915 she was torpedoed by German submarine *UB-14* whilst in the Aegean Sea. She made it to Mudros safely with the assistance of HMS *Racoon*, and repairs were made. In August 1916 she re-entered the White Star-Dominion Line service on the Liverpool-Montreal-Quebec route. By the time the United States entered the war in April 1917, she was used for trooping duties on Eastbound Atlantic crossings, but this was short-lived. On 4 June 1917, whilst underway from Liverpool to Philadelphia, she was hit by two torpedoes from the German submarine *U-70* and sunk 140 miles north-west of Tory Island, off the coast of County Donegal, Ireland in position 56° 01′ N, 12° 14′ W. Four of her crew were lost with her.

BRITANNIC (II)

(1914)
48,158 grt; 852 ft BP 6 in (903 ft OA) x 94 ft
Quadruple Expansion SR Engines + LP Turbine,
Triple Screw, 60,000 ihp, 22 knots
Passengers: 790 First class, 830 Second class,
953 Third class
Harland & Wolff, Belfast. Yard No. 433

Originally ordered for White Star as the third ship to follow the *Olympic* and *Titanic*, the *Britannic* was laid down at Harland & Wolff's as Yard No. 433 on the slipway previously occupied by the *Olympic*, on 30 November 1911. The name *Gigantic* had been tentatively chosen for the new liner but, in the light of the *Titanic* disaster, it was abandoned. That event was, however, to have an even more profound effect on the *Britannic*. Construction on the third ship of the series had hardly begun when the *Titanic* collided with an iceberg on her maiden voyage and staggered the world with the terrible news of the enormous loss of life. Construction was halted immediately, and many additional safety measures were incorporated into her design, following the Public Enquiry into the disaster. Around this time Harland & Wolff's yard was plagued by myriads of starlings which roosted on the huge gantries at night. The mess from their droppings was not only extremely unsightly, but also so slimy as to be actually dangerous to the workforce which swarmed over the large structure. So an early gang was brought in at about 5.30 am each morning to wash it away with high pressure hoses before the main labour force arrived. When work was suspended on the ship, she was soon in an indescribable state

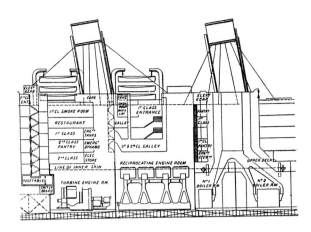

Above: **Arrangement showing the *Britannic*'s after dummy funnel placed over the turbine room. For the sake of appearance, cast iron whistles and dummy pipes were often fitted to dummy funnels.** *Richard de Kerbrech Collection.*

of filth and this had to be cleared off when the work resumed. The *Britannic*, as she had now become, was given much increased compartmentalisation to 16 by the extension of transverse bulkheads one deck higher, five being extended to 40 ft above the waterline. She was also fitted with a double skin to her hull that extended up beyond her bilges, up the ship's sides as wing walls to between the middle and upper decks in the area adjacent to the engine and boiler rooms. By doing so the *Britannic*'s beam increased by some 30 in more than her sisters.

The *Britannic* was launched on 26 February 1914 and as completion took place noticeable differences between her and the two former sisters were more apparent. The layout of the passenger spaces was similar, but like the *Titanic*, half of promenade deck 'A' was enclosed by large glass windows, slightly taller than those of *Titanic* and with a glazing bar near the top of each window. Unlike either the *Titanic* or the *Olympic*, the *Britannic* had this arrangement repeated on the deck below, bridge deck B for 132 ft of its length. The rest of the deck was given over to a larger number of First class staterooms and suites, all with private bathrooms. These staterooms had square windows, like those on the *Titanic*, but shorter and distributed in close pairs. Near *Britannic*'s stern the well deck was enclosed. The other major alteration was the provision for extra lifeboats. Originally the *Britannic* was to be fitted with eight sets of a new form of girder crane davits which, it was said, would transfer their boats from one side of the ship to the other, as necessary. These would have enabled her to carry 48 lifeboats, but the five sets eventually fitted (together with other boats under conventional davits) looked rather odd and completely spoiled her appearance. With all the emphasis on safety of life at sea, a White Star brochure stated:

'The vessel is equipped with the latest and most approved type of electrically-driven, boat-lowering gear, by means of which a very large number of boats can, one after the other, be put over the side of the vessel and lowered in much less time than was possible under the old system of davits... One

Above: **The launch of the *Britannic* at Belfast on 26 February 1914.** *William J. Nelson.*

of the advantages of the new system is that the passengers take their places in the boats expeditiously and with perfect safety before the boats are lifted from the deck of the vessel, and the gear is so constructed that the fully laden boats are lowered at a very considerable distance from the side of the ship, thus minimising risk in bad weather. Moreover, the whole of the boats on board can be lowered on either side of the vessel which happens to be clear, and the gear has been kept so far inboard as to give a wide passage at either side of the ship for promenading and for marshalling the passengers in the event of an emergency.'

Harland & Wolff's original rigging plans showed eight sets of gantry davits capable of handling six boats apiece. Provision was made to float 12 boats forward on the upper deck, 24 aft on the upper deck and 12 boats aft on the poop deck, making a total of 48 boats, some of which were motorised. The description 'gantry' may seem odd but that is by the way. The *Marine Engineer & Naval Architect* of March 1914 carried quite a feature on the *Britannic's* boats and gear, much of which repeats the foregoing quotation, but continued to state:

'These boats, instead of extending right along the boat deck(they did carry them in this configuration when the *Britannic* entered service), are arranged in four separate groups with abundant space for marshalling passengers etc. The system of davits used differs from that in any other preceding ship. There are two davits on each side of the deck where the boats are placed. These do not slew, the space apart being sufficient to pass the boats through. They are of lattice girder construction with a swan-necked top turned towards each other in each pair. They more resemble sheer legs in their action than davits or cranes, being pivoted at their base and moving from a vertical position to a

considerable angle inboard or to a considerable angle outboard. Indeed, the angle is so great that the davits command one half of the deck of the ship while, when outboard, they would enable the boats to be lowered vertically into the sea even if the vessel has considerably heeled over. This arrangement is such, too, that the boats may be traversed across the deck so that all the boats may be lowered on the one side of the ship at the will of the Captain. The davits are inclined inboard or outboard by means of powerful screw gear. The height and outreach of the davits enables the boats to be mounted one over the other in tiers and to facilitate the placing of several tiers in the width of the ship…limit switches are provided so that in the event of any accident, or any temporary aberration on the part of a man manipulating the gear, the motion of the davits, or both, will be arrested before damage can take place, thus making the gear practically mistake-proof. Another feature is the arrangement by which boats can be lowered on an even keel even in the event of the ship being down by the head or the stern. A further advantage of this davit, which is made by the builders of this vessel, is the fact that the boats can be all open lifeboats of good type, thus dispensing with the troublesome collapsible type.'

An encouraging boast in the wake of the *Titanic* disaster, but in any event even though the publicity blurb stated: '…the davits command one half the deck of the ship', was partially correct in that any lifeboats being transferred across the decks or the davits extending too far inboard would hit the first and fourth funnels! The *Britannic's* completion was delayed owing to the start of World War 1 which led to priority Admiralty orders from Harland & Wolff. These included the conversion of 15 cargo ships into dummy battleships to deceive the Germans of the actual strength of the fleet. By May 1915, White Star was doing its best to fend off suggestions from the Admiralty that the *Olympic* and the virtually complete *Britannic* be 'utilised for military or transport purposes… the suggestion

has not been viewed with favour'. The torpedoing of the Cunard liner *Lusitania* off Ireland that month must also have put an end to any plans to run the *Britannic* on the transatlantic service. Towards the end of her completion on 8 November 1915 a compromise was struck whereby the *Britannic* would be used as a hospital ship and requisitioned by the Admiralty on 13 November. Her accommodation was modified such that she could carry around 3,300 casualties, medical staff made up of 52 doctors and officers, 101 nurses and 336 orderlies, together with a crew of 675.

The *Britannic* was completed to a new specification with a white hull and superstructure, green band, buff funnels without the White Star black tops and together with three prominent red crosses distributed between the green band along both sides of the hull, in accordance with the Geneva Convention. The poop deck gantry davits and the port side forward gantry davits were not installed. Instead, the open spaces on the boat deck were fitted with 12 boats mounted under Welin davits, with further collapsible lifeboats underneath. A further two sets of lifeboats and collapsibles were placed on the poop deck. So despite all the lifeboat hyperbole the final decision reverted to relying quite heavily on the 'troublesome collapsibles'. The Dardanelles campaign had been opened up in April 1915 with the invasion of the Gallipoli Peninsula by Great Britain and France, the object being to force a supply route through to Russia via the Bosphorus and the Black Sea. The operation turned out to be a costly blunder and the offensive collapsed with the allegiance of Bulgaria passing to the enemy states. When the smaller Balkan countries of Serbia and Montenegro were overrun in the autumn of 1915, it became necessary to release French and Italian warships covering the landings in order to render assistance in the evacuation of Serbian and Montenegrin troops to Corfu. In consequence of this, there was no alternative to the withdrawal from Gallipoli that was underway by November 1915.

The *Britannic* began storing with medical equipment on 13 November 1915 and was handed over in her International Red Cross livery, following trials, on 8

December. She commenced her hospital ship role when she sailed from Belfast to Liverpool on 11 December 1915, under the command of Captain Charles Bartlett. The *Britannic* was ready for her first voyage by 23 December 1915 and sailed from Liverpool for Mudros (on the island of Lemnos), which lies some 50 miles west of the Dardanelles between Greece and Turkey, and had been established as the Allied Headquarters for the Gallipoli campaign. After four days at Lemnos she returned to Southampton on 9 January 1916 with 3,300 sick and wounded aboard. These casualties would have been disembarked at Southampton's old Netley Hospital on Southampton Water. The Dardanelles evacuation ended early in 1916, but the *Britannic* was used for three more voyages mainly on round trips between Naples to Mudros, with periods of layup in between and being returned to Harland & Wolff, Belfast. On 6 June 1916 she was released from Government service, albeit temporarily. The *Britannic* was recalled again in August and two more return voyages were completed to Naples and Mudros (with an occasional call at Marseilles).

The *Britannic* left Southampton on 12 November 1916 on what was to be her final voyage, her scheduled destination was to be Salonika (Thessaloniki) where she was to embark more casualties. She called at Naples en route to re-bunker, arriving there on 17 November and remaining there for the next two days as she was delayed by a severe storm. On 21 November, at around 08.15 hours, (8.15am), (precisely at the same time as the engine room watches would be handing over), when nearing the end of her voyage outwards, she struck a mine off Port St. Nikolo, the principle port of the small island of Kea which is situated south-east of the Gulf of Athens, in the Aegean Sea. At first there was some dispute about whether it was a mine or whether in fact she had been torpedoed. The *Britannic* was painted quite clearly in the internationally accepted hospital ship colour scheme. The probable cause of her loss was indicated later by Lieutenant

Commander Siess of the German submarine *U-73*, who stated in his log that his vessel (boat) had laid mines in the Kea Channel, through which the *Britannic* had been passing some hours before the fatal explosion occurred. As if to confirm this, Union-Castle's *Braemar Castle*, another hospital ship, also struck a mine in the same area two days later and was only saved from sinking by being beached.

The explosion caused by the mine was against her starboard hull near the main transverse bulkhead between cargo holds 2 and 3, and the rate of flooding that resulted was nearly the same in extent as the *Titanic*. Reports from survivors state that there was a severe hull whipping experienced by the *Britannic* and a large hole was punched into the shell on both the starboard and port sides. The fireman's passage was destroyed, and since the access door to Boiler Room No 6 was left open due to a change in watch, Boiler Room No 6 flooded. Shock damage to the watertight door mechanisms on the main transverse watertight bulkhead between Boiler Rooms 5 and 6 prevented the door closing, which resulted in Boiler Room No 5 flooding. Likewise, the transverse bulkhead at the after end of the forepeak tank, known as the collision bulkhead, was also damaged by the whipping. Like on the *Titanic*, the vulnerability of her hull plates following the explosion had split riveted seams where the rivets had popped and had allowed the ingress of water, resulting in the flooding of the first two compartments. Some of the wing tanks outside the boiler rooms also began to take in water and the *Britannic* started to trim by the bow and develop a list to starboard. In theory, because the *Britannic* had a greater beam and improved subdivision, she should have remained afloat with her first six compartments flooded. However years later, divers on her wreck revealed that many of the portholes had been left open to air the cabins prior to picking up a full complement of wounded service personnel later that day. In addition, many port glasses in the vicinity of the explosion would also have been shattered, thus increasing the ingress of water. All these porthole openings increased the unsymmetrical flooding and caused the rapid increasing list to starboard. In the confusion following the explosion, Captain Bartlett made an attempt to beach his ship on a nearby coast but the steering failed. The *Britannic* heeled over to starboard and sank at 9.17am, just over an hour after striking the mine. Since she sank in about 300 ft of water, her bow pivoted on the seabed, causing severe structural damage to the bow section which had already become weakened by the explosion. This in turn bent the bow some 85° upwards or away from the main hull. Of the 1,125 medical staff, Royal Army Medical Corps personnel and crew on board, 21 lost their lives and another 28 were injured. Most of the deaths occurred when two lifeboats launched from the poop deck were smashed by the *Britannic*'s still revolving propellers which had risen clear of the water as the ship's head had sunk deeper. It appears that the gantry and Welin davits proved their worth, especially in so limited a time.

The survivors were picked up by the cruiser HMS *Heroic* and destroyers HMS *Foxhound* and HMS *Scourge*. Amongst those saved were two very remarkable individuals, a nurse named Mrs. Violet Jessop and a 29-year-old fireman, John Priest. Four years earlier both had survived the *Titanic* disaster; Mrs Jessop in the capacity of stewardess, and with this second experience they were to be the sole witnesses of the tragic demise of two of the White Star Line's giant ships.

A later forensic analysis of the ship's loss, published in March 1995, attributed the loss of the *Britannic* to the following factors:

- Shock damage to equipment such as to the machinery to close the watertight doors and the steering gear. Pumps in Boiler Rooms 5 and 6 were also unable to function properly and control the inflow of water.
- The hull plating appeared to be as notch sensitive (i.e. tending towards being brittle), as the steel in the *Titanic* and *Olympic*, but this could only be confirmed if hull samples were ever taken from the wreck.
- The open or damaged portholes and flooding of the wing tanks on the starboard side were sources of unsymmetrical flooding that caused water to flood into the starboard side, which led to the capsizing.

The loss of the *Britannic* was a tragic one, the more particular since she struck a mine as a hospital ship, thus was not by any stretch of imagination a specific target of the enemy. As such she was typical of so many fine resources wasted by the exigencies of war. She had been meant to enter White Star's Southampton to New York service in the spring of 1915, but as things transpired she lasted less than a year as a hospital ship. Her furnishings and decorations which had never been installed were auctioned off on 4 July 1919. The *Britannic* was the largest liner to be built in the British Isles until the *Queen Mary* entered service in 1936. She was the largest four-funnelled liner ever built, while her triple-expansion steam reciprocating engines were the largest of their kind ever to be fitted in a ship. On a sadder note, the *Britannic* was the largest ever British merchant ship lost during wartime.

BELGIC (IV)

(1917-1921)
24,547 grt; 670 ft 5 in BP (696 ft 6 in OA) x 78 ft 5 in
Triple Expansion SR Engines + LP Turbine,
Triple Screw, 18,500 ihp, 17 knots
Passengers: 500 First class, 600 Second class,
1,500 Third class.
Harland & Wolff, Belfast. Yard No. 391

In the wake of the success of Red Star's *Lapland* of 1909 led them in 1912 to order a newer and much larger ship for their service from Antwerp, in the hope that she would be ready to enter service in 1914, under the name *Belgenland*. The ship was laid down at Harland & Wolff's at Belfast but with the impending threat of war and its eventual outbreak

Above: **Although registered in the name of the International Navigation Co., the *Belgic*, the fourth ship to bear the name, was managed by White Star. She is seen here following her completion in June 1917 and painted in her World War 1 dazzle pattern.** *Tom Rayner Collection.*

in August 1914, resulted in a slowing down of passenger ship construction while priority was given to more urgent naval work. As the berth on which the *Belgenland* was being built was required for warship construction, the new Red Star liner's hull was rapidly completed and launched on 31 December 1914; only to be laid up incomplete at Belfast until 1917. As the war claimed its heavy losses from British merchant shipping it became apparent that there was an increasing need for a greater number of ships of all types. This led to the hurried completion of a number of future passenger ships, without their superstructure and accommodation, as large carriers of food and munitions. The *Belgenland* was one such ship and she was handed over to White Star by the IMMCo as a cargo carrier, named the *Belgic*, on 21 June 1917. As completed the *Belgic* was given two well-raked oval funnels with two tallish raked masts of full height, and a lofty mizzenmast. This gave her the appearance of being long, low and rakish. No superstructure had been fitted above the bridge deck except for a house for the officers' accommodation and the navigating bridge above it. She went to sea dazzle painted in black, sky blue, dark and light grey camouflage. When completed for war service she had a gross tonnage of 24,547 tons and a very large deadweight capacity of around 17,000 tons on a draught of 36 ft 4 in. Her hull was subdivided by 11 bulkheads and she was built with seven holds, two boiler rooms, an engine room and two peaks. There were three overall decks with an orlop deck in the three forward holds, a shelter deck with a long bridge deck above it.

The *Belgic* was probably one of the earliest of Harland & Wolff's ships to have been designed with a cruiser stern and what would eventually become a trademark of the builders. Her steering gear, winches and windlass were all steam driven. The *Belgic* was installed with the then popular Harland & Wolff combination machinery arrangement in which there were 4-cylinder, triple expansion steam reciprocating engines coupled to her two wing propeller shafts, exhausting into a low pressure turbine directly driving the centre shaft propeller. The steam engines had cylinders of 35½, 56, 64 and 64 in. bore and a stroke of 60 in. and each developed some 6,000 ihp. The LP turbine drove the centre

shaft direct, without gearing, and developed some 6,500 shp. The turbine ran ahead only as there was no astern blading, so that as with the other combination machinery ships of the day, the ship manoeuvred as a twin screw vessel. In the astern mode the turbine was short-circuited by a changeover valve leading the exhaust steam from the reciprocators direct to the condenser. The total shaft horsepower developed was around 17,000 which gave her a speed of 17 knots. Steam at 215 psi was provided by 10 double-ended, unsuperheated, coal burning boilers, each with six furnaces.

Operating under the Shipping Controller from 1917 onwards, the *Belgic* ran principally on the Liverpool to New York route, with a call at Halifax. On 11 August 1917, she had a near miss when she was unsuccessfully attacked by the German submarine *U-155* off the south of Ireland. In 1918, she was hurriedly converted into a transport at New York with accommodation for over 3,000 troops, and in fact during January 1919, whilst repatriating United States troops, she made a voyage to New York with 3,141 aboard. The White Star Liverpool service to New York was resumed after the Armistice by the *Baltic*, *Cedric* and *Celtic* and the *Belgic* was employed as an extra ship, which by this time had been painted in Red Star livery. However, by April 1921, the *Belgic* was laid up at Liverpool as no shipyard had a berth free in which she could be fitted out and completed in accordance with the original plans for her completion as a passenger liner. So the *Belgic* had to wait her turn.

Nearly a year later in March 1922 a berth became available at Belfast and she sailed there for her completion. The work took a year and in this time her superstructure and passenger accommodation were built up, with two extra promenade decks, and the opportunity was taken to convert her boilers to oil burning. She was given a third dummy funnel, equally spaced with the other two and her mainmast was removed. When originally built she was intended to carry 660 First,

Above: **Following the war and prior to being rebuilt in 1922, she operated between Liverpool and New York. She is photographed here in her Red Star Line livery.**
Tom Rayner Collection.

350 Second and 2,000 Third class passengers, but this was altered to carry 500, 600 and 1,500 respectively. This, in turn, was quite soon altered to 453, 638 and 970. By the standards of the day the accommodation was good and comfortable and of a very high standard generally, though not particularly outstanding. The Third class had two dining saloons which seated 303 and 253 persons respectively. The completed ship emerged as the 27,132 gross ton liner *Belgenland,* registered at Liverpool under the ownership of the International Navigation Company and flying the Red ensign. Her appearance was as she had originally been planned and she bore an uncanny similarity to Holland America's new *Statendam.* (The previous one building when war broke out had been lost as the *Justicia*).

She was completed and arrived at Antwerp on 17 March 1923 and sailed on her maiden voyage finally as a Red Star liner on 4 April. The Antwerp to New York service had been resumed in 1920 and the *Belgenland* ran in consort with the *Zeeland* and *Lapland.* During 1924, the following year, the River Scheldt had become silted up and required dredging below Antwerp so it was necessary for ships the size of the *Belgenland* and *Lapland* to switch to London as their European terminus. At the time the *Belgenland* became the largest ship to use the Thames. Another first in that same year was that she became the largest liner to embark on a 'Round the World' cruise. By 1925, the dredging operation had been completed and the Red Star ships returned to Antwerp. The post-war trio was joined on the service by the *Pittsburgh,* later *Pennland,* and the *Arabic (III).* This well-served route meant

that the *Belgenland* could remain on the mail service in the season and switch to cruises when not on the North Atlantic.

During 1928, the International Navigation Company was disbanded and the registered ownership of the Red Star ships passed to Frederick Leyland & Co. Ltd still within the IMMCo Group. By 1929 the *Regina* was renamed *Westernland* and replaced the *Arabic (III)* on the Antwerp service. The change of ownership made no difference to the ships' livery for they still retained their Red Star funnel colours. The world depression was beginning to manifest itself into the shipping industry causing a considerable fall off in passenger traffic. As this was felt the *Belgenland* was employed more extensively on cruising and for this some Second and Third class accommodation was re-graded as Tourist. In December 1930, she departed New York on another round the world cruise, which arrived back at the end of April 1931, and in this she catered for the really wealthy clientele in the United States. However the squeeze from the Depression began to be felt and there became less demand for this expensive type of cruise, so instead the *Belgenland* ran on shorter excursions out of New York to the Caribbean and even offered day trips out of New York for liquor-starved American passengers. In January 1932 she made her final Antwerp to New York crossing and was then employed on full time cruising from Antwerp, although this proved a limited success for she was then laid up at Antwerp during March 1933.

Later in July that year she made three Mediterranean cruises before being laid up again in London in September 1933. The Red Star Line was suffering from low passenger receipts. Whereas in 1913 the company had carried well over 117,000 passengers, in 1934 it had carried fewer than 4,000! They decided to throw in the towel. In 1935 Red Star sold the *Pennland* and *Westernland* to Arnold Berstein of

Hamburg. The other consort, *Lapland*, had been sold for demolition in 1933 and the ships chartered from the Atlantic Transport Line, disposed of. The *Belgenland* was sold in January 1935 to the Atlantic Transport Company of West Virginia and renamed *Columbia*. She was given an all-white hull but still retained her Red Star funnel colours, and placed on the Panama Pacific Line's New York to California service via the Panama Canal. This proved unprofitable as any migration west across the continent was by rail and road rather than by ship, and the service was cancelled after a few months. She was then placed on running from New York to the West Indies but this too failed. Apparently, although her First and Second class were fully booked, for some reason American passengers were not keen on the former Third re-graded as Tourist so she did not operate with full capacity. She only managed a voyage or two on this route before sailing from New York on 22 April 1936 to Bo'ness on the Firth of Forth, where she arrived on 4 May to be broken up by P. & W. McLellan. Had she managed to survive the operational losses for another three years or been laid up she might well have proven valuable as a troopship in another war.

JUSTICIA

(1917-1918)
32,234 grt ; 740 ft 6 in BP (776 ft OA) x 86 ft 5 in
Triple Expansion SR Engines + LP Turbine,
Triple Screw, 22,000 ihp, 18 knots
Passengers: 800 First class, 600 Second class,
2,030 Third class
Harland & Wolff, Belfast. Yard No. 436

Harland & Wolff's Yard No 436 was originally ordered as the *Statendam* for the Holland America Line in 1912. She was launched on 9 July 1914 but after World War 1 had begun on 4 August, work on her proceeded at a much slower pace. Then, following negotiations with her Dutch owners, she was requisitioned when almost complete and purchased by the British Government for conversion to a troopship.

On 7 April 1917 she was handed over to White Star to manage her for the British Government under the name *Justicia*. The original intention had been to award her to the Cunard Line to replace the lost *Lusitania*, and it was for this reason that she was given a name ending in *-ia* instead of *-ic*. Apparently Cunard's initial choice of name had been *Neuretania* before *Justicia* was settled on. (As an intention to replace the *Lusitania*, the word was to give the impression of 'Justice'). However, all this proved to be of little consequence because, in the event, Cunard did not have the officers and men with which to man her anyway. The *Justicia* was therefore re-allocated to White Star who had spare manpower from the lost *Britannic*, for them to manage for the duration of the War. It is uncertain whether the ship would have been returned to the Cunard Line after the war or transferred back to the Holland America Line who ordered her in the first place.

The *Justicia's* gross tonnage was 32,235 with an overall length of 776 ft. In passenger service she would have carried 3,430 passengers in three classes: 800 First, 600 Second and 2,030 Third, whilst the crew would have numbered 600. Although Holland America Line's projected flagship was of modest proportions compared with the ships then being built or planned for the Hamburg America, White Star and Cunard Lines, this was certainly not the case with regard to public rooms and standards of interior décor. Indeed, it is widely held that, had the *Statendam* been completed for the express mail service as scheduled, the quality and spaciousness of her interiors would have exceeded that of any of her contemporaries. For example, she would have boasted a First class social hall over 20 ft high, which would have been amongst the tallest of its day. Both her First class Dining Saloon, which would have been capable of seating 563 at one sitting, and the huge palm court were designed with the kind of creative freedom of style that would be more apparent in the late 1920s.

Like all Harland & Wolff liners of the period, she was a triple screw vessel fitted with combination machinery. In the *Justicia's* installation the outer shafts were driven by 4-cylinder triple expansion engines, and these exhausted into a large direct acting low pressure turbine which drove the centre screw, the maximum indicated horsepower (ihp) being 22,000. Steam was supplied by 12 double-ended

Below: **Justicia** in 'dazzle paint'. *Richard de Kerbrech*

boilers, each with six furnaces, with a working pressure of 215 psi. This gave the *Justicia* a designed service speed of 18 knots.

She had four overall decks; an orlop deck forward and a long bridge deck which had been carried right forward to the foremast. Above this were two decks, the lower of which was plated in for most of its length. In a similar fashion to the *Olympic* and *Britannic* there were double-tiered ports along her main deck. As with White Star's larger ships, the aftermost funnel was a dummy, which contributed to a well balanced profile.

Following the United States' entry into World War 1, the *Justicia* commenced on her first trooping voyage and arrived in New York on 25 April 1917 escorted by the *Adriatic*. Initially, she was painted all grey but later, some time early in 1918, she was given a dazzle-painted scheme. An Admiralty working group under the leadership of Norman Wilkinson, the marine artist, had contrived this camouflage idea during October 1917, and its application was soon widespread. Unlike later camouflage paint schemes, the principle of dazzle painting was not necessarily to conceal the ship against her background. Instead the object was often to break up her silhouette by contrasting areas of light and dark paints, making it difficult to identify ships and, more particularly, their sizes and the direction in which they were heading, especially in poor visibility and, in general terms, to distort perspective. The *Justicia's* dazzle paint consisted of patches of black, blue and light grey and was intended to disguise her as a single-funnelled cargo ship. As mentioned, her first trooping voyage was in April 1917. This was followed by several round trips to Halifax, after which she switched to the Liverpool to New York run following the United States' entry into the war.

The *Justicia* could carry some 5,000 troops as well as 15,000 tons of supplies, and it is reported that on one occasion she carried a large contingent of around 12,000

Below: **The first geared turbine to be built by Harland & Wolff was installed in White Star's *Vedic*, essentially a cargo ship. She could double up as a third class passenger carrier depending on the demands of the trade.** *B&A Feilden.*

together with their full kit. Ironically, in her new dazzle livery, her first brush with the enemy was on 23 January 1918 when she was attacked by U-boats in the Irish Channel. On this occasion the torpedoes missed. The beginning of her end came on Friday morning on 19 July 1918, for when she was 23 miles off the Skerryvore Rock in the Hebrides, in a convoy bound from Liverpool to New York, she was attacked by *UB-64* and torpedoed at 2.30pm in the engine room. Two hours later another two torpedoes were fired by *UB-64* but failed to hit their target, one being diverted by the gun crew's fire and, later in the same day, all but a skeleton crew was taken off. HMS *Sonia* then took her in tow for Lough Swilly on the north coast of Ireland. At around 8pm, the *UB-64* again attacked and fired another torpedo which was deflected by the *Justicia's* gunners once more. The *UB-64* had to break off the engagement when she herself was damaged by a depth charge dropped by the trooper's escort vessels. Early on the morning of the following day the attack was resumed, this time from *U-124*. A torpedo fired at around 4.30am missed and although the *Justicia* had been flanked by some 20 naval escort vessels, two more fired at around 9am proved more decisive in her fate. With two fatal hits in her port side, Nos 3 and 4 holds, she sank by the stern and finally disappeared below the surface at 12.40pm in position 55° 38′ N; 07° 39′ W.

The *Justicia* had been carrying no passengers or troops at the time of the attack, but she had a crew of between 600 and 700 aboard. Of these, 15 engine room ratings and the 3rd Engineer were killed when the first torpedo exploded in her engine room. The survivors were transferred to the escorting ships and the destroyers HMS *Marne*, *Milbrook* and *Pigeon* succeeded in sinking the submarine *U-124*. Apparently this U-boat under Lieutenant Wutsdorf had developed so many leaks from the depth charges dropped around her that she made a desperate attempt to escape by diving right under the stricken liner. All bar two of the crew were taken prisoner. The *Justicia* had taken a good deal of punishment and took a considerable period of time to sink; of the seven torpedoes fired at her, three had found their mark. The German High Command were said to be particularly jubilant over the sinking of the *Justicia*, having

Above: **Although initially employed on the Glasgow to Boston route and on the Canadian emigrant trade the** *Vedic* **was also utilised on the Australian run. Here she is photographed at Cape Town.** *A. Duncan.*

mistaken her for the ex-*Vaterland*, their luxury liner 'stolen' from them by the Americans. This vessel, which had been interned in New York for over two years, had been seized along with many other German ships on 4 April 1917. The *Justicia's* original owners, Holland America Line, were compensated for her loss with 60,000 tons of steel, which in part was put towards a new *Statendam* and ordered as a replacement from Harland & Wolff in 1921.

VEDIC

(1918-1934)

9,302 grt; 460 ft 6 in BP (461 ft 6 in OA) x 58 ft 4 in
Single Reduction geared Turbines, Twin Screw,
4,500 shp, 14 knots
Passengers: 1,250 Third class
Harland & Wolff, Govan. Yard No. 461

The *Vedic* was laid down and constructed at Harland & Wolff's Govan yard during 1913, when, following the outbreak of World War 1, work on her was suspended, while priority was given to more urgent warship construction. However, as merchant ship losses became more critical as a result of enemy attacks, work on her resumed. She was intended to be operated by IMMCo as an emigrant ship out of Europe but in the event she was completed as a cargo ship, as a replacement for the old four-masted classes.

The *Vedic* was launched on 18 December 1917 and later towed from Govan to Belfast to have her engines installed. She had seven holds and hatchways, and 14 winches handled her cargo. She had three overall decks; upper, main and lower, together with a forecastle, a bridge deck 130 ft long and a poop. Her hull was subdivided by 11 main bulkheads. She had a deadweight capacity of 11,840 tons and a displacement tonnage on a load draught of 31 ft 6 in of 18,750. In addition she had a depth of hold of 37 ft 4 in,

giving her a large cargo carrying capacity. It was whilst she was fitting out that she was modified to carry troops. She ran her trials on the Clyde on 28 June 1918 after which she was handed over on 10 July 1918 and taken up under the Liner Requisition Scheme. Upon completion she was dazzle-painted in shades of black, blue and light grey to camouflage her. Another innovation was that the masts and derricks were hinged and could be laid flat on the deck, leaving the smallish funnel and an off-centre signal mast as salient features. This, it was hoped, would help to deceive any German submarine as to her true course. All in all her appearance was one of utility and austerity.

Her twin screws were driven by a high-pressure and a low-pressure turbine, both single reduction geared on each shaft. Two double-ended boilers supplied steam to the turbines which produced 3,800 shp that gave a speed of 13 knots, or a maximum of 4,500 shp that produced 14 knots. As such the *Vedic* was White Star's first ship to be fitted with geared turbines and also the first with this type of machinery built by Harland & Wolff. In fact, up until the entry of the *Doric* in 1927 this would be the only turbine driven ship owned by White Star. The *Vedic* departed on her maiden from Belfast on 11 July 1918 for the Clyde, and sailed on to Boston on her inaugural trooping trip.

By August she was released from the Government's Liner Requisition Scheme and purchased by White Star and made her first commercial voyage for them, sailing from Glasgow to Boston on 28 December 1918. The following year in 1919, she made two voyages on the Liverpool to Quebec and Boston service. Later that year because of her large troop capacity, she was used for repatriating 1,000 British troops from Russia, where they had been used to quell revolutionary elements. Having left Archangel in mid-September, by 20 September 1919 she was in British waters and went aground in the Orkney Islands. She remained stranded for some 3½ hours but warships and tugs soon arrived, and she was pulled clear with their assistance. No damage was sustained and after being towed into deep water the *Vedic* continued on her voyage.

Her turbines gave a fair turn of speed and reliability in service and White Star decided to refit her for Third class on the post-war emigrant run to Canada. Accordingly she was refitted at Middlesbrough during 1920 to carry 1,250 passengers. The refit was quite an investment for the Company and greatly improved the external appearance of the *Vedic*. She was given a larger funnel, fore and mainmasts, taller derrick posts, extra deckhouses and six extra lifeboats. Once painted in new White Star livery she looked like a new ship. The forecastle, bridge deck and poop were painted white with the usual gold (or sometimes referred to as yellow) sheer line painted at the upper deck level, after which she took on the appearance of a rather classy cargo liner with some well balanced lines.

Upon her re-entry into service she left Liverpool in August 1920 for her first White Star voyage to Quebec and Montreal. As such she sailed to the St. Lawrence on the emigrant service and on to Portland, Maine in summer and to Halifax and New York in winter. Because of her purpose-built interiors and non-ostentatious internal appointments, shipping agents in the United States marketed her as 'the ship of democracy', thereby avoiding the 'emigrant' connotation. As she catered for Third class only, it essentially gave passengers unrestricted access to all decks, such as they were. But it was US immigration laws that later put an end to her 'democracy' service and trade.

A reshuffle of tonnage followed by the end of 1921 and the *Vedic* made her last voyage from Liverpool to Halifax and Portland on 6 April 1922. The following month she inaugurated a new trial emigrant service from Europe along with Red Star Line's *Poland*. She commenced on this service on 17 May 1922 from Bremen, Southampton, and Cherbourg to Quebec and Montreal when the St. Lawrence

was clear and to Halifax and New York in winter. All this took advantage of the depleted German passenger ship fleet occasioned by the War. She made four round voyages on this service, the last leaving from Bremen on 11 October 1922, after which she and the *Poland* were replaced by the larger *Canopic* and *Pittsburgh*, until the Germans ran their own service from Hamburg.

In 1925, the *Vedic* went to Harland & Wolff at Belfast for a refit to suit her for the Australian emigrant service, via South Africa. During this her gross tonnage was altered to 9,180. She made her first sailing on this route on 31 October 1925, from Liverpool to Cape Town, Sydney and Brisbane. On one voyage she replaced the *Runic's* schedule. Later she joined a White Star-Blue Funnel-Aberdeen Line joint service on the Australian route via the Cape. In this capacity the *Vedic* made frequent voyages under charter to the Salvation Army, by carrying many hundreds of hopeful emigrants from distressed areas of unemployment and social deprivation. As such, when leaving Liverpool or in the Mersey, she flew the Salvation Army flag at her foremast and would usually be accompanied down the Mersey by the Salvation Army band playing from the deck of a tender.

After a relatively short career of 16 years with White Star, her active service came to an end. Following a series of withdrawal of several ships from the Australian trade such as the *Persic*, *Medic*, *Suevic* and *Runic*, the *Vedic* was in turn laid up at Milford Haven on 26 February 1930. Ironically she joined a near sister, also built at Govan at the same time, the Leyland Line *Bostonian* (ex-*Rimouski*). The following year 1931, the *Vedic* broke adrift from her mooring and grounded, and two years later she was involved in a collision during November 1933. Following the merger between Cunard and White Star she became surplus to requirements and she was sold in July 1934 for £10,400 to Metal Industries Ltd of Rosyth for scrap. Although the *Vedic* was a one-off for White Star in both design and propulsion, it is for consideration

Below: **Built at the neighbouring yard of Workman, Clark as the *War Argus*, she was bought by White Star in 1920 for their Australian trade as the *Gallic*.** *Nautical Photo Agency.*

that her design may well have been a template for other emergency standard vessels of World War 1.

VEDIC: *Of or pertaining to Veda, one of the Sanskrit books forming the oldest sacred literature of the Hindus.*

GALLIC (II)

(1920-1933) 7,914 grt; 450 ft BP (465 ft OA) x 58 ft 3 in
Triple Expansion SR Engines, Twin Screw, 5,800 ihp,
12.5 knots
Passengers: None. Cargo only.
Workman, Clark & Co. Belfast. Yard No. 436

This ship started life as one of 22 Standard 'G' type emergency ships for the rapid wartime production of cargo vessels. She was built by Workman, Clark & Co. of Belfast, launched on 19 October and completed on 12 December 1918 as the *War Argus* for HM Shipping Controller, a month after the Armistice. As such she was placed under White Star management until she was surplus to requirements in the year following World War 1. White Star purchased the *War Argus* in August 1919 and renamed her the *Gallic*. She entered the Australian service for White Star as a cargo-only ship. When trade was rationalising on that route she was used on the Atlantic cargo service. After 14 years service with White Star and with the impending merger of the Company with Cunard Line, the *Gallic* was sold to Clan Line Steamships of Glasgow during October 1933 for £53,000, and renamed *Clan Colquhoun* and deployed on the same route. Following another 14 years with Clan Line, having proved a valuable refrigerated cargo carrier during World War 2 with the MoWT, she was sold in February 1947 to the Zarati Steamship Co. of Panama, and renamed *Ioannis Livanos*. She was again sold during 1949 to Dos Oceanos Compania de Navegacion SA of Panama and renamed *Jenny*. She was purchased by Djakarta Lloyd NV of Indonesia during 1951 who initially named her *Imam Bondjal* and later in 1952, *Djatinegra*.

Three years later and after 37 years in service she was sold

for scrap to Japanese breakers. On 1 December 1955 whilst on her last voyage from Djakarta to Osaka under tow, she put in at Lingayan near Manila in the Philippines with her engine room shipping water. She was refloated on 21 February 1956 and towed to Hong Kong for scrapping.

BARDIC

(1919-1925)
8,010 grt; 450 ft 5 in BP (465 ft OA) x 58 ft
Triple Expansion SR Engines, Twin Screw, 1,138 nhp,
12.5 knots
Passengers: None. Cargo only.
Harland & Wolff, Belfast. Yard No. 542

Built in 1918 as a sister to the *Gallic* under the World War 1 emergency standard ship programme, she was named *War Priam*. She was launched on 19 December 1918 for HM Shipping Controller. Whilst fitting out she was bought by White Star and handed over on 13 March 1919 as the *Bardic*. She sailed on her maiden voyage from Liverpool to New York on 18 March 1919. Between June 1919 and April 1921 she was switched to the Atlantic Transport Line to fill the gaps left by the wartime losses of refrigerated vessels. Still retaining the name *Bardic*, she operated on the London to New York service. Whilst on this service on 21 January 1920, the *Bardic* went to the assistance of a disabled steamer, the *Powhattan*, and attempted to take the stricken vessel in tow. However, the strain on the line proved too great and it snapped, leaving the trailed line to wrap around one of the *Bardic*'s propellers. The resulting damage caused her to put into Halifax, Nova Scotia for repairs.

In May 1921, she reverted to White Star operations, being transferred to their Australian service for the carriage of frozen beef, wheat and baled wool. Three years into a regular service, the *Bardic* departed Sydney on 6 August

Above: **The *Bardic* lies stranded on the Maenheere Rocks off the Lizard with her starboard propeller out of the water. Salvage attempts are seen in progress. She must have proved an interesting tourist attraction during August 1924.** *Richard de Kerbrech Collection.*

1924 under the command of Captain Charles Graeme. The return journey to the UK across the Indian Ocean via Suez took nigh on three weeks and she arrived in Liverpool on 26 August 1924, a fast passage for its day. Having discharged part of her cargo there she then sailed for London to land the remainder of her cargo, on the night of 29 August. As she approached the coast of Cornwall she encountered heavy fog and reduced speed and kept extra vigilance. Notwithstanding this, at 1 am on 31 August 1924, she ran aground on the Maenheere Rock (several hundred yards from where the *Suevic* had gone aground in 1907), near the Lizard.

The *Bardic*'s hull was gashed and her Nos 1, 2 and 3 holds had flooded, in addition the swell and current caused her to be further pounded against the rocks. The Master requested tugs and 80 of the *Bardic*'s crew were taken off by the Lizard lifeboat. With the Master and a couple of Engineers remaining aboard to keep the pumps going, two attending tugs failed to move the stricken ship, and with the outlook for the *Bardic* deteriorating by the hour, White Star called in the salvage experts. On 1 September, the Liverpool & Glasgow Salvage Association's vessel *Ranger* was in attendance but by now the *Bardic* was trimming by the bow with a list to port. The *Bardic* was lightened and in a period of six days her cargo was discharged into two 60 ft lighters. Another salvage vessel, the *Trover*, joined in the rescue and ran her pumps in tandem with those that were still operating on the *Bardic* with steam still available. These, together with air compressors, managed to stem the flooding which was gushing in through an 11 ft hole in her bow and 140 buckled and sprung plates along her keel area. Ironically, some of the refrigerated holds had maintained their watertight and frozen integrity. Eight days later, on 9 September, with strong gales threatening to hamper the

rescue, all salvors were taken off the *Bardic* and the pumping ceased to allow her to resettle back on the rocks in an effort to minimise damage. The storms off the Cornish coast did not abate until the 25 September, when the salvage attempt resumed. It was decided to try and pull the *Bardic* off the Rock at the next high water spring tide which was expected at 3.45pm on 29 September. On this day the *Ranger* and *Trover*, aided by four tugs and what power the *Bardic* could offer managed to drag her free. She was towed slowly with a heavy list to port, and beached temporarily near Falmouth before being drydocked by R. H. Green & Silley Cox on 3 October. Badly buckled and ripped plate damage was temporarily shored up and the *Bardic* finally sailed for Belfast under her own steam on 17 October where Harland & Wolff would effect more permanent repairs.

The salvors had saved another White Star ship for further trading and by the end of 1924 the *Bardic* returned to the Australian service. From then on the *Bardic*'s career became more chequered for on 22 August 1925 she was sold for £242,086 to the Aberdeen Line. Although it was mooted that she become the *Hostilius*, she was in fact renamed *Horatius*. White Star's partner on the New Zealand run, Shaw Savill, then purchased her on 3 August 1932, renaming her *Kumara*. However she proved rather slow for Shaw Savill's service schedule and she was laid up in the Gareloch during 1936 to await disposal. She was sold in 1937 to the Greek shipowner John S. Latsis of Piraeus and renamed *Marathon*. While trying to keep up with her convoy during World War 2, she was sunk by the German battlecruiser *Scharnhorst* on 9 March 1941, in a position north-east of the Cape Verde Islands. Apparently she had difficulty in maintaining the convoy speed and had become a straggler proceeding at her own speed. She had signalled RRR to the main convoy to inform them as such. All 38 of her crew were saved.

BARDIC: *Of or pertaining to a Celtic minstrel. Also pertaining to a Welsh or Cornish poet, particularly at the Eisteddfod.*

Titanic, war years and aftermath

In January 1912, prior to the *Titanic* disaster three months later, J. Bruce Ismay had indicated to the Board of IMMCo that he wished to stand down from the presidency of the combine. He would receive adverse press coverage, especially in the American newspapers for having survived the sinking of the *Titanic*, an incident that was to haunt him for the rest of his life. His resignation was accepted on 2 January 1913 and he relinquished his presidency on 30 June that year, being succeeded in the post by his friend and colleague Harold Sanderson. In the wake of the *Titanic* disaster he indicated that he wished to remain a director of the White Star Line but IMMCo turned this request down. He did, however, remain a director of IMMCo and on its British Committee, but without any hope of re-election to the Oceanic Steam Navigation Co, he resigned from these positions in June 1916, effectively bringing down the curtain on the Ismay family links with the White Star Line.

In March 1913, John Pierpont Morgan died. He too had been devastated by the loss of the *Titanic*, which had been the largest vessel in his combine. He was succeeded as head of the Morgan empire by his son J. P. Morgan Jr, known as Jack.

For White Star the *Titanic* disaster had done untold damage to the Company's reputation and dented the confidence of the ocean-travelling public. This confidence was slowly clawed back only by the improved safety features and the luxury and regularity of the *Olympic* and her consorts; also with the introduction in 1913 of the largest steamer on their Australian service, the *Ceramic*.

With a surge in emigration to Australia shortly before the 1914 War, the *Gothland* was transferred from the Red Star Line and renamed *Gothic*, although ironically she had originally been built as the *Gothic* for White Star in 1893 for their joint service with Shaw Savill, to New Zealand. She transferred to Red Star in 1907. Between 1911 and 1913 she augmented the five 'Colonial' class liners maintaining the service before reverting to Red Star once more.

When World War 1 broke out, White Star had many useful ships to contribute to the war effort. The express service from Southampton was immediately suspended and from Liverpool only the *Adriatic* and *Baltic* continued on the North Atlantic service. The requisition of four liners to be turned over to Armed Merchant Cruisers (AMCs) was quickly made; the *Oceanic* on 8 August, the *Celtic* on 20 October, *Cedric* on 4 December and *Teutonic* on 12 September; the latter was eventually purchased outright by the Admiralty on 16 August 1915. All were to serve in the 10th Cruiser Squadron, otherwise known as Cruiser Force

B, which comprised converted liners, many still manned by their Merchant Navy officers and crews as members of the Royal Naval Volunteer Reserve (RNVR). The 10th Cruiser Squadron was used to maintain the blockade of the North Sea, its patrol area extending from the Norwegian coast far out into the Atlantic and covering all approaches to the European continent from a northerly direction. In all, throughout the period of its existence, no fewer than 42 different passenger liners served with the squadron for some length of time, each armed with guns of up to 6 in calibre.

The *Olympic* was taken over in 1915 as a transport whilst the *Cevic* was taken over in late 1914 and disguised as the battleship HMS *Queen Mary*. Twice in 1915 she was a marine casualty and in 1916 became the auxiliary *Bayol* with circular tanks fitted for the carriage of oil. In 1917 she moved to HM Shipping Controller and was purchased later by the Anglo-Saxon Petroleum Company in 1920 and renamed *Pyrula*.

War losses for White Star, as with other shipping companies, were heavy and their first ship to be sunk was the AMC *Oceanic* which ran aground in the Shetland Islands by navigational error on 8 September 1914. The first loss to enemy action was the *Arabic (II)*, a victim of a torpedo from *U-24* off the Old head of Kinsale on 19 August 1915.

During 1916, three ships were lost; the *Britannic* by a mine in the Aegean Sea, the *Cymric* on 8 May (torpedoed by *U-20* 140 miles west north west of Fastnet) and the *Georgic* on 10 December, sunk by the surface raider *Moewe*, 590 miles east-south-east of Cape Race. She was carrying wheat and 1,200 horses.

Moving on to 25 January 1917, the *Laurentic* left Liverpool for Halifax with £6.5 million of gold bullion on board. She struck a mine off Malin Head, County Donegal and sank in 20 fathoms of water. Later, over a period of seven years, 3,186 of the 3,211 gold bars were recovered. A month later on 12 February, the *Afric*, the first of the Colonial class ships on the Australian run, was sunk by a torpedo from *U-66*, 12 miles west of the Eddystone whilst later on 17 August 1917, their New Zealand service ship *Delphic* was torpedoed and sunk 135 miles from Bishop Rock.

Also, in 1917, Harland & Wolff hurriedly completed for trooping a ship they had on the stocks when war broke out. Named *Belgic*, she was managed by the Company until 1923 when she was returned as the *Belgenland* to the Red Star Line by whom she had been originally ordered. Delivery was taken in 1918 of a single cargo ship, the *Vedic*. Three standard ships were also taken over after the War. These were the *War Argus*

(*Gallic*), *War Priam* (*Bardic*) and *War Icarus* (*Delphic (II)*). They were employed on the Atlantic cargo service until disposed of, the *Bardic* being transferred in 1925 to become the *Horatius* of the Aberdeen Line whilst the Clan Line bought the *Gallic* and *Delphic (II)* in 1933, these becoming the *Clan Colquhoun* and *Clan Farquhar* respectively.

An event that passed almost unnoticed owing to the war was the appointment, in April 1915, of a receiver to handle the affairs of the IMMCo. At the time the market value of the stock was approximately $26.5 million (c£5.3 million), whereas the paper value was almost $172 million (£34.4 million). Thanks to the efforts of the receiver Mr P. A. S. Franklin, and the boom in shipping brought about by the War, barely a year later the market value had risen to $165 million (£33 million). In recognition of his invaluable services, Mr Franklin was appointed President of the company, succeeding Harold Sanderson, who was then demoted to the European chairmanship of the combine.

In 1919 ships began to be released from Government requisition and White Star, as with other shipping companies, began the urgent replacement of their decimated fleets. With only the *Olympic* left on the planned Express service, a 40,000-ton liner to be named *Germanic*, later changed to *Homeric*, was at first considered. After prolonged consideration, the inflated building costs of the time decided the Company against having new tonnage constructed and instead they looked to ex-German ships that had been ceded to Britain under the Treaty of Versailles, as war reparations. The capital of the Oceanic Steam Navigation Co. was increased on 29 May 1920, to £5 million, having not long been raised by £3 million above the 1872 figure of £750,000. The first ship purchased was the *Berlin*, which had distinguished herself as the minelayer which had caused the sinking of HMS *Audacious*, to be renamed *Arabic (III)*. She was not seen very often at Southampton, but the others, notably the *Columbus*, which became the *Homeric*, and the *Bismarck*, which was completed as the *Majestic (II)*, augmented the *Olympic* on the much delayed three-ship Express service from that port.

Other confiscated, captured and ceded German vessels that were placed temporarily under White Star's management following the war were the *Hunslet, Alexandra Woermann, Frankfurt, Ypiranga* and *Zeppelin*. By 1922, these had all been sold on for further trading with other companies.

With this service in place White Star claimed to have the largest liner in the world (although this was hotly contested by the United States Line's *Leviathan*) in the *Majestic*, which was also the world's largest quadruple screw vessel. They boasted the world's largest triple screw and largest British built ship, the *Olympic*, and also the world's largest twin screw ship and the largest driven by reciprocating engines, the *Homeric*. On the run to Australia they owned the largest triple screw ship on that route, the *Ceramic*.

In the immediate post-war years there was a boom in emigration to North America form Europe and to this end in the spring of 1922, a service was started from Bremen by White Star to fill the vacuum left by the much-depleted German liner companies. The new service called at

Southampton and Cherbourg to Quebec and Montreal, in a joint arrangement with American and Red Star lines. The emergency built *Vedic* called at Southampton on 17 May running in consort with Red Star's *Poland*, but at the end of that year when the St. Lawrence closed, the North American termini were changed to Halifax and New York. Other ships also served the same route such as the *Canopic*, which called at Southampton on 10 November 1922 and American Line's *Pittsburgh*, replacing the former vessels. In November 1923 Hamburg replaced Bremen as the terminal, but by the mid-1920s the German North Atlantic trade had recovered and White Star withdrew the service.

In the years following World War 1, shipping companies in competition on the Atlantic withdrew their ships one at a time for conversion to oil. The liquid fuel adopted for steam raising in boilers was petroleum, either in its crude state or more often after it had gone through a refining process, giving a treacly (viscous) black tar known as 'Bunker C oil'. The hydrogen content of oil fuel, being about eleven per cent, was higher than that of coal, which gave it an added advantage. The value of fuel as a heat producer is measured by its calorific value, i.e. the number of (Imperial) heat units contained in one pound of the fuel. For coal an average figure would be 13,500 British Thermal Units, and for oil 18,500, so that 0.73 lb. of oil was equivalent to 1 lb of coal as a heat producer. Thus for a given steam production less oil fuel was required than coal. Oil fuel being a liquid could be stowed in places where coal could not, e. g. in the tanks formed by the double bottom of the ship and in existing coal bunker spaces that had to be modified to make them oil tight. All bunker 'snap head' rivets had to be punched out and holes countersunk for flush head rivets to make them leak-proof; a system of wash bulkheads was installed to restrict sloshing and free surface effect and heaters incorporated into the tanks to increase fluidity (less viscous). The bunker space required was less, due to the smaller quantity required for a given voyage, and also because less space is occupied per ton. The shipping of fuel oil and the handling of it on board were practically noiseless, and unaccompanied by any dust or mess.

It took eight months to convert a large ship; yet the resulting economies in manpower, speed of bunkering and maintenance more than offset the temporary loss of revenue. The labour required for supplying oil to the burners in the furnaces was reduced by about seventy-five per cent. In a coal-burning ship one fireman would attend to three furnaces, but with oil fuel one fireman could look after 12 furnaces, and with much less manual effort! In a large passenger ship as many as 200 men could be redundant in the engineering department; for those men who had once performed the back-breaking task of keeping up steam to maintain the schedules, this was to be their reward; to be consigned to history. For those firemen who survived the conversions and were taken on to oil-burning ships, they would acquire a white-overalled respectability that their blackened predecessors had never attained.

Considering the combustion of oil, it was continuous and uniform, with a corresponding uniform production of steam

Above: **A rare photograph of the *Mobile* in White Star livery. Her post-war operational performance proved so unsatisfactory that White Star only chartered her for two round voyages.** *Richard de Kerbrech Collection.*

and no residue, unlike with coal in which ash was continually formed in the furnaces which had to be removed and the firebed remade. All this had a bad effect on the boiler and on the quantity of steam raised. Anything from three to twenty per cent of the weight of coal could be left in the furnaces as ash. Oil-fired boilers could be more effectively controlled by shutting off the burners, so gone would be the distinctive, sulphurous reek of coal smoke around the ports and the clouds of filth and coal dust when bunkering by coal chutes.

The fuel changeover, which lasted into the 1920s, precipitated a crisis in Britain's strife-torn collieries but their loss was a gain to New York, where oil was cheaper, and it became the major bunkering centre for the Atlantic liners. Notwithstanding all this progress the *Ceramic* plodded on as a coal-fired ship to the end of its days.

In 1919 the British Mercantile Marine Uniform Act came into being with recommendations for standard uniform insignia for certified or other qualified officers. Although not adopted by White Star, they did drop the 'executive curl' for navigators. Engineers, as had previously been, were identified by purple inset between gold braid, (as were pursers with white and surgeons with red).

Post-war emigration was on the move by the early 1920s but it was the United States Immigration Act of 1924, which introduced Annual Quotas, that would have a drastic effect on steamship passenger revenue. The standpoint of the British shipowner was that an 'open door' policy should be followed, and that the emigrant passenger should have complete freedom of choice of route and steamer. Put another way, the emigrant with, say, £20 in his pocket, as the price of his steamer ticket, should be free to travel by the same routes as those followed by the more wealthy American tourist.

The passing of the US Quota Law brought about a radical change in the transatlantic movement. The quotas

established limited the immigration of aliens into the United States to a figure corresponding to two per cent of the foreign-born population of each nationality resident in the United States at the time of the 1890 census. At the time, the exception to the rule was the immigration of farm labourers, of which there was a world shortage! The US quotas are listed in Appendix I.

Notwithstanding this, it was safe to assume for the prospective developments of the passenger movement by sea that certain trends were manifesting themselves. As far as the North Atlantic was concerned, the shipowner saw a steadily increasing movement of American tourists to Europe, also the immigration movement to Canada had made a healthy recover since the immediate post-war years. With the radical diminution in the immigration movement to the United States, the tendency, so far as Third class US traffic was concerned, was more in the direction of encouraging two-way traffic; of which there was great potential and it went some way towards attempting to fill the gap created by the Quota Law.

Some mention should be made to the important factor that the Jewish race played in the passenger movement by sea between nations. It was felt at the time that Palestine couldn't absorb anything like the numbers of Jews anxious to emigrate, more particularly from countries like Poland, Romania and Russia (which had become the Soviet Union). On the political front, in 1922, Home Rule was granted to Ireland and the island partitioned to form Northern Ireland and the Irish Free State. The main transatlantic port of Queenstown became Cobh.

MOBILE

(1920)

16,960 grt; 588 ft 11 in BP (607 ft OA) x 65 ft 4 in
Quadruple Expansion SR Engines, Twin Screw,
11,500 ihp, 15. 5 knots
Passengers: 250 First class, 390 Second class,
2,550 Third class
Blohm & Voss, Hamburg. Yard No. 197

The *Mobile* (pronounced Mobeel), a former German liner, was one of the first vessels to be handed over to the Allies as a war reparation under the Treaty of Versailles. Blohm & Voss of Hamburg originally built her as the *Cleveland* for the Hamburg America Line and she was launched on 26 September 1908. The *Cleveland*, when completed on 16 March 1909, had a net tonnage of 10,267 and a deadweight tonnage of around 12,000. Her displacement tonnage was approximately 23,000 on a draught of 32 ft 8 in. Her hull was subdivided by 11 main bulkheads and with a double bottom for the full length of the ship. The *Cleveland* had three overall decks, with an orlop deck below outside machinery spaces and a long bridge deck above, on which a central enclosed promenade deck and boat deck were situated. This gave the liner the appearance of having a huge box-like superstructure amidships. The *Cleveland* had eight hatchways served by derricks on the four masts; the derrick on the mainmast was a heavy lift one capable of a maximum load of 20 tons. The masts were evenly disposed either side of her two funnels, and her hull had a gentle sheer with a flare at the bow at one end and a counter stern at the other. In the luffing davits she carried 28 varnished mahogany lifeboats. The bridge front and wheelhouse were also finished in mahogany.

Her twin quadruple expansion steam reciprocating engines consisted of 4 cylinders of 29½ in, 43 in, 61½ in and 86½ in bore with a stroke of 55 in. Steam was generated in three double-ended and three single-ended cylindrical coal-fired boilers. These supplied steam and gave her engines a total of 11,500 ihp, capable of giving the *Cleveland* a speed of 15.5 knots. All boiler uptakes exhausted through the fore funnel, the after one being a dummy. Her original accommodation as built catered for 239 First, 224 Second and 2,391 Third class passengers with a crew of 443. One of the innovations apparently accredited to the *Cleveland* was that instead of the long central tables that had hitherto traditionally been fitted to ocean liners in the main dining saloons since Victorian times, her main saloon was distributed around with numerous small tables. The *Cleveland* sailed on her maiden voyage from Hamburg to New York via Southampton and Cherbourg on 27 March 1909 and firmly established herself with the travelling public. During the winter low season, low occupancy caused Hamburg America (HAPAG) to send her on a world cruise with a revised accommodation for 650 passengers. After leaving New York the *Cleveland* sailed via Cape Horn to San Francisco, thus linking two United States ports with a

foreign flag vessel and breaking United States Intercoastal Reservation laws, but this was resolved without acrimony.

The *Cleveland* continued over the following three years to operate on the North Atlantic during the summer high season and switched to innovative cruising during the low season. On one of these embarked on during January 1912, she sailed from Hamburg via Suez to the Far East, then north to Japan. From Japan she crossed the Pacific via Honolulu and terminated at San Francisco. From here her passengers could travel across the United States by the Union Pacific Railway to New York and return to Hamburg by the earliest available HAPAG liner. On 10 July 1913, the *Cleveland*, along with her sister the *Cincinnati*, was switched to sail between Hamburg and Boston via Boulogne and Southampton. Retained on this service towards the end of July 1914, the *Cleveland* was moored at Hamburg when World War 1 broke out, and remained there idle throughout the duration of the war. Following hostilities and under the Treaty of Versailles she was surrendered to the Allies, and in a neglected state, she sailed during 26 March 1919 under HM Shipping Controller from Hamburg to Cowes Roads. Here she was allocated to the US Navy, and was fitted out as a troop transport by them and renamed *Mobile*. She repatriated US troops from mainland Europe, mainly from Brest to New York. Despite her main engines proving troublesome as a result of a lack of maintenance during her period of idleness, by the late summer of 1919 the bulk of the repatriation work had been completed.

Following this, the *Mobile* was transferred back to HM Shipping Controller, who in turn offered her for sale to White Star. White Star, wary of the great cost and expenditure needed to bring the *Mobile* up to scratch, did not purchase her but instead chartered her during 1920. She was repainted in White Star livery, her mahogany lifeboats being painted white and double banked on the amidships boat deck. The white paint was extended down from the superstructure to the upper deck level. Resplendent in her new colours she sailed from New York to Liverpool on 10 July 1920. Following this she made two more round voyages from Liverpool to New York via Queenstown on 6 August and 17 September respectively.

The *Mobile*, although augmenting the *Lapland* and the *Belgic (IV)* on the Liverpool run, proved unsatisfactory in performance and expensive to run, so by October that year her charter was terminated. The *Mobile* was sold to the Byron Steamship Company of London, part of the Embiricos Company for use on their National Greek Lines subsidiary between Piraeus and New York, and renamed *King Alexander*. She was a large vessel for the run and her large passenger capacity could cater for vast numbers of emigrants during each voyage. The US Immigration restrictions curtailed a lot of the Mediterranean trade and on one occasion she arrived in New York to find that along with another ship, their total Greek passengers landed had exceeded the year's quota (*Old 3% Quota, 3,063*)! Sadly the *King Alexander* had to return some of her hopeful passengers. After this she became more readily available for cruising and special charters, one of these undertaken between New York, San Francisco and Honolulu during April 1922 was by the Society of the Mystic Shrine.

The *King Alexander* was sold in the summer of 1923 to the United American Line. This was a United States owned, Panama Flag organisation and was the main catalyst to regenerate HAPAG operations on the North Atlantic once more (quite apart from circumventing the American Prohibition laws). She was reinstated with her original name *Cleveland* and sent for a refit to her builders Blohm & Voss of Hamburg. She was converted to an oil-fired ship and her accommodation was updated and re-designated as a Cabin class vessel with a capacity for 600 Cabin and 1,146 Third class passengers. In the course of the conversion her gross tonnage was modified to 15,746. She emerged as a reconditioned ship and sailed on her first post-war voyage from Hamburg to New York on 21 October 1923, and by 1925 a call at Halifax was added to her itinerary.

The pilot service proved so successful that by the following year HAPAG was in a financially stronger position, enough to buy back their former ship on 26 July 1926, still retaining her original name. In effect, HAPAG bought out the United American Line and the three liners it owned for 10 million marks and assimilated them into their reborn service. She ran on the Hamburg, Southampton to New York run. By 1929 she was again refitted and installed with a Bauer-Wach system exhaust turbine; this restored her service speed to 15.5 knots and improved her fuel economy as well as raising her gross tonnage to 16,971. Following the Wall Street crash and the Depression which permeated through to Germany there was a surge in passenger traffic in 1931. With the effects of this and the stiff competition from North German Lloyd's *Bremen* and *Europa*, the *Cleveland* was laid up in Hamburg in 1931, never to sail again. On 1 April 1933, she was sold to her builders, Blohm & Voss, for demolition.

HAVERFORD

(1921)
11,635 grt; 531 ft BP (550 ft OA) x 59 ft 2 in
Triple Expansion SR Engines, Twin Screw,
4,157 ihp, 14 knots
Passengers; 150 Second class, 1,700 Third class
John Brown & Co. Ltd., Clydebank. Yard No. 344

The *Haverford* was built by John Brown, Clydebank for the American Line of Liverpool, and launched on 4 May 1901. She was one of a pair of vessels, the other being the *Merion*, and was completed later in August that year. Her original accommodation provided for 150 Second and 1,700 Third class, but this was later changed to 216 Second and 1,308 Third. The *Haverford* and *Merion* were essentially emigrant and cargo ships, although Second class was the highest class carried as the term Cabin class had not been coined in 1901.

The *Haverford* had a net tonnage of 7,493 and a deadweight tonnage of 11,096 and a loaded draught of 30 ft 10 in. Her bridge deck was 150 ft long which included the Officers' accommodation and No 4 hatchway. Above this was the boat deck. The weather deck was a shelter deck and below this were the upper and main decks. The ship was built with seven holds and hatchways; the hull itself was constructed with web frames and subdivided by 11 bulkheads. Her twin screws were driven by triple expansion steam reciprocating engines with cylinder bores of 29 in, 46½ in and 75 in, with a stroke of 51 in. Her two single-ended and two double-ended boilers consumed 90 tons of coal a day. Their working pressure was 160 psi which gave the engines a total ihp of 4,157. At full output they could

Below: **American Line's** *Haverford* **was only in service with White Star for a year. This photograph shows her at sea in her White Star livery.** *Richard de Kerbrech Collection.*

produce 5,000 ihp which gave the *Haverford* a turn of speed of 14 knots. Her bunker capacity was 2,212 tons.

Although the *Haverford* was built for the Liverpool to Philadelphia service she was routed to Southampton and sailed on her maiden voyage on 4 September 1901 from there to New York via Cherbourg for the single round trip. Following this she undertook four round voyages for the Red Star Line on their Antwerp to New York route, between 9 November 1901 and 8 March 1902. During 1902 and following the formation of the IMMCo, there was much transferring, swapping and shuttling of ships between the main companies that formed the combine, i.e. White Star, American Line, Red Star Line, Dominion Line and Atlantic Transport Line. On 5 March 1902 American Line's *Waesland* was sunk in a collision off Anglesey, North Wales with the British steamer *Harmonides*. However the *Haverford* had been rescheduled to take her place on the intended Liverpool service and she commenced her first voyage from Liverpool to Philadelphia via Queenstown at the beginning of April 1902. For a time she ran in consort with her sister ship the *Merion* on this route and on one of these returning trips, on 13 June 1906, she was discharging cargo in Liverpool when an explosion occurred in one of her holds, killing eight men and seriously injuring 40 others.

On 17 December 1908, the *Haverford* made two round voyages for the Dominion Line, another of the IMMCo group, this time between Liverpool, Halifax and Portland, Maine. Upon completion of these on 21 January 1909 she returned to her service with the American Line along with the *Merion* and Dominion Line's *Dominion*. On 29 May 1913, whilst on one of her scheduled voyages, the *Haverford* ran aground on Carrigadda Rock when leaving Queenstown and flooded two holds before being refloated the next day. Following the outbreak of World War 1 on 4 August 1914, she continued on her North Atlantic commercial service until January 1915 when she was used as a troopship at Mudros during the Dardanelles campaign, until 1916. On 12 June 1917, she was attacked by a German submarine off the south of Ireland but escaped unharmed. A fortnight later on 26 June she was torpedoed again by a German submarine off the West Coast of Scotland with the loss of eight lives. The *Haverford* was beached to prevent further flooding and subsequently repairs kept her out of service for almost six months. The following year, on 17 April 1918, she was attacked yet again by a German submarine whilst in the North Atlantic, but the two torpedoes fired narrowly missed her. After the end of the war she was used to repatriate US troops, before returning to the American Line service between Liverpool and Philadelphia in January 1919. On this route she was joined for a time by the *Zeeland* but later sailed on her own until February 1921. With effect from 1 April 1921, White Star took over the Liverpool-Philadelphia service from the American Line and IMMCo transferred the *Haverford* to White Star. She was painted in White Star livery with her bridge deck side plates painted white, although the International Navigation Co. of Liverpool still officially owned her. She sailed on her first

voyage on 1 April 1921 on the revised Liverpool to Philadelphia service, making seven round voyages, the last on 6 November that year. From 18 January 1922 she made three round voyages from Hamburg to New York for the American Line, completing the last on 15 April 1922. A month later, on 16 May, she made her first voyage for White Star on the revised Liverpool to Boston and Philadelphia route and was joined on 6 June by the *Pittsburgh* which had been taken over by White Star from the American Line.

On 19 September 1923, the *Haverford* was in collision at sea with the American steamer *West Arrow*, which was en route from Liverpool to Boston. The *West Arrow* sustained a twisted stem and buckled plates from her forecastle head to below the waterline. Repairs carried out in Boston drydock cost around £10,000. She made her last voyage on 27 August 1924 from Liverpool, calling at Belfast and Glasgow before steaming on to Philadelphia. Upon her return she was laid up and sold in the December that year. She was purchased for £29,000 by Italian breakers and sailed for Italy where she was scrapped during 1925.

ARABIC (III)

(1921-1926)
16,786 grt; 590 ft 2 in BP (613 ft OA) x 69 ft 8 in
Quadruple Expansion SR Engines, Twin Screw,
16,000 ihp, 17 knots
Passengers: 266 First class, 246 Second class,
2,700 Third class
A. G. Weser, Bremen. Yard No. 164

In 1919 ships began to be released from the British Government requisition and shipping companies began the urgent replacement of their decimated fleets. After careful consideration, the inflated building costs of the time influenced White Star against having new tonnage constructed, and instead they looked to ex-German ships which had been handed over to them under the Treaty of Versailles. The first ship to be acquired was the *Berlin*, to be renamed *Arabic*.

A. G. Weser at Bremen built the *Berlin* during 1908 for the North German Lloyd. She was launched on 7 November 1908 and completed on 25 April 1909.

The *Berlin* sailed on her maiden voyage from Bremen to New York via Southampton and Cherbourg on 1 May 1909. She then entered the lucrative Italian emigrant market for North German Lloyd, departing from New York on 15 May 1909 for Naples and Genoa. She was deployed successfully on the Mediterranean service until she made her last voyage on this route on 14 May 1914 from Genoa and Naples to New York. Departing on 4 June 1914 from New York and returning to Bremen on which route she continued until her final departure over a month later on 18 July, just prior to the outbreak of World War 1. She was converted during August 1914 for war service and on 18 September 1914 was commissioned as an Auxiliary Cruiser (Hilfskreuzer) 'C' for the Imperial German Navy. As such she was fitted with 2,000 EBER mines and painted in (British) Anchor Line livery. The *Berlin* took up her station, laying a minefield off Tory Island in the North Channel between the north of Ireland and Scotland.

On 26 October 1914, one of the mines laid by the *Berlin* was struck by and sunk the battleship HMS *Audacious*. The *Berlin* had to return to Germany from her tour of duty, but owing to a shortage of coal she was unable to make it to a German port, so on 17 November she entered Trondheim in Norway and was interned there on 18 November 1914. She remained idle there for the next five years but removed from the conflict and any sabotage. Following the War's end, a year later on 13 December 1919, she was handed over to HM Shipping Controller for use as a troopship. She retained her name and was refitted for trooping at Smiths Docks, Southbank-on-Tees. She was managed by P&O and undertook some trooping voyages to Bombay but by November 1920 she was surplus to the Controller's requirements and purchased by White Star. She then went to Portsmouth Dockyard where she was refitted for further passenger service and her gross tonnage was revised to 16,786, and in 1921 was renamed the *Arabic*. She sailed on her first voyage for White Star on 7 September 1921 from Southampton to New York via Cherbourg for a single trip. Then, by way of a strange coincidence, she repeated her itinerary when she first entered service for her German owners. The *Arabic* then departed New York on 20 September and sailed for Naples and Genoa to replace the

Canopic on White Star's New York-Mediterranean service, for the next two years. By 1922 some of her machinery was giving trouble; the *Arabic's* steam steering engine, which controlled the chain mechanism to the rudder quadrant, broke down and she also suffered from leaking boilers and decks. Quite apart from this the US Immigration restriction legislation was compounded by the efforts of the Italian Government to keep their American-bound passengers in their own ships. White Star decided that the Mediterranean service that had proved so fruitful was no longer worth its time and investment. Thus the *Arabic* concluded her service on the Mediterranean route, sailing from Genoa and Naples to Boston and New York during October 1923.

In August 1924, the *Arabic* was converted to carry 500 passengers in the newly styled Cabin class and 1,200 Third class and on 16 August that year was placed on the Hamburg-Southampton-Cherbourg-Halifax-New York route. She again replaced the *Canopic* which had been on that run and which was then switched to the Liverpool secondary service joining the *Haverford*. Ten days later on 26 August 1924, whilst on this voyage the *Arabic* was hit by a hurricane off the US eastern seaboard. So tempestuous was the sea that four life rafts and one lifeboat were swept away while other boats were smashed in their davits. So many porthole glasses were smashed that deadlights were put down or smashed ports stuffed with pillows in order to prevent flooding. The windspeed and current were so great that the *Arabic* made little or no headway into the hurricane. Casualties mounted in the engine room as 17 engineers, 40 firemen and 6 greasers were thrown off their feet, many sustaining injury by falling into the rotating machinery. Passageways were flooded and a single wave shattered the library windows and caused fear and confusion to the 100 persons therein at the time.

Below: **The *Arabic* was originally built in 1909 for the North German Lloyd as the *Berlin*. As a minelayer in World War 1, her mines sank HMS *Audacious*.** *B&A Feilden.*

When the *Arabic* arrived in New York she had a 10° list to port and her much traumatised and seasick passengers were met by seven ambulances. The Company's *Homeric* arrived in New York not long after the *Arabic*, having been struck by an 80 ft wave in the same hurricane. Following its baptism of 'hell and high water', the *Arabic* settled into its Hamburg service for the next two years and one return leg on 9 November 1925 arrived at Hamburg from New York with a fire in a starboard bunker that was later put out with only minor damage occurring. However, by 1926 the German steamship companies had re-established themselves after the war and White Star withdrew from the route, just as they had previously done in the Mediterranean. So once more the *Arabic* was bumped from a regular service and she made her last voyage on this run from Hamburg on 11 October 1926. Whilst at New York on 29 October 1926, she was chartered to Red Star Line for the Antwerp to New York service and she sailed on their schedule the following day from New York to Antwerp via Plymouth and Cherbourg.

On 12 January 1927 following calls at Plymouth and Cherbourg, she arrived back in Antwerp with a fire in her bunkers. Some damage was sustained but it was eventually extinguished. At first the *Arabic* retained her White Star livery but during April 1927 she was repainted in Red Star colours. This service continued for three years up to 27 December 1929 when the *Arabic* made her last voyage from Antwerp to New York via Southampton and Cherbourg for Red Star. From New York on 11 January 1930, she departed on her eastbound crossing to Cobh (formerly Queenstown) and Liverpool, having reverted to

White Star. Her accommodation was re-graded so that she could carry 177 Cabin, 319 in the new Tourist and 823 Third class passengers. Two months later on 15 March she made her first voyage from Liverpool to Cobh and New York on their restyled 'intermediate' service. Owing to the effects of the Depression, the Canadian trade was seriously affected also and the *Arabic*'s itinerary was short-lived, for she completed only five round voyages on the service before making her last from Liverpool on 16 July 1930 and was subsequently laid up pending disposal.

As 1931 drew to a close White Star's showed a further financial loss of £450,777 and following a year of idleness the *Arabic* was sold to Italian shipbreakers of Genoa, in December 1931, for £17,000. But this and the sale of the *Cedric* for £22,150 did little to offset the Company's deficit.

HOMERIC

(1920-1936)
34,351 grt; 751 ft BP (774 ft OA) x 83 ft 4 in
Triple Expansion SR Engines, Twin Screw,
32,000 ihp, 18 knots
Passengers: 529 First class, 487 Second class,
1,750 Third class
F. Schichau, Danzig. Yard No. 891

Concurrent with the construction and brief career of the *Britannic*, another large liner was forecast for the White Star Line. Listed as a forthcoming new building in the Company's 1913 list of new tonnage, and bearing the name *Germanic*, she was originally intended to be a replacement for the recently lost *Titanic*. Measuring 33,600 grt, the *Germanic* was to be built by Harland & Wolff at Belfast. Following the outbreak of war, the projected vessel's name was prudently changed to *Homeric* but, by the time of the Armistice, no progress had been made on the new liner. With only the *Olympic* surviving the intended pre-war express service, White Star looked at more large liners which had been building in Germany at the start of the War, but on which work had been delayed.

One such ship that had been laid down by F. Schichau of Danzig (Gdansk), for the North German Lloyd just before the war and had been launched on 17 December 1913 as the *Columbus*. Completion was delayed during the war and on 28 June 1919 she was ceded to HM Shipping Controller as a war reparation under the Treaty of Versailles. In June 1920 White Star bought the new ship at her builders and renamed her *Homeric*. The building to the Company's specifications continued under Harland & Wolff's supervision, much to the disdain of the German shipyard. She was built with five decks and her twin triple expansion, 4-cylinder engines were supplied by 12 double-ended cylindrical boilers with steam at 210 psi. This developed

some 32,000 ihp which gave her a service speed of 18.5 knots. For her size her draught was 35 ft 3½in, which probably contributed to her stability in service.

The *Homeric* was quite a prize, being at the time, the largest twin screw reciprocating engined ship in the world, and she arrived at Southampton from Germany on 21 January 1922 to join the Express service. On 15 February 1922, she sailed on her maiden voyage to New York via Cherbourg. In the meantime the *Homeric*'s former sister, the *Hindenburg* one of the few half-built German ships not commandeered by the Allies, was completed for the North German Lloyd. She eventually sailed on her maiden voyage in 1924 under the *Homeric*'s original name *Columbus* and the two ships rivalled one another to some extent. When the *Majestic* arrived in May that year, White Star's weekly Atlantic service was finally established. Together with the *Olympic* the trio operated in direct competition to Cunard's *Berengaria*, *Aquitania* and *Mauretania*, and they were marketed as the 'De Luxe' service in the 1920s sailing schedule.

Trying to maintain the Atlantic Express service along with the *Olympic* and the newly-acquired *Majestic*, proved difficult for the *Homeric* with her speed of 18.5 knots. She was considered too slow and difficulty was frequently experienced in fitting her into a regular timetable. Notwithstanding this, her imposing appearance did gain her a popular following among regulars on the North Atlantic and her stiff motion in rough weather gained her a good reputation among her passengers. The disparity in a regular schedule meant that White Star experimented with placing her on winter cruises and a Mediterranean cruise on charter to Thomas Cook & Son. On one of these, on 12 February

Below: **This photograph shows the *Homeric* underway in the Solent. She had been ordered as North German Lloyd's *Columbus* but ceded to Britain as war reparation.** *Richard de Kerbrech Collection.*

Above: **Although the *Homeric* helped augment the Southampton to New York service, her reciprocating machinery handicapped her performance as an express liner.** *Richard de Kerbrech Collection.*

1923, from Syracuse to Alexandria, the *Homeric* was in collision with a coastal brigantine off Chanak Kalesi, Turkey. In this the *Homeric*'s gangway ladder was torn off and some windows on the Second class deck broken.

Between October 1923 and April 1924, the *Homeric* was refitted by Harland & Wolff in which she was converted to burn oil and her accommodation re-arranged to 540 First, 840 Second and 320 Third class. After her conversion her engine room staff had been reduced by two-thirds to a muster of

around 100 but upon her return to service on 19 April 1924 her speed had increased to 19.5 knots. Although this increased speed reduced her Atlantic crossing time by 24 hours she was still considered slow by comparison with her consorts and caused further scheduling problems. On 26 August 1924, the *Homeric* arrived late in New York after having sailed through a hurricane off the East Coast of the United States. In this she had been hit by an 80 ft wave. Seven people were injured, ports and windows were smashed in by the impact, and one of the lifeboats was carried away. In her lounge and other public rooms, chairs had snapped from their fastenings.

Below: **The *Homeric*'s First Class lounge.** *C. R. Hoffmann.*

The following year the *Homeric* was again riding another storm in the Atlantic when she picked up a SOS on 19 April 1925 from the Japanese cargo ship *Raifuku Maru*. The 5,867 ton freighter, with a crew of 48, had sailed the day before from Boston for Hamburg with a full cargo of wheat. She was pounded by high seas and developed a heavy list after what is thought to have been a shift of cargo. The *Homeric*, under the command of Captain Roberts, was some 70 miles away when the distress call was received and she ploughed through mountainous seas at 20 knots to the position of the stricken ship. Just as the *Homeric* reached the *Raifuku Maru*, the Japanese wireless operator transmitted: 'Now very danger. Come quick'. The cargo vessel's crew had tried to get off in their boats but the high seas smashed them and they were swept away. Captain Roberts positioned the *Homeric* as near to the *Raifuku Maru* as he could safely do but she had now heeled to a list of 30°. He was powerless to effect any type of rescue and the ship sank with all hands. He signalled Camperdown wireless station (Canada) 'Observed steamer *Raifuku Maru* sink in latitude 41° 43′ N; longitude 61° 39′ W. Regret unable to save any lives.'

As a consequence of the US immigration controls introduced in 1924 the *Homeric*'s Third class capacity was felt to be too great to be considered profitable and in April 1926 it was re-graded between the newly introduced Tourist and Third class. From 1927, she was chartered for five seasons to Messrs Thomas Cook & Son for January cruises commencing from New York. These were six-week cruises starting from the United States to the Mediterranean via Madeira and terminating at Southampton. These cruises normally catered for 500 passengers but during the 1928 charter only 400 or so berths were taken up. This meant that Thomas Cook had chartered her at a loss but they met their professional obligations with alacrity. Later that year on 9 July 1927, whilst outbound to New York, having left Southampton en route to Cherbourg, the *Homeric* collided with an Italian schooner, the *Giacomo*. No damage was sustained by the *Homeric* but the schooner was dismasted by the collision. The *Homeric* left one of her lifeboats with the schooner for her assistance. Again, just over a year later, on 26 November 1928, as she sailed from Southampton she encountered heavy weather and rough seas in the English Channel. No 2 hold had its hatch cover stove in, forward promenade deck windows were smashed and railings at the forecastle head were torn away. These were one of the advantages of her being a 'stiff' ship, but slightly less uncomfortable for the passengers in this type of weather.

By 1930, the *Homeric* was the Company's first ship to abolish Second class by re-grading it as Tourist. Her accommodation was altered to 523 First, 841 Tourist and 314 Third class. In effect the Second class and the best cabins in Third class had been renamed, all in an attempt to make her more appealing to a travelling clientele. To suit her role better for cruising she was fitted with an outdoor swimming pool and Lido deck which when installed necessitated the removal of four lifeboats down aft. She was then advertised as: 'The Ship of Splendour - Famous for her

Above: **Homeric's grand staircase.** *C. R. Hoffmann.*

size, steadiness and wonderful appointments…public rooms unsurpassed for spacious elegance…numerous staterooms with private baths…wireless telephone service…new open-air bathing pool and Lido deck'. All of which she was.

But back in 1930, the affects of the Depression had begun and the *Homeric*, and indeed the rest of the White Star fleet felt the financial difficulties biting. The number of passengers aboard the express three dwindled continually even in the normally peak summer months. However the *Homeric* was gradually easing out of the Atlantic express service and she was engaged more in cruising from Southampton and Liverpool, with rates as low as £1 per day. Other trips were offered to the Canary Islands, West Africa and the Mediterranean. During the August Bank Holiday weekend in 1931, the *Homeric* sailed from Southampton on a 'Cruise to nowhere', which in fact was a cruise to Southern Ireland and back. The fares for the mysterious trip ranged from £3 to 7 guineas (£7.35p). The following month the *Homeric* was used as an accommodation ship during the Schneider Cup Seaplane Trophy which took place over the Solent that September.

During 1932, it was decided to switch her to fulltime cruising and she made her last Atlantic crossing from Southampton on 1 June 1932 to New York via Cherbourg,

Above: **Homeric's verandah café.** *C. R. Hoffmann.*

departing New York on 10 June and returning to Southampton. Having just settled into her cruise mode, on 28 September 1932, the *Homeric* was involved in a minor collision whilst anchored off Santa Cruz, Tenerife. Cia Transmediterranean's 5,334grt steamer *Isla de Tenerife* rammed her when the Spanish ship's steering failed as she was circling the *Homeric*. The Spanish ship's stem was twisted but neither vessel was badly damaged and they were both able to resume their respective voyages. Apparently the *Isla de Tenerife* offered the *Homeric* an immediate payment of £5,000 to settle the matter, which was declined. Later, when dealt with in the orthodox insurance claim manner, the damage was found to be much greater than the 'on the spot' offer of £5,000.

Early in December 1932, the *Homeric* became the first liner to berth at Southampton's (then incomplete) New Docks extension, and on 21 December she made the first departure from these New Docks when she sailed on a Christmas cruise. The decision to place her on fulltime cruising was prudent for as it turned out 1932 was a boom time for cruising with more than 100,000 Britons spending their holidays at sea. During that period more than 200 cruises were operated from British ports and White Star had earned its share of the market. But even the demand and success of the cruise market could not hide that White Star's losses for 1932 amounted to £152,045. The following year whilst on an Atlantic cruise, on 12 June 1933, the Staff Captain John Foyster reported that whilst in latitude 32° 53′ N and longitude 9° 45′ W, she was 'In company with German airship *Graf Zeppelin*. Exchanged courtesies.'

At the time of the merger of Cunard and White Star in February 1934, she became an integral part of the newly formed fleet. On a Christmas and New Year cruise sailing from Southampton on 21 December 1934 to Portugal, Madeira and the Canary Islands, the tailor shop owner and diarist, Sir Montague Burton, observed: 'I have tea in the magnificent lounge. The absence of pillars adds to its stateliness and spaciousness'. And in another rather confusing entry: '…the dining room, which is larger than that of the *Empress of Britain*, although the *Homeric* is a smaller ship. This is a great convenience for the staff, as it enables all the passengers to be accommodated at one sitting for meals. However, if the full complement of 550

passengers had turned up, there would still have to be two sittings on this cruise, but, owing to the bad weather reports, about 150 people cancelled their reservations…'

Following the merger with Cunard, White Star's contribution to the combined fleet was 12 ships including those on the New Zealand service. There had to be a rationalisation of the fleet because of the surfeit of tonnage and berths available and one of those earmarked for disposal was the *Homeric*. However this decision was postponed and she was left on cruising as it had captured a valuable clientele. Together with the *Berengaria* and *Lancastria*, the *Homeric* represented the Merchant Navy at the Naval Review at Spithead, on 16 July 1935, to mark King George V's Silver Jubilee. The following month on 18 August, the *Laurentic*, which was on a cruise, collided with the Blue Star liner *Napier Star* in which six of her crew were killed. The *Laurentic* had to return to Liverpool where the passengers who were booked on the cruise were transferred to the *Lancastria* and the *Homeric*. The *Homeric*'s cruising days ended when she returned to Southampton on 25 September 1935 on what was believed to be a successful cruise. Her programme was taken over by the *Franconia* with effect from 28 September and the *Homeric* was laid up off Ryde, Isle of Wight for the winter, pending disposal. On 27 February 1936 she was sold to Thos. W. Ward of Sheffield for £74,000 and sailed for Inverkeithing during March for breaking up. It had been rumoured that her former owners, North German Lloyd, had been interested in purchasing her as a consort to her near sister, the *Columbus*, thereby achieving what World War 1 had prevented. The speculation was scotched by her sale for demolition.

Much has been written about the *Homeric* being too slow for the North Atlantic service and the fact that she was the largest ship in the world installed with large 4-cylinder triple expansion steam reciprocating engines and the largest twin screw steamer. The volume and deadweight taken up by the steam reciprocating machinery would have contributed to a slightly larger metacentric height, which would restore her to the upright when rolling in a seaway far quicker. This made her a 'stiff' ship in a rough seaway and gave her the reputation of being 'steady'.

Below: **The *Homeric* was employed on occasional cruises. On a 'Cruise to Nowhere' in 1931 fares started from £3. From 1932 she was switched to full time cruising**. *A. Duncan.*

Above: **On 12 June 1933, the German airship *Graf Zeppelin* flew over the *Homeric* whilst on a cruise. The airship can be seen to the right above the boat deck. The *Homeric* is blowing her whistle in salute.** *Peter Roberts.*

It is pure conjecture to ponder on whether re-engining her with steam turbines would have given her the speed to maintain the weekly schedule or not. After conversion to oil fuel, her 32,000 ihp engines could manage a maximum speed of 19.5 knots. Her sister, North German Lloyd's *Columbus*, was originally engined in the same fashion as the *Homeric*, was re-engined in 1929 with geared turbines, in an attempt to bring her up to speed with the *Bremen* and *Europa*. Her increase from 32,000 ihp to 49,000 shp gave her a maximum speed of 21.5-22 knots. The prohibitive cost

of refitting with turbines was high and existing maintenance costs low on *Homeric*'s power plant, and any re-engining would no doubt have affected her stability; this made the exercise financially unviable. Captain Walter Parker, who was the *Homeric*'s Master during 1928, said of her: '…as a sailor, she is all that one could desire; the largest twin screw steamer in the world…'

HOMERIC: *Of, pertaining to or in the style of Homer or the poems attributed to him.*

Below: **A post-merger photograph of the *Homeric* entering the Ocean Dock at Southampton on 2 August 1934.** *A. F. Williamson.*

POLAND

(1922)
8,282 grt; 475 ft 6 in BP (492 ft OA) x 54 ft 2 in
Triple Expansion SR Engine, Single Screw,
4,300 ihp, 13 knots
Passengers: 120 First class
Furness Withy & Co. West Hartlepool Yard No. 231

Originally the *Poland* was one of five ships built by Furness, Withy & Co. of West Hartlepool during 1897. She was launched on 31 July 1897 as the *Victoria* for Wilson's & Furness-Leyland Line which had been incorporated in 1896. The *Victoria* was a steel 4-masted ship, originally of 6,849 gross tons, with deadweight and net tonnages of 8,150 and 4,384 respectively. She had a displacement tonnage of between 13,000 and 14,000 on a draught of 27 ft 6½ in. She had three steel decks, a long bridge deck with boat deck above and her hull was divided by 10 bulkheads, giving her seven holds and 'tween decks. Only First class passengers were carried and were accommodated in the bridge deck space and on the promenade deck. Horses and cattle could be transported in the long upper 'tween deck.

Her single screw was driven by a triple expansion steam engine with cylinders of 32, 54 and 90 in bore with a stroke of 66 in. They were supplied by steam at 190 psi from two double-ended and two single-ended boilers, this developed 4,300 ihp which gave her a sea speed of 13 knots, possibly 14 maximum. Permanent bunker capacity was for 1,100 tons of coal with a reserve space for another 1,050 tons, as she consumed some 65 tons per day. The *Victoria* sailed on her maiden voyage on 9 January 1898 from Newcastle to New York, and returned to London for her first voyage in her intended service from there to New York on 12 February 1898. This was short-lived as in September 1898 the entire company fleet was sold to the Atlantic Transport Line and they were chartered to the US Government for trooping duties during the Spanish-American War. As such her first sailing was from London to New York on 4 August and she completed another two round voyages before being renamed *Manitou.*

In 1902, IMMCo absorbed the *Manitou* along with the rest of the Atlantic Transport fleet and she completed her last voyage from London to New York for ATL on 9 February 1905. She was then transferred to the Red Star Line for service on the Antwerp to Philadelphia route. As such she was painted in Red Star livery, and made her first voyage for them during August 1905, from Antwerp to Philadelphia, her accommodation having been downgraded to Second class. During 1906, whilst outward bound for Philadelphia and off Land's End, her single shaft cracked forward of the thrust block and disabled her. She had to put back into Falmouth for repairs.

In July 1914, she added Boston to her itinerary but the following month, August 1914, Belgium and Antwerp were invaded. The *Manitou* resumed the London-New York run for ATL from 31 October until 22 December. In 1915 she was transferred to Liverpool for conversion to an emergency transport. Here she was modified to carry 1,106 Third class passengers in what had been the cattle decks. All the lifeboats were doubled and an extra pair carried between the fore and mainmasts. Having survived the War, on 20 January 1921, she was renamed *Poland* and reinstated Red Star's Antwerp-New York service, although she was still registered as being owned by ATL. On her return trip her itinerary was changed and she sailed from New York on 17 February to Hamburg, Danzig and Libau. On 25 May 1921, she made her last voyage from Philadelphia, New York to Danzig. Whilst there she was transferred to White Star for an emigrant service. This commenced on 26 April 1922 from Bremen to Southampton, Quebec and Montreal. She made three round voyages in consort with the *Vedic* and on the completion of these she was laid up in July 1922. It was not until June 1925 that she was sold to the Italian breakers Ardito & C. Beraldo for £18,000. She was renamed *Natale* for her final voyage to Italy to be broken up and arrived at Genoa on 13 June 1925 for demolition.

MAJESTIC (II)

(1922-1936)

56,551 grt; 912 ft BP (955 ft 10 in OA) x 100 ft 1 in
Steam Turbines, Quadruple Screw, 86,000 shp, 23.5 knots
Passengers: 700 First class, 545 Second class, 850 Third class
Blohm & Voss, Hamburg. Yard No. 214

The fate of three German ships, laid down in the immediate pre-war years as replies to the 'Olympic' class, was decided when White Star took over the *Bismarck* and Cunard Line, the *Imperator*, as the *Berengaria*. Both companies had a half-share in the ownership of each, an arrangement that was later nullified and full ownership assumed by the respective companies to whom they had originally been allotted. (A third vessel, the *Vaterland*, went to the United States Lines as the *Leviathan*). The *Bismarck* was the third of Hamburg America Line's giants and as such was the last of an era of mammoth liners planned before World War 1. The *Bismarck* had been laid down in 1913 at Blohm & Voss's Hamburg yard. The late Chancellor Bismarck's granddaughter, the Countess Hannah von Bismarck launched her, on 20 June 1914. At the climax of the ceremony, the Countess experienced some difficulty in breaking the champagne bottle on the *Bismarck*'s hull. Kaiser Wilhelm II, who was also present for the naming ceremony, stepped forward and broke the bottle for her.

Within weeks of the launch, the outbreak of war interfered with the *Bismarck*'s progress as all shipyard labour was diverted to the more urgent German war effort. So she languished in an incomplete state for the duration of the War. In this state most of her brass and copper fittings were cannibalised for use elsewhere. On 28 June 1919, under the Treaty of Versailles, the British Reparations Committee awarded her and the *Imperator* to Great Britain to replace the sunken *Britannic* and *Lusitania*. To this end, White Star, aided by Harland & Wolff technical staff, tactfully set about the task of supervising the completion of *Bismarck* to their own specifications at the Blohm & Voss shipyard in Hamburg. On 5 October 1920, her completion was delayed considerably by fire. Sabotage by the German shipyard workers was at first suspected, as they were understandably reluctant to part with her. Notwithstanding this the 1,200 shipyard workforce turned to, to complete her construction.

Initially the *Bismarck* had been bought under a package deal by the Cunard and White Star Lines, but as Cunard were already operating the *Imperator* the *Bismarck* became a White Star ship during February 1921. On 28 March 1922, the *Bismarck* was completed and White Star crew and officials under Captain Bertram Hayes arrived at Hamburg to take her around to Liverpool and trials. They found the liner alongside at her dock painted in Hamburg America Line livery and boldly displaying the name *Bismarck*. This had been allowed to happen to assuage German feelings. On board, the Master found his cabin being used for the storage of ship's fittings. Furthermore, they found that Royal suites had been built into the *Bismarck* to carry the entire German Imperial family on a round-the-world Victory cruise!

Above: **The *Majestic*, not long after she had entered service, being manoeuvred by four tugs in The Solent en route for New York.** *Richard de Kerbrech Collection.*

Members of the German public and the shipyard workforce were reported to have lined the dockside and banks of the River Elbe, in silence, when the *Bismarck* sailed from that port for Liverpool. According to Captain Hayes, upon the *Bismarck* clearing Cuxhaven he had the name *Bismarck* painted out on the bows and stern and the name *Majestic* painted in its place.

On 1 April, she started on a series of trials in the Irish Sea which lasted over a period of 10 days and upon the completion of these she was officially renamed *Majestic* on 12 April. From Liverpool she sailed around to Southampton

Below: **This full stern view shows the *Majestic* in the United States Navy drydock at Boston on 16 November 1922. She would use this facility until Southampton's floating dock came into service in 1924.** *Royal Navy Museum.*

to be stored and painted in White Star livery prior to her maiden voyage. The *Majestic* was marketed as the World's largest Liner and she sailed on her maiden voyage from Southampton on 10 May 1922 to New York via Cherbourg, under the command of White Star Commodore Sir Bertram Hayes. The *Majestic* had nine decks and her hull was subdivided transversely by watertight bulkheads into 14 compartments, the doors being controlled from the bridge; while her hull consisted of cellular construction which gave great strength to the vessel. The boiler uptakes did not lead directly into the funnels through the central part of the ship; instead, the boiler uptakes for the two forward funnels were divided and led up the sides of the ship to rejoin just below the funnel base above the level of the boat deck. The after funnel was used solely for ventilation purposes.

This configuration gave a vast, uninterrupted area of open space on the promenade deck and was used to great advantage in her magnificently-decorated public rooms. Her interior space was said to be equivalent to 400 eight-roomed

houses. Of her decks, the five lowest ran the full length of the ship and the watertight bulkheads extended up through them. The First class dining room, which was also the Central hall, was situated on F deck and was the largest ever built in a ship. The middle part had an area of 2,300 ft², was 31 ft high, topped by a lofty, frescoed dome supported on slim Ionic pillars and the total area was 11,350 ft², and had a seating capacity for 678 passengers. The dining room was surrounded by tall windows which helped illuminate the area. Above the fifth deck were the four decks which contained the cabins and public rooms like the lounge, á la carte restaurant and palm court. One of her luxury amenities was the swimming bath in the Pompeian style of ancient Rome. It was furbished with rich marbles and brilliant red mosaics and had an area of 820 ft², with a depth range from 3 to 9 ft. The depth from her keel to the boat deck was 101 ft.

The *Majestic* was powered by quadruple screws direct-driven by Parsons steam turbines, with an astern turbine on each shaft. The four turbines normally worked in triple combination. Steam entered the high pressure turbine on the inner port shaft, then flowed to the intermediate pressure turbine on the inner starboard shaft, and then exhausted

Left: **Here the *Majestic* is seen going astern after departing from her pier at New York on 2 June 1923, during the high season on the Atlantic.** *Richard de Kerbrech Collection.*

equally between the low pressure turbines on the two outer shafts. The turbines developed a total of around 80,000 shp. Steam at 260 psi was supplied by 48 Yarrow-Normand water tube boilers with a total heating surface area of 220,000 ft². The boilers were fired with oil fuel on the J. Samuel White system, with five burners fitted to each boiler. Bunker compartments in tanks on each side of the boiler room, a cross bunker forward and in double-bottom tanks provided for 9,000 tons of oil fuel. The fuel consumption on each Atlantic crossing was around 5,700 tons. Her screw propellers were four-bladed, of 16 ft 5 in diameter and rotated at 200 rev/min. This power plant gave the *Majestic* a normal speed of about 25 knots, and in speed only Cunard's *Mauretania* surpassed her. She had also been fitted with Frahm anti-rolling tanks in an attempt to dampen any roll in a rough seaway.

Accommodation was provided for 700 First class passengers. The Second class, of whom there were 545, were accommodated aft of the First class in two, three and four-berth cabins. The 850 Third class were accommodated on four decks aft of the Second class. During the first week of August 1922, the *Majestic* arrived back in Southampton in the afternoon to disembark her passengers. The next day she sailed to Cowes and anchored alongside the Royal Yacht *Victoria & Albert*. Here King George V and Queen Mary inspected her during their visit to the Cowes Week Regatta. Now at last the Big Three express service, the *Majestic* together with the *Olympic* and the *Homeric*, was underway. Sailing on a Wednesday, usually at noon, arrival and departure from Cherbourg were the same day and at dawn the ship was usually clear of the Lizard. Quay to quay, Southampton to New York, the transatlantic voyage was roughly six days and with four days in port, the round trip took 16 days. Arriving in New York on Tuesday, the ship was re-stored and turned around the following Saturday.

Below: **This photograph shows the Majestic in Southampton's Floating Dock on 7 April 1925.** *Richard de Kerbrech Collection.*

Later that year on 23 December 1922 while docking during a strong gale at Southampton, the *Majestic* collided with her sister, the *Berengaria*, which had its starboard quarter railings wrenched away. The following year, during September 1923, the *Majestic* made her fastest eastbound Atlantic crossing between Ambrose Light vessel and Cherbourg with a crossing time of 5 days, 5 hours, 21 minutes at an average speed of 24.76 knots. On another crossing she departed New York on 28 June 1924 with 480 First, 736 Second and 1409 Third class passengers, a total of 2,625, the most ever carried by White Star in a single crossing. A good sign especially when one considers that White Star's big three were in competition with Cunard's express three, the *Mauretania*, *Aquitania* and *Berengaria*.

In early 1924, during a routine inspection when removing a ceiling, a deck plating fracture on the *Majestic's* 'C' deck port was discovered. It was forward of the uptakes of the middle funnel in the First class foyer. The ⅝in thick deck plating between the uptakes had split. At first repairs were not immediately carried out as it was felt to be attributed to a design fault that Blohm & Voss had built in the split uptakes to the funnels, and it had occurred in light plating. The forward end of these uptakes were in line with a pair of lifts and because the corners of the lift shafts or the uptakes had not been rounded, this had been sufficient for high stress concentrations to be set up, which propagated the crack. By December that year, in a rough crossing, the crack had spread rapidly enough to raise serious concern. The *Majestic's* sister, the *Leviathan* also suffered this defect. In August 1925's *Marine Engineering,* it was highlighted that the crack had spread and travelled down the port side of the *Majestic.* Apparently, during a westbound crossing and whilst rolling heavily to starboard, it had added greatly to the strain on the port shear strake. The crack began amidships, working its way outboard from both uptakes, spreading to the butt straps and then propagating rivet by rivet until finally C deck was completely cracked on both sides, thus placing all the strain on all the light inboard plating between the funnel uptakes. At that point, the crack on the port side spread its way down to the top of the first 16 in diameter porthole it came to. By the time the article on the crack appeared in this journal, during July 1925 the *Majestic* was undergoing her semi-annual overhaul. In this her deck plating on both sides was doubled for strength which arrested the crack, but this occurrence brought the strength of her midships structure into question and a watching brief was kept on it at all times. She was ready in time for her scheduled sailing on 12 August.

Above: **The** *Majestic*'**s first class dining saloon.** *C. R. Hoffmann.*

In May 1925, the *Majestic* had made another fast passage time of 5 days, averaging a speed of 25 knots and reaching 27 knots for five hours. Before the advent of the *Queen Mary* in 1936, the *Majestic* was fast becoming a popular ship and as such she became known as the 'Queen of the Western Ocean' and amongst seafarers as the 'Magic Stick'. At first drydocking became a problem for the *Majestic*, as it had not been possible for her to enter the Trafalgar Drydock at Southampton, because she was 37 ft longer that the maximum length for a ship to enter that dock, (even though it had been modified for the *Berengaria*). Instead, when required, she used the United States Navy drydock at Boston Navy Yard. The first time she used this facility was on 16 November 1922 for maintenance and to have her name properly mounted and again 17 months later when she left Southampton on 9 April 1924 and arrived at Boston on 15 April for drydocking. A year later, however, she was able to take advantage of the Southern Railway's new 60,000 ton floating dock which was moored off Southampton's Town Quay. She entered this for the first time for routine maintenance and overhaul on 26 March 1925.

The following year, on 5 June 1926, she sailed with her accommodation re-graded as First, Second, Tourist and Third

Below: **The** *Majestic*'**s palm court.** *C. R. Hoffmann.*

class. By January 1928 she underwent a major refit and overhaul in which she was reboilered, by Harland & Wolff of Southampton. During this overhaul the black tops to her funnels were extended further down the funnel and the hull black paint extended up one deck with just her spirket plate forward painted white. Following this refurbishment, which was carried out in seemingly record time, she was ready for service by 29 February. During the summer of 1930, when the Depression began to be felt in Britain, the *Majestic* was sent across the Atlantic to operate on cruises from New York. These were 3½-day mid-week excursions to Halifax, Nova Scotia, or on 'cruises to nowhere', often in partnership with the *Olympic*, when both ships had to stay in New York for a seven day stopover. These excursions were thinly disguised to lure American clientele from the restrictions of prohibition and were dubbed 'Booze Cruises'.

White Star was feeling the squeeze from the Depression and also in staff cutbacks resulting in reduced maintenance and upkeep on their liners. Sadly the outcome was that the *Majestic* occasionally entered port streaked with rust. In October 1931, the *Majestic*'s accommodation was again revised to First, Tourist and Third. 1930 had witnessed a large decline in passenger traffic on the North Atlantic, which in 1931 saw a virtual collapse, for westbound passenger receipts alone decreased by 240,000. The unpleasant fact emerged that British lines, including White Star, were losing more passengers than their Continental rivals. Prospective clientele were booking aboard the latest liners in service, like North German Lloyd's *Bremen* and *Europa* which had the benefit of operating on a state subsidy, which of course White Star did not. In fact by the end of December 1931, White Star showed a financial loss of £450,777. In the summer of 1932, the 1932 Great Britain Olympic Team, bound for Los Angeles, sailed in the *Majestic* on its five-day crossing and continued on by Union Pacific Railway for a further five days across the American continent until they reached Los Angeles. This gave White Star a bit of a fillip but again at the end of 1932, they incurred a loss of £152,045. However, as 1933 drew to its close, there were

Above: **The First class lounge entrance on the** *Majestic.*
C. R. Hoffmann.

definite signs that the worst of the slump was over but no great improvement in the North Atlantic trade where the competition of the newer, palatial Cabin ships had cut into the profits of the more expensive express liners, which ran at a considerable loss. White Star's losses for 1933 amounted to £353,552. On the brighter side was the impending merger of White Star with the Cunard Line in 1934 and that by then total westbound traffic had bottomed out.

On 19 January 1934, the *Majestic* became the first liner to use the newly-completed King George V Graving Dock at Southampton. Later in July 1934, the *Majestic* became part of the larger, merged Cunard White Star Line Ltd which was formed on 1 January that year to take over the trade of the former rival companies, now at last partners for all future services, but the merger effectively brought an end to the White Star Line. The *Majestic*, along with the *Olympic, Homeric, Georgic, Britannic, Adriatic, Albertic, Laurentic (II), Doric* and *Calgaric* was White Star's contribution to the new company. Upon the merger, White Star's Australian and New Zealand interests, represented by the Ceramic and the Ionic, were hived off to Shaw Savill & Albion. The *Majestic* was still the world's largest liner and the largest in the combined fleet. Notwithstanding her size, during that September 1934, she encountered a huge Atlantic wave which struck the liner and poured tons of water onto her upperworks. The Master, Commodore Edgar J. Trant, was badly injured and the Staff Captain had to resume command for the rest of the voyage. Commodore Trant never sailed again. Later in the same month, during the spring tide season, the *Majestic* missed the tide and ran aground on the Bramble Bank off Calshot, in the Solent. She was eventually floated on the next tide under her own power and without damage.

At first the *Majestic* formed part of the North Atlantic express service in company with the *Mauretania, Aquitania, Berengaria* and the *Olympic,* but on 27 March 1935 the *Olympic* made her final round trip from Southampton after which she was withdrawn from service. From this time the *Majestic,* which remained on the run, maintained the express service along with the *Aquitania* and the *Berengaria,* which by then had replaced the *Mauretania.* The service was operated

until the summer season. When French Line's *Normandie* entered service on 20 May 1935, she became not only the fastest liner in the world, capturing the Blue Riband from Italy's *Rex,* but also at 79,280 gross tons, the world's largest liner. The *Majestic* had lost its heavyweight crown, being displaced into second place. The *Majestic's* 207th and last voyage took place from Southampton to New York on 13 February 1936, and later departing New York on 21 February to arrive back in Southampton via Cherbourg for lay up. The *Queen Mary* took her place on the New York run when she entered service on 27 May 1936.

With all the hyperbole surrounding the *Queen Mary's* maiden voyage, these events overshadowed the *Majestic's* disposal. After three months' layup at Southampton she was sold for scrap on 15 May 1936 to Thos. W. Ward, for £115,000. Subsequently she was stripped of most of her external fittings and her masts and three funnels were shortened to facilitate her passage under the Forth Railway Bridge to the breaker's yard at Inverkeithing. However, around this time the Admiralty Board had decided that a training facility for new entry Boy Seamen and Artificer Apprentices should be sited at Rosyth in Scotland. As a shore establishment would take some time to build they sought a stopgap measure. The huge *Majestic* was ideal for a floating training establishment because she could accommodate the 1,500 new entry seamen and 500 apprentices, and the Admiralty decided to acquire her. It is believed that the Royal Navy could not buy the liner even at her scrap price, so an

Below: **A 50-ton electric gantry crane at work on the** *Majestic* **in the King George V graving dock at Southampton.** *Stothert & Pitt.*

exchange deal was brokered. The Royal Navy would trade 24 old warships whose tonnage was equivalent to that of the *Majestic*, for scrap instead. The exchange was agreed and the *Majestic* became the property of the Royal Navy. John I. Thornycroft of Southampton took her in hand under Admiralty supervision, for extensive alterations. An intensive programme started in which some 2,000 shipyard employees worked for up to 13 hours a day, seven days a week, for almost eight months to complete the conversion. In this, the First cabin dining saloon was turned into the Seaman Boys' Mess and the oak-panelled lounge was converted into a Gymnasium complete with a boxing ring with main recreation spaces. The *Majestic*'s former elegant Pompeian swimming pool became the baths on board and was one of the luxury fittings retained from her liner days. In addition to these alterations she was also fitted with seven guns and range finding equipment. The cost of conversion to the Royal Navy was estimated to be £472,000, and she emerged as the newly refurbished HMS *Caledonia*. The new training ship left Southampton for Rosyth on 8 April 1937 under her own power with Captain J. W. Binks in command, the former Master of the *Olympic*. On Saturday 10 April 1937, she anchored just below Inverkeithing until the tide was low enough to allow her safe passage under the Forth Bridge, aided by eight tugs. Once under the bridge she was inched into the Dockyard basin where she was to remain for the next two years. All her machinery remained intact and the *Caledonia* was capable of producing her own heat, light and domestic

Above: **The** *Majestic* **in the King George Graving Dock, Southampton.** *Richard de Kerbrech Collection.*

hot water. However fresh water had to be piped aboard and her sewage disposal system was linked to shoreside.

On St. George's Day, 23 April 1937, she was officially commissioned as the fourth HMS *Caledonia*. As such she was the Royal Navy's largest warship in commission and also ranked as the third largest passenger liner ever built with a capacity for 2,500 personnel. On 1 September 1939, Britain declared war on Germany and for safety reasons the boys and apprentices were moved from HMS *Caledonia* to temporary shoreside billets on 2 September. Because of her size, she was considered a potential hazard to the dockside, especially if she was bombed. So during the same month she was towed out of the basin to a point west of the Forth Railway Bridge and a good distance away from the main shipping channel. She then had water pumped into her bilges so that she settled on an even keel on the bottom of the Forth. This precaution was taken in case of an air raid, so that if hit, she could not break adrift and obstruct the

Below: **From the world's largest liner to the Royal Navy's largest 'warship' on active service. The former** *Majestic* **as HMS** *Caledonia* **with divisions on the parade ground on the occasion of a visit by King George VI around 1937.** *HMS Sultan.*

Above: **An unusual photograph of the** *Majestic* **alongside the berth at Halifax, Nova Scotia. It is thought that this view might have been taken in the summer of 1930 during one of her 3½-day excursions from New York.** *Royal Canadian Air Force Photo.*

main channel to Rosyth. Any thoughts of seriously considering her for use as a troopship were forestalled when on 29 September 1939 she caught fire and was gutted.

In March 1940, the Royal Navy sold her back to Thos. W. Ward for scrapping at Inverkeithing and during October 1942, Ward's began the job of salvaging the remains of HMS *Caledonia*. They lightened her by removing the superstructure and hull of the ship down to the main deck, which was one deck below the gunwales, then to the waterline leaving the forepeak intact to assist towing. Once lightened on 17 July 1943, the remains of her hull were raised and towed by three tugs to Inverkeithing where the

hulk was beached. However, during beaching, the last 250 ft of her stern section broke away. This was salvaged and towed away to Dalgety Bay where it was beached and finally broken up during 1943. Apparently when the bottom plates were cut out from between the webbings, they were of such high quality material that they were in remarkably good condition. They were deemed suitable for further use in the construction of new tonnage and perhaps one of the earliest examples of recycling.

MAJESTIC: *Characterised by majesty; imposing, stately.*

Below: **The ex-**-*Majestic* **fully converted to HMS** *Caledonia* **in the New Docks on 16 January 1937, with the** *Laurentic* **moored forward of her. Note the** *Caledonia*'s **masts and funnels have been cut down to enable her to pass under the Forth Bridge.** *P. A. Vicary.*

Above: **The** *Pittsburgh* **berthed at her pier in New York.**
Eric Johnson.

PITTSBURGH

(1922-1926)
16,322 grt; 574 ft 5 in BP (601 ft OA) x 67 ft 10 in
Triple Expansion SR Engines + LP Turbine,
Triple Screw, 12,000 ihp, 15 knots
Passengers: 600 Cabin class, 1,800 Third class
Harland & Wolff, Belfast. Yard No. 457

In 1913, two new intermediate liners were ordered from
Harland & Wolff's Glasgow and Belfast yards, the *Regina*
for the Dominion Line and the *Pittsburgh* for the American
Line. By August 1914 on the outbreak of war, the *Pittsburgh*
was not far enough advanced to be hurriedly sent to sea as a
cargo ship, as was the *Regina*. Instead, work was suspended
for six years and she was not launched until 11 November
1920. Both ships were built as the first of a series of similar
liners by Harland & Wolff around this period. The others
similarly constructed were White Star's *Doric* and *Laurentic
(II)* and Holland America's *Volendam* and *Veendam*, the
latter two being slightly smaller editions.

The *Pittsburgh* was laid down in November 1913 and was
not completed until 25 May 1922. She had a net tonnage of
9,855 and a deadweight capacity of around 14,040 tons.
Her displacement was 22,600 tons on a load draught of 28
ft. Her depth of hold was 40 ft 11 in. There were four full
length decks, an orlop deck in the cargo holds, and
promenade and boat decks above. With a forecastle, bridge
and poop, the well decks were decked over which gave her

the appearance of a flush-decker. She had seven holds and
hatchways and together with two boiler rooms, the engine
room and cross bunker were 12 main bulkheads.

Very prominent in the *Pittsburgh* and also the *Regina* and
Doric were the large gantry-type Topliss davits at each end of
the boat deck. The *Pittsburgh* had ten 30 ft lifeboats in the
tier under the forward set and 12 under the after; the theory
being that all these lifeboats could be launched with a good
outreach on either side of the ship. The system may have
seemed good on paper, but from a practical seaman's point-
of-view it was far from satisfactory. One has only to imagine
the ship (if only in a calm sea) with a heavy list and the
feelings of those occupants allotted the last boat of the 12 to
see why, bearing in mind also the possibility of a power
failure. The rest of the davits were of the more familiar Welin
type. It is thought that the Topliss davits were later removed
from all three of the ships in about 1927.

The *Pittsburgh* had three screws. The wing shafts were
driven by 4-cylinder, triple expansion engines with cylinders
of 28, 44, 49½, and 49½ in bore and a stroke of 54 in; they
exhausted into the low pressure turbine which drove the
centre propeller direct. Since there was no astern turbine,
the wing propellers were used for manoeuvring. The
reciprocating engines produced 8,360 ihp and the turbine
about 4,300 shp which gave the ship a sea speed of 15.5
knots with a maximum of 16.5. Six double-ended boilers
with six furnaces each occupied the two boiler rooms, all
their uptakes leading to the forward funnel; the after one
was a dummy. Originally intended as a coal-burner, but
probably due to a change in design during her long period
awaiting completion, the *Pittsburgh* was fitted for oil fuel
from the start; 2,790 tons could be bunkered and at full
speed she burnt about 120 tons a day.

Her passenger accommodation had a capacity for around 600 Cabin class and 1,700 Third class originally with the Third class rising later to over 2,000. The Cabin class accommodation was comfortable if not luxurious, with the drawing room, lounge, smoking room, gymnasium and children's room all on the promenade deck. Third class was situated on the shelter, upper and main decks forward and aft. Following her completion at Belfast she arrived in the Mersey on 26 May 1922. The American Line had practically ceased to exist by then and the *Pittsburgh* was transferred to White Star and completed in White Star livery, although she retained her name and was registered under the International Navigation Company of Liverpool. Her dimensions and machinery were exactly the same as those of the *Regina* except that the *Pittsburgh* differed from her near sister in having two hatchways and an extra pair of derrick posts in the gap between the navigating bridge and officers' deck and the main midships superstructure. This was probably due to her change over to oil and use of the former coalbunkers for cargo or stores. The fairly heavy rake to her masts and funnels and gradual sheer to the hull gave the *Pittsburgh* a well-balanced and attractive profile with the funnel placing being aft of amidships.

The *Pittsburgh* sailed on her maiden voyage on 6 June 1922 from Liverpool to Boston and Philadelphia on the same route as the *Haverford*. At 0445 (4.45am) on 1 November 1922 whilst on a return voyage from New York, she received an SOS signal from Libera Triestina's new steamer *Monte Grappa*, then 185 miles away. She sighted the stricken ship around 1800 hrs (6.00pm) and after manoeuvring around in the darkness sent two boats across the heavy swell to the Italian ship; in the meantime floodlights on the gantry davits were illuminated. The boats were successful in bringing off all 45 men on board and returned safely to be re-hoisted. A month later on 1 December 1922, the *Pittsburgh* made her first sailing from Bremen to Southampton, Halifax and New York, mainly engaged in the emigrant trade before the 1924 Quotas came into force. On this route she ran in consort with the *Canopic*. On Good Friday in April 1923, she was struck by a large wave in the Atlantic that demolished her wheelhouse and injured all inside, but left the bridge wings intact. On 25 November, the terminal was switched to Hamburg on the complete withdrawal of the American Line.

From 20 January 1925, the *Pittsburgh* was transferred with the *Arabic (III)* to the Red Star Line service from Antwerp to Southampton, Cherbourg and New York and departed for her first Red Star voyage on that date. Also operating this service for Red Star were the *Lapland* and *Belgenland*. On 18 February 1926, the *Pittsburgh* name changed to *Pennland* in keeping with Red Star nomenclature and commenced her first voyage under her new name on the same route on 2 April. She had been painted in Red Star livery when she joined the service and it is believed that soon after this her innovative Topliss gantry davits were removed and replaced by ordinary luffing davits instead. Also in that year, the International Navigation Company was disbanded

and the *Pennland, Lapland* and *Belgenland* were transferred within the IMMCo group to Frederick Leyland & Co. Leyland already owned the *Regina* and by 1929 she was renamed *Westernland*. As such she joined the others during 1930 on the Antwerp service and replaced the *Arabic (III)*. In January that year, the *Pennland's* accommodation was re-graded as Tourist and Third for by this time the world slump was disrupting shipping and bringing an end to many old established companies.

The Atlantic Transport Line ended its London service and its latest ships, the *Minnetonka* and *Minnewaska*, were transferred to Antwerp in Red Star livery only to be taken off the run after about a year and laid up. The *Pennland* and the *Westernland* made a few more voyages in 1934, the last for the *Pennland* being on 16 November, before Red Star itself collapsed. In January 1935, both ships were sold to Arnold Bernstein of Hamburg. He continued to employ them on the Antwerp-Southampton-New York route and retained the company title of Red Star Line, but as a new German company. As such she was reconditioned at Kiel and in this the white band on the funnels was doubled in depth and a red star painted in the centre of each. The number of boats was reduced by discarding the upper ones at the ends of the boat deck and those on the poop. She was refitted to carry only 486 Tourist class passengers, while considerable space in the vacated 'tween decks was given over to the carriage of uncrated cars. The *Pennland* commenced service for her German owner on 10 May 1935 from Antwerp.

Unfortunately for Arnold Bernstein he was a Jew in Nazi Germany. In 1937, he was arrested and imprisoned and his ships disposed of, although the *Pennland* and *Westernland* continued running until May 1939. Ironically, they were sold to the Holland America Line a year prior to this with authority to continue operating them on the old Red Star service with effect from June 1939. As a Holland America liner the *Pennland* was repainted in the Dutch company's livery and the yellow riband around the hull of her White Star days was reinstated, if only 3 ft lower than before. On the outbreak of World War 2 in September 1939, the *Pennland* and *Westernland* had their name and 'Holland' painted in large white letters on their sides amidships. The *Pennland* sailed from Antwerp on 10 March 1940 to New York, departing the American port on 26 March to return to Antwerp, before the Netherlands and Belgium fell to the invading Germans.

The following month on 27 April 1940, the *Pennland* left Antwerp for New York with a large complement of passengers and general cargo. After discharging she left under charter to the Ministry of War Transport for Liverpool with a cargo of war material. Upon arrival she was converted to a troopship. After the 8 July attack to immobilise the French battleship *Richelieu* based in the Vichy French port of Dakar in Senegal, the *Pennland* sailed on 31 August on the Dakar expedition with General de Gaulle and 1,200 Free French troops on board. However, the landing was not carried out due to the unforeseen resistance and, instead, she disembarked her troops at Douala.

Above: The *Doric* was the only turbine-driven passenger liner purpose built for White Star, as completed in 1923, with Topliss davits. *A. Duncan.*

Her next assignment was to carry 640 German and Italian POWs to Jamaica for internment before proceeding on to Canada to embark 2,000 Canadian troops for the UK. In 1941, her next mission was to transport 2,500 troops from Glasgow to Suez, followed by 3,000 Australians from Alexandria to Piraeus for the defence of Greece. She made a second run with more troops, but at the time of their landing the Germans were already over-running the country and the situation was hopeless. Accordingly, the *Pennland* on her return to Alexandria was recalled to help in the evacuation of British and Australian soldiers. On 25 April 1941, whilst bound from Alexandria to Athens, she was attacked by German aircraft. She was hit by no less than eight bombs with many more near misses, the first of which shattered the windlass and smashed the steering gear, while another sprung a serious leak in the hull in way of a bulkhead. Another bomb penetrated the engine room and exploded, killing four engine room staff. The doomed *Pennland* was abandoned and sunk shortly afterwards, her survivors from 251 crew and 100 troops being picked up by HMS *Griffin* and landed at Crete. According to Lloyds records she was sunk off Bela Pouli, near the San Giorgio Islands.

Although the *Pennland* as the *Pittsburgh* missed being used for troop-carrying duties in World War 1, up to the time of her sinking in 1941 she had carried a total of some 15,000 troops, no mean feat considering her limited passenger-carrying capacity. She was one of the last of Harland & Wolff's triple-screw liners to be installed with the well-proven combination machinery and seems to have proved reliable during her 19-year career.

DORIC (II)

(1923-1925)
16,484 grt; 575 ft 6 in BP (601 ft OA) x 67 ft 10 in
Steam Turbines, Twin Screw, 9,000 shp, 15 knots
Passengers: 583 Cabin class, 1,688 Third class
Harland & Wolff, Belfast. Yard No. 573

The *Doric* was the third of a series of four built to a pre-war design by Harland & Wolff for companies within the IMMCo group. The first was Dominion Line's *Regina*, built at Govan, which entered service on the Canadian route in 1922. The second one, the *Pittsburgh*, was built originally for the American Line for service on various Atlantic routes. The *Doric* was the third and the slightly larger *Laurentic (II)* followed it in 1927.

Although laid down in 1921, the *Doric* was launched by Harland & Wolff on 8 August 1922. The *Doric's* gross tonnage was 16,484 but carried a deadweight tonnage of 14,230 on a draught of 33 ft 11 in. This gave her a displacement tonnage of 28,480. She had a moulded depth of 45 ft 6 in and also four continuous decks. Cargo could be carried in nine holds served by eight hatches, with a total capacity of 439,148 ft³. The *Doric* had the distinction of being the only turbine-driven passenger ship ever built for White Star. She was installed with two sets of single reduction geared Brown-Curtis turbines which developed 9,000 shp. These were supplied by steam at 215 psi fed from six coal-fired boilers which could give her a maximum speed of 16 knots.

The *Doric* was initially completed to carry 583 Cabin and 1,688 Third class passengers and as an intermediate liner her internal appointments were quite impressive. An attempt was made to give an air of elegance but not too ostentatious décor with a lightness of touch and colour. Top of the list with regards to luxury were two three-room suites on the bridge deck, the bedrooms of which were in Louis XVI period style and had pearl grey walls with white mouldings.

Accommodation for Third class comprised 2, 3 and 4-berth cabins 'fitted with the finest of bedding and wash cabinets of the most approved type'. Another claim was that the orchestra played daily in the Third class dining saloon during meal times, and later doubled as a public room in which passengers had at their disposal the use of a piano and a gramophone with a large selection of records for their entertainment. Another apparent Cabin class innovation was that the *Doric* carried 'conductresses to care for and assist unaccompanied ladies'. In addition to these matrons were also part of the permanent crew 'whose duty it is to have special regard for the comfort of women and children'.

Upon her completion the *Doric* was handed over on 29 May 1923. Her appearance was like that of the *Pittsburgh* with two funnels and masts and the Topliss lifeboat davits fore and aft of the funnels. The *Doric*, along with the *Vedic*, were the first White Star liners to be built with a cruiser stern; that would for many years become the hallmark of ships built at Harland & Wolff's. With this type of stern a larger waterline length was obtained, improving hull flow through the water and aiding propulsive efficiency. It also gave better protection to the screws in harbour as well as greater buoyancy aft in a seaway. The *Doric* sailed on her maiden voyage from Liverpool to Quebec and Montreal on 8 June 1923. On this voyage she called at Belfast to pick up a large quantity of Irish passengers. She was originally advertised as being on the White Star-Dominion Line service, but with the demise of the Dominion Line it was re-advertised as the White Star Canadian service. She ran in consort with the *Regina*, which started life with the Dominion Line but later became a White Star ship.

On 10 June 1926, the *Doric*'s passenger accommodation was re-graded to take 320 Cabin, 657 Tourist and 537 Third class passengers. It may be around the same time that her Topliss lifeboat davits were replaced by the more popular Welin style davits. On 14 September 1927, the *Doric* was in a minor collision with the British steamer *Barrie* at Montreal in a bow-to-bow bump. The *Barrie* had her stem

Above: **A fine photograph of the Doric under speed. Her once-innovative Topliss davits have been replaced by more conventional Welin gravity davits.** *B&A Feilden.*

bent and two plates damaged while the *Doric* had a bow plate buckled. Temporary repairs were made before she departed for Liverpool. Again, on 14 May 1928, the *Doric* was in a narrow scrape at Montreal when a grain carrier, the *Judge Kenefick*, brushed the *Doric* with minor damage to No3 lifeboat's lower blocks of the falls. For 1930, the *Doric* would extend her itinerary during the winter months when the St. Lawrence River was frozen. She left Liverpool on 22 February and on 22 March to New York, calling at Belfast, Glasgow and Halifax en route. The return voyages from New York sailed on 8 March and 5 April respectively, returning to Liverpool via Halifax and Cobh (formerly Queenstown). Winter Cabin fares eastbound and westbound were £35 each way. Tourist Third cabin was £25 one way all year round while other offers in this class were £46 round trip in the off season, up to £50 for the summer season. Third class fares were £21 eastbound, £22 westbound with reduced round trip fares of £39.

Below: **The *Doric* is seen here following her 1930 refit dressed overall and being towed into the River Mersey in readiness for sailing to New York.** *John Clarkson.*

On 8 December 1930 whilst undergoing an annual overhaul at Liverpool, fire broke out on board and destroyed the interiors of five 'C'-deck cabins before being brought under control. On 27 May 1932, the *Doric* made her last transatlantic crossing and from October 1932 until April 1933 she was laid up at Liverpool, later re-entering service cruising to the Mediterranean. She survived in this capacity operating at first for White Star then for Cunard White Star after the amalgamation in 1934. She was employed on tourist cruises out of Southampton at a minimum rate of £12 for 13 days afloat.

Whilst returning from one of these cruises with some 736 passengers and 350 crew aboard, she had exited the Mediterranean and was heading north along the Portuguese coast. At 0400 hrs (4.00am) on 5 September 1935, she was in collision with Chargeurs Reunis's *Formigny* on passage to Oran, in thick fog off Cape Finisterre. The *Doric* was damaged starboard, forward of the bridge, following the collision, with a 10ft long by 5 ft wide hole opening her No3 hold to the sea. The hold started to flood and a list to starboard developed. Her Master, Captain A. C. Greig, ordered the watertight doors shut and the *Doric* sent out an SOS at 0530 hrs (5.30am). P&O's *Viceroy of India* arrived at the scene and took off 250 passengers. Later, Orient Line's *Orion* which was returning from a shakedown cruise to the Mediterranean with First class guests aboard also arrived at the scene. She was able to take off 486 passengers and 42 of the crew. The *Formigny* made for Lisbon while the more seriously damaged *Doric* proceeded to Vigo for temporary repairs, which included the fitting of a watertight cofferdam. Following these repairs, the *Doric* sailed from Vigo at 1500 hrs (3pm) on 12 September for Tilbury, where she arrived on 15 September. All the passengers' baggage and belongings that had been left aboard since the collision were forwarded on to their owners. At Tilbury she was surveyed by Cunard White Star's marine department and notwithstanding her being only 12 years old and given the newly-merged

company's excess tonnage and diminished passenger receipts, she was considered uneconomical to repair and declared a total constructive loss. She was sold to John Cashmore Ltd. as scrap for £35,000. Later, on 7 November 1935, she sailed for Newport, Monmouthshire, for breaking up. Her fixtures and fittings were removed and sold at public auction which raised £7,500 funds for the Royal Gwent Hospital.

DELPHIC (II)

(1925-1933)
8,006 grt; 450 ft 5 in BP (465 ft OA) X 58 ft 3 in
Triple Expansion SR Engines, Twin Screw,
5,100 ihp, 12.5 knots.
Passengers: None. Cargo only
Harland & Wolff, Belfast. Yard No. 540

Another wartime emergency-standard 'G' type ship built by Harland & Wolff at Belfast and a sister of the *Gallic* and *Bardic*. She was built during 1916 as the *War Icarus* for HM Shipping Controller and launched on 19 September 1918. When completed on 18 October, she was managed by the Liverpool-based Booth Line, but this was for a short interlude in her career. During May 1919, she was purchased by the Atlantic Transport Line who renamed her *Mesaba*. After six years of service with them she was transferred within the IMMCo to White Star in 1925. She was refitted at Belfast and renamed *Delphic*, and placed on the Australian cargo service along with the *Gallic*. She replaced the *Bardic*, which had grounded near the Lizard during 1924.

After eight years with White Star and with the Cunard and White Star merger imminent, like her sister the *Gallic*, she was sold to Clan Line Steamers of Glasgow in October 1933 for £53,000, after being laid up at Milford Haven. Clan Line renamed her *Clan Farquhar* and continued to operate her on the Australian service until July 1948, when after 30 years trading, she was broken up at Milford Haven.

White Star did not use the name Delphic *again, which became a Shaw Savill & Albion nomenclature.*

Above: The First World War delayed the completion of the *Regina* as a purpose-built passenger ship. This view highlights the Topliss davits showing their complex arrangement.
Richard de Kerbrech Collection.

REGINA

(1925-1929)
16, 313grt; 575 ft 5 in BP (601 ft OA) x 67 ft 10 in
Triple Expansion SR Engines + LP Turbine,
Triple Screw, 12,000 ihp
Passengers: 631 Cabin class, 1,824 Third class
Harland & Wolff, Glasgow. Yard No. 454

The *Regina* was built by Harland & Wolff at Glasgow as a sister to the *Pittsburgh*. She was originally laid down in 1913 for the Dominion Line and was the first of a class of six intermediate liners for Dominion, Leyland, White Star and Holland America Line.

She was launched on 19 April 1917 and towed to Belfast for installation of the power plant comprising twin four-cylinder, triple expansion steam reciprocating engines coupled to the two outer shafts – the resulting steam was forced into a large low pressure turbine that drove the centre shaft. Due to her early construction she was coal-fired and because of the desperate need for emergency tonnage, she was completed in austerity fashion devoid of any furnishings and upper promenade deck. She was partially completed on 26 October 1918 with only one funnel and mast and no passenger accommodation and was put into service on the Liverpool to Boston run repatriating US troops and emigrants. On completion of her post-war duties, she returned to Harland & Wolff's at Belfast in August 1920 for completion as a passenger liner to the builders' original design. However by 1921, the Dominion Line fleet transferred its ownership to Frederick Leyland & Co., but in order to retain the company goodwill, the title White Star-Dominion Line remained in use for marketing the ship. She emerged following her conversion sporting two funnels and masts together with the innovative Topliss davits which were vogue at the time on others of her class. She underwent her trials on 2 March 1922 before sailing to Liverpool from

where she sailed on her maiden voyage in Dominion Line colours on 16 March between Liverpool, Halifax and Portland, Maine, on the White Star-Dominion Line Joint Service. Two weeks following this, the *Vedic* commenced her last passenger voyage from Liverpool before being transferred to the White Star service between Bremen, Southampton, Cherbourg and Quebec. Following this, the *Regina* together with Dominion Line's *Canada* and White Star's *Megantic* and *Canopic,* operated a weekly service from Liverpool to Quebec and Montreal.

On 17 February 1923, the *Regina* sailed from Liverpool and made her only call at Bermuda to disembark naval personnel on the island before sailing on to New York. On 21 June 1924, the *Regina* sailed from Montreal and Quebec for Liverpool with 572 Cabin and 652 Third class passengers. All of the latter comprised mainly American and Canadian college students going to Europe on holiday. The Third class accommodation allocated for this purpose became referred to as 'College Tours'. Other shipping companies keen to capitalise on this new type of clientele soon copied this innovative move by White Star. This probably gave rise in April 1925 to the official term 'Tourist Third cabin' being introduced by the North Atlantic Passenger Conference, and taken up by all the lines belonging to the Conference until 1931 when 'Tourist class' was adopted. For this new type of traveller, improved food and amenities with a lot more passenger space was provided.

On 6 November 1925, the *Regina* made her last voyage from Liverpool to Quebec and Montreal for the White Star-Dominion Line. Upon her return and following the demise of the Dominion Line, she was painted in White Star colours and made her first voyage for them on 12 December 1925 from Liverpool to New York via Halifax under the banner White Star Line (Canadian Services). The *Regina's* accommodation was re-graded in June 1926 to Cabin, Tourist and Third. She maintained the New York service during the winter months and the Canadian run to Quebec and Montreal during the summer months. However, the sale of IMMCo to the Royal Mail Group in 1927 substituted one labyrinthine organisation for another and the *Regina* made her last voyage for White Star on 1 November 1929 from Liverpool to Quebec and Montreal via Belfast and Glasgow. Although technically still owned by Frederick Leyland, in 1929 she was transferred back to them and allocated to Red Star Line and renamed *Westernland*. She was then repainted in Red Star colours and joined the *Pennland* (ex-*Pittsburgh*) and *Belgenland* on the Antwerp service, thereby replacing the *Arabic (III)*.

The *Westernland* made her first Red Star voyage commencing from Antwerp to Southampton, Cherbourg and New York on 10 January 1930 with accommodation for 350 Cabin, 350 Tourist and 800 Third class passengers. The service lasted barely a year prior to Red Star Line's collapse in 1934. On 30 November that year, the *Westernland* departed on her last Red Star voyage from Antwerp to Le Havre, Southampton and New York arriving on 10 December 1934. She departed two days later, returning to Antwerp via Le Havre and London. Upon her arrival at the terminus she was laid up for three months pending the uncertainty of the Red Star Line. At the beginning of 1935, Arnold Bernstein of Hamburg bought the *Westernland* and the *Pennland* and continued to operate them on the Antwerp-Southampton-New York route, retaining the title and goodwill of the Red Star Line (but suffixed by GmbH). Following a minor refit to accommodate 486 Tourist class passengers only, she made her first voyage for her new German owners on 29 March

1935 from Antwerp to New York via Southampton. In addition to passengers she also loaded more and more cars for the US. Nine months later on 31 December 1935, the *Westernland* rescued two crewmen of a sinking French trawler, the *Satanile*, which sunk in a gale. Again, almost a year later, on 8 November 1936, she rescued the sole survivor of Hamburg America's *Isis* which had sunk in a storm with the loss of 39 lives.

Red Star Line GmbH's owner Arnold Bernstein was arrested and imprisoned under Germany's anti-Semitic laws during 1937. However, the *Westernland* continued the service departing on her last voyage for them on 6 May 1939. The Company was sold to Holland America Line who continued to operate her on this route on which she ran from June 1939 from Antwerp to New York via Southampton. When the Germans invaded Belgium and the Netherlands in April 1940, the *Westernland* sailed from Antwerp on 10 April for Falmouth. It was here on 10 May that she became the headquarters ship for the Dutch Government in exile, until more permanent quarters could be found. During July 1940, she was requisitioned as a troopship and sailed for Liverpool for refit and conversion. She was used for this purpose until November 1942 and purchased by the Admiralty from Holland America at a cost of £450,000 for conversion into a destroyer repair and depot ship. This plan did not come to pass and she was decommissioned in 1945 and laid up in the River Blackwater. During October 1946, the *Westernland* was sold to Christian Salvesen of Leith who intended to convert her for further use as a whaling ship. This was thought to be too expensive for a 30-year-old coal-burning ship and the idea was dropped. On 15 July 1947, she was finally sold to the British Iron & Steel Corporation for scrap, and on 1 August 1947, arrived at Blyth to be broken up by Hughes Bolckow.

Left: **A collision during September 1935 brought a premature end to the *Doric*'s career. This photograph of her being towed into Liverpool Docks was taken in her halcyon days.** *Tom Rayner Collection.*

A shipping empire cannot be conquered from without unless it destroys itself from within.

1920-1932

Class of travel, takeover, money matters and Depression

One of White Star's staunchest allies, Lord Pirrie, the former Chairman of Harland & Wolff, died of pneumonia, aged 77, on 7 June 1924, whilst transiting the Panama Canal on board the Pacific Steam's *Ebro*. His embalmed body was shipped home to Belfast aboard the *Olympic*. Harland & Wolff were in the process of enlargement and improvement to meet the demands of the post-war shipbuilding boom when Lord Pirrie died, but by then orders had greatly diminished. Harland & Wolff was reconstituted as a public company under the Chairmanship of Lord Kylsant and further orders were received from his Royal Mail Group, financed by loans under the Trades Facility Acts (and Northern Ireland's Loans Guarantee Acts), as was indeed part of the yard's modernisation.

Around 1926 or 1927, White Star's Passenger Traffic Manager, Major Frank Bustard OBE, gave a lecture to Liverpool's City School of Commerce in which he identified six classes of accommodation provided on the North Atlantic. Changing passenger trends during the 1920s and some of the passenger classifications that were developed as solutions to these problems had a considerable bearing on the prosperity or otherwise of shipping lines at this time. In this context, Major Bustard's observations on social stratification make interesting reading and are quoted as follows:

(a) First class by the express steamers from Southampton, used particularly by businessmen and others to whom time is of monetary consideration; also by members of the theatrical profession and film industry, who for publicity purposes cannot afford to travel other than on the 'monster' steamers.

(b) Some of the companies are still running similar steamers, though not quite so large or fast and at slightly lower rates, from other ports, especially Liverpool. Their patrons are mainly business travellers and the American tourist class, to whom time is not of primary importance, and who have learnt by experience the estimable sea-going qualities that prevail on the type of steamer of 20,000-30,000 tons making the passage to and from New York in just over the week.

(c) Cabin class. This class is supported by many passengers who formerly travelled First class, but who desire to combine economy with their travels, and there are also many travellers who previously crossed Second class in the three-class ships, who prefer Cabin accommodation because there is no better class above them on the ship. The Cabin fares are only slightly higher than the Second class rates.

(d) Second class retains its popularity, particularly on the 'monster' steamers.

(e) Tourist Third Cabin is an entirely new class, and it is to this particular traffic that the steamship lines look to take the place of the reduced emigration movement brought about by the US Quota Restrictions (United States Immigration Act, 1924). The Tourist Third Cabin quarters afford most comfortable accommodation to passengers to whom economy in travel is the primary consideration; and the development of this travel since 1925 shows clearly the possibilities of an increase in this movement of Americans desiring to visit Europe. Efforts are also being made to encourage the Tourist Third Cabin movement from Great Britain and Ireland to the United States, but it is expected that the bulk of this traffic will emanate from America.

(f) Third class continues to be maintained more particularly for the emigrant type of passenger, and the worker in the United States or Canada when returning home on seasonal or occasional visits.

Although Frank Bustard was a White Star official, his lecture gave a general picture of the classes of accommodation offered by most of the major companies of the day. And so it was by the late 1920s that styles of travel considerably changed with the introduction of the new Cabin class which proved popular and very much in demand. This term had been chosen by the Atlantic Conference of all companies engaged in the North Atlantic trade, which included White Star. Many passengers who formerly travelled First class but wanted to travel more economically supported the new class. Also many travellers who had previously crossed Second class in three-class ships preferred Cabin accommodation because it was the best class on these ships. In effect, Cabin class meant First class treatment in slower vessels.

Early in the 1920s, Mr P. A. S. Franklin, President of the American-owned International Mercantile Marine Company (IMMCo) had wanted the combine to divest itself of some of its foreign-flag shipping companies, chief among these being the Oceanic Steam Navigation Company Ltd, owner of White Star. An offer for all the British-flag ships was made by Lord Pirrie and Sir Owen Phillips (later Lord Kylsant in 1923) but this was vetoed by the American President. In 1926, an offer by Furness Withy & Co. Ltd to buy White Star was thwarted by the General Strike in Britain and by the requirements of IMMCo with respect to the New York terminals. But in November 1926, Lord Kylsant had bought up all the assets and shares of the Oceanic Steam Navigation Co. Ltd. He had considerable standing as he had already obtained control of Harland & Wolff during 1924. Throughout 1926, negotiations had taken place for its sale and brokered by Mr Franklin of IMMCo who had driven a hard bargain in demanding the then huge sum of £7 million for the Company and its goodwill.

On 1 January 1927, Lord Kylsant (formerly known as Sir Owen Phillips), the adventurous shipping magnate and head of the Royal Mail Steam Packet Co. Group of companies (Royal Mail Group) purchased the Oceanic Steam Navigation Company Ltd (OSNCo). In this deal the Royal Mail Group paid the asking price in instalments at four per cent interest, the last instalment of £2.5 million being due by 31 December 1936. This in effect pushed the total cost up to £7,907,661. The Royal Mail Group then became one of the world's largest shipping concerns with a total tonnage of over 2 million gross tons. The Group, however, had heavy financial commitments and the effect of the impending Depression had not been foreseen. Lord Kylsant became President and Joint Managing Director of OSNCo with Mr Harold Sanderson appointed as Chairman and Joint Managing Director.

The Royal Mail Steam Packet Group's financial resources were insufficient to underwrite the purchase of OSNCo, so a new company known as the White Star Line Ltd was registered as a public company on 12 January 1927 to hold the shares of OSNCo. Lord Kylsant became Chairman of the newly-formed company with Harold Sanderson as his deputy, and in order to raise the necessary working capital of £9 million, a share issue was floated. The capital was made up of £5 million in £1 Preference shares issued to the public and guaranteed as to capital and dividend by the Royal Mail Group. The balance of £4 million in £1 Ordinary shares was issued to other companies within the Group, i.e. Royal Mail Steam Packet Co, Union-Castle, Nelson Line, Elder Dempster and the Pacific Steam Navigation Co. Of the capital raised by the public issue the Royal Mail Group was reimbursed £4,650,000 by White Star Line Ltd towards the purchase of the OSNCo shares, the balance being due by 31 December 1936. For the £1 Ordinary shares, however, the Group companies actually paid up only 2/- (10p) per share, in effect raising only £400,000 of their anticipated £4 million.

The White Star Line began its days with the Royal Mail Group with a working capital deficit of forty per cent. The public issue of Preference shares would also become a major contributor to White Star's downfall. Unknowingly, White Star had swapped one complex and labyrinthine organisation for another and in hindsight, from the day the Royal Mail Group acquired White Star, it inadvertently put into place a chain of events that eventually sealed White Star's fate some eight years later. With only two vessels, the *Doric* (1923) and *Laurentic* (1927), ordered since the end of World War 1, it was clear that some more competitive tonnage would be needed to replace the ageing Edwardian 'Big Four': the *Celtic*, *Cedric*, *Baltic* and *Adriatic*. Like Lord Pirrie before him, Lord Kylsant was a champion of the motorship and diesel propulsion and from the time he gained control of the Group he planned the inclusion of motor vessels in the White Star fleet. Indeed, since 1926, Royal Mail's liners *Alcantara* and *Asturias* had been diesel driven, and had a proven operating performance on the long-haul route to South America. In addition to this, the first motorship on the North Atlantic, Swedish America's *Gripsholm*, built by Armstrong-Whitworth on the Tyne in 1925, had given remarkable reliability on her North Atlantic ferry service.

To this end White Star placed an order for a new liner at Harland & Wolff as Yard No 807. The keel was laid at Belfast on 14 April 1927 on was to become the *Britannic*, the third ship of that name to be built for the Company. White Star also had ambitious plans for the world's first 1,000 ft liner, to be named the *Oceanic*. Building had progressed as far as laying the first keel plates in Harland & Wolff's Musgrave Yard on 28 June 1928. The vessel was planned to have a gross tonnage of 60,000 and an overall length of 1,010 ft. White Star could not finance the project on its own and the government of the day was not prepared to forward a loan towards the estimated cost of £3.5 million on such an innovative project, especially when the Cunard Line was also seeking a loan for its 1,000 ft liner, later to emerge as the *Queen Mary*. Due to the labyrinthine and complicated nature of the Royal Mail Group of companies, White Star Line's fate was intertwined with those of the holding group. Perhaps some of White Star's declining fortunes may be attributed to a chronology of events since its rebirth in the Royal Mail Group.

White Star's representation and marketing in the United States, including all banking arrangements for passengers and freight and terminal facilities continued to be handled by Mr P. A. S. Franklin of IMMCo. Mr Franklin's growing interest in the operation of American flag tonnage left White Star at a serious disadvantage compared with Cunard and all other North Atlantic lines which benefited from their own full representation in North America. The IMMCo retained the White Star agency up until 30 June 1934. The White Star was immediately absorbed by Royal Mail. Two of their liners, the *Ohio* and the *Orca*, which were employed on Royal Mail's New York service, were sold within the Group to White Star Line for £1 million. Renamed the *Albertic* and the *Calgaric*, they were employed on the Canadian service. They did not, however, prove successful on the route, probably due in part to the fierce competition from other British companies and also from foreign-flag ships, for the passenger traffic that was available.

Early in 1928, Lord Kylsant, in the name of White Star Line, bid £1.9 million for the ailing Australian-owned Commonwealth Line which had incurred losses in its seven ship fleet. Four years later, White Star had managed to pay only £1,000,850 to the Australian Government. Impatient that the balance was slow in coming, the Australian Government terminated the purchase agreement by calling in the mortgages. The Commonwealth Line ships were sold on 8 March 1933 to Shaw Savill & Albion for £500,000. White Star made a capital loss of £1,487,807, but it was later revealed that with accrued interest, together with the cost of improvements to the Commonwealth Line ships, the total cost was around £2,712,994: a net loss of £2,212,994. In order to raise further capital, in June 1928 the public were invited to subscribe to a Second Debenture stock in the Royal Mail Group for £2 million. The prospectus issued for the stock floatation was worded in such a way as to give the impression that the Royal Mail Group was operating at a profit. In fact it had been 'fudged' by including taxation reserves that were not required. It was this misleading prospectus that was to lead to Lord Kylsant's eventual downfall and his ultimate removal as head of the Royal Mail Group. The ramifications for White Star were that Lord Kylsant began to siphon off OSNCo's earnings for the use in the rest of the Royal Mail Group, albeit temporarily, in the expectation that the financial situation would improve. Against the background of these events perhaps a look at White Star's dividends would indicate the Company's financial troubles. In 1927, the Company declared a dividend of £450,000; in 1928 a dividend of £400,000 with a bank overdraft of £337,839 and for 1929, a dividend of £400,000 but with a bank overdraft of £896,844. (At this time Mr Harold Sanderson relinquished his seat on the Board). In order to try to increase White Star's working capital to £11 million on 16 May 1929, 2 million extra £1 Ordinary shares were created but never issued.

White Star's total passengers carried on the North Atlantic for 1928 was 172,000 which faired poorly with their major rival Cunard who carried 231,000. By the following year these figures had dropped significantly to 157,930 and 202,161 respectively for both companies. On 29 July 1929, work on White Star's planned *Oceanic* stopped and the project was abandoned; however, their first motorship *Britannic*, was launched a week later on 6 August. Another unnecessary heavy expense incurred was the forced removal in July 1929 of White Star's long-established Head Office and staff from Liverpool to the Kylsant Headquarters at Royal Mail House, Leadenhall Street, London. This was a demoralising move for its staff. The high point of their first motor ship taking to the water occurred just two months before the Wall Street stock market crash of October 1929 when the financial bubble of the Roaring Twenties finally burst. At this point the weakness of White Star and Cunard's ship replacement policy became apparent. Not only were White Star and Cunard suddenly confronted with drastically reduced demand for their oversized fleets, but their front-line express units were ageing. As a result of acquiring second

hand tonnage, neither company had built a major new passenger liner since the start of World War 1. Three of the 'Big Six' were ex-German and all were of pre-war vintage, while the three British-built liners ranged from 15 to 22 years in age.

A further complication was the fact that White Star and Cunard were also facing competition from a new generation of modern passenger liners introduced by the leading continental passenger companies. These shipping companies had the luxury of state operating subsidies that British vessels did not, consequently they were to some extent cushioned from the fullness of the Depression's cold draught. In the four years following 1929, Britain was in the grip of the Great Depression and world seaborne trade declined by nearly a third. At that time there were more passenger ships afloat to carry fewer travellers than there had been in 1914. Consequently, passenger traffic was equally affected. Every North Atlantic line suffered a sharp drop in passenger receipts and to this end White Star and its rival Cunard were no exception. Ocean liners were meeting their schedules but sailing with greatly reduced occupancy. Shipowners were thus faced with the necessity of severely retrenching or going out of business. Most opted for the former and in those lean times hundreds of ships were laid up and many thousands of seafarers laid off.

On 10 June 1930, a group that handled the Royal Mail Group's financial and banking affairs met to try to resolve the Royal Mail Group's complex financial predicament with losses exceeding some £50 million, a staggering sum for that time. One of its recommendations was that three trustees with voting rights were co-opted to the board of the Royal Mail Group. One of these was the Rt. Hon. Walter Runciman MP. Their brief was to examine and rectify Royal Mail's liabilities. These further deteriorated over the next two years and in June 1932, an application was made to the High Court for a Scheme of Arrangement. One of the scheme's edicts was the creation of new ship operating companies to which the ships of certain companies within the Royal Mail Group could be transferred. By this action it was intended that shipping activities could be carried on by the separate shipping companies unhindered by financial restraint. Each company would have a moratorium (freeze) until 31 December 1934.

In July 1930, a month after its formation, Mr Walter Runciman together with the newly appointed trustees of the Royal Mail Group felt that some of White Star's problems could be resolved by the sale of its assets and discharge of its liabilities to the Cunard Steamship Company. As this would be seen as a takeover with a loss of the White Star name, the trustees returned three months later and asked the Cunard directors to investigate the possibility of a merger between Cunard and White Star Line. The Cunard Steamship Company offered around £3.25 million for some of White Star's Atlantic fleet, partly in cash and partly in the assumption of liabilities. As this fell short of a desired merger and no money was forthcoming from the British Government, the negotiations fell through.

Above: **The *Albertic* passed to White Star in 1927 and was formerly Royal Mail's *Ohio*. She had originally been laid down in 1914 as the German liner *München*.** *John Clarkson.*

In 1930, White Star Line declared a 'nil' dividend. With a bank overdraft of £1,239,382, for the first time in the 61 years of its existence White Star's accounts showed a loss, of £379,069. Another depressing statistic was that the total number of passengers in all classes carried both ways by all companies operating on the North Atlantic in 1930 had been at a near peak of 1,002,353. By the following year, this had plummeted to 685,456. With the bite of the Depression and intensive competition on the North Atlantic, White Star was doomed. Could the impending merger with Cunard save the situation? In the same year, Harland & Wolff, which was also under Lord Kylsant's control, had lost more than £12 million but managed to survive by capital re-structuring. At the beginning of 1932, they had effectively run out of major work and after the delivery of the *Georgic* in June that year, most of the huge yard was placed on a care and maintenance basis. Work was not resumed until the autumn of 1933.

In July 1931, Royal Mail Group's Chairman Lord Kylsant was tried for fraud at the Old Bailey. He had been arrested on charges under the Larceny Act but found not guilty on two counts of issuing false annual reports and accounts; however, he was proven guilty on one charge of issuing a false prospectus. He was jailed for 12 months. From this point the fortunes of the White Star Line were on a downturn. By the end of December 1931, White Star made a loss of £450,777 and was unable to meet its interest repayments for that year amounting to £94,000. The Royal Mail Group was unable to repay a similar sum to IMMCo. Further losses were accrued by White Star; £152,045 in 1932 and £353,552 in 1933.

ALBERTIC

(1927-1934)
18,940 grt; 590 ft 10 in BP (614 ft 6 in OA) x 71 ft 6 in
Quadruple Expansion SR Engines, Twin Screw,
16,000 ihp, 17 knots.
Passengers: 229 First class, 523 Second class,
690 Third class
AG Weser, Bremen. Yard No. 209

In 1926, the Royal Mail Steam Packet Co. had negotiated and secured the entire share capital of White Star Line from the IMMCo and on 1 January 1927, White Star once more became a wholly owned British company. To prevent needless competition on the Atlantic, Royal Mail transferred two of their ships, the *Ohio* and the *Orca*, to White Star, becoming the *Albertic* and the *Calgaric*. The Albertic was originally laid down in 1914 at the AG Weser yard at Bremen; she had been ordered as the München for North German Lloyd and her keel was laid but further construction was suspended for the duration of World War 1. On 28 June 1919, she was designated by the Treaty of Versailles to be handed over to Great Britain as reparation, and construction on her resumed. The *München* was launched on 23 March 1920 and the Royal Mail Group purchased her from the Shipping Controller. She was fitted out over the following three years and completed in Royal Mail colours on 26 March 1923. The following day she was renamed *Ohio* and at the time of her trials was Royal Mail's largest liner and ready to enter service. After World War 1 and with the absence of German competition on the North Atlantic, the Royal Mail Steam Packet Co. (RMSP) decided to enlarge and diversify its passenger carrying services, hitherto confined to the East coast of South America, on a new route from Europe to the United States. The new service was to operate from Hamburg to New York via Southampton and Cherbourg.

Owing to the opening in 1914 of the Panama Canal, which gave quicker access to the West coast of South America, two ships from the kindred company, the Pacific Steam Navigation Co, namely the *Orbita* and *Oropesa*, were used to inaugurate the new North Atlantic run. These vessels had recently been made temporarily surplus and along with the *Orduna*, that had just finished service on the Atlantic for Cunard Line, were ideal to trial this new route. The first sailing from Hamburg was made by the *Orbita* on 30 April 1921 and was followed by the *Oropesa* and *Orduna* in fortnightly sailings. As this route started to pick up, Royal Mail persevered further with the service. During the autumn of 1923, the *Oropesa* was returned to Pacific Steam Navigation Co's South American service as the RMSP's liner *Orca* was completed from her war service at Belfast to make her entry on the route as a passenger liner. She was later joined by the *Ohio*. The *Ohio* sailed on her maiden voyage from Hamburg on 3 April 1923 to New York via Southampton and Cherbourg. Her speed of 17 knots enabled her to complete the crossing in eight days compared with 10 days of other similar ships on that route.

Her twin screws were driven by quadruple expansion, four-cylinder engines which were supplied by steam at 220 psi from two boiler rooms with six double-ended and one single-ended boilers developing 16,000 ihp. She was built of steel with five decks and 10 watertight compartments. In addition to carrying 1,442 passengers and 400 crew she had six cargo holds. By 1925, German passenger ships began re-establishing themselves on the Atlantic, using Hamburg as their main port. In light of this the *Ohio*'s European terminus was switched to Southampton. Also in 1925, she made two voyages from New York to Naples with pilgrims for Holy Year. She proved a popular ship with the travelling public and fitted in well with the Royal Mail's slogan 'The Comfort Route' in which she offered excellent accommodation in all three classes, coupled with good food, service and reasonable fares.

She continued in this service with an occasional cruise programme from New York until 1927, when the Royal Mail Group purchased White Star from IMMCo and the former withdrew their North Atlantic service. With immediate effect during February 1927, the two Royal Mail liners *Ohio* and *Orca* were sold within the Group to White Star for £1 million. As a hint of her future service, the *Ohio* was renamed *Albertic* and the *Orca* was renamed *Calgaric* and together they were placed on the Liverpool to Canada route. The ship's original over-tall masts were shortened by 37 ft and completed with 20 ft telescopic poles. This was to enable her to pass under the Quebec Bridge to reach

Above: **A full broadside view of the *Albertic* outward bound in the River Mersey with the Royal Liver building in the background.** *Richard de Kerbrech Collection.*

Montreal. The *Albertic*, newly painted in White Star colours, departed Liverpool on 22 April 1927 for Quebec and Montreal. When she sailed on her second voyage from Montreal on 3 June 1927, she carried 704 passengers, of which some 300 or so were Manxmen and women and their descendants, who were returning to the Isle of Man for the first time since emigrating to Canada and the United States.

Six months later, on 5 December 1927, the *Albertic* was the first liner to enter Liverpool's Great Gladstone drydock that had been closed since 1921 pending the completion of the Gladstone Dock system. She was also reputed to be the first liner in Liverpool to be drydocked without the customary side shores, the ship's hull being supported entirely on keel blocks. The following year, on 31 March 1928, the *Albertic* made a trip from Liverpool to New York, departing there a fortnight later for London via Southampton and Le Havre. From this new terminus on 5 May 1928 she made her first sailing on the London-

Below: **By all accounts the *Albertic* proved to be highly unsuited to the North Atlantic trade but came into her own when she replaced the *Celtic* on the Liverpool-New York run in 1929. In this photograph she is turning in the River Mersey and flying the Royal Mail pennant.** *Richard de Kerbrech Collection.*

Above: **The *Calgaric* was originally constructed as a cargo vessel in 1918. She was later completed as the liner *Orca* initially for PSNC then Royal Mail. In the photograph she is at anchor with bunting flying and two lifeboats in the water.** *Tom Rayner Collection.*

Le Havre-Southampton-Quebec-Montreal route in consort with the *Megantic*. On 2 February 1929, the *Albertic* was transferred to the Liverpool to Boston and New York run to replace the *Celtic* on that route which had been lost off Cobh at the end of 1928. On 21 May 1929, a large pin connected with the *Albertic*'s steering gear and disabled her rudder off Cobh. The after conning position was engaged to enable her to reach port. As an added precaution a tender was dispatched from Liverpool to escort her to the Mersey. She was repaired in drydock at Liverpool.

The next year, on 9 May 1930, she reverted to the Liverpool-Quebec-Montreal itinerary for the summer months only up until 29 August and she was subsequently laid up in the Clyde for the winter months. She repeated the same service schedule for the following two seasons and during March 1933 she was taken out of service and laid up in the Firth of Clyde at Holy Loch. In 1934, after the amalgamation of Cunard and White Star she was put up for sale. In July 1934, the *Albertic* was sold to Japanese shipbreakers for £34,000 and sailed the following month for Osaka. She arrived at Osaka on 29 November to be broken up after only 11 years service.

ALBERTIC: *Of or pertaining to the Canadian province of Alberta.*

CALGARIC

(1927-1934)
16,063 grt; 550 ft 4 in BP (574 ft OA) x 67 ft 4 in
Triple Expansion SR Engines + LP Turbine,
Triple Screw, 11,900 ihp, 15 knots
Passengers: 190 First class, 220 Second class,
480 Third class
Harland & Wolff, Belfast. Yard No. 442

Originally ordered for the Pacific Steam Navigation Co. and laid down in 1914, work was suspended on her until 1916. She was eventually launched on 5 April 1917 as the *Orca* and completed as an emergency-style cargo vessel for the

Shipping Controller. She was handed over on 25 May 1918, without any superstructure other than the bridge. As built she had a single funnel and mast without any rake and her two stump masts and Samson posts were hinged to lie along the derricks when at sea. The *Orca*'s original grt was 15,120 and she was painted in dazzle paint pattern and placed into transport service for the Shipping Controller.

Following her release from the Controller, she returned to Harland & Wolff at Belfast on 18 February 1921 to be completed to her original specification as a passenger ship with an accommodation for 190 First, 220 Second and 480 Third class passengers. Upon her final completion in December 1922, she had a deadweight tonnage of 11,380 and a load draught of 36 ft 4 in. Her combination machinery consisted of two triple expansion engines on the outer shafts, the steam from which exhausted and operated the low pressure turbine on the centre propeller shaft. Steam was supplied to the reciprocating engines by six double-ended boilers with 36 furnaces.

Since 1910, the Pacific Steam Navigation Co. had been controlled by the Royal Mail Steam Packet Co., and following World War 1 with the opening of the Panama Canal, the PSNC lacked a profitable outlet for its newest ships. The RMSPCo transferred them within the holding group to take advantage of the vacuum left by German shipping companies on the North Atlantic. So it was that Royal Mail placed some ships in service on the new route between Germany and New York. This had been inaugurated during May 1921 by the *Orbita*, which was later joined by the *Oropesa* and *Orduna*. The *Orca* arrived at Southampton on 18 December 1922, and on 1 January 1923 was sold within the group to Royal Mail with the same name. She sailed on her maiden voyage from Southampton on 3 January to Hamburg, and then from Hamburg to New

York and in doing so replaced the *Oropesa* on this route. She was joined three months later by the *Ohio* (ex-*München*). A call at Halifax was later added to her itinerary. She was re-designated as a Cabin class ship in 1924 and her accommodation altered to suit, but by 1925, with German tonnage re-entering the market the *Orca* discontinued her call at the Hamburg terminus. She continued on the New York run partly through 1926, after which the Royal Mail Group purchased White Star from IMMCo and from 10 January 1927 she became part of the enlarged group. The *Orca*, along with the *Ohio*, were sold within the Royal Mail Group to White Star for £1 million during February 1927. The *Orca* was subsequently renamed *Calgaric* (a hint at her intended route) and her passenger accommodation altered to carry 290 First, 550 Tourist and 330 Third class. She sailed on her first voyage in White Star colours on 4 May 1927 from Liverpool to Quebec and Montreal along with the *Albertic* and during the rest of her career interposed cruises between her regular itinerary. It was on one of these cruises to the Mediterranean on 1 March 1929 whilst at Algiers that high winds caused the *Calgaric* to part from her moorings and collide with the British steamer *Tintern Abbey*, whose superstructure was damaged. The *Calgaric* was able to continue on her cruise. Some seven weeks later, on 20 April 1929, she switched to the London to Canada route sailing to and from London, Le Havre, Southampton, Quebec and Montreal, along with the *Megantic*.

Whilst calling at Gibraltar on a cruise on 28 February 1930, the *Calgaric* was in collision with the British Admiralty tanker *Fortol*. The *Calgaric* was manoeuvring when she collided with the tanker, which was coaling at the wharf. After temporary repairs both ships resumed their respective voyages. Following two round voyages to Canada in the summer of 1930, the *Calgaric* was laid up at Milford Haven on 6 September 1930 as a standby reserve ship. On 9 June 1933, she resumed the Liverpool-Quebec-Montreal service for one round voyage only, and between 12 August and 29 August 1933 she undertook a 17-day cruise on charter to the Scout and Guide Associations for a Scouting and Guides cruise to North European ports. It is said that Lady Baden-Powell had originally approached White Star about the charter with some trepidation as to the cost liability falling on the Guide Movement if expected numbers failed to materialise. Representatives of White Star assured her that: 'You will incur no obligation whatever. Your name and that of Lord Baden-Powell are sufficient guarantee. We are willing to undertake any risk, and we are quite sure your people will follow you.'

Above: **A slightly 'touched up' photograph of the *Calgaric* taken in the River Mersey by Southampton photographer C. R. Hoffmann. A tug and towlines to her bow have been brushed out and her houseflag appears lower than normal on her mainmast.** *C. R. Hoffmann.*

And so it was when the *Calgaric* sailed from Southampton on 12 August 1933 under the command of Captain F. J. Burd and First Officer J. G. Boxall, she had embarked 100 Scouts, 475 guides and 80 non-Scouts or Guides. In addition were Lord and Lady Baden-Powell. The cruise visited the Baltic States of Latvia and Estonia, Finland and Sweden via the Kiel Canal and took in nine ports – then via Oslo and across the North Sea, through the Pentland Firth to Oban before terminating at Liverpool on 29 August for a total distance of 3,424 miles. It proved to be a highly successful cruise, so much so that the last of the 'Big Four', the *Adriatic*, was chartered by the Boy Scouts Association for the same purpose the following year. However, following this eventful cruise, on 9 September the *Calgaric* was laid up at Milford Haven once more.

As 1933 drew to its close, there were definite signs that the worst of the slump was over. There was an improvement in the price of steel and consequently of scrap metal and many British shipowners took the opportunity to dispose of their surplus tonnage at the elevated scrap value. The general improvement in financial conditions in Britain had been

Right: **The *Calgaric* departs Southampton on 12 August 1933 on her Baltic cruise on charter to the Scouts & Guides Association.** *B. A. Butt.*

Above: **The tug/tender *Magnetic* eases alongside the *Laurentic* at Liverpool on 14 July 1928.** *Tom Rayner Collection.*

brought about by trade agreements concluded during the year. However, there was no great improvement in the North Atlantic trade where the competition of the newer palatial Cabin ships had cut into the profits of the more expensive express liners and these had, for the most part, run at a considerable loss. Against this, White Star's losses for 1933 amounted to £353,552. In July 1934, the *Calgaric* was one of 12 ships owned by White Star that transferred to the newly merged Cunard White Star Line. With a glut of berths available to the new company, the *Calgaric* was considered surplus to requirements and was put up for sale. She was sold 'as lies' to shipbreakers in Rosyth for £31,000 and sailed from Pembroke on 20 December 1934, arriving at Inverkeithing on 25 December. She was stripped of all fittings and fixtures at Rosyth before being broken up in 1935.

CALGARIC: *Of or pertaining to Calgary, the largest city in the Canadian province of Alberta.*

LAURENTIC (II)

(1927-1940)
18,724 grt; 578 ft 2 in BP (600 ft OA) x 75 ft 5 in
Triple Expansion SR Engines + LP Turbine,
Triple Screw, 15,000 ihp, 16 knots
Passengers: 594 Cabin class, 406 Tourist class,
500 Third class
Harland & Wolff, Belfast. Yard No. 470

The news that the White Star ships belonged once more to a British company was at first received with delight but was soon found to be a disaster. In 1927, when the newly constituted White Star Line Ltd was formed it soon became embroiled in the financial difficulties of the Royal Mail Group. The 'O' ships of the RMSP and PSNC dropped their North Atlantic service and two, renamed *Calgaric* and *Albertic*, were placed on White Star's Canadian run. In 1928, to obtain new capital for the huge commitments of his shipping group, Lord Kylsant issued new White Star shares although his empire was already beginning to crumble. As the world slump was reaching its peak, White Star operated at a loss during 1930 and no dividends were paid but the following year the crunch came when Lord Kylsant was arrested, tried and gaoled for issuing a prospectus for the 1928 shares knowing it to be false. New directors were appointed, but there was already chaos within the Royal Mail Group.

Against this backdrop the *Laurentic*, the second of the name, was born and originally ordered by IMMCo who apparently did not want her. With the costs of shipbuilding rocketing, the contract with Harland & Wolff was for the first time with White Star on a 'fixed price' basis and not a 'cost plus' as had been the previous arrangements. Mr Franklin had originally intended her to be the finest 'cabin' ship on the Canadian service but later dictated that there was to be no unnecessary expenditure on her. In effect she was launched and delivered to a company already in serious financial trouble and due to crash within three years. Concurrent with these internal problems, the Depression worldwide was building up to its peak, with the shipping industry at rock bottom. This was a dismal outlook indeed for a new ship to enter this arena. It is difficult to comprehend why she was ordered at all.

She was similar to the *Doric* of 1923, a ship with geared turbines driving twin screws, but the *Laurentic* reverted to the earlier combination machinery of three screws with steam reciprocating on the wing shafts and a low pressure turbine driving the centre propeller. She was also a coal burner at a time when the trend was for oil-fired boilers. It is pure speculation but with a Yard No 470 and the earlier *Doric*'s of 573, she may well have been ordered before the *Doric*! Quite apart from the difference in machinery selection, the *Laurentic* was not a sister ship of the *Doric* with respect to the hull as there was an increase in beam of 7 ft for the same length. Such an addition to the beam would mean a significant change in the lines, design and construction of a ship, not merely the widening of public rooms and promenade decks. So if ordered before the *Doric*, it would have meant some unorthodox procedure in the Belfast yard, with the centre girder of the *Laurentic* occupying a berth for some five years and her reciprocating engines and turbine stored over that period. One hint of the delay in the decision to go ahead may be found from Harland & Wolff's yard number reference in which both *Germanic* and *Homeric* had been proposed before the name *Laurentic* was chosen. *Germanic* seemed an unlikely choice in view of the recent conflict and *Homeric* was allocated to North German Lloyd's *Columbus* (q. v.).

Due to the General Strike of 1926, the construction of the Laurentic was delayed by nine months; she was eventually launched without ceremony on 16 June 1927 and completed in just under five months to be ready for trials on 1 November. The completed ship had a net tonnage of 11,103 and a deadweight capacity of 11,170 tons on a load draught of 29 ft 3 in. She had three overall decks counting the weather or shelter deck, an orlop deck outside the machinery spaces and promenade and boat decks amidships. There were six holds and 'tween deck spaces for cargo, including large refrigerated spaces and 10 main bulkheads.

Below: **The *Laurentic*, the last coal-burning transatlantic liner, leaves Belfast Lough after her delivery to White Star.** *Harland & Wolff.*

Her machinery consisted of two 4-cylinder triple expansion reciprocating engines with cylinders of 29, 46, 52 and 52 in bore and a stroke of 54 in on the wing shafts, the steam from which exhausted into a low pressure turbine driving the centre shaft direct. From the turbine the steam exhausted into two regenerative condensers. Manoeuvring was by means of the wing propellers alone. The engines developed a total of around 16,000 ihp which gave the ship a service speed of 16.5 knots, with a maximum of 17.

Steam was supplied by four double-ended and four single-ended cylindrical boilers with superheaters, but under natural draught and burning coal. Three 100 kW turbo generators and an emergency generator were also installed. The machinery system was virtually the same system that had been installed in the *Laurentic* of 1908 and later in the *Olympic* and her sisters. Its adoption in 1926-27, especially after the *Doric* had been fitted with steam turbines, seemed a retrograde step, but it may well have been on account of its reliability and low maintenance, being a tried and tested arrangement. Ironically by the time she came into service, the Bauer-Wach system, in which the LP turbine was geared to the main shaft, and obtained all the advantages only very much more simply, was gaining in popularity at the time.

Passenger accommodation catered for 594 Cabin class, 406 Tourist or Tourist Third Cabin (as it was then called) and 500 Third. Around 100 passenger berths were interchangeable between Cabin and Tourist. The Cabin class facilities included a drawing room, lounge, smoking room, card room, veranda café, gymnasium and a children's playroom, with a saloon capacity for 310. All public rooms were in various styles of decoration, ranging from an Italian Renaissance lounge with a large fireplace to a Jacobean smoke room, and with the several suites for Cabin passengers in Louis XIV to XVI styles. In addition there were a number of 2-berth rooms for the Tourist class, the rest for Tourist and Third being 4- or 6-berth. For these two classes there were three dining rooms, a ladies' room, a

Above: **A rather deceptive photograph which attempts to show the *Laurentic* underway at speed. In reality she has the 'blue peter' flying at her foremast, indicating that she is ready to sail.** *Real Photographs Co Ltd.*

lounge, a general room, two smoking rooms and a children's room.

The *Laurentic* was the fourth in a series of intermediate Atlantic liners ordered by the IMMCo group from Harland & Wolff. The first was the *Regina*, laid down in 1913 but rushed into service as an emergency cargo vessel-cum-troopship during 1918 and later completed as a passenger liner in 1922. This was followed by the *Pittsburgh* for the American Line. After her was the *Doric*, very similar to the earlier two but with twin screw geared turbines. The *Laurentic* was generally similar in layout but not a sister of the preceding three vessels. She reverted to the machinery system of the first two but differed from them all in having 7 ft 6 in more beam and being 3 ft longer to give her over 2,000 grt more space. Unlike the others, she was never fitted with the large gantry davits with which the earlier three had begun their careers and instead had a double tier of seven lifeboats each side under luffing davits.

Like the earlier three ships, the *Laurentic* had an island bridge but differed slightly in that her promenade deck was continuous from the fore part of her superstructure to its after end, with No 3 hatchway trunked through it, while the promenade was glassed in for about 65 ft under the forepart of the boat deck. The *Laurentic* and the earlier trio gave the appearance of being flush-deckers but they actually were constructed with a forecastle, bridge and poop with the wells decked over. Although the *Laurentic* was built for the Canadian service, her masts were too lofty for the voyage up to Montreal and these were later reduced in height by 25 ft. The *Laurentic* ran trials on 1 November 1927, then made a 'trial trip' from Belfast to Liverpool with representatives of White Star, Harland & Wolff and other guests on board. She sailed on her maiden voyage on 12 November 1927 from Liverpool to New York followed by a second round voyage on 31 December. Early in 1928, she was booked for two cruises to the Mediterranean in January and March.

She was eventually placed on the Canadian service when she left on her first voyage on 27 April 1928, from Liverpool to Quebec and Montreal, joining the *Doric*, *Regina*, *Calgaric* and *Albertic* on this route. Between then and 1932 the *Calgaric* was utilised more on cruising and the *Albertic* was switched to the New York service, which left the *Laurentic* and *Doric* to maintain the service with a degree of regularity. However, the trade depression was reaching its peak with more ships being taken off the Atlantic run to try and find alternative employment in the cruise business. So it was that during 1932 the *Doric* was entirely switched to cruising, leaving the *Laurentic* solely to maintain the Canadian service. On 3 October 1932, she collided with Mountain Steamship Co's steamer *Lurigethan* in Belle Isle Strait. Both ships were damaged above the waterline and they were both able to proceed on their journeys. However, in a later enquiry the *Laurentic* was apportioned to be fifty-five per cent to blame for the collision.

Following this mishap she continued on the Canadian run until the end of the 1934 season with some intermittent cruising up until 25 February 1934 when she made her last voyage as a White Star liner, from Boston to Halifax and Liverpool. During March 1934, the *Laurentic* sailed from Dublin with 700 pilgrims aboard to witness the ceremony of closing the holy door in St. Peter's in Rome by the Pope on Easter Monday. For this cruise, ten altars were fitted in the ship as many priests were aboard, as well as a cinema for entertainment. 1934 saw the merger of Cunard and White Star and the *Laurentic* was one of 12 White Star ships in the newly merged fleet. In July 1934, she made the first of two round voyages under the new Cunard White Star ownership from Liverpool to Quebec and Montreal, completing these on 25 September. After this she was utilised on full-time cruising. In 1935, she was advertised along with the *Doric*, *Homeric* and *Lancastria* for spring and summer cruises, her first being a fortnight's cruise to the Mediterranean. Returning to London she then took a party of Rover Scouts to Sweden, returning to Liverpool. From 13 July, these cruises had fares starting from as little as £1 a day.

On Sunday 18 August that year, the *Laurentic* was outward bound from Liverpool to the Northern Capitals with 620 passengers on board when she collided with the Blue Star liner *Napier Star*. The accident occurred in the Irish Sea off the Skerries at 3am in the morning in foggy weather. Six members of the *Napier Star*'s crew were killed and another four injured in the collision. The Blue Star ship had rammed the *Laurentic* in her starboard side just forward of the foremast. In doing so she tore a huge hole 20 ft wide which extended down to 6 ft below the waterline and smashed 12 of the crew's cabins in the forecastle head. All passengers were ordered to don lifejackets and muster at their boat stations, but no panic ensued and they were allowed to return to their cabins when it was learnt that there was no danger of sinking. Both vessels returned to Liverpool and arrived on the Monday, with the *Laurentic* entering the Gladstone Graving Dock for repairs by Harland & Wolff.

Her cruise was cancelled and the passengers could opt for a fare refund or were transferred to the *Doric*. In drydock the damage revealed that some 20 shell plates, 18 frames and

numerous plates and beams on five decks had to be replaced at a cost of £20,000. The subsequent inquiry into the collision found both ships equally to blame. By September, repairs were completed and the *Laurentic* was ready in time to resume her sailing schedule and take a booked cruise of pilgrims from Dublin to Lourdes, possibly calling at Bordeaux. On the conclusion of this cruise she returned to the Mersey and from December 1935 was laid up in the Bidston Dock at Birkenhead for almost a year. By the following year all the former White Star ships except the *Laurentic*, *Britannic* and *Georgic* had been disposed of by the Cunard White Star Line after two years of merger. In September 1936, the *Laurentic*, in a rather shabby and neglected state was towed across the Mersey and moved into the Gladstone Graving Dock for survey and overhaul before sailing for Southampton. She had been chartered by the Government as a troopship for the transportation of troops to Palestine (now Israel) to help augment the Palestine Police in the mandated territory. Her original accommodation for 600 Cabin, 400 Tourist and 500 Third class passengers was stripped and on 14 September 1936 she left Southampton in this role for a single trooping voyage and upon her return was laid up at Millbrook from January 1937.

Following the abdication of King Edward VIII and the accession to the throne of the Duke of York to become King George VI, another Naval Review took place at Spithead on 20 May 1937. For this event the *Laurentic* was revived to carry sightseers to view the spectacle, along with the *Aquitania*. Following this she was moved in April 1938 to join the tiers of idle ships laid up in the River Fal. Another bugle call again revived her fortunes, for with the impending war she was commandeered on 24 August 1939 to be converted to an Armed Merchant Cruiser (AMC) at

Below: **This photograph shows the *Laurentic* at anchor in the River Mersey. She became a 'Holy' ship when she made a special cruise to Rome during Easter 1934.**
Tom Rayner Collection.

Devonport Dockyard. Her mainmast was removed along with most of her numerous lifeboats leaving only three on each side. An after control position was built at the after end of the engine room casing and she was armed with seven 5.5 in guns, which apparently were stamped on their barrels 'Made under licence in Japan 1912'. In addition she was armed with three 4 in AA guns. She was initially painted with a black hull and funnels and a dull brown (ochre) superstructure which may later have changed to AMC grey. As an AMC she was one of 56 passenger liners, mainly twin screw vessels with a service speed of at least 15 knots, that were requisitioned between 1939-40, and she may well have been one of the last 'deep sea' coal burners in the Royal Navy. As such she was employed on Northern patrols in the Orkneys and Shetlands and on convoy duties in the North-west Approaches under the command of Captain E. P. Vivian.

Mr J. Evans, a young marine engineer, joined the *Laurentic* for the first year of the war before he was due to take his Second Engineer's certificate of competency. Of the *Laurentic*'s engines, he observed: 'The engines were, of course, quite out of date by 1927 standards. Engaging the centre exhaust turbine and its propeller appeared to have little effect on the vessel's speed. One of the senior engineers, who knew the vessel, claimed it had no effect on the speed, but 'it took the knocks out of the engines'. Among the engineers were some ex-Cunarders who looked down their noses at the reciprocating engines, not to mention coal.' And of her performance on patrol and engine room crew he went on to add: 'Even steaming at very reduced speed, about 20 days on patrol was the limit. The *Laurentic* would return to Liverpool and take on 4,000 tons of coal…We had a black gang of around 120, mostly Liverpool men. They did not take kindly to Navy discipline. On sailing day, I was relieved of my engine room duties in order to stand guard at one of the ship's side doors, complete with pistol. I was supposed to stop firemen from jumping ship. Some did get away, by disguising themselves as the shore gang, carrying a length of pipe on their shoulders.'

Her first encounter with the enemy was on the night of 29 November 1939, when off Iceland she intercepted the Hamburg America cargo ship *Antiochia*, which did not reply to signals sent by the *Laurentic* but hove to after a warning shot was fired. Her crew abandoned ship and were picked up after hurriedly scuttling her. The sinking vessel was used as target practice by the *Laurentic*'s gun crews. Early in 1940, while returning from patrol and making for Liverpool, dense fog had been experienced for several days, such that the *Laurentic* ran aground on the Island of Islay one night. When dawn broke it revealed the Island's cliffs towering over the forecastle head. Tugs were dispatched from Glasgow to help refloat the stricken vessel and she was towed to Belfast to undergo extensive repairs to her hull that took six weeks.

Whilst resuming her patrol station off the west coast of Ireland on the evening of 3 November 1940, the *Laurentic* steamed to the aid of the torpedoed and sunk Elders & Fyffes ship *Casanare*, in order to pick up survivors. The *Laurentic* was off the Bloody Foreland, County Donegal, in position 53º 55′ N; 14º 30′ W at 22.50 hours (10.50pm) when she was struck by the first of three torpedoes from U-99. Another AMC, Blue Funnel's *Patroclus*, moved in to rescue the crew and at 02.00 hours (2am) on 4 November was also hit with the first of five torpedoes and sank with

Above: **The *Laurentic* laid up at Southampton in 1937 following her trooping trip to Palestine. Here she has been reprieved to take part in Merchant Navy week from 17 to 24 July that year.** *Southampton City Museum.*

the loss of 79 lives. The *Laurentic* was subsequently hit again at 04.53 hours (4.53am) and sank with a loss of 49 lives. Her Master, together with 51 officers and 316 ratings were saved. All three ships were the victims of U-99, commanded by Otto Kretschmer, who was later decorated by Adolf Hitler when Oak Leaves were added to Kretschmer's Knight's Cross. The action of the *Patroclus* stopping to rescue survivors when a U-boat was in the area raised some controversy.

So the *Laurentic* was spared the post-merger rationalisation and only made four Atlantic crossings for Cunard White Star before becoming a victim of a U-boat ace. In retrospect she was probably a fine ship from a passenger's point-of-view: comfortable, reliable and steady. With the exception of the engine-room firemen, her crew may well have felt the same. However, from a shipowner's point of view, when it was difficult to find occupation for any ship to run at a profit, she proved a liability. Her machinery, though reliable, was uneconomical with the inconvenience of continuous coaling. Within three years she had two collisions, the one with the *Napier Star* being highly expensive. Despite this unfortunate chain of events, Cunard White Star probably retained her as the *Napier Star* was their third newest ship.

OCEANIC (III)

60,000 grt; 1,010 ft OA x 120 ft
Diesel-Electric, Quadruple Screw, 275,000 ihp,
30 knots
Passengers: N/A
Harland & Wolff, Belfast. Yard No. 844

As far back as 1880, Sir Edward Harland had proposed a design for a liner with a length of 1,000 ft. In the late 1920s just prior to the Wall Street crash, the renaissance of such a project was becoming more of a reality, although not Sir Edward Harland's original concept. With White Star Line having returned to British ownership within the Royal Mail Group, it found in Lord Kylsant a champion of diesel propulsion. Due mainly to his influence, the new express liner planned was to be propelled by diesel-electric engines, a revolutionary innovation for the adoption of which there was no proven precedent. For this reason, the installation of these marine engines in the *Oceanic* would have been a greater gamble than the installation of steam turbines in the *Lusitania* and *Mauretania* had been in 1907. For them the liner *Carmania*, built two years earlier, had acted as something of an engine testbed for the two Cunard record breakers.

Quite obviously White Star and Harland & Wolff were fully aware of the immensity of the decision to install such engines, but their precaution and protracted hesitation in deciding firmly whether the generating machinery for the liner's electric drive should be diesel instead of turbine only contributed to her eventual cancellation. The question of the *Oceanic*'s engines was finally resolved in favour of diesel-electric propulsion and by this time the stage reached with the *Oceanic* was the furthest of any of the pre-*Normandie* 1,000 ft liner projects, for her construction had actually started. Knowledge of the Oceanic project first came to the maritime world in August 1926, when an announcement indicated that a giant 25-knot liner to replace the *Homeric*, whose service speed was inadequate, was under consideration by the White Star Line. The press statement also suggested that the new vessel would bear a 'family resemblance' to the *Olympic*. This was somewhat misleading because the final design showed a liner with three squat motorship-type funnels and the now more familiar cruiser stern. Her appearance, in fact, had far more in common with the smaller *Britannic* of 1930 and with the Royal Mail liner *Asturias* that entered service in March 1927: the first of a long line of Harland & Wolff-built motor vessels propelled by double-acting 4-stroke diesel machinery.

Work on the *Oceanic*'s design took two years and eventually the contract for her construction was placed on 18 June 1928. In their historic announcement, White Star declared that their new liner, to be named *Oceanic* after the Company's pioneer ship, was to be built by Harland & Wolff at Belfast. The building was expected to take between three to four years and the final cost to be in the region of £7 million. The *Oceanic* was to measure 60,000 gross tons with an overall length of 1,010 ft, a beam of 120 ft and a draught of 38 ft. The ship would be employed on the Southampton to New York route and she would be 'fitted and furnished in the most luxurious manner'. The first keel plates of the giant *Oceanic*, Yard No 844, were laid on 28 June 1928 at the famous Musgrave yard on Queen's Island. The details of her engines were released many years later by Mr Cuthbert Coulson Pounder, Director and Chief Technical Engineer of Harland & Wolff, after World War 2. From his definitive work *Diesel Engine Principles & Practice*, he described the intended power plant as follows: 'The propulsive power was 200,000 shp total for four screws, and there were 47 exhaust turbo-charged, 4-stroke single-acting trunk engines each having 6 cylinders 670mm (26.38 in) bore, 930mm (36.61 in) stroke delivering 3,400 bhp at 260 rev/min. Most of the engines were arranged end-to-end, in pairs, forming 12-cylinder units with the dynamos at the ends. The propulsion motors were 24 ft in diameter, the engine dynamos and the propulsion motors being direct-

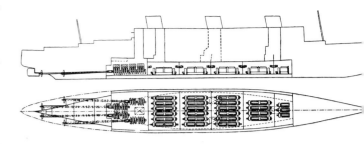

Engine arrangement of the diesel-electric liner OCEANIC (courtesy of Harland & Wolff)

Above: **Engine arrangement for the proposed 1,000 ft diesel-electric liner *Oceanic* (1929). 200,000 shp.** *Harland & Wolff.*

current machines. The total installation weight was 17,000 tons.'

Before any substantial progress could be made with her construction, the effects of the Great Depression began to be felt and the slow pace of the work was a clear indication that something was amiss. The fears were eventually substantiated on 23 July 1929 when all work was stopped on the *Oceanic*'s almost complete keel structure. A formal announcement two months later on 6 September confirmed that further work was to be deferred temporarily pending final decisions on her propulsive machinery. Meanwhile, the keel section was to remain undisturbed on the slipway. In effect the project was cancelled. White Star could not finance the project on its own, and so the giant *Oceanic* was discarded and priority given to a more economic sister ship of the Britannic, namely the *Georgic* of 1932. Meanwhile, the *Oceanic*'s keel structure was broken up discreetly and the giant liner was gradually forgotten, denying Harland & Wolff the honour of building the first liner of over 1,000 ft in length. Of this Mr Pounder wrote: 'Thus was a history-making engineering achievement lost for the nation.'

Below: **Mr John H. Isherwood's profile of White Star's proposed *Oceanic*. The concept metamorphosed into the smaller liner *Georgic*.** *J. H. Isherwood.*

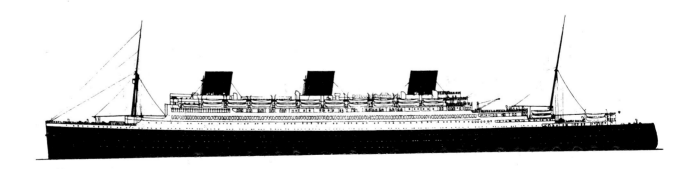

BRITANNIC (III)

(1930-1960)

26,943 grt; 683 ft 8 in BP (712 ft OA) x 82 ft 6 in
Double-acting diesel engines, Twin Screw,
23,000 ihp, 17 knots
Passengers: 504 Cabin class, 551 Tourist class,
498 Third class
Harland & Wolff, Belfast. Yard No. 807

By 1927, White Star's *Celtic* and *Cedric* were 25 years old, the *Baltic* 23 and the *Adriatic* 20. In the interceding years styles of travel had considerably changed. Cabin and Tourist classes became the popular vogue in this period and the two oldest of the 'Big Four' had re-graded as 'Cabin class' in 1926, the others followed suit two years later. With the increasing Depression, cruising had become an important means of keeping otherwise idle ships employed and it became apparent that modern, more competitive tonnage was needed to replace the Edwardian 'four'.

So it was that the *Britannic*, the third ship of the name to be built for the Company, was ordered and her keel was laid on 14 April 1927. Lord Kylsant was a champion of the motorship and diesel propulsion was selected as the Britannic's power plant. This seemed ironic as White Star had not espoused the trend towards steam turbines, with the *Doric* being their only liner so fitted. With the *Laurentic* of 1927 they had regressed to steam reciprocating machinery, but then that was under the old IMMCo order. With new ownership new ideas abounded as under the Royal Mail Group, the *Asturias* and *Alcantara* of Royal Mail and Union-Castle's *Winchester Castle* had pioneered the way with the installation of diesel propulsion on long-haul routes. So for White Star it was a quantum leap that their new ships should be diesel-driven. The *Britannic* would be the first motorship in the fleet, the largest under the British flag and the second largest in the world, after the Italian liner *Augustus*. She was designed for Cabin and Tourist class travel on the Liverpool to New York service, with alternative use as a cruise ship.

With the cessation of the 1,000 ft *Oceanic's* construction in July 1929 and the accidental loss of the *Celtic* in December 1928 on the rocks off Cobh, greater priority was given to the building and completion of the *Britannic* and she was launched on 6 August 1929. In the meantime, the *Celtic's* schedule was covered temporarily by the *Albertic*. In addition to her gross tonnage, the *Britannic* had a deadweight capacity of 16,440 tons on a draught of 32 ft 9 in. This later increased within a year or so to 17,050 tons on a new draught of 34 ft 3in. Her displacement tonnage was 36,800 and her fine underwater hull form gave her a block co-efficient of 0.71. Her depth to C deck was 43 ft 9 in and from her keel to the boat (sun) deck the depth was 78 ft 11 in. The Britannic's forecastle was 110ft long and the bridge deck 325 ft. The forward well was decked over with Nos 2 and 3 hatchways trunked down to B deck. Clear of the machinery space there were eight decks, the sun or boat deck, promenade deck, bridge deck A, upper B, main deck

C, middle D, lower E and orlop decks with a lower orlop in holds 2, 3 and 8. Of these, decks B, C, D and E ran the full length of the ship. The boat deck overhung the ship's sides by 1 ft 6 in.

The *Britannic's* eight holds and hatchways were served by fifteen 10 ton Safe Working Load (SWL) and one 15 ton SWL derricks operated by 16 electric winches. The ship's 12 watertight bulkheads extended up to C deck with the exception of the fore peak bulkhead which was extended up to B deck. Watertight doors could be electrically operated from the bridge or locally by manual operation, the power being taken from the main generators or from the emergency generator on C deck. No 4 hold below the orlop deck had a smooth inner skin installed for the carriage of palm oil; No1 lower orlop 'tween deck was made 11 ft deep to transport uncrated cars, and Nos 2 and 3 orlop and lower orlop 'tween decks were insulated for refrigerated cargo. 'A' deck was the strength deck over the midship half length, its sheer strake 1 in thick with a ⁹⁄₁₆ in doubling plate over the midship area and a deck stringer plate of two 1 in thicknesses. Three expansion joints were fitted in the superstructure above this midship area. The double-bottom tank top was extended flat out to the ship's sides so that there were no bilges as such; the tank itself was 4 ft 9 in deep and 7 ft 6 in under the engine room. There were four lines of girders each side of the centre keel, one of them watertight,

Below: **The *Britannic* enters the water after being launched on 6 August 1929.** *Ulster Folk & Transport Museum.*

Above: **The *Britannic*'s port engine completed in the builder's engine shop. It is seen here linked to a dynamometer, a device that measures the engine's brake horsepower (bhp).** *Ulster Folk & Transport Museum.*

Below: **A section through a Harland & Wolff double-acting, four-stroke crosshead engine as installed in the *Britannic* and *Georgic*.** *Richard de Kerbrech Collection.*

thus giving four separate tanks athwartships. Under each main engine were two pairs of fore and aft girders, each pair forming a cofferdam, and through the top of each of these spaces passed the large engine holding down bolts which were open to inspection at all times.

The *Britannic*'s 43-ton rudder was a semi-balanced type and actuated by electro-hydraulic gear. She carried 24 lifeboats, two motor boats and two 'accident' boats. All were carried under Welin McLachlan luffing davits except four sets aft which were of the 'over arm' type. To assist in shipping the lifeboats were twenty 10hp electric boat winches. The *Britannic* was a

top air inlet

camshaft

top exhaust pipe

bottom air inlet valve

bottom air inlet

bottom fuel valve

bottom exhaust valve

bottom exhaust pipe

Double-acting, four-stroke crosshead engine

twin screw vessel driven by two 10-cylinder, 4-stroke cycle, double-acting Harland & Wolff-Burmeister & Wain oil engines. The cylinder bore was 840 mm (33 in) with a stroke of 1,600 mm (65 in) with air injection provided by four independent injection air compressors. The engine cylinders were cooled by fresh water and the pistons internally oil cooled. At a speed of 102 rev/min, each engine had an indicated horsepower of 11,500, which could produce 10,000 bhp at the engine shop dynamometer and deliver 9,250 shp. This gave her a normal sea speed of 17 knots with a maximum of 17.5 to 18 knots. The injection air compressors were driven by 4-cylinder trunk-type diesel engines and not by the main engines themselves.

These engines were the largest of their type constructed, of colossal proportions and of great complexity; in fact an engineer of just less than average height could stand comfortably in the cylinder space with the piston at bottom dead centre. An all mechanical device with air inlet, fuel and exhaust valves at the top and bottom of the cylinder operated by camshafts, push rods and rocker arms. For their day they would be the most advanced type of diesel engines, which only the design and engine building personnel could fully understand, and it was difficult finding engine-room staff with the necessary operational experience and technical expertise unless they had worked at Harland & Wolff. This may well be one of the contributing factors why two of the *Britannic*'s precursors, the *Asturias* and the *Alcantara*, were re-engined in 1934. The *Britannic*'s fuel capacity was 2,050 tons bunkered in deep tanks between the engine rooms and forward of the auxiliary engine room. With a fuel consumption of 88 tons per day, this bunker capacity was sufficient for two Atlantic crossings, which no doubt gave some credence to the builder's claim that 'a thimbleful of oil would be sufficient to drive one ton of her weight through a mile of water.' The *Britannic* was built at a time when the shipping industry was at a low ebb, and every point of possible economy had to be considered.

The main engine room was below the after funnel and contained besides the main engines, four 500 kW, 220-volt, diesel driven generators, together with various bilge, ballast, cooling and fire pumps. The auxiliary engine room, forward of the main one, contained four 850 hp diesel driven air compressors, numerous pumps and seven boilers. There were four Clarkson upright, thimble-tube vertical boilers which used exhaust gas from the main engines to raise steam at 100 psi for heating and cooking purposes, and one similar using the gases from the auxiliary diesels. There were also two single-ended, oil-fired Scotch boilers with a working steam pressure of 150 psi – these were donkey boilers for

Above: **A rare photograph taken of the *Britannic* on 25 May 1930 during her trials.** *Harland & Wolff.*

use in port or at sea. Despite all this power plant the main engine room needed to be heated and this was effected by eight large vertical steam heaters. Her forward funnel was a dummy with half of its area given over to the Engineers' smoking room and the other half containing fresh water and hot water tanks. Her passenger accommodation originally catered for 504 Cabin class, 551 Tourist Third Cabin and 498 Third class. These terms were originally chosen by the Atlantic Conference to even out the passage charges in international liners of much varying luxury and comfort. Tourist Third Cabin became shortened to 'Tourist' and Cabin class was effectively First without the over ostentation of the big mail liners.

The *Britannic*'s Tourist class was almost up to the Cabin standard as she had also been designed with cruising in mind with the Cabin and Tourist merged into one class with a fair degree of interchangeablity between the two classes. Her accommodation throughout certainly introduced new standards on the Liverpool to New York route. The Cabin class area occupied the midships section of the ship, while the Tourist class was positioned aft and the Third forward. Of the 500 crew, most were billeted forward while the ship's officers and engineers had the whole of the long deckhouse on the boat deck for their accommodation, smoking and mess rooms. The navigating officers were messed forward and the engineers round the engine room casing with a lift down to the machinery space.

In the Cabin class the public rooms on the promenade deck consisted of a card room right forward, entrance hall, lounge, long gallery on the port side with children's and ladies' rooms to starboard. There was the smoking room and veranda café with the gymnasium at the extreme after end of the deck. On A deck were Cabin staterooms and two suites, mostly with private bathrooms. On B deck below was a large entrance hall, shops and more staterooms, while the saloon was on C deck. Down below on E deck was the swimming pool. The *Britannic*'s décor was essentially English Period with the lounge in the style of an 18th century English room, being two decks high and surmounted by a large dome. The ladies' drawing room was in the Old Colonial style while the smoking room was of Tudor décor and the card room forward was in Gothic. Her dining saloon was on C deck and extended the full width of the ship, and in the centre extended into the deck above, and was decorated

in Louis XIV period style. The Tourist class accommodation included two smoking rooms, a lounge, the saloon on C deck and a smaller lounge on the port side with staterooms on both C and D decks. Third class, forward, had promenade space on the fore deck and also on B deck where the sides were open in the forward well. Their smoking room and ladies' rooms were on C deck abreast and abaft No 2 hatchway. All the Tourist and Third class public rooms were panelled with the exception of the children's playrooms, which were decorated with murals of nursery rhymes and fairy tales. Cabins were on D deck and the saloon was at the after end of the Third class space, almost below the forward funnel. Cabin Nos 1, 2 and 3 were up against the collision bulkhead and may have proved uncomfortable during a rough winter crossing when the ship pitched violently.

Galleys and bakeries were all electric. Ventilation was afforded throughout by 87 electric pressure fans that varied from 10 in to 5 ft in diameter, which drew the fresh sea air into all the public rooms and cabins. The flow of cool air could be regulated or stopped at will in any room. The heating was provided by means of Pleno units that passed warm fresh air around through ducts, the air being heated by steam heaters. It is not surprising that when the *Britannic* first entered service she was the largest and probably the finest Cabin class liner in the world. On 25 May 1930 she underwent builder's trials over three days in the Firth of Clyde. During this time a temporary wireless telegraphy system linked the vessel with Harland & Wolff in Belfast. Following these, she returned to Belfast for completion and departed on 21 June with a distinguished party aboard bound for Liverpool, completing her sea trials en route.

The *Britannic* left Liverpool on 28 June 1930 on her maiden voyage under the command of Captain F. F. Summers and watched by 14,000 people who had turned out to witness the event. She sailed for New York via Belfast and Glasgow but had to reduce her speed on route owing to fog. On the homeward bound journey she averaged a comfortable speed of 17.04 knots. She soon settled into the North Atlantic run along with the ageing consorts, the *Adriatic* (1907), *Baltic* (1904) and *Cedric* (1903). During the summer months, the

Above: **One of White Star's earlier impressions of the *Britannic's* cabin lounge.** *Richard de Kerbrech Collection.*

Britannic operated on the North Atlantic service and in the winter season she was employed on cruises to the West Indies and the Old Spanish Main out of New York. From December 1930 to April 1931, she cruised some 23,220 miles and for 1931 her average speed for the year was 17.58 knots, with a fastest voyage average of 19.95 knots.

The appearance of the *Britannic* was also unique, her two squat motorship funnels starkly contrasting with the tall, natural draught funnels of the steamships of the day. As with other new Cabin class liners being brought into service during the Depression, the *Britannic* proved a popular ship and she maintained a full quota of passengers trip after trip, while other ships were crossing half empty. In fact, all new Cabin liners that entered service during that economically inclement period were among the few vessels that continued to carry economically viable passenger loads. It was well known that the newest ships attracted the most customers. The *Bremen* in 1929 and the *Europa*, which entered service in the same year as the *Britannic*, showed this, but with respect to Cabin class ships there was more to it than that. The modern Cabin ships were certainly not as fast as the express liners but they provided practically everything else at lower fares, and in less prosperous times that was a determining factor for the seasoned traveller. The *Britannic's* cheapest fare was £19 one way.

In June 1932, the *Britannic* was joined by her sister the *Georgic*, the *Cedric* having been sold to the breakers at the end of 1931, while the *Baltic* was laid up for sale in October 1932. During May 1933, she made a record voyage at 19.5 knots with the largest number of passengers carried by an Atlantic liner that year, a total of 1,103. Later in December that year the *Britannic* ran aground in Boston Harbour in dense fog, although without damage. She only had 250 passengers on board at the time and was refloated after 12 hours. On 11 May 1934, White Star Line officially merged

under the North Atlantic Shipping Bill with the Cunard Line to form Cunard White Star. White Star's initial contribution to the enlarged company was 12 ships. They retained their White Star livery and flew the White Star houseflag above that of Cunard. The *Adriatic* was sold in November 1934 and the following month on 13 December while at New York, the *Britannic* suffered a small fire in her fan space but it was quickly brought under control. From November onwards, the *Britannic* and the *Georgic* shared the Liverpool service with ships of the Cunard Line, but the following year they were transferred to operate out of London's King George V Dock to New York with calls at Southampton and Le Havre. The *Britannic* commenced on this service on 19 April 1935 and was to be the largest liner ever to navigate the River Thames.

On 4 January 1937, engine trouble held the *Britannic* in Quarantine at New York for 45 minutes; however temporary repairs enabled her to dock. She entered drydock the next day where more permanent repairs were carried out. By the end of year much of the former White Star fleet had been disposed of and only the *Britannic*, *Georgic* and *Laurentic* remained. The latter was continually laid up and apart from a trooping trip to Palestine, she never re-entered commercial service. On 13 August 1939, the *Britannic* arrived in New York with Earl Baldwin of Bewdley and his wife on board. As Stanley Baldwin, he had been British Prime Minister from 1923-29 and 1935-37. With the impending declaration of war, the *Britannic* was requisitioned as a troop transport on 29 August, firstly with the Ministry of Shipping and later for the Ministry of War Transport (MoWT). As such she was hastily fitted out to carry around 3,000 men which was later increased to 5,000 before the war ended.

A week later on 5 September 1939, she left Greenock in a convoy of 17 ships via Suez for Bombay and returned home with key British personnel. In the following seven voyages she was engaged on commercial Atlantic voyages to New York before being commandeered again on 23 August 1940 for a round-Africa voyage from Liverpool to Suez and back via Cape Town. This was followed by a voyage to Port Tewfik and Bombay before returning to the Clyde. Throughout 1941 and 1942, she was routed to Bombay via Cape Town and return. When the *Britannic* sailed from Liverpool on 19 June 1943 with 5,000 troops on board, she was the convoy's Commodore ship. These troops were disembarked at Algiers in preparation for the Sicily campaign. She then sailed on to Freetown and embarked some 3,500 West African troops for the onward voyage to Bombay. Following this she returned via the Mediterranean to Liverpool where she arrived on 5 November. Between 19 November 1943 and 16 May 1944, she undertook four round voyages from Liverpool to Boston then later to New York transporting some 20,000 US soldiers and equipment to the UK for the build up to D-Day. On the subsequent voyages during 1944 and in the first months of 1945, in which British troops were taken to Italy before the ships proceeded to Egypt to embark troops for the UK, the *Britannic* was Commodore ship of her convoy on four more occasions.

British wives and children of Canadian servicemen were the passengers during April and May 1945 on the ship's next two voyages between Liverpool and Halifax. Special menus were prepared for the children and the extra stewardesses who were drafted to the ship were kept busy. After these trips the *Britannic* again reverted to trooping to the Near East, sailing from Liverpool on 28 June 1945 for Port Said with over 3,000 troops on board. Her next voyage was to Canada, and 15 August 1945 found her in Quebec disembarking 3,000 Canadian troops carried home. By the close of 1945, the *Britannic* since the outbreak of war had transported some 175,550 people and travelled 324,972 miles – her Harland & Wolff engines had proven themselves over a gruelling period. She was released in March 1947 after repatriation work and was sent to Liverpool where Harland & Wolff gave her a complete refit as a two-class ship suitable for the Liverpool-New York service. This work took until mid-May 1948 and in this time her passenger and crew accommodation were almost entirely rebuilt, having been stripped to the hull. New shops and a new pool were incorporated on C deck and decoration for both classes made more in tune with cruising requirements. Most rooms were provided with private toilets and the passenger numbers became 429 First and 564 Tourist, numbers which changed in her last year to 369 First and 608 Tourist. The interior décor and furnishings used were the most modern for the day – in effect the fashionable pre-war Art Deco style was incorporated throughout the public rooms. In addition, ventilation, fire detection and fire fighting systems were updated. Outwardly, the Britannic was altered by having the bridge deck plated in and the whole of the promenade deck below the boat deck glassed in with large windows. The open side in the forward well was also plated with the exception of a very small opening. During this refit her gross tonnage rose from 26,943 to 27,666, her net tonnage became 15,811 and her deadweight capacity decreased to 13,240 on a draught of 32 ft 9½ in.

On 22 May 1948, she left Liverpool on her first post-war voyage to New York via Cobh and continued on this run for the next 10 years or so, although winter cruising became an

Above: **The *Britannic*'s long gallery.**
Richard de Kerbrech Collection.

ever more part of her work. Almost two years after she had re-entered service on 1 June 1950, she collided with the United States Lines' *Pioneer Land* in the Ambrose Channel; little damage was done and both ships proceeded on their way. In January 1953, the Britannic made a 59-day winter cruise to the Mediterranean calling at 22 ports. The cruise terminated at Southampton on 30 March where 200 passengers disembarked, others had landed at Cherbourg. She then left for Liverpool to resume her North Atlantic sailing schedule. Later that year while at Southampton in December there was a minor fire on board. A similar cruise to the aforementioned was undertaken in January 1955 while her sister, the *Georgic*, was withdrawn from service that year, leaving the *Britannic* as the last White Star liner in commercial service. When three days out from New York on 23 April 1955, a fire in No 4 cargo hold destroyed 559 bags of mail and items of passengers' luggage. It was brought under control by the crew after six hours.

Below: **One of the twin-berth cabin class bedrooms on the *Britannic*.** *Braynard Collection.*

Above: Having arrived in the River Mersey from her builders, the *Britannic*, dressed overall, weighs anchor and is towed to the Gladstone for victualling. *John Clarkson.*

Right: Dressed overall, the *Britannic* prepares to depart on her maiden voyage on 28 June 1930. *Cunard.*

Below: The *Britannic* departs on another voyage from the Prince's Landing Stage at Liverpool. This view shows clearly the lines of her cruiser stern. *Real Photographs Co Ltd.*

During the 1959 off-season period, First and Tourist class one-way fares on the *Britannic* were £95 10s (£95.50) and £62 respectively. These then rose in the summer season period to £111 10s (£111.50) and £71 10s (£71.50). By this time, her now rather outdated air-injection diesels that were so innovative and pioneering back in 1930 had inevitably aged and required constant attention from the ship's engineers and shoreside maintenance staff. The engines had frequently suffered from cracking of the bedplate girders underneath the main crankshaft bearings. These had always been repaired by heavy sandwich plate reinforcement and a watching brief kept on crankshaft deflections. The *Britannic* sailed on 22 January 1960 on what was to be her last winter cruise from New York to the Mediterranean via Madeira. Its duration was 66 days taking in 23 ports with fares ranging from £455. When the ship called at Larnaca in Cyprus on 17 February, Sir Hugh Foot, British Governor of Cyprus and Archbishop Makarios, later the island's first president, visited the ship. One of the members of her crew at the time was John Prescott, who later went on to be one of the UK's longest serving Deputy Prime Ministers. The cruise terminated at Southampton on 21 March.

The *Britannic*'s much patched and reinforced engine bedplates inevitably resulted in her final demise. While on a trip to New York at the beginning of May that year, an unusual 'clonk' from the vicinity of one of the crankshafts was reported by the engineers. Detailed examination at Pier 92 in New York revealed that one of her main crankshafts had severe fatigue cracking in way of the webs. On 10 May, the sailing scheduled for the following day was cancelled and it was decided to attempt engine repairs at her berth. Her 770 passengers were transferred to other vessels. Temporary repairs were carried out at New York in which two of the main units were dismantled and fitted with huge clamps and bolts across the webs in way of the damage. These temporary repairs enabled her to sail on 8 June without passengers and return to the UK firing on nine of her ten cylinders. Upon her safe arrival back in Liverpool a further survey was made. During an eight-week lay-up further temporary repairs were made to the crankshaft and webs as Cunard felt that more permanent repairs were not economically viable. In addition, the unofficial seamen's strike in Britain a month earlier sought only to hasten her end and towards the end of the 1960 summer season Cunard reached the decision to withdraw the *Britannic*, removing the last vestige of the White Star Line from service.

She returned to North Atlantic duties for five more round voyages. On the last of these, she left Liverpool for New York on 11 November 1960 and following her turnaround, left New York on 25 November. She arrived in Liverpool on 4 December, upon which she was sold to Thos. W. Ward, shipbreakers of Inverkeithing. Finally on 16 December 1960, the *Britannic* left Liverpool under her own power for berthing at Inverkeithing where she arrived three days later. She had been the last ship of the White Star Line to be in service and the last to wear their colours.

GEORGIC (II)

(1932-1943/1956)
27,759 grt; 682 ft 9 in BP (712 ft OA) x 82 ft 6 in
Double-acting diesel engines, Twin Screw,
23,000 ihp, 17 knots
Passengers: 479 Cabin class, 557 Tourist class,
506 Third class
Harland & Wolff, Belfast. Yard No. 896

As a way of consolation after the abandonment of the 1,000 ft *Oceanic* project in July 1929, the keel of a sister ship to the *Britannic* that was later to be the *Georgic* was laid down at Harland & Wolff's as Yard No 896 on 30 November. It cannot be confirmed but it is possible that some of the steel cut for the *Oceanic* may have been used in her construction. The finance to build the *Georgic* had been partially raised by White Star Line making use of the Trades Facility Acts and mortgages raised by Harland & Wolff through the Northern Ireland's Loans Guarantees Acts. Against the backdrop of the mounting financial crisis within White Star, the imprisonment of Lord Kylsant, head of the Royal Mail Group and the grip of the depression, the *Britannic*'s slightly larger sister was launched without ceremony on 12 November 1931. She was the second ship in the Company's history to be named *Georgic* and at 27,759 grt was the largest British motorship and largest vessel to be launched by a British shipyard that year. More significantly she was the last liner to be built for the White Star Line.

It had been some 16 months since the *Britannic* entered service and even with the effects of the Depression she proved a tremendous success, therefore much was expected of her slightly modified sister. The *Georgic* took two years to build, employing some 2,000 men in her construction. During her construction, some 650 tons of rivets were driven into her hull, 13 miles of piping were used in her plumbing and four miles of air ducting utilised for ventilation. 200 miles of electric cable was installed and the electricity generated for one night's consumption was apparently sufficient to supply a town of 30,000 inhabitants. The *Georgic*'s cast stern frame weighed 30 tons and was built up from four pieces that together measured 65 ft by 37 ft 11 in. The strengthened cast steel rudder weighed 40 tons with a forged steel stock of 20 in diameter. The engines were the largest installation of the Harland & Wolff, double-acting, 4-stroke oil engines and the last to have blast injection. Another detail revealed at the time of the *Georgic*'s launch calculated that every 24 hours each screw would turn 144,000 revolutions and each piston would travel 286 miles in its cylinder!

The *Georgic* had a depth of 48 ft 7 in and a load draught of 35 ft. Her net and deadweight tonnages were 16,839 and 16,834 respectively. She had nine decks, labelled from the top, boat, promenade and A to E decks. A was the strength deck over the central portion of the ship and B the uppermost continuous deck. An orlop deck was fitted in all holds except No 6 and a lower orlop in the forward three.

There were 12 main bulkheads dividing the ship into eight holds, two engine rooms and the two peaks. Refrigerated cargo capacity was provided in Nos 2 and 3 lower 'tween decks and orlops and 16 electric winches worked the cargo. Her two bow anchors weighed 10 tons each and the cables were 3⁷⁄₁₆ in. Electro-hydraulic steering was fitted, together with all the latest navigational appliances, a very comprehensive fire-fighting system and 30 lifeboats including two motorboats stowed in quadrant davits. Her machinery was the same as the *Britannic's* and were the most powerful of their type with twin 10-cylinder oil engines – at 100 rev/min, they could develop 20,000 bhp which produced a service speed of 18 knots, although during her early days the *Georgic* averaged 18.5 knots over an entire voyage.

The air compressors were independent and four of them, together with the main generators and other auxiliary machinery were situated in the auxiliary engine room forward of the main engine room in which the main engines were. There were also two oil-fired and four exhaust gas boilers, the uptakes from which were in the after funnel with the main engine silencers. The fore funnel was a dummy and housed the radio room and the Engineers' smoke room. A total of 2,050 tons of oil fuel could be carried in double bottom tanks and in deep tanks at each end of the auxiliary engine room. The passenger accommodation in the *Georgic*, as in the *Britannic*, had been very carefully thought out. The great saving in space taken by the propulsion machinery, together with considerable planning, gave an unusually ample area for public rooms and created a general air of spaciousness throughout the vessel. This lavish scale made the Cabin class more than equal to First in most of the smaller Atlantic liners of the day. Rooms were mostly 2-berth, many with private bathroom. And besides the main saloon there was a lounge, palm court, card room, smoke room, veranda, long gallery and gymnasium. Tourist and Third were also well catered for.

The *Georgic* reflected the modern style of interior design of the day – now referred to as Art Deco, so popular in the ODEON cinema buildings in the 1930s – whereas the Britannic had been decorated in various period styles popular in the 1920s. As the largest Cabin class ship yet built, the *Georgic* was also probably the best appointed. In appearance the *Georgic* was rather massive and distinctive looking with her short stumpy motorship funnels. She differed from the Britannic in that the fore part of her superstructure and bridge was rounded, instead of straight as in her sister; in addition she had considerably more of her promenade deck plated in. As with the *Britannic*, the *Georgic* had a distinct sheer forward to a straight stem. There was no topgallant forecastle but a small deckhouse between the stem and the bridgefront, out of which rose the foremast. Below this on the lower deck was a tonnage opening. Gone was the traditional counter stern previously favoured by White Star. Instead both sisters sported the cruiser stern which almost became a 'hallmark' of Harland & Wolff during this era. The *Doric* of 1923 had introduced it into White Star and its longer waterline length improved hull flow through the water and aided the efficiency of the propulsion. The cruiser stern also gave better protection to the screws in harbour as well as greater buoyancy aft while underway.

With guests who had been taken to the ship by the Belfast Steamship Co's *Ulster Monarch* that had been chartered for the occasion, the *Georgic* commenced her sea trials on 4 June 1932 and was handed over on 11 June. She left Belfast the following day and later anchored off the Mersey Bar that evening. Although not anticipated at the time, her debut ended the long association between Harland & Wolff and the White Star Line, the *Georgic* being the last liner to be built for the Company. She commenced her maiden voyage on 25 June 1932 from Liverpool to New York and on the outward journey made an average speed of 16.46 knots, while homeward achieving an average speed of 17.72 knots. Upon her entry into service she ran in consort with the Britannic. As with other new Cabin class liners being brought into service at the height of the Depression, both the *Georgic* and *Britannic* proved popular ships and maintained a high quota of passengers trip after trip while other ships were crossing half empty and being withdrawn from service. At the time it was rumoured in Liverpool that these two motorships were the only British-owned passenger liners running at a profit on the North Atlantic. Towards the end of 1932, the *Olympic* developed cracks in her port crankshaft during a homeward bound voyage from New York. Consequently her sailings were cancelled, her machinery surveyed and the *Olympic* was withdrawn from service for 3½ months and given a refit. The *Georgic* was switched from Liverpool to Southampton to cover the *Olympic's* sailings on 11 January and 1 February 1933. When the *Olympic* resumed service on 1 March, the *Georgic* returned to her Liverpool-based itinerary. In April 1933, the *Georgic* made a westbound voyage in 8 days 45 minutes at an average speed of 18.43 knots. Six months later, she discharged a 3,000 ton consignment of fruit in 51,687 cartons at Liverpool.

Left: **The launch of the *Georgic* on 12 November 1931, the last White Star liner to be built by Harland & Wolff.** *Ulster Folk & Transport Museum.*

In the winter seasons she undertook some cruises to the West Indies, but following White Star's merger with Cunard on 10 May 1934, the *Georgic* and the *Britannic* were part of the merged fleet and retained their White Star livery and houseflag, but with the addition of Cunard's houseflag. In January the following year whilst at New York, the *Georgic* experienced a small fire from a cargo of cotton stowed in her forward hold that delayed her sailing for some hours. This was quickly brought under control and damage negligible. Three months later, the *Georgic* and *Britannic* were transferred to the London to New York service in which their itinerary included Southampton and Le Havre both outward and homeward. As such they became the largest liners to sail up the River Thames and use the Port of London. The *Georgic* commenced on this service on 3 May 1935 and, along with the *Britannic*, maintained this route until the outbreak of war in 1939.

At the declaration of war the *Georgic* was not immediately commandeered along with the *Britannic*, but instead reverted to the Liverpool-New York service in September 1939 and made five round voyages on commercial service before being requisitioned for trooping duties on 11 March 1940. She arrived back in Liverpool on 14 April 1940 from New York. During the next six days she was hastily converted to accommodate 3,000 men and provisioned for such. She departed Liverpool on 20 April for the Clyde and remained there anchored on stand until 24 May when she sailed for Norway to assist in the evacuation of British troops from Andesfjord and Narvik in which destroyers ferried out 4,700 soldiers to waiting liners. They sailed from Harstad on 4 June and reached Scapa Flow four days later. From here the *Georgic* proceeded to the Clyde. Following this she assisted in the evacuation of Brest and then St. Nazaire and it was at this latter port on 17 June that the Cunard liner *Lancastria* was bombed and sunk with a loss of 2,833 lives.

Right: **The *Georgic* alongside in readiness for her maiden voyage. Note the Post Office gangway in place to the right of the ship's bow.** *Tom Rayner Collection.*

Between July and September 1940, the *Georgic* made a trooping voyage to Iceland then on to Halifax, Nova Scotia to embark Canadian soldiers. From then on she made voyages from Liverpool and Glasgow to the Middle East via the Cape followed by several between Liverpool, Bermuda, New York and Halifax. On 22 May 1941, the *Georgic* left the Clyde with the 50th Northumberland Division on board bound for Suez via the Cape under the command of Captain A. G. Greig. She was in a convoy that was lightly protected at the time and she eventually reached Port Tewfik on 7 July. Her troops and stores were disembarked and loading and embarking for home had commenced. On 14 July, whilst the convoy was at anchor off Port Tewfik in the Gulf of Suez, waiting to embark 800 Italian internees, the port was heavily attacked by German bombers shortly after midnight. Their first principal targets were the shore installations, after which they turned their attention on the *Georgic*, the largest ship anchored in the bay. After several misses, one bomb glanced

Above: **The *Georgic*'s cabin class dining saloon.**
Richard de Kerbrech Collection.

off the ship's side, exploded in the water and did considerable damage to the hull in No 4 hold that caused heavy flooding. A second struck the after end of the boat deck, penetrated five decks and exploded in a lift shaft. Heavy damage was caused to No 5 hold and fire started in the after accommodation. Oil fuel from ruptured double bottom tanks ignited and time-expired ammunition stowed in the after holds for the return home exploded. The fire reached the ship's 6 in gun ammunition magazine that also exploded and the whole after end of the ship was engulfed in a mass of flame.

By 3.30am, Captain Greig decided to attempt to get the ship under way and try and beach her clear of the busy channel that she was in danger of blocking. Although the ship was heavily down by the stern and listing to port, the engineers managed to start the engines. By this time the fire had spread forward to the bridge and cut all communication, but the Georgic was eventually driven onto a reef off Kal ar Kabireh, in the centre of Suez Bay and clear of the channel. In doing so she was involved in a collision with HMS *Glenearn*, which severely damaged and twisted the *Georgic*'s stem. Miraculously her engineers and all on board somehow managed to escape from the burning vessel in the ship's lifeboats. The *Georgic* now lay listed 17° to port, flooded with water up to her after deck and finally filling the engine room to above the tops of the main engines and burning fiercely. The fire burnt itself out after two days, leaving the whole superstructure in a blackened and twisted condition.

Captain Greig and a small party re-boarded to inspect as far as possible the damage and try to discover if salvage was at all possible. Cunard White Star's marine superintendent, Captain F. W. Manley, and a Lloyd's Register surveyor, Mr Douglas Ray, arrived and on 14 September it was decided to attempt salvage. The basic hull structure was not too severely damaged and since the machinery and shafting had operated

until the ship grounded it was assumed that these were capable of overhaul and fit for further service. Work started on 15 September and the ultimate success in bringing the *Georgic* home must rank as one of the greatest feats in the history of salvage. The first efforts were directed to getting the *Georgic* off the reef where she was subjected to all the alternating stresses caused by the rise and fall of the tide. The only salvage vessel available was the small *Confederate*, which was not equipped for such a major job. However, much of the debris was cleared, bulkheads shored up, temporary patches and plugs on the hull were attempted and a pump operated by power from a tractor engine was installed on board. With this and the Confederate's pumps, pumping started on 9 October. On 24 October, the ship began to rise and three days later moved to an anchorage. The *Confederate* was withdrawn for more urgent work ten days later. The improvised pump was kept going continuously and by 5 December the temporary plugs over leaks in the hull had been replaced by more permanent cement boxes.

Once seaworthy, it was decided to tow the ship to Port Sudan. No tugs were available but two British cargo ships

Below: **One of the twin-berth cabin class bedrooms on the *Georgic*. Note the mural and the modernistic carpet and bedheads.** *The University Archives, The University of Liverpool.*

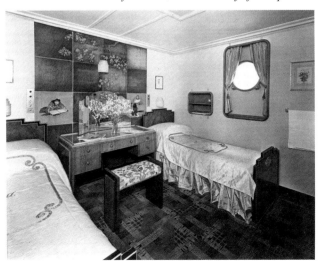

were allocated to perform this task. Since the *Georgic* had no power, light or accommodation, it was decided to tow her as an abandoned hulk. Towing began on 29 December with the *Clan Campbell* pulling on an 8 in wire and 60 fathoms of the *Georgic*'s port cable, while the *City of Sydney*, attached astern by two heavy wires, helped the steering. The speed of this curious little convoy was about 6 knots and some strong winds were encountered. The dead hulk, with her rudder deliberately jammed amidships, sheered about wildly to such an extent that on 3 January 1942 she carried away both wires to the *City of Sydney*. By 10 January, the ship that was leaking had developed a 10° list. A party of volunteers boarded and restarted the pump that eventually

Above: **A clear photograph of the *Georgic* arriving back in Liverpool. This view gives a good study of the ship's lines.** *B&A Feilden.*

reduced the list to 5°. On the same day, the *City of Sydney* made contact again and with the help of a tug from the port, the *Clan Campbell* successfully brought her unwieldy charge to anchor in Port Sudan after a 13 day tow. The *Georgic* remained at Port Sudan for almost eight weeks and pumping operations were more or less continuous. The cement boxes on the hull were rebuilt and strengthened, her jammed rudder was freed and the ship was made seaworthy for a long voyage to Karachi.

On 5 March 1942, the *Georgic* left Port Sudan in tow of the Harrison liner *Recorder*, assisted at first by the tug *Sampson*. However, the *Sampson* proved too small for the task and had to slip next day. On the eighth day, the British India ship *Haresfield* took over the steering position and the tug *Pauline Moller* helped with towing. Eventually on

Below: **With effect from May 1935 the *Georgic* joined the *Britannic* on the London to New York service. In this rather poor photograph she is seen alongside the Tilbury Landing Stage.** *Richard de Kerbrech Collection.*

31 March, after 26 days, they arrived at Karachi. Here, it was decided that the ship's engineers, with the aid of shoreside engineering firms, should carry out all essential work that did not require drydocking. In the engine room, everything had been covered with oil as the water had risen. This was cleaned and the main engines painstakingly restored to working condition. One of the generators was cleaned and dried out by means of heating coils from the ship's galley, then started. With this generator back in service, power and light was once more restored to the *Georgic* and progress on her was able to proceed at a greater speed. A remarkable if not unique repair was undertaken on the badly bent stem. The ship was trimmed so heavily by the stern that the damage forward was raised clear of the water. A controlled fire was then built around the twisted stem – to make the steel in this vicinity more malleable – that was then straightened by means of purchases, levers and heavy sledgehammers.

Some accommodation was built up on board and an Indian crew was hired. On 11 December, the *Georgic* left for Bombay under her own power, her engines giving her a speed of 11 knots. She had been at Karachi for over eight months, but with the limited resources available for the engines and auxiliaries to achieve this turn of speed after what the ship had been subjected to was surely a remarkable feat of engineering. By 13 December, the *Georgic* arrived at Bombay where she was drydocked. The hull damage was repaired and a further overhaul given to the machinery – in addition, she was loaded with 5,000 tons of pig iron ballast. Five weeks later, on 20 January 1943, she left for the UK via the Cape at a speed of 15 knots. For those on board it must have been an uncomfortable and hair-raising voyage, but the ship arrived safely at Liverpool on 1 March, having undertaken the entire journey unescorted. On 16 March 1943, after a survey by the Admiralty and the Ministry of War Transport officials, it was decided to rebuild the *Georgic* as a troopship. Cunard White Star was asked to take over management of the ship on behalf of the Ministry of War Transport. On 19 March, she left for Belfast for conversion by Harland & Wolff. There was no berth available in the yard at first and until 5 July she anchored in Bangor Bay where little work could be done other than

cleaning up and removing debris.

Once in the repair berth work went ahead. Over 5,000 tons of steel were removed from the gutted upperworks, large sections of the machinery went ashore for overhaul and repair, new upper decks and superstructure were built and on 12 December 1944 the work was completed. It had taken about 19 months but the *Georgic* had been transformed into what was probably the best-fitted troopship in the world with the best amenities and fittings for servicemen. There was plenty of space and special attention had been paid to ventilation; military personnel dubbed her as the 'Super Trooper'. The improvements built into the *Georgic* became the pattern for future troopships. In some earlier troopers, servicemen had complained bitterly about the conditions on board and several walk-offs had occurred. The *Georgic* was a very changed ship in appearance, still all grey, but without her fore funnel and mainmast and with the foremast cut down to a stump. Abaft her bridge a light signal mast had been erected. She underwent her sea trials on 13-16 December and arrived at Liverpool on 17 December.

For the next three years she was a busy trooper with voyages at first to Italy, the Middle East and India, arriving at Liverpool on 25 December 1945 with troops from the Far East. In 1946, she repatriated 5,000 Italian prisoners of war on one voyage and later brought home some 5,000 RN and RAF personnel from Bombay. In June, she brought more home from India, both civilian and military personnel, and had some trouble aboard between the 'service' and civilian women. Throughout 1947 and most of 1948, the *Georgic* continued with trooping and repatriation duties. In 1947, the £10 assisted passage for emigrants to Australia and New Zealand was introduced, creating a demand for ships with adequate Tourist class accommodation to cater for the growing number of emigrants. In 1948, with troopship requirements falling off, the Ministry of Transport (formerly MoWT) decided to convert the *Georgic* once again for the emigrant run, having completed less than four years as a trooper. In September 1948, she arrived at Palmer's yard at Hebburn-on-Tyne to be refitted as an emigrant ship with an accommodation for 1,962 with the proviso that she could be switched to trooping duties if the needs arose. During the refit, the *Georgic*'s original White Star colours were restored. Although she was resplendent in her new livery giving an illusion to the former luxury liner that she once was, she was in effect a 'papered over' troopship and utility vessel.

On 11 January 1949, the *Georgic* began carrying settlers to Australia under the auspices of the Australian Government but was managed and operated by Cunard White Star. She left Liverpool and sailed to Fremantle, Melbourne and Sydney via Suez, becoming part of quite a large fleet of elderly liners, some owned by the MoT and some chartered. Among them were such ships as the *Ormonde, Cameronia, Asturias, Ranchi, Empire Brent* and the *Oxfordshire*. On the return leg of one of those voyages via New Zealand, the *Georgic* departed Wellington during May 1949 with 396 passengers and 3 stowaways. She reached Balboa in Panama on 8 June and became the largest liner to transit the canal since 1939.

To help meet the rising demand for Tourist class crossings, Cunard chartered the *Georgic* from the MoT in 1950 for six round voyages to New York, Tourist Third only, in the high season commencing on 4 May. Temporarily withdrawn from the UK-Australia emigrant trade, the *Georgic* ran in consort with her sister once more, out of Liverpool. She was again chartered by Cunard on 22 March 1951 and the following year for seven summer round voyages. During 1951-52, the number of British emigrants arriving in Australia had reached a peak of 73,082 (45,113 on assisted passage) and by 1952-53 this had fallen to 46,559 (26,250 on assisted passage). With the demand for passage at its lowest since the introduction of the Government sponsored service, and with the Korean War at its height, the number of vessels on the Australian route was reduced by withdrawal from service or switching to trooping. Thus by March 1953, the fleet serving the Australian emigrant route had been reduced to two vessels with the *Georgic* and Shaw Savill's *New Australia*, but the *Georgic* was again chartered for the North Atlantic service the following month. The ship was taken on a charter by Cunard White Star for seven round trips to assist with the additional summer traffic anticipated for the coronation of Queen Elizabeth II in June that year. The *Georgic* sailed on the first voyage of this charter on 11 April from Southampton via Cherbourg and Cobh with 620 passengers for Halifax and 440 for New York.

On 6 August 1953, the *Georgic* left Southampton for New York with 750 passengers, with another 580 booked to join her at Le Havre and 290 at Cobh; this must have been a record for that year. Cunard's seven-round-voyage charter of the *Georgic* in 1953 from the Government ended on 19 October when she arrived from New York without passengers. On 11 November, she resumed her trooping deployment when she left Southampton with 1,800 troops and families for the Far East. A further charter of seven voyages for Cunard was repeated during 1954's high season. The *Georgic* made her last voyage on charter to Cunard departing from New York on 19 October 1954 for Southampton via Halifax, Cobh and Le Havre.

By January 1955, it was announced by the MoT that the *Georgic* would be withdrawn from service in the August of that year. The ship had made another trooping voyage and arrived back in Liverpool from Japan on 16 April to be put up for sale, but was withdrawn from sale in May when the Australian Government chartered her for one more season on the emigrant run. Her machinery, however, was proving somewhat troublesome at this time and there had also been some adverse publicity about the indifference of her crewmen drawn from the 'pool'. The *Georgic* bore the scars of wartime service, and any thought of restoration to a full passenger ship status was totally uneconomic. She sailed on her last voyage to Australia in August 1955 and upon her return to Liverpool on 19 November, she was withdrawn from service pending disposal. She was sold to the British Iron & Steel Corporation and allocated to Metal Industries Ltd. in January 1956. On 1 February 1956, the *Georgic* arrived at Faslane for breaking up. A sad, but inevitable end, for the last liner built for White Star.

Below: **The *Georgic* as a post-war passenger ship seen here departing Southampton outward bound for New York via Halifax.** *Richard de Kerbrech Collection.*

1932-1934

Merger, absorption, loss of identity and demise

Originally during the early discussions of Cunard's proposed takeover of White Star, the Northern Ireland Government had not been very happy about the exclusion of the *Georgic* from any negotiations. They had hinted that if debts accrued by the ship's construction were not liquidated it was within their interests to run the *Georgic* and *Britannic* as a business themselves. Their anxiety could well be appreciated as they were major creditors of White Star with first and second mortgages on the two motorships of £534,300 and £995,650 respectively. In addition the British Treasury had provided a third loan on both vessels to the tune of £800,000, and also Harland & Wolff were owed £107,000 secured by a long-term mortgage. These, together with White Star's other financial difficulties, were a veritable minefield of liability for any bidder.

On 2 March 1932, Sir Percy Bates, Cunard's Chairman, told Mr Walter Runciman, the President of the Board of Trade, that he would make the following offer, although it was really in the nature of an explanatory proposal: the Government to finance two Cunard ships at 2.75 per cent, then cash for the *Georgic* £1,350,000, the balance in Income Debenture stock (the amount of the latter to show some improvement on earlier offers). This was the first time that Cunard had actually suggested that the Government should provide the finance for their new ships, as all previous offers had laid down that the Bank of England should 'facilitate it'.

Below: **A rare occasion. The *Britannic* (left) and the *Georgic* together in the Gladstone Dock, Liverpool. They were the last liners to be built for White Star.** *Ulster Folk & Transport Museum.*

The discussions, both formal and informal, on all levels continued. All the time Sir Percy Bates was pressing the Government for financial assistance to get work restarted on Yard No 534 (later to become the *Queen Mary*) on Clydebank. While the Government 'backed with that persuasion which naturally arises in those who have the power of the purse' as Neville Chamberlain was to phrase it, was trying to bridge the gap between the two sides. They let it be known that some satisfactory agreement between the two companies was an essential requirement to any offer of financial help towards the completion of No 534. Ironically in June 1932 as the *Georgic* was preparing for her maiden voyage, White Star's Director and General Manager Mr Arthur Belcher Cauty stated: 'She was laid down when the world depression might well have discouraged us, but happily she comes into service when we are, I hope, without being unduly optimistic, on the verge of better times.' A bold statement in light of subsequent events.

Later in October of the same year, Neville Chamberlain, then Chancellor of the Exchequer, had asked Lord Weir to conduct a confidential enquiry into the trading and financial positions of British shipping companies operating mail and passenger services on the North Atlantic. He was also required to make a special survey of building and operating subsidies paid by foreign governments to their national operators. Lord Weir took just eight weeks to deliver his secret report. Some 27 years later he said: 'It was my firm belief that the British Government should guarantee a building loan to the Cunard company on condition that the two companies (Cunard and

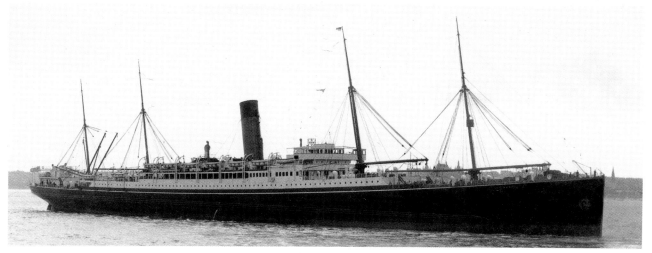

Above: **The *Ceramic,* once the largest ship on the Australian run found further employment with Shaw Savill.**
Tom Rayner Collection.

White Star) merged into one, united front against the opposition.' This report was to pave the way to an amalgamation of the two rivals and the forwarding of a Government loan to complete No 534. In August 1933, the Bank of England and the Treasury reconsidered the position and the White Star credit continued as there was no hope of repayment and to insist on it would have involved a receivership. This was the very thing that the original advance had been given to prevent.

As 1933 drew to a close, there were signs that the worst of the slump was over. There was however, no great improvement in the North Atlantic trade where the competition of the newer and palatial Cabin ships had cut into the profits of the more expensive express liners which had, for the most part, run at a considerable loss. White Star's losses for 1933 amounted to £353,552. At the end of December 1933, an agreement between the Government, Cunard and OSNCo was reached for a merger between Cunard and White Star. On 1 January 1934, the Cunard White Star Line Limited was formed to take over the trade of the two former rival companies. Cunard was allocated sixty-two per cent of the capital and White Star thirty-eight per cent. On 27 March, a Bill was passed in the House of Commons (the North Atlantic Shipping Act of 1934), under which the British Government proposed to lend a sum of £9.5 million to the new Cunard White Star Line. This comprised £3 million for the completion of the *Queen Mary,* £1.5 million working capital and £5 million towards the construction of the *Queen Elizabeth.* The new company was registered on 11 May with a working capital of £10 million in £1 shares. Following the merger, 300 employees of both former lines were made redundant resulting in a total of £50,000 severance payouts.

One of the consequences of the 1932 Scheme of Arrangement with its moratorium was that the outstanding £2.5 million instalment due to IMMCo guaranteed by the Royal Mail Group on behalf of White Star was no longer operative. Also, at the time of the purchase of OSNCo and the re-formation of the White Star Line Ltd, the Royal Mail Group had guaranteed the dividend on White Star's Preference shares. Until 1 July 1930, these were paid out, but under the Scheme of Arrangement £1 Preference, shareholders were issued with five per cent Deferred shares in lieu of payment. This in effect made White Star Line former Preference shareholders, unsecured creditors of the Royal Mail Group. With no half-yearly dividend paid from December 1930 to July 1934, these unsecured creditors were owed around £5 million. In addition, IMMCo was also a major creditor and White Star Line was forced into liquidation. The White Star Line was eventually wound up by a High Court Order dated 8 April 1935. In this the White Star Line had a total financial deficit of £11,280,864.

The merger with Cunard in effect brought an end to the White Star Line. What is not generally known is that one of the eventual outcomes of the merger was that White Star officers effectively lost their seniority and, with the possible exception of a few, would never achieve high station in the new company. White Star uniform insignia was gradually replaced with that of Cunard. Regular White Star passengers found their choice of White Star vessels somewhat limited by the merger and yet many of them kept their allegiance to the White Star ships. In this manner, at least up until World War 2, the *Britannic* and *Georgic* carried the old White Star goodwill with them. These two innovative motorships together with the *Majestic, Olympic, Homeric, Adriatic, Albertic, Laurentic, Doric* and *Calgaric* were White Star's contribution to the new company. The ships on White Star's Australian and New Zealand services, namely the *Ceramic* and the *Ionic,* upon the merger, were transferred to their former partner on the joint service, Shaw Savill & Albion Co. Ltd. All retained their White Star livery and houseflag, but also flew the Cunard lion beneath it.

J. Bruce Ismay, whose name was synonymous with White Star and whose life was shattered by the loss of the *Titanic,* retired from the public limelight. In his latter years he verged on being a recluse and died on 17 October 1937 aged 75, outliving the Line founded by his father. In 1947, the Cunard Steamship Company Ltd, which owned sixty-two per cent of the share capital of Cunard White Star Ltd, bought the balance at £2 for each £1 share. Thus that year, Cunard White Star Ltd became a wholly owned subsidsiary of the Cunard Line.

Above: **The *Olympic* photographed in the 1920s. She was White Star's standard-bearer for quarter of a century.** *A. Duncan*

EPILOGUE

The White Star Line traded across the Atlantic for 75 years and to the Antipodes for 51, mainly in joint service with Shaw Savill & Albion. During that period the Company enjoyed much success, but had also suffered great tragedies. The White Star Line became a prestige line of Britain's merchant fleet and along its history many achievements stand out against the background of normal trading. The first was the formation of the Company itself by Thomas Henry Ismay. Then there was the *Oceanic (I)* that led the way in affirming steam propulsion, iron construction and moving passenger accommodation amidships in this type of ship. Then came the introduction of cargo liners, in whose progressive design the White Star Line was involved, and which later developed into the cargo-passenger ship. The plan for the construction of 'Olympic'-class luxury liners was never fully realised for only one remained after World War 1.

There are reminders or outstanding voyages which are on record. The *Britannic (I)*, which made her 318th voyage in a time of 7 days 6 hours 55 minutes during 1890. The *Oceanic (I)*, which in 1889 arrived in San Francisco from Yokohama after breaking the trans-Pacific record by 14 hours. Mention must also go to the solid workmanship put into these ships as exemplified in the *Germanic* of 1875 that survived a sinking in New York in 1899 due to the topweight of ice on her decks. Later in 1915, she was raised after being torpedoed in the Sea of Marmara under the Turkish flag. She survived on another occasion after running ashore once more in the Sea of Marmara and was finally scrapped at Messina in 1950 at 75 years of age.

And in 1934, when White Star merged with Cunard, the Company could boast ownership of the world's largest vessel, the *Majestic*; the world's largest triple-screw and British-built ship, the *Olympic*, and the world's largest twin screw ship and the largest driven by steam reciprocating engines, the *Homeric*. On the Australian run, White Star owned the *Ceramic*, the largest triple screw ship on that route and they also owned the *Georgic*, the world's largest cabin liner, Britain's largest motorship and the largest ship sailing out of Liverpool. Not a bad achievement in the lifespan of a Company that has now passed into history.

Bibliography

Anderson, Roy, *White Star* (T. Stephenson & Son Ltd, 1964)

Barnaby, K. C., *Some Ship Disasters and Their Causes* (Hutchinson & Co, 1968)

Benstead, C. R., *Atlantic Ferry* (Methuen & Co. Ltd, 1936)

Bonsor, N. R. P., *North Atlantic Seaway Vol I & II*, 2nd Edition (David & Charles, 1975/Brookside Publications, 1978)

Bowen, Frank C., *A Century of Atlantic Travel* (Sampson Low, Marston & Co. Ltd, N/D)

Bowen, Frank C., *The Flag of the Southern Cross* (Shaw Savill & Albion Co. Ltd, 1939)

Burton, Sir Montague, *Globe Girdling Vol I & II* (Privately published by author, c1935)

Cooper, Gary, *The Man Who Sank the Titanic?* (Witan Books, 1992)

de Kerbrech, Richard P., *Shaw Savill Line-Images in Mast, Steam & Motor* (Ship Pictorial Publications, 1992)

de Kerbrech, Richard P., *The Last Liners of the White Star Line* (Shipping Books Press, 2002)

de Kerbrech, Richard P. & David L. Williams, *Cunard White Star Liners of the 1930s* (Conway Maritime Press, 1988)

Dunn, Lawrence, *Famous Liners of the Past, Belfast Built* (Adlard Coles Ltd, 1964)

Eaton, John P. & Charles A. Haas, *Falling Star* (Patrick Stephens Ltd, 1989)

Griffiths, Denis, *Steam at Sea* (Conway Maritime Press, 1997)

Hughes, Tom, *The Blue Riband of the Atlantic* (Patrick Stephens, 1973)

Isherwood, J. H., *Steamers of the Past* (Sea Breezes, 1966)

Kludas, Arnold, *Great Passenger Ships of the World* (Patrick Stephens Vol 1 & 2, 1975/76)

Lightoller, Commander (Charles E.), *Titanic and Other Ships* (Bay Tree Books N/D)

Lord, Walter, *A Night to Remember* (Longmans, 1956/Penguin Books, 1976)

Louden-Brown, Paul, *The White Star Line* (The Titanic Historical Society, 2001)

Mallett, Alan S. & Andrew M. Bell, *The Pirrie Kylsant Motorships 1915-1932* (Mallet & Bell Publications, 1984)

Marcus, Geoffrey, *The Maiden Voyage* (New English Library, 1976)

Maxtone-Graham, John, *The North Atlantic Run* (Cassell & Co. Ltd, 1972)

McCaughan, Michael, *Steel Ships & Iron Men* (The Friar's Bush Press, 1989)

McCaughan, Michael, *Titanic* (Ulster Folk & Transport Museum, 1982)

McCluskie, Tom, Michael Sharpe, Leo Marriot, Titanic & Her Sisters Olympic & Britannic (PRC Publishing Ltd, 1999)

Milson, C. H., *The Coal was there for Burning* (Marine Media Management Ltd, 1975)

Mitchell, W. H. et al, *A History of the White Star Line at Southampton* (World Ship Society, Southampton Branch, 1980)

Oldham, Wilton J., *The Ismay Line* (The Journal of Commerce, 1961)

Parker, Walter H., *Leaves from an Unwritten Log-Book* (Sampson Low, Marston & Co. Ltd N/D)

Pounder, C. C., *Human Problems in Marine Engineering* (I Mar E Transactions, March 1960)

Pounder, C. C., *Machinery and Pipe Arrangement on Shipboard* (Emmot & Co. Ltd, 1922)

Pounder, C. C., *Diesel Engine Principles and Practice* (George Newnes Ltd, 1955)

Rentell, Philip, *Historic White Star Liners* (Blue Water Publications, 1987)

Robinson, Annie, *The White Star Line* (Allerdale District Council, N/D)

Sanderson, Basil, *Ships & Sealing Wax* (William Heinemann Ltd, 1967)

Shipbuilder, *The Ocean Liners of the Past: Olympic & Titanic* (Patrick Stephens, 1976)

Spratt H. P., Marine Engineering-Part II Catalogue (HMSO Science Museum, 1953)

Spratt H. P., *Outline History of Transatlantic Steam Navigation* (HMSO Science Museum, 1950)

Todd, John A., *The Shipping World* (Sir Isaac Pitman & Sons, 1929)

Vale, Edmund, *Shipshape* (J. M. Dent & Sons Ltd, 1931)

Waters, Sydney D., *Shaw Savill Line: One Hundred Years of Trading* (Whitcombe & Tombs Ltd, 1961)

Williams, David L., *Salvage* (Ian Allan Ltd, 1991)

Williams, David L., *Wartime Disasters at Sea* (Patrick Stephens Ltd, 1997)

Williams, David L. & Richard P. de Kerbrech, *Damned by Destiny* (Teredo Books Ltd, 1982)

White Star Line Official Guide (Sea Breezes – Reprint, 1989)

Periodicals, Technical Papers & Websites

Isherwood, J. H., *Steamers of the Past* articles, which were featured in the *Sea Breezes* magazine from September 1949 to December 1987

Brown, David K, MEng, CEng, FRINA, RCNC et al, *The Titanic & Lusitania, A Final Forensic Analysis* (SNAME Chesapeake Section, 1995)

The Times *Titanic* Souvenir issue, 1998

www.red-duster.co.uk

www.shawsavillships.co.uk

www.photoship.co.uk

Appendix I

THE SHIPPING WORLD

UNITED STATES IMMIGRATION ACT, 1924—ANNUAL QUOTAS

	Old 3% Quota	1924 Quota 2%		Old 3% Quota	1924 Quota 2%
British Isles			*British Empire*		
Britain & N. Ireland . .		34,007	Africa (South) .		100
Irish Free State		28,567	Africa (S.W.) .		100
			Australia. .	279	121
Total .	7,342	62,574	Bhutan . .	—	100
			Cameroons .	—	100
			India . .	—	100
Other European			Iraq . .	—	100
Albania . .	288	100	Nauru . .	—	100
Andorra . .	—	100	Nepal . .	—	100
Austria . .	7,342	785	New Zealand .	80	100
Belgium . .	1,563	512	New Guinea .	—	100
Bulgaria . .	302	100	Pales.ine. .	57	100
Czecho Slovakia	14,357	3,073	Samoa (Western)	—	100
Danzig . .	301	228	Tanganyika .	—	100
Denmark .	5,619	2,789	Togoland. .	—	100
Esthonia .	1,348	124			
Finland . .	3,921	471	Total .	416	1,521
France . .	5,729	3,954			
Fiume . .	71	—	*Asia*		
Germany. .	67,607	51,227	Afghanistan .	—	100
Greece . .	3,063	100	Arabia . .	—	100
Hungary. .	5,747	473	Armenia . .	230	124
Iceland . .	75	100	China . .	—	100
Italy . .	42,057	3,845	Japan . .	—	100
Latvia . .	1,540	142	Muscat . .	—	100
Lithuania .	2,629	344	Persia . .	—	100
Luxemburg .	92	100	Syria . .	882	100
Liechtenstein .	—	100	Siam . .	—	100
Monaco . .	—	100	Turkey . .	2,654	100
Netherlands .	3,607	1,648	Yap . .	—	100
Norway . .	12,202	6,453	Other Asia .	92	—
Poland . .	30,977	5,982			
Portugal . .	2,465	503	Total .	3,858	1,124
Rumania .	7,419	6ɔ3			
Russia . .	24,405	2,248	*Africa*		
San Marino .	—	100	Atlantic Islands	121	—
Spain . .	912	131	Cameroons		
Sweden . .	20,042	9,561	(French) .	—	100
Switzerland .	3,752	2,081	Egypt . .	18	100
Yugo Slavia .	6,426	671	Ethiopia . .	—	100
Other Europe .	86	—	Liberia . .	—	100
			Morocco . .	—	100
Total .	275,944	98,748	Iruanda & Urindi	—	100
			Togoland		
			(French) .	—	100
			Other Africa .	104	—
			Total .	243	700
			GRAND TOTAL .	357,803	164,667